The Parish Chest

The first Register of Filey, Yorks. (1571–1646), which was surrendered to the Society of Genealogists after having been in private possession for over sixty years. The Society had it repaired and restored to the Church. (*See p.* 54.)

The Parish Chest

A Study of the Records of Parochial Administration
in England

BY

The Late W. E. TATE

Third Edition

CAMBRIDGE
AT THE UNIVERSITY PRESS
1969

PUBLISHED BY
THE SYNDICS OF THE CAMBRIDGE UNIVERSITY PRESS

Bentley House, 200 Euston Road, London, N.W.1
American Branch: 32 East 57th Street, New York, N.Y. 10022

First printed in Great Britain at the University Press, Cambridge
Reprinted by photolithography by Unwin Brothers Limited,
Woking and London

Contents

Illustrations

The illustrations are by permission of the following: *Frontispiece* (The Society of Genealogists), IV (Mr A. Cossons and the Historical Association), V (Mr Cecil Farthing and the National Buildings Record), VIII (Mr A. M. Buck and the Luton Public Museum), XI, XII, XIII (Essex County Records Committee).

Preface to the Third Printing and to the Third Edition

Again and yet again my book has gone out of print very soon after it was re-issued. This new version of it is offered in response to the requests of numerous correspondents who found the study useful in their original historical work, or in history teaching at various levels. These correspondents included a great many parochial clergy, who wished to know more of the records in their care, tutors of W.E.A. and other local history groups, and fellow-teachers in colleges of education and University training departments, who believed, as I do, that English history at any rate is usually best approached from the local point of view. Most of all I have valued the letters I have received from my colleagues the masters and mistresses of village schools, and those from a few boys and girls, pupils usually in grammar schools which have adopted the local approach, not so much as a means of teaching history as of infecting their youngsters with a passion for it. It has pleased me a great deal to respond to these requests, and to prepare this revised text of the book. Again it must necessarily be a somewhat limited one, so I hope my correspondents will obtain their copies while these are still available, or if they fail to do this, address their very flattering importunities not to me but to my Publishers.

Again I have to thank a great many correspondents who have responded to the invitations in my earlier prefaces, that readers should offer notes of any corrections they think called for. I do not think I can reasonably hope to include further archival exemplification of points already made in the text, for so there would be no end of the work until the records of some 10,000 parishes had all been scrutinised, and the book had expanded into a library. But where, on some point of law or history, a reader thinks me wrong, I shall be most grateful if he will say so, and set me right. Similarly I have not thought it necessary to record transfers either of parish records from their parishes, or of diocesan register transcripts (p. 52) from the diocesan registries, to county or diocesan record offices, especially if these have taken place, as a great many have, between 1946, when my book first appeared, and this present year, 1968. For if I did, my work of revision would never be finished. So, e.g. the sentence 'There is in the Little Piddlington parish chest...' may on occasion have to be interpreted 'There was in the parish chest, but is now in the Loamshire county record office...', and so on. I do not think any misunderstanding can possibly arise through this, for now that every English county but two has a proper record office, anyone seriously interested in the history of an English parish will at some stage quite early in his inquiries address himself for information and advice to the County Archivist (usually to be found at the local county hall or shire-hall).

For corrections incorporated in later editions I am indebted (in addition to correspondents already named) to: Mr W. K. Ford of Worthing, Mr I. R. Gee of Alton Barnes School, Wilts, Mr J. T. Gould of Aldridge, Staffs, Sir R. de Z. Hall of West Coker, Somerset, Mr E. Ingram of Sewerby, E.R. Yorks, Mr S. Price of Pontesbury, Salop, the Registrar of the National Register of Archives, the Reader in Palaeography (as Head of the Department of Palaeography and Diplomatic) in the University of Durham, and the Head of the Department of English Local History in the University of Leicester. When new versions of the book were proposed, I twice circularised, through the respective Clerks of the Peace, all the County Archivists in England. I have to thank for their response (either with notes of correction or with the very gratifying reply that in their use of the text they had seen no statement, general or local, to which they took exception) the County Archivists of Bedfordshire, Buckinghamshire, Cambridgeshire, Cornwall, Cumberland, Devonshire, Dorset, Essex, Gloucestershire, Hampshire, Hertfordshire, Huntingdonshire, Lancashire, Leicestershire; the Lincolnshire Archives Committee; and the County Archivists of Middlesex, Salop, Somerset, Staffordshire, West Suffolk, Surrey, Worcestershire, and the North Riding of Yorkshire. It will be evident that, even more than their predecessors, the later printings and now this new edition owe much to the work of many others besides their titular author. But even so, it may well be that my work still contains some remaining errors, or some statements, which, correct now, may be incorrect in the future. So I venture again to repeat my invitation, and to say that I shall be very much indebted to any reader who accepts it.

1967   W. E. TATE

Preface to the Second Printing

My book was much more successful than I had dared to hope—hence the need for this new edition, concerning which I ventured to hint, not very hopefully, in the preface to the first.

In it I have corrected a few printer's and author's errors, and I have brought up to date the list of statutes and Church Assembly measures cited. I am much obliged to numerous correspondents who accepted the invitation to supply from their learning the gaps in my own. I am particularly grateful to: Mr Geoffrey Beard of Stourbridge, the Rev. R. Bloxam of Ealing, Mr E. J. Brinkworth of St Catherine's College, Oxford, Mr John Coplow of Worcester, Mr F. Crowder of Manchester, the Rev. Dr G. R. Dunstan of Hawarden, Professor C. J. Fordyce of the University of Glasgow, Dr D. V. Glass of the London School of Economics, Miss Joyce Godber of Bedford, Dr A. H. John of Stoke-on-Trent, the Rev. Canon B. F. Relton of Gillingham, Kent, the Rev. J. M. Turner of Washfield, Devon, and Mrs J. Varley of Lincoln.

Several reviewers in England and in America who were very generous in their assessment of the value of my book, put me further in their debt by offering suggestions about corrections and improvements for a future edition. Particularly I have cause to thank for their kindness in proffering help of this kind the reviewers in *Blackfriars*, the *Church Times*, the *Church Quarterly Review*, the *Economic History Review*, the *English Historical Review*, the *Lincolnshire Historian*, the *Listener*, *Notes and Queries*, *Theology*, *Time and Tide*, the *Times Literary Supplement*, the *University of Toronto Law Journal*.

I wish very much that it had been possible for me to include in this edition all the valuable new matter which correspondents have sent to me. However, the fact that this volume was being produced by a photo-lithographic process made it necessary to restrict alterations to the minimum, and to save other material for a future edition to be prepared by the more usual processes. Even so the book is much bettered by our joint work on it. I am not foolish enough to think it incapable of further improvement. The invitation in the preface to the first edition still stands, and I shall be very grateful to any other readers who are moved to accept it.

1951   W. E. TATE

Preface to the First Edition

For some years I have been the tutor of a Workers' Educational Association class and study group working at local history, and on two or three occasions lately I have had the pleasure of lecturing at various summer schools to groups of local history enthusiasts. My colleagues and I have many times been asked for a text-book which should indicate the principal classes of record available for the use of the parish historian, and should give him some help in interpreting these records. We were obliged to reply that so far as we knew there was no such book, and that, in fact, one was very much needed. The present work is an attempt to supply this need.

Evidently such a book must necessarily be very much of a compilation. I hope this one contains very little original matter, since the chances are that what there is will be wrong!

In writing it I have quoted freely from Dr J.C. Cox's admirable works upon Parish Registers and on Churchwardens' Accounts, from Mr Toulmin Smith's *The Parish*, Mr J.S. Burn's *History of Parish Registers*, Mr R.E. Chester Waters' *Parish Registers in England*, Mr Thiselton Dyer's *Old English Social Life...* and Miss Eleanor Trotter's *Seventeenth Century Life...*, from the Rev. R.W. Muncey's *Romance of Parish Registers*, and from the only large-scale printed inventories of parish records with which I am acquainted. These are Mr M.W. Barley's *Parochial Documents of the East Riding*, Archdeacon Fearon and the Rev. J.F. Williams' *Parish Registers and Parochial Documents in the Archdeaconry of Winchester*, the Rev. W.E. Buckland's *Parish Registers and Records in the Diocese of Rochester*, the Rev. C.E. Woodruff's *Canterbury Diocesan Records*, Messrs E.C. Peele and R.S. Clease's *Shropshire Parish Documents*, Miss D.L. Powell's *Guide to Archives relating to Surrey—List of Parish Records* (Publication XXVI of the Surrey Record Society), the *Parochial Records Exhibition Catalogue* compiled by the Bishop of Lincoln's Committee for the Survey of Parochial Documents in the Diocese and County of Lincoln, the late Dr J.E. King's *Inventory of Parochial Documents in the Diocese of Bath and Wells and County of Somerset* (Mr E.J. Erith's *Essex Parish Records*, 1950, and Dr F. Hull's *Kent County Archives*, 1958). I have also used various lists of parish records in *Sussex Archaeological Collections* and *Sussex Notes and Queries*, in *Lincoln-*

shire Notes and Queries, in *The Local Historian*, published by the Lindsey Local History Society, every issue of which contains an inventory of the records in one Lincolnshire parish chest, and in the numerous publications of my friend Mr F. G. Emmison, late Bedfordshire county record keeper, now county archivist of Essex. I have used these last works so freely, by permission of the authors or their representatives, that I have thought it unnecessary to repeat an acknowledgment by each citation. I take this opportunity of stating that all Bedfordshire, Essex, Hampshire, Kent, Lincolnshire, Shropshire, Somerset, Surrey, Sussex and East Riding references, unless otherwise noted, are from these invaluable works. The references to manuscript records in Nottinghamshire, Staffordshire and the other two Ridings of Yorkshire are usually from personal examination of the documents.

I am very particularly indebted to my friends Mr T. M. Blagg, Mr A. Cossons and Mr F. G. Emmison. Mr Blagg has put at my disposal the encyclopaedic knowledge of everything relating to parish registers which he has gathered during many years' work in their transcription and printing; Mr Cossons has aided me in a host of ways, and in particular has supplied all the black-and-white drawings and has verified all the numerous citations of Acts of Parliament in the text and the footnotes; Mr Emmison has given me the benefit of his labours among the parish records of Bedfordshire and Essex. The Rt. Rev. the Lord Bishop of Peterborough has revised my very amateurish renderings into English verse of the Latin verses found in many registers. I am obliged also to the following gentlemen who have read the text in whole or in part, and have helped me to deal with points upon which their specialised knowledge has been most valuable: Fr. M. Bevenot, S.J., Mr C. C. Blagden late of Chapel Chorlton, Staffs., now of Calcutta, Mr A. Caldicott of Beaudesert, Warws., Professor J. D. Chambers, formerly of Ashby-de-la-Zouch, Leics., of the University of Nottingham. Dr G. G. Coulton of Cambridge, Mr W. E. Doubleday of Northwood, Middlesex, Mr E. E. Edwards of Washington D.C., U.S.A., Dr J. King of Chilton Polden, Som., Prof. V. Lavrovsky of Moscow, now at Tashkent, U.S.S.R., Mr L. E. H. Lee of Bramhall, Ches., Mr J. Meeds, B.A., now of H.M. Forces, but formerly of Kirklington, Notts., Dr and Mrs C. S. Orwin of Oxford, Dr Peyton, formerly of Reading University and now of the University of Sheffield, Col. L. Tebbutt of Cambridge, Mr H. R. Thomas of Wolverhampton, Dr J. A. Venn of Queens' College, Cambridge, and Fr. R. Walsh of Cresswell, Staffs. My sister and my brother-in-law Drs Mary Tate and John Roberts have read pp. 156–60, and have given me technical information as to the modern treatment of scrofula.

The extract from *Humanity in Politics* on p. 9 is reproduced by permission of Mr A. Bryant and the late editor of *The Observer*, Mr J.L. Garvin, the text from *The Nottinghamshire Guardian* on pp. 109–12 and 255 I owe to the courtesy of Mr W.E. Doubleday, and the editor, Mr W.B. Louvois. That on pp. 267–8 is from my book elsewhere cited, and the paragraphs on pp. 264 and 267–8 are from Mr T.M. Blagg's introduction to it. These are used with Mr Blagg's permission. A few sentences in Part II, chap. v are from articles of mine in various periodicals. These are reproduced by permission of Mr E.L. Guilford and the other editors concerned. I am obliged to the representatives of the late Dr J.C. Cox, and to his publishers, Messrs Methuen, for the sentence of excommunication reproduced on p. 147, to Dr J.A. Venn and his publishers, the Cambridge University Press, for the lengthy quotations on pp. 135–7, and to H.M. Registrar-General and the Controller of H.M. Stationery Office for the quotation from *The Story of the General Register Office* on pp. 58 and 285. I tender my thanks to Mr F. Roe and to Mr A. Valence who have read my chapter on 'The Chest Itself', and to Mr N. Kerr, Reader in Palaeography in the University of Oxford, who has revised my Note on Handwriting.

I am grateful to Miss Margery Fletcher, late Assistant Secretary to the Institute of Historical Research, for information as to printed parish records, and to the following parish historians, who have been good enough to give me permission to use their work, and some of whom have put me still further in their debt by checking the extracts with the original documents: The Rev. C.C. Brooke of Middle Aston, Oxon, Mr G.W. Church, schoolmaster of Stowmarket, Suff., the Rev. F.C. Clair of Harpenden, Herts., the Rev. H.S. Cochrane of Wimbledon, Mr S.A. Cutlack of Gnosall, Staffs., the Rev. R.G. Dudding of Saleby, Lincs., Mr J.S. Elliot, late of Luton, Mrs B. Ewing, representing the late Mr Guy Ewing, of Edenbridge, Kent, the Rev. J. Gurney of Cleasby, formerly of Myton-on-Swale, Yorks., the Rev. J.V. Haswell of Sunderland, the Rev. E. Jauncey of Heswall, Ches., Mr C.D. Linnell of Pavenham, Beds., Mr E.H.S. Longhurst of Rolleston, Notts., the Rev. Canon K.H. Macdermott of Uckfield, Sussex, the Rev. A. Midwinter of Tunstall, Kent, the Rev. G. Paget of Hedenham,

Norf., the Rev. J.D.H. Patch of Ashill, Som., the late Rev. S.P. Potter of East Leake, Notts., Mrs M.C. Sketchley of Marston Mewsey, Wilts., the late Miss I.D. Thornley of Highgate, Mr F. Warriner of Millom, Cumb., the Rev. H.W. Watson of Teignmouth, formerly of Feniton, Devon, and Mr C.A. White of Stevenage, Herts. I am obliged also to these gentlemen who have sanctioned the use of illustrations of which they hold the copyright, and some of whom have assisted me still further by lending me the blocks: Mr A. Cossons and the Historical Association for fig. 4, Mr Cecil Farthing and the National Buildings Record for fig. 5, Messrs W.P. Phillimore for fig. 7, Mr C.E. Freeman, Mr A.M. Buck and the Luton Public Museum for fig. 8, Mr F.G. Emmison for figs. 11–13. Mr Cossons has drawn for me figs. 1, 2, 3, 6, 9, 10. I am particularly grateful to the Essex County Records Committee, who have supplied the photographs for figs. 11–13, and to the Society of Genealogists which has allowed me the use of the very interesting plate adopted as frontispiece.

Since whatever merits this book may possess are so largely due to the work of others, I think I ought to state also that responsibility for any inaccuracies in points of fact and for any opinions advanced is mine and mine alone. In particular the two Roman Catholic clergy noted do not of course agree with me upon many matters concerning the medieval Church and the Reformation, and the two medical practitioners disagree with me wholeheartedly as to the value of the ancient method of treating scrofula.

I am very conscious of the limitations of my knowledge, and of the fact that these limitations must have reflected themselves in this work. I hope that my readers will regard this book as the essay of a fellow student rather than as the authoritative treatise of an expert, and that they will be so good as to notify me of any errors of fact that they notice. Such errors will be corrected, and such assistance acknowledged in a future edition, if indeed I am so fortunate as to find that one is needed.

I think I may appropriately conclude a note partaking alike of justification and of apology by the observation that if this book is soon superseded by a better, its author will be delighted.

1946   W. E. TATE

B

INTRODUCTION

The English Parish

THE MODERN VILLAGE. If one were to ask a number of intelligent travellers, familiar with the appearance of rural England, what they considered the typical features apparent upon the face of the English countryside and in its villages, it is likely enough that their answers would have a good deal in common.

They would probably mention the broad highways zigzagging from village to village, between their boundaries of hedges, banks, or fences, and narrowing and becoming still more tortuous in the village centres. Then in the villages themselves they could hardly fail to have noticed the old manor houses, the ancient parish churches, and snug respectable Georgian vicarages and rectories standing each in the heart of its settlement. Very evident, too, are the rows of labourers' cottages and the old houses which have been degraded into such, although obviously they were originally designed for the occupation of persons of a different class. They must have noticed also the isolated farmsteads, each standing in the middle of its own farmland, sometimes several miles from a centre of population.

If in the interest of research into village economy a student had gone so far as to live for a year or two in one of such typical villages, he would have discovered that even in the mid-twentieth century the social structure of the place was one of clearly marked stratification, such as to a townsman would appear almost inconceivable. The crown of the local society is the lord of the manor or squire, resident in the local hall or manor house (when indeed economic circumstances have not forced him to make way for a 'new' business man from the town). To some small extent his income is drawn from the land, although even if the entire village is his freehold, in very many instances the real proprietor is the bank which holds his mortgage deeds. In other places the titular squire owns perhaps not an acre, save the grounds of his manor house, and probably the land of the manor farm; and industrial shares, Government stock, and other gilt-edged securities (if indeed he is fortunate enough to have inherited such, or to have married prudently), form the economic basis of his generally happy and by no means altogether useless existence. Next only to the squire comes the incumbent—rector or vicar—the spiritual head of the little local society. He is rarely the owner of any great area of land save his glebe farm, still more rarely the actual farmer of land.

He is now, and every year is becoming more fully, the recipient of grants, benefactions and donations from various national and diocesan societies which exist in order to make up his income to something approaching a living wage; above all, he is often the dependant, and eventually he seems likely to become the mere employé, of the Church Commissioners (the great ecclesiastical corporation formed by the amalgamation of the Queen Anne's Bounty Office with the Ecclesiastical Commissioners). Some share of the administration of the estates which form the endowment of his office he may still be permitted to discharge in person, or to entrust to the local 'Tithe and Glebe Agency'. But for the rest the connection between the individual parson and the land is now but a faint one, and it is daily becoming more exiguous.

Next in the order of rustic society come the larger farmers, rarely freeholders (save under the handicap of heavy mortgages), gradually merging into the middle and small farmers, and all alike in that their production is mainly for market, not for subsistence, and in the fact that the actual operations of husbandry are entrusted by them to a dependent wage-earning class of landless labourers.

Then come the village shopkeepers, seldom producing what they sell, but in actual fact the mere distributing agents for Indian tea, Canadian flour, Danish bacon, and Dutch condensed milk. In the same way the publican in his tied 'tenanted' or 'managed' house is hardly ever a brewer, but is the dependant, sometimes even the employé, of the brewery company. A few semi-independent producers and craftsmen still survive here and there. The saddler, the shoemaker, the blacksmith still contrive to gain a precarious livelihood. To their numbers has often been added in the last few years the garage proprietor; and in special districts the followers of some such rustic craft as basket making, wood turning, or handloom weaving have shown some sign of reversing the downward career it has pursued for so long. But these are all divorced from the land, and, given a slump in their own particular industry, those who practise it have no alternative to removing to the towns. Here, if they can secure employment for a time, they may well speedily become eligible in sickness for wage-related benefits, and if family men, in unemployment for other social welfare payments, giving a gross income considerably exceeding a fully-employed farm labourer's normal wage. The base of the whole structure is the class of farm labourers, employed at low wages and often housed in 'tied' cottages, with neither house nor land of their own, and with an extremely remote possibility of ever owning either. Law and order in this rustic community are maintained by a member of the county police force. The highways between it and its neighbours are cared for by county road-men. Such culture as it needs is purveyed by the county library supporting until very recently the devoted labours of the village schoolmaster. A somewhat anomalous part of the local society, necessary, one likes to think, but hardly lending himself to ready classification, was this village schoolmaster, suspended socially (*teste me ipso*), much after the fashion of Mahomet's coffin. He was paid (by the County Council, not by the villagers) very much worse than his colleagues in the towns, and again he was quite divorced from the land and all appertaining to it. Incidentally one may remark that soon in many villages the squire will have vanished and his estate been sold up in bits to urban investors; the parson will have disappeared (as he is doing daily through the amalgamation of parishes, so that future generations of villagers will have perhaps a quarter of a rector or $33\frac{1}{3}$rd per cent of a vicar). The village school and schoolmaster will by then have gone into oblivion through the activities of the somewhat bureaucratic reorganisers of the county education authorities, with their arrangements for carrying off children in 'bus loads to the palatial new 'county secondary' or 'comprehensive' schools of the towns, so it is difficult to see where can be the centre of community life and culture. Perhaps as the squire's functions have often lapsed to the parson, and his again to the schoolmaster, this last in turn may have had to hand them on to some other individual or organisation—probably the Women's Institute!

Swift[1] pointed out two centuries ago that there were social advantages in any arrangement which ensured that in every village of the country there should be at any rate one person able to read and write, and it seems not unreasonable to think that nowadays each community needs at least one resident with rather more lofty academic attainments.

CONTRAST WITH THE VILLAGE OF FORMER DAYS. Of all the features of the countryside and the village to which we have referred above there is hardly one which is not of comparatively recent growth. The broad highways a couple of centuries ago were undefined dirt tracks. The hedges and fences, save in the immediate neighbourhood of each village, throughout the Midlands and Eastern England at any rate, have grown up largely since 1700. The old houses in the main street two centuries ago were the dwellings of farmers, not of labourers: the isolated farmsteads did not exist. The land of the lord of the manor and the incumbent was in minute parcels in the open fields, interspersed with that of a host of other proprietors under a variety of tenures, freehold, copyhold, leasehold, and yearly tenancy at will: and both lord and parson were often mainly practical farmers. The parson's income was largely paid in tithe, which he often collected for himself: the remainder of it came from the glebe which he farmed in person. There were fewer large farmers and many more small ones: and, if one may believe some of the historians, in some villages there was no such thing as a landless labourer. Two centuries ago there was little scope for a village shopkeeper, since farmers large and small produced for subsistence rather than entirely for market. The publican was an independent producer, brewing his ale in his brewhouse, and he, like such craftsmen as blacksmith, saddler and shoemaker, held land as well as exercising his craft. Even the schoolmaster, when a village was so fortunate as to possess such an amenity, was a village officer, paid partly by fees, partly from an endowment of land, and very often carrying on in his spare time a little farming (plus occasionally some land surveying, appraising, book-keeping and such semi-legal work as will-making). In short, the villagers were then a closely knit and finely graded community, rather than a mere heterogeneous collection of discrete individuals.

THE VILLAGE COMMUNITY. Moral supervision of the entire community was in the hands of the parish priest, with the elected and nominated churchwardens as his principal officers. The law was enforced by the parish constable, the poor were cared for by the overseers elected by the ratepayers, the highways were maintained (or neglected) under the supervision of the surveyor elected indirectly by the villagers themselves. The commons and open fields were managed in accordance with the general sense of the community, either by an elected officer, or by the parish itself meeting in a kind of petty parliament, the vestry meeting. The central authorities could act if the constable was so neglectful as to make his village a menace to the welfare of its neighbours, or the overseers actually allowed the poor to starve in the streets. There would be trouble if the surveyor of highways neglected his duties so grossly as to damage the horses or coaches of the county notabilities who had occasion to use the parish roads, or if the modest demands of county and national authorities were not met when they imposed county rates or national taxes upon the place. If nothing of this kind occurred, the vestry was left to manage its affairs very much after its own liking. How it managed them is recorded in the archives still to be found in the parish chests of England, and it will be clear that these documents have an interest and a value all their own.

In the recent revival of interest in public records, local records in general have received a good deal of very much overdue attention. Every year the county records are becoming better known and better arranged. Virtually every English county has now a proper county record office, and some more progressive ones have published either directly, or through local record societies, indexes, lists and calendars of their records, or excerpts from them. Even the bishops and archdeacons are at length managing to put their records into something approaching order. It is still true to say, however, that until very recently the parish itself often neither knew nor cared what records it owned, so, naturally enough, until very recent years at any time it might cease to possess them. The parish is, however, the ultimate unit of local government in

England, which has been for many centuries most closely connected with the social and economic development of the country.

Here and there an enlightened incumbent might arrange and
classify the parochial records. Or a historically-minded bishop or
archdeacon might use his influence to check gross neglect, to
ensure that at any rate some kind of inventory was made for the
chest of every parish within his jurisdiction, and to ordain that
this inventory should be checked at intervals, especially at each
change in the incumbency. Too often, however, the incumbent's
work was lost when, in process of time, he left the parish. In the
minds of ecclesiastical officials, too, the parish registers often
loomed so large that they dwarfed in importance all other parish
records of every sort. These documents, particularly the civil
records of the village community, were often much neglected in
areas where every proper care was taken of the parish registers.
Fortunately in general now the inadequacies of the minor local
authorities are being made good by the major ones. The County
Councils[2] have long had a statutory duty of supervision, but till
lately their attempts to discharge it were often somewhat half-
hearted. Many of them contented themselves by issuing at
intervals a questionnaire to each local clergyman, or to the clerk
or chairman of each parish council or meeting. These last were—
indeed, still are—in many instances profoundly in the dark as to
the historical evolution of the communities they helped to govern,
so for all the good the inquiry did it might as well be addressed to
the headmen of the South Sea islanders, and couched in Double
Dutch.

Consequently until quite lately invaluable documents disappeared wholesale, much to the indignation of historians, amateur
and professional. In Bedfordshire, e.g. six parishes lost records
of one sort or another between the time of the County Council
survey (1928–33) and 1937. In Somerset an early and most
interesting volume of churchwardens' accounts at Croscombe,
printed in 1890, cannot now be found. In the same county 'many
years ago' the parish books of Bathealton (1754–87) in a dispute
were thrown into the fire by one of the contestants; those of
Brockley were used 'in the past' for lighting fires; at Creech
St Michael a number of old papers as well as other relics were
destroyed 'on the ground of their age'; and at Holford the records,
being mouldy and illegible, were all burnt 'a year or so ago'. The
'salvage drives' of the last two wars have caused much havoc. At
Chinnor, Oxon, the tithe book 1750–5, with a good deal more of

the parish records, was salved from the 'salvage', and restored to
the church by an enlightened and public-spirited village schoolmaster.

Each of the 10,000 parishes existing at the beginning of the last
century should have (to quote Mr Sidney Webb),[4] as well as the
registers, 'Churchwardens' Accounts from the fourteenth century
at least, Surveyors of Highways' Accounts from the seventeenth
century, vestry minutes possibly from the sixteenth and certainly
from the seventeenth or eighteenth centuries, and poor relief
accounts for at least a couple of centuries',[5] but in fact 'perhaps
half of them possess no records earlier than the beginning of the
nineteenth century',[6] 'and the preservation of a representative
series of parochial records in any recognised custody is a rare
exception.[7] Even so, however, there is in the aggregate a colossal
quantity of priceless historical material. County archivists are
busy men, and parish authorities have often a remarkable inertia.
So even when a county records committee has decided in principle
to invite deposit in the county record office[8] of all the parish
records of its area, and when the county archivist has been able
to give a degree of priority to the mass of work, clerical, archival
and diplomatic, which such deposit entails, a good deal of archival
matter still remains physically in its parish of origin. Throughout
most of England therefore, for many years to come, the pastime
of ferreting out the whereabouts of parish records will still be
available to those having a taste for it. Parish-record searching is
a fascinating sport, though the taste for it is, no doubt, an acquired
one. The most inviting church may have been swept clean of
every vestige of record, save the registers, by the reforming zeal
of some parish official, or the spring-cleaning fervour of some
vicar's wife or daughter, while some much restored and apparently
quite unpromising church turns out, upon inquiry, to have
preserved hundredweights of material, dating back perhaps in
substantial proportions even to mediaeval times.

Often an incumbent will flatly (and of course quite *bona fide*)
deny his possession of any records whatever except the registers,
when in actual fact treasure untold is stuffed away in a dark cup-
board of the vestry, packed in a forgotten chest in a corner of the
belfry, or reposing beneath piles of antique hymn books, disused
vestments, and harvest festival leaflets in the ancient parish chest,
designed for its accommodation but certainly not for that of its
companions.

So there is scope for diplomacy in meeting with a smiling and well-concealed scepticism the invariably courteous and friendly, but often very misleading, statements of the incumbent as to his lack of records beyond the registers. With tact one may induce him upon some excuse or other to permit one access to wherever the registers are kept, and on an admiring inspection of these, with suitable comments, contrive to pry among the remaining documents of the collection. Or if one is well assured that the church is really bare of all manuscripts, a tactful inquiry as to the whereabouts of the registers, the tithe award, or the oldest terriers of the benefice, may possibly give one the opportunity for a personal investigation whether or not any other records survive in their company.

Even if, one having first assured oneself that the parish records have not been collected by the county archivist, for deposit in the county record office, and the church and parsonage alike prove bare, it is still possible that the records in whole or in part may survive. The churchwardens may have them, they may be at the manor house or in the estate office. Or it may possibly be (although on the face of it this is most unlikely) that the civil records of the parish are in the hands of their legal custodians, the chairman of or clerk to the (secular) parish meeting or parish council.

By the Vestries Act of 1818,[9] the duty of determining the custodian and place of deposit of all parish records except the registers was entrusted to the vestry, and by the Local Government Act of 1894[10] this duty was transferred to the newly established parish councils and parish meetings. The definition of the records so transferred is 'all public books, writings, and papers' with the exception of the registers and 'books and documents containing entries wholly or partly relating to the affairs of the Church, or to ecclesiastical charities'. Section 14 contains the definition of an 'ecclesiastical charity'. Apparently if an overseer's account book contains a single record of church charity accounts, or of churchwardens' expenditure among a century of poor-law accounts, the book is still legally in the custody of the incumbent. Such documents as enclosure and tithe awards, however (a very delicate point this last, and one which has led to some litigation), are vested entirely in the civil authority. Fortunately it is not often that any difficulty arises; when there is one it is generally due to some ill-feeling between the incumbent and the secular parish council. So usually the legal question is tacitly left upon one side. The parish council has rarely anything of the least

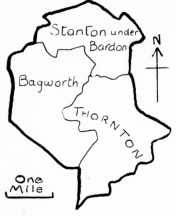

The Parish of Thornton, comprising the townships of Thornton, Stanton under Bardon and Bagworth, the last of which was also a chapelry. (All in Sparkenhoe Hundred.)

I.   The Parish of Thornton, Leics. (*See pp.* 9 & 10.)

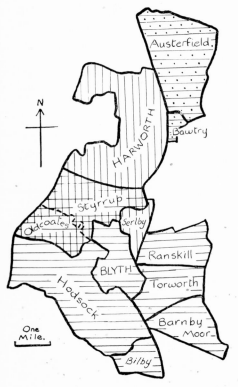

Key

Vertical lines: Parish of Harworth, with detached part, Serlby. *Horizontal lines:* Parish of Blyth, comprising the townships of Blyth, Ranskill, Torworth, Hodsock, Barnby Moor with Bilby, Austerfield, and Bawtry.

Dots: Townships of Blyth parish in the West Riding of Yorkshire; remainder in Notts.

Crossed lines: Hamlets of Styrrup and Old-coates forming the township of Styrrup with Oldcoates, jointly in Blyth and Harworth parishes.

II.   An anomalous case of interlocked Parishes, Harworth, etc., Notts. and West Riding of Yorks. (*See pp.* 9 & 10.)

1. Arkendale
2. Marton cum Grafton
3. Lower Dunsforth
4. Upper Dunsforth with Branton Green
5. Great Ouseburn
6. Little Ouseburn
7. Kirby Hall
8. Allerton Mauleverer with Hopperton
9. Whixley
10. Thorpe Underwoods
11. Widdington
12. Green Hammerton
13. Nun Monkton

III. Variations in the size of parishes according to the fertility of the soil. The five parishes on the left are in the barren moorland district of West Yorkshire, the thirteen on the right in the fertile Vale of York in the same county. (*See pp.* 9 & 10.)

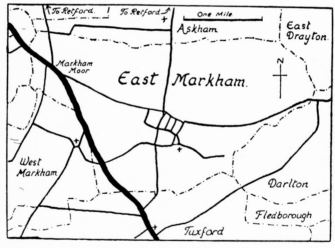

IV. Parish roads and turnpikes at East Markham, Notts. (*See p.* 247.)

interest in its actual custody, save usually its minute book, and occasionally a tithe or enclosure award wrung from the hands of a protesting vicar, although legally almost everything in the chest is in its keeping.

As parish meetings and councils go, this is probably a very good thing, and it is good, too, that the records should be kept together in the hands of a person always well known, and generally easily accessible, always of some education, and often a scholar; usually to some extent interested in the history of his parish, sometimes deeply versed in it; and as a rule, from the nature of his office, of conservative leanings, so that he will be unlikely to part with any item of the records in his care. With some regret then we admit that until parish meetings and councils are a great deal more enlightened than they are in general at present, or seem likely to be in the near future, it would be a disaster to give them any more powers in this matter. It would be a mistake even to call to their attention the very considerable powers they already possess.

THE ENGLISH PARISH AND ITS OFFICERS

A distinguished English historian[1] has said: 'The cradle of our liberties was the village.... Centuries before universal suffrage was ever dreamt of, we were governing ourselves...the local community was the only real authority; the parish was the unit of government.... Every householder had to serve his year as an administrator of the nation's business. Unpaid, with little option of escape,...and almost certainly reluctantly, he had to take his turn in one of the parish offices or to provide an efficient substitute.... For a year the mantle of authority rested on his humble and unlettered shoulders. As much as the king on his gilded throne he became for the time being an essential part of the national machinery. During his year of office he may not have shown himself a particularly good administrator—often he must have been a ludicrously bad one—but he learnt a great deal. At the end of his year he went back into the general body of the village community with what he had learnt. He transmitted it to his children.'

Before dealing with these officers of the parish, and the records they have left behind them, it would be convenient to define the term 'Parish' and to inquire what is the relation the parish bore and bears to the other historic ultimate units of local government. This is, however, a matter of some difficulty. Ecclesiastically the traditional definition is 'that circuit of ground which is committed to the charge of one person or vicar, or to other minister having cure of souls therein'.[2] Civilly a parish is, or was until a late 'reform' of local government, 'a place for which a separate poor rate is or can be made, and for which a separate overseer is or can be appointed'.[3] It would however be hardly correct to think of the parish, as quite famous scholars have done, as the 'township in its ecclesiastical capacity', since many parishes, especially in the northern and least fertile districts, contain several townships, while, especially in old corporate towns, it is not unusual for a township to contain a great many parishes. In some counties it is the exception for the parish and the township to be co-extensive. The relation between the parish and the manor is still more obscure, though there *is* a relation, as we shall see later. If Blackstone[4] may be believed 'the boundaries of a parish were originally determined by those of a manor or manors. With the spread of Christianity the lords began to build churches upon their own demesnes or wastes ...and obliged all their tenants to appropriate their tithes to the maintenance of the officiating minister'. And later developments have complicated the story still further.[5]

Perhaps the best of all definitions is this: 'The parish is the territorial basis of community service.' It was long held that this basis was established by the great Archbishop of Canterbury, Theodore of Tarsus,[6] who first created parishes in connection with his plans for reforming and overhauling the church's machinery. It is generally agreed nowadays, however, that the *parochiae* attributed to him correspond to modern dioceses—in fact, that the words diocese and parish have each been degraded. As Christianity spread, the original dioceses became provinces (there is still a correspondence between the provinces of modern ecclesiastical organisation and the *provinciae* of imperial Rome), the original parishes became dioceses, while the term parish was eventually applied to the ultimate unit in the whole organisation.

When these parishes began it is difficult to say. Probably they are antedated by the tithe system[7] which so long maintained their ecclesiastical functions, since it is almost certain that originally tithes were diocesan. In 1095, at the Council of Clermont, appropriations to particular parishes were recognised, though by no means encouraged, and it seems that in England, at any rate, the parochial system was developed in its essentials before the Norman Conquest. Sir Henry Hobart suggested that parishes

probably date from the Lateran Council of 1179: Blackstone[8] himself is inclined to think the latter date too late, the former too early,
and so we may for the time rest content with his suggestion that
the truth probably lies between these two extremes. There is some
evidence in favour of the traditional ascription of the erection
of the normal parish church to the manorial lord, who erected a
church for his tenants and himself, giving his own tithe and compelling his tenants to give theirs, and reserving in his own hand the
appointment of the incumbent who was to receive this tithe. A
century or so after the Conquest the system had attained a stability
which in all essentials it preserved for six centuries or more. The
parishes, rural deaneries and archdeaconries of e.g. Pope Nicholas'
Taxation[9] in 1291, and of *Valor Ecclesiasticus*,[10] 1534–5, do not
differ a great deal from those immediately before the reorganisation
of church and state carried out by the Reform Parliaments from
1832 onwards.

A number of such parishes were divided for convenience after
the Restoration, when an act[11] was passed allowing partitioning,
provided that each part taken off had been not a mere hamlet or
district, but a vill or township by reputation when the poor law of
1601 was passed. In actual practice this meant that a district could
demand its independence if it could prove it had enjoyed the
services of its own constable. Roughly speaking it might be said
that the constable 'made' the township, just as the churchwardens
'make' the parish. By 1844 it was said that in all 5355 townships
had been so severed from the parent parishes. In the other
direction there were a few unions of parishes, generally urban ones,
by special acts beginning in the reigns of William and Mary and
Queen Anne. Still more unions were made after the passing of
Gilbert's Act in 1783, and by 1834 there were from sixty to seventy
'Gilbert Unions', i.e. voluntary partial amalgamations of parishes
for poor-law purposes only. Each of the vast new county boroughs,
and the boroughs of our modern local government system was of
course from the legal point of view—and we suppose still is—
normally one civil parish, though it may contain dozens or scores
of ecclesiastical parishes.

How far it is safe to suppose that the making of parish records,
apart from the registers, came virtually to an end with the 'strangulation of the parish' by the Poor Law of 1834 it is difficult to say.
Strong evidence in support of this view is afforded by such records
as those of East Clandon, Surrey, where a series of accounts from

1590 to 1836, almost complete except for 1641–9, has as its last entry
in the old records a note that the New Poor Law was then (1836)
coming into force in the parish. In 1839 was passed an act[12] providing for heavy penalties upon those who destroy or injure parish
records, etc., but punishment seems unhappily, however often it
has been deserved, rarely to have been imposed. Nevertheless
English parishes have, in the aggregate, an enormous mass of
'record' material, and it is our endeavour in the pages which
follow to direct the attention of the reader to a few of the classes
of record which either from their historical importance, or
because of their outstanding human interest, are likely to prove
a fruitful field for his labours.

THE MINISTER OF THE PARISH AND HIS CIVIL AND ECCLESIASTICAL DUTIES

The incumbent[1] was no doubt originally the nucleus around
which the whole parochial organisation was to develop.[2] In the
sixteenth century, at any rate until 1536 or 1552, he was still regarded as the person whom the relief of the poor mainly concerned.
In mediaeval times[3] it had been enacted that, upon the appropriation of a parish church, the diocesan should ordain a suitable
proportion of the fruits thereof to be distributed annually to the
poor parishioners for ever. Tudor statutes reiterate the injunction
to the minister 'to exhort and stir up the people to be liberal and
bountiful', 'to exhort the parishioners to a liberal contribution',
'gently to exhort' those who decline to respond to the collector's
appeals, and 'if still they refuse', to notify such refusal to the bishop
of the diocese, who is 'to certify the matter to the justices'.[4] Later,
however, with the development of rates,[5] the incumbent's powers
and duties gradually passed to other persons. In 1609 he is ordered
to certify to the justices the constable's account of vagrants apprehended;[6] towards the end of the century he is found attending the
constable when rogues are whipped, 'to register the same', and
registering the testimonial of any servant leaving his employment;[7]
and, by the middle of the next century, his certificate of good
character is needed by a parishioner desiring to perform any one
of a wide variety of actions, from leaving his employment in
husbandry for labour in another parish,[8] to opening an alehouse,
or even a slaughterhouse.[9]

Although sadly shorn of his ancient glories he still retains many important duties, privileges and immunities. He is a 'corporation sole with perpetual succession'.[10] Until comparatively recent years he could have the benefit of his clergy in a case of felony without being branded in the hand, and unlike a layman he could have it more than once.[11] If he wishes he may decline to accept any such temporal duty as that of bailiff, reeve, or constable. He is not bound to serve in war, to appear at a court or view of frankpledge, or to serve on a jury. He is privileged from arrest in civil suits, while going to, continuing at, or returning from divine service, or while carrying the sacrament to the sick. On his parochial duty he is exempt from toll. Unless there is a custom to the contrary he nominates one of the churchwardens.[12] By common law he is, if present, chairman of the vestry meeting.

For more than four hundred years he has been entrusted with the registration of the baptisms, marriages and burials of his parishioners. It is with the records of his activities in this matter that the next chapter is concerned.

On the first page of the Register I of Lenham, Kent, is a summary of the minister's and the wardens' duties in this respect which, modernised, reads as follows:

...The Minister, Churchwardens and Sidesmen must subscribe their names to all christenings, marriages and burials that are celebrated every year before a true copy be taken out of the same. And it is to be remembered that at the Archdeacon's Visitation, which commonly he holdeth about Easter, the Churchwardens of the year past are to put into his office at that Visitation a true copy of all marriages, christenings and burials for one whole year beginning and ending the xxvth day of March whereunto the Minister's and Churchwardens' hands are to be subscribed. And at the Visitation held about Michaelmas the like copy of this register must be sent into the Archbishop's[13] Court of Consistory, beginning at Michaelmas and ending the Michaelmas twelvemonth.

THE VESTRY MEETING

In the study of parish records one is constantly coming across notes of decisions arrived at by 'the inhabitants', 'the inhabitants in vestry assembled', 'the parish', 'the town meeting', 'the principal inhabitants', 'we, the inhabitants whose names are undersigned', and so on.

These deal with every aspect of parish life and communal affairs. It is necessary here then to pay some attention to the origin and growth of the vestry meeting.

It is difficult to say at what date this became generally established.

Mr and Mrs Sidney Webb found the first mention of the term 'vestry meeting' in 1507. Mr Toulmin Smith[1] argued with great enthusiasm for the substantial identity of the vestry meeting with the early mediaeval juries, empanelled to inquire upon a wide variety of matters of local concern. He endeavoured to establish the unbroken continuity of free democratic institutions through these, from the supposed folk moots of the early English village community to the vestry meetings still existing in every parish in England, though now almost wholly bereft of their ancient powers. This, however, like his similar identification of the modern church-wardens with the communal officers of early days, is not generally accepted by modern historians.

Probably the most reasonable explanation of the vestry's origin is that advanced by the Webbs.[2] From at any rate the sixteenth century the hundredal and manorial courts were beginning to decay. The vestry meeting, established at least as early as the fourteenth century for the management of ecclesiastical affairs, was the natural successor to their duties. An assembly which could impose a church rate[3] had not far to go before it could levy other rates for purposes of public welfare. So the vestry, which began after the parish officers had been established, became gradually a kind of parochial parliament claiming to control them in at any rate some of their activities. In many parishes and manors, courts baron existed side by side with vestries for centuries, and matters which in one parish are dealt with in vestry minutes, in others are recorded on court rolls. The time when the transfer was effected in any particular parish depended upon local circum-stances.

Before Tudor times the tendency was developing, and the application of parochial funds to purposes included in or arising from the *trinoda necessitas* had already gone very far in some parishes. Often this involved the temporary or permanent diversion of chantry or gild endowments for such purposes. The numerous duties which were cast upon the parish by Tudor legislation helped to develop still further the use of the parish as the ultimate unit of local administration. So, by gradual stages, the provision of arms for soldiering, and the relief of maimed soldiers and wayfarers, came within its purview. With the highway act of Philip and Mary, the vestry was on the way to becoming a local highway board, appointing the waywardens, and levying its highway rates. The poor law of Elizabeth led to its becoming in some parishes—it is difficult to say how many—a sort of parochial 'social welfare' committee. When a body was already discharging such important duties, the further decay of manorial jurisdictions led it naturally enough to claim a share in the appointment of the constable, and often to assume entire responsibility for the choice of his assistants, the haywards and fieldmasters, and the maintenance of the stocks, the cage and the pinfold.

Churchwardens, constables, waywardens and overseers were all understood to be to some extent parochial officers, submitting their accounts to be 'allowed' at the vestry meeting which appointed or had a share in appointing their successors. So the vestry began to claim, as other auditors do, the right to control policy by allowing or disallowing items, as they were felt to be in accordance with, or in opposition to, the general sentiment of the ratepayers who furnished the funds. It was natural enough that the vestry should develop and extend its ancient right of making by-laws, binding the parishioners generally, upon every conceivable subject. These range from fining persons bringing paupers into the parish or turning scabbed beasts upon the common or refusing to accept public office, to administering such common property as the pound, the common and the wastes of the parish. They include regulating the communal husbandry, stinting the pastures, and occasionally even recasting the whole field system of the parish, selling scraps of waste to the highest bidder, or employing a surveyor to make a general enclosure.

The vestry's interest in preventive medicine is shown by such records as the minutes of the vestry at Clifton, Beds., including a list of eighty-five persons vaccinated in 1825. Its care of parochial property is well illustrated by an agreement of 1773 in the churchwardens' accounts of Pertenhall, in the same county, giving the conditions under which it will lend the fire-engine to a neighbouring parish, 'in case of any accerdent should happen by fire'.

An interesting example of the vestry assuming functions and powers it had not the least right to exercise occurs at Nempnett Thrubwell, Som., where the vestry on many occasions after 1836 fined overseers and churchwardens for non-attendance. The select vestry of Hinton Charterhouse, Som., agreed in 1830 at its first meeting that every member missing a meeting should be fined five shillings. At Newport, Essex, in 1704, the vestry took on itself to enter into an agreement with the vicar for the commutation of

C

all the small tithe in the parish, giving in exchange the produce of a sixpence in the pound rate. At Sundon and Streatley, Beds., in 1791, the vestries of two neighbouring parishes, according to a memorandum in the register of the latter, following the enclosure adjusted the parish boundaries, and agreed that all old charitable donations payable from Sundon lands to Streatley poor, and *vice versa*, should be extinguished.

Vestry minute books are among the most interesting of parish records. No one knows how many early ones are still extant, and the inquirer may quite possibly find that the volume now in use for recording the minutes of the formal vestry referred to below contains the transactions of its predecessors for two or three centuries. To take a few examples from but one county—that of Lincoln: early vestry books are known to exist at Addlethorpe 1542–1826, Aslackby 1628–1933, Boston 1705–66, Frampton 1597–1855, Heckington 1560–1729, New Sleaford 1653–1760, North Somercotes 1670–1809, Stamford St John's 1588–1675, Waddington 1642–1805, and Whaplode 1678–1838.

Strictly speaking, the vestry,[4] as representing the inhabitants generally, had the power to administer common property and to make by-laws on all matters of public concern. It had absolute control over the assessment, levy and expenditure of the poor rate and the church rate, and over the election of at least one of the churchwardens. An interesting example of a vestry which (apparently quite improperly) regarded the elected warden as holding an office different from that of the vicar's warden, occurs at Kettering, Northants., where the vestry minutes include:

December 9th, 1819. The Churchwardens accounts were in part examined, those disallowed struck from the book—some referred to the parish churchwarden for enquiry, and others allowed....

The participation of the vestry in the appointment of the waywardens was somewhat shadowy, and, according to legal theory, in that of overseers and constables it had no share whatever. In actual practice, however, it often had a good deal.

THE INHERITANCE OF FUNCTIONS BY THE VESTRY FROM THE COURT BARON. The date at which the manorial election of some officers lapsed, and the vestry replaced the court baron, varied enormously from parish to parish. At Kettering, Northants., e.g. the manorial officers were elected at the court leet with court baron until well into the nineteenth century.[5] The officers were constables and headboroughs (not elected after 1841), fieldmen and pinherds (disappearing after the enclosure of 1805, but the latter being appointed again from 1812 onwards), chimney searchers, flesh searchers (fish and flesh searchers from 1826), leather searchers, aletasters and bread and butter weighers.

The vestry met at Easter to appoint churchwardens, according to the rules laid down in the canons, 'in *Easter* week or within one month after Easter', as laid down by the act of 1601 to choose overseers, and on 22 September, in accordance with the act of 1555, to compile the list from which the waywardens were nominated by the justices. In 1835[6] this date was changed to that of the meeting at which the overseers were appointed. By the Parish Constables Act of 1842[7] it was enacted that the vestry meeting to nominate constables should be held between 27 February and 24 March.

What happened if the rates demanded by the parish functionaries, or the accounts submitted by them, after allowance by the justices, were not approved by the vestry, it is difficult to say. Probably as a general rule the officers of the parish made sure of the acquiescence of the vestry before visiting the local magistrate, to get him to 'allow' the rate. Comparison of the data given in old vestry books as to the days on which rates were 'agreed' by the vestry and 'allowed' by the magistrate seems to suggest this.

At Keston, Kent, the certificate of the vestry that the assessment is a fair one precedes that of the justices allowing the rate, and the vestry's note of allowance at the end of the year precedes the justices' certificate. Sometimes the parishioners here would give a final warning before disallowing an expenditure of any particular type, e.g. in 1714 the overseers' accounts include: 'Spent at the bonfiers 07s. 06d.' Against this is the note, in the rector's hand: 'Allow'd now but never to be so any more.'

The vestry of Caddington, Beds., in 1760, adopted resolutions disallowing the payment of any casualty bill incurred by the constable. Twenty years earlier it had limited to 1s. 6d. the expense to be allowed to the constable for a journey to any sessions.

It is not clear either what happened if a magistrate declined to allow the rate. Apparently the contingency rarely arose. Church rates, of course, needed no such allowance.

It was less uncommon for the accounts to be disallowed by the justices, apparently generally upon appeal to them by the vestry. The procedure then was by way of surcharge, as may be seen from an entry in the parish book of Laxton, Notts., 7 June 1739:

Whereas complaint was made unto me one of His Majestys Justices of the Peace...by several inhabitants of the Parish of Laxton against yᵉ accounts of Thomas Skinner and Gervas Cullen in yᵉ last three preceding pages of this book, particularly against the two last articles of forty shillings and 3 pounds pretended or said to be paid to John Hunter & Mr. J. Keyworth, and whereas it appears to me upon a full hearing of ye said Inhabitants Skinner and Cullen that yᵉ said sums are not justly charged, the same being pᵈ by them upon their own acts only and not upon act of yᵉ Inhabitants or by or with their consent and privity. I do therefore disallow of the sᵈ two articles and adjudge that they are Debtors to the sᵈ Inhabitants upon yᵉ balance of ye sᵈ Accounts yᵉ sum of four pounds six shlgs and fourpence farthing, and do order them to pay yᵉ same to yᵉ present Overseers of yᵉ poor.

E. A. W. Becher.

Since there was generally a debit balance to be met by the new officer, probably the old functionary found it wise to keep upon good terms with his neighbours, and in actual practice the system —unreasonable as it seems—worked fairly well. The duties heaped upon the justices gave ample scope to the most energetic of them, and apart from occasionally presenting a parish or its waywardens for gross and persistent refusal to repair its roads, or, more often, ordering relief upon a more generous scale than the parish officers thought wise,[8] the magistrates seem to have interfered very little in the minutiae of parish government. They were quite content to certify the rates almost automatically, leaving the parish officers to administer their miniature republic in accordance with their own wishes and the general sense of the community, lubricating their debates with an ample supply of the traditional solvent of disputes among Englishmen.

Even in early times, both legislators and judges had harboured a notion that 'inhabitants' implied 'chiefest', 'most substantial', 'principal', 'more sufficient', 'most discreet', 'having served parish offices',[9] or, in short, that aristocracy, plutocracy, or oligarchy, not pure democracy, was the fundamental basis of the parochial organisation. Many parishes therefore came to be governed by 'select' vestries.

These remarkable organisations consisted of bodies of one to two dozen persons—having no organic connection with the inhabitants at large—but, together with the incumbent and the usual parish officers, acting in all respects on their behalf. They appear in records as the 'ancients', the 'elders', the 'gentlemen or company of the Four and Twenty', the 'Kirk masters', the 'Masters or Governors of the Parish', etc. The election of parish church-wardens was in their hands, they assessed and levied the rates, they exercised the same undefined supervision over constables, overseers and waywardens as did the 'open' vestrymen, and like these they were subordinate to the magistrates. Like the ordinary vestry they administered the parish property and controlled the parish expenditure. In short, as Mr and Mrs Webb say, they 'formed a fragment of the parish which conceived itself to be endowed with all the legal powers of the whole'. It has been suggested that there may be an unbroken continuity between some select vestries of Stuart and Georgian times and the 'sworn men' used in the fourteenth century for tax assessment, but this is, to say the least of it, doubtful.

Select vestries seem to have existed in great numbers in old corporate towns, where they were obviously analogous to the old close 'corporations', and in such cities as London, Westminster and Bristol, but they occur especially, perhaps, in the North and in the West of England. Possibly they originated because, as the manorial jurisdictions decayed, with them disappeared their juries of twelve or twenty-four of the homage, empanelled by the stewards, not by the inhabitants at large. Naturally enough, some of the new governing bodies, arising from their ruins, tended to resemble them in constitution.

It seems clear enough that the usage often alleged by select vestries, when their privileges were called in question, 'from a time whereof the memory of man runneth not to the contrary', may have been well founded in a few cases. As a rule, however, the select vestry began at some time in the late sixteenth or early seventeenth century by a resolution of parishioners at the open Easter vestry appointing a sort of committee. This, with or without the consent of its constituents, contrived to recruit itself by co-option long enough to claim a prescriptive right to do so. Where by immemorial usage and prescriptive custom the practice has grown up of the parishioners leaving the management of parish affairs in the hands of a few of their number, the custom has been held to be a 'good' one still.[10]

There came a tightening up of Anglican control of the country in general in the reign of James I, and still more with the re-enthronement of Anglican supremacy after the Restoration. With this there came also a tendency to use the machinery of the select vestry in order to exclude a dissentient party—even sometimes one forming a numerical majority of the parishioners—from all share in the government of the parish.[11] Apparently the bishops considered that the vestry meeting was essentially an ecclesiastical affair. Hence, like the rebuilding of a church, the allocation of pews, or the disposal of the glebe, it could be regulated by a faculty issuing from the consistory court, the chancellor, the vicar-general, or the commissary. It was largely upon such grounds that several bishops took upon themselves to issue faculties establishing or confirming such select vestries.[12] In fact they had not the slightest authority to do anything of the kind.[13] During the eighteenth century this fact became generally recognised, and many of the parishes having select vestries by faculty found it expedient to 'lose' their faculties and depend upon their alleged prescriptive right. Where a faculty contained references to the open vestry or the 'meaner parishioners' who before its issue had governed the parish, it was worse than useless to its possessors. Its power to establish a select vestry was non-existent, and its references to the open vestry were conclusive proof against the immemorial usage which alone could be taken as sound basis for its own existence. Apparently the creation of select vestries by faculty ceased after the Revolution of 1688.

Attempts to reform the select vestries still existing began about the same time. In 1693 a bill was introduced 'for the better governing and regulating of vestries'. In 1697 an unsuccessful attempt was made to insert a clause 'to prevent the poor's being cheated ' (by select vestrymen!) in the Poor Law Amendment Bill sent up from the Commons to the Lords. Again in 1710 the House itself ordered a Select Vestries Bill. This, however, was wrecked in the storm created by the impeachment of Sacheverell. Yet another was brought forward in 1716, but inadvisedly its promoters had included in it a whole series of attacks upon clergy and churchwardens, so it fell before the unanimous opposition of the Lords.

It is curious that to this day the dummy bill introduced every session into the Lords, as an assertion of the House's right to debate before the reading of the Queen's Speech (corresponding to the Commons 'Bill to prevent Clandestine Outlawries'), is one entitled 'A Bill to reform Select Vestries'. It is understood to be at least a couple of centuries old.

Occasionally, select vestries owe their origin to legal enactments of undoubted validity. Various Church Building Acts, whether

applying to specific parishes, or to such as might be determined
on by an executive commission, ordered that in new parishes the
government should be in the hands of a limited number of persons,
whether the 'principal inhabitants', those who had served certain
parish offices, persons to be nominated by the bishop, or persons
having the same qualifications as the (select) vestrymen of the
mother parish. The Church Building Act of Queen Anne[14] expressly
authorised the commissioners it set up to appoint select vestrymen
for each parish created.[15] Numerous other acts created such
vestries for particular parishes, very rarely, however, troubling to
lay down exactly which functions were to reside in the new
vestries, and which were to remain in the vestries of the mother
parishes, but leaving this to be wrangled out by the parishes
concerned. And local acts of Parliament, having no relation to
church building, often included provisions as to the election of
select vestries, and the transfer to them of both the properties and
the powers of the open vestries.

The colossal rise of poor rates (concerning which we shall have
something to say later),[16] from rather more than two millions in
1785 to five and one-third millions in 1802, and to more than ten
millions in 1817–19, led to the appointment of select committees
by both Houses of Parliament to consider the working of the poor
laws. The Commons Committee had, as chairman, the Rt Hon.
Sir William Sturges Bourne, who held strong views as to the reorganisation of local government, especially by the substitution
of select vestries for open ones. While the Committee did not
venture to recommend anything quite so sweeping as the total
abolition of the open vestry, it did recommend very drastic alterations in the vestry constitutions, and these were embodied in two
acts—the Sturges Bourne Acts[17]—passed in 1818 and 1819 respectively 'for the Regulation of Parish Vestries' and 'for the Relief
of the Poor'.

The former act applied compulsorily to all parishes outside
London and Southwark, except such as were governed by vestries
under local acts or peculiar customs. It laid down rules for the
conduct of meetings, disfranchised persons who had not paid
rates, gave votes to non-resident occupiers and joint-stock companies, and it introduced the principle of plural voting.[18] To the
student of local records it is important in so far as it provided that
a vestry must have a chairman to sign the minutes, and that these
must be kept in a book reserved expressly for the purpose. The

1819 act, like its predecessor, was not to interfere with vestries existing by local act or established custom. Unlike the 1818 act, it was adoptive, and it authorised any parish wishing to do so to establish a standing committee of 5–20 persons to deal solely with poor relief, the existing vestry retaining all the rest of its powers. The open vestry could appoint a salaried overseer, but when he was appointed he was to conform to the instructions of the parish committee, if any. In short the entire management of the poor was entrusted to the committee for a year, but at the year's end the committee came up for election again by the open vestry.[19] This meant that the standing committee's policy could be changed by changing the personnel, or that, if necessary, the close vestry could be entirely discontinued at the year's end. Clearly there were excellent points about the whole idea.

However, to damn the scheme from its inception the parish committee was burdened with the name 'Select Vestry', which had by now become a byword for jobbery and corruption, but nevertheless, by 1828, 2868 select vestries had been established under the 1819 act. Traces of its operation are to be found in many parish chests, e.g. at Claverley, Salop, where there is a vestry minute book containing 'The Orders and Resolutions of Several Committees of the Parish of Claverley' 1771–89, followed by a vestry minute book 1807–27, which merges into the minute book of a select vestry.

For a variety of reasons the number of select vestries soon began to decline, and by 1832 it had fallen by 500. The 1818 act was found to have resulted virtually in giving each parish the power of referendum upon any matter remotely connected with the public interest. Clearly this was a very dangerous weapon to place in the hands of the radical masses of the great manufacturing towns during the era of Reform agitation, and it was probably in consequence of this, plus a series of vestry scandals in London, that in 1831 another enthusiast for the reform of local government, (Sir) John Cam Hobhouse, later Lord Broughton, very astutely passed through Parliament Hobhouse's Act.[20] This gave universal suffrage, annual elections (though one-third only of the vestry was to retire each year), the single vote, and a host of other concessions to the democratic spirit of the age. In fact almost the only 're-actionary' clause in the whole act was that imposing a fairly high property qualification for vestrymen.

The act, like the second Sturges Bourne Act, was adoptive. In actual fact it was very rarely adopted, such few parishes as did set up vestries under it being almost entirely select vestry parishes in London. Perhaps this was as well, for this act, unlike its predecessors, entirely abolished the old open vestry. In any case it will concern us little here, since it was restricted to parishes having 800 ratepayers, a limit which would exclude by far the greater part of rural parishes, even if the parishioners had heard of the act and felt inclined to take advantage of it. Moreover, 1831 is but three years before 1834, and in 1834 took place the great poor law reform which is dramatically but not unjustly characterised by the Webbs as 'The Strangulation of the Parish'. Until 1818–19 the right of attending the vestry was in every parishioner, and in no one else. The alterations which were made by Sturges Bourne's Acts will be dealt with later.

The right of convening the vestry resided primarily in the churchwardens with the consent, express or implied, of the incumbent. It is by no means certain, however, that a vestry summoned without the incumbent's consent would be void. The notice of meeting since the Parish Notices Act of 1837 must be signed by *either* incumbent *or* warden.

There are some few special acts ordering the convening of vestries for special purposes by particular officers: the overseers for vestries to pass constables' accounts, or to make out lists of persons qualified to serve as constables; the churchwardens for the election of inspectors under the Lighting and Watching Act; and the churchwardens and overseers to nominate members of a select vestry.

But these acts are all of comparatively recent date, and extant vestry books show that on occasion vestries were convened by any of the officers named, by constables, by waywardens, by resolution of a previous vestry, by the chairman of a vestry committee, or by the requisition of several inhabitants. A famous judge was 'not prepared to say that a notice of vestry signed by any parishioner alone not being either minister, churchwarden, or overseer would be absolutely void'.

The chairman of the vestry meeting is, by common law, the minister of the parish, whether rector, vicar, or perpetual curate, and this right of the minister to be the chairman is indirectly recognised in Sturges Bourne's Act (providing that if he is not present a chairman shall be elected by a majority vote). Generally the vestries, open and close, seem to have worked fairly harmoniously from the last decade of the eighteenth century onwards except in the larger towns, where their unwieldy organisation offered an ideal opportunity for aspiring politicians, and in the country generally during the acrimonious religious controversies of the 1840's and 1850's. Nonconformists then flooded the vestry meetings, elected dissenters as churchwardens (as they were quite entitled to do, according to law), and made themselves very much of a nuisance to the clerical chairmen. An instance of dispute in much earlier times occurs at Gnosall, Staffs., where keen controversy arose as to the proper scale of relief in 1717.

1717 Dec. 3rd. Agreed at this time that there shall be allowd to Jessey Hancox 3s. & 6d. ye week for bread & 6d. ye week for Cloathing & 17/- for Coles.
Agreed by us being ye major part at a parish meeting.

> (Signed Thos. Hawke.
> (Signed) Sam¹. Hawke.
>
> (A third person has begun to sign.)

Memorand. At this time Edward Millington snatched away this book & refused to suffer ye parishners to Subscribe their Names.

Towards the latter part of the period when party feeling ran high, the losing party in the vestry very often demanded a poll in the hope that by so doing they would be able to reverse the decision. At Kettering, Northants., a poll was successfully demanded as to whether or not the roads should be repaired with Mountsorrel granite. The vestry of Nottingham St Mary's was full of contention and threw the town into periodical convulsions by holding polls—arousing more party feeling than a general election, and almost as much as a miniature civil war—upon such questions as whether the Whig or Tory candidate should be appointed as e.g. organist or even pew-opener in the parish church.

The vestry still meets, of course, in every parish in the country, at least once a year for the election of churchwardens. The recent legislation for 'democratising' the Church of England did not take away such of its ancient powers as still survived. It extended them to a composite body made up of the vestry and the parochial church meeting, sitting together. To be a member of the parochial church meeting a parishioner must be a baptised person of eighteen years or more, not belonging to any rival religious organisation. For attendance at the vestry one must be merely a ratepayer in the parish.

There will rarely be very much business to transact, apart from the election of churchwardens, though the vestry has still the right to control or to be informed of the expenditure of certain parish funds, and the management of parochial property. It has also the right to express the views of the parishioners upon faculty applications. Generally, however, it consists merely of a five-minute meeting for the election of churchwardens, immediately before the annual parochial church meeting.

Even so, however, there is some pleasure for the historically minded parishioner in sharing the proceedings of a democratic governing body whose story in England is at least six hundred years old, and which, if Toulmin Smith was right, is of such immemorial antiquity that compared to it the Mother of Parliaments herself is a mere chicken.

RATES AND RATING

The question of rates can hardly fail to have a melancholy interest for the English householder. He may derive some consolation concerning the demands regularly made upon his purse from the reflection that, since every government must be financed somehow, they are a necessary concomitant of the self-governing institutions to which he is attached, though probably he rarely troubles to voice his attachment. Clearly if local taxation were abolished, local government also would perish eventually, and our affairs would necessarily fall into the hands of a remote bureaucracy in the capital. This could not but be far less conscious of local needs and much less responsive to local opinion than the present local bureaucracy, which shares with its national confrère the management of so large a proportion of our affairs.

Although the definition of a rate as 'a local tax' is unsound theoretically,[1] it is practically a convenient one and will serve here; nevertheless until recently there were local taxes which were not rates, and there are still national 'rates' which are not in the ordinary sense of the term 'taxes'.[2]

In mediaeval times, such 'public' services as were carried on were largely undertaken by private charity,[3] occasionally by the more or less voluntary service of the persons they were supposed to benefit,[4] or sometimes by charges laid upon the occupiers of specified houses or lands.[5] Examples of local levies of labour for the maintenance of sea walls in Romney Marsh are known as early as 1250, and the rate may have originated in the bailiffs' power to execute work, and charge the person liable with double the cost for neglecting to carry out his obligation. Within the next century this custom had hardened into one for the gathering of a drainage rate. About the same time as this first drainage rate there appears the first bridge rate, in an ordinance that Chester bridge, repairable originally by the men of the county, one man from each hide, be repaired at a cost to be apportioned amongst those responsible. The ancient 'Fifteenths' and 'Tenths' had originally been a true 10 per cent tax on movables in boroughs and upon ancient demesne, and a true 6⅔ per cent upon the capital value of goods in the rest of the country. After 1334 the charge became stabilised, or was supposed to be, and each grant was conditional upon its being apportioned in exactly the same way as the previous levy, i.e. a tax became levied in rate fashion. This meant, of course, that with the varying development of different parts of the country the levies became widely disproportionate as between one area and another, although fairly assessed as between one inhabitant and another in the same place.

As we have already pointed out, church rates as a means of meeting occasional deficits in the parish accounts had developed by the fourteenth century,[6] and in the mediaeval borough even fortifications might on occasion be repaired from the produce of a rate. Sometimes burghal poll taxes were levied, especially in early times, but by the fifteenth century the fairer method of levying the sum required by a rate upon possessions had been generally adopted. Professor Cannan[7] quotes a most interesting series of entries from the Ipswich records showing the gradual growth of the governing body's practice of levying rates upon the same assessment as that used for the royal fifteenths. By the fifteenth century an accurate assessment was made and regular rate collectors were appointed. In the sixteenth a proper assessment committee was in being, and levies were made for a whole variety of purposes, from repairing the mills or removing nightsoil, to repaying the town debts or paying a preacher's wages. Apparently real and personal property alike were assessed, since either was evidence of 'substance', and therefore of ability to pay rates. For details upon the long drawn out controversy on this point which arose in later years the reader is referred to Professor Cannan's book,[8] which is a mine of information upon all topics connected with rates and rating, and on which the following notes are very largely based. Here it will be enough to remark that from time to time attempts were made to clear up the question whether or not personal property should be assessed. As late as 1807 Whitbread's Poor Bill[9] definitely authorised the rating of *personalia*, but the promoter himself deleted this clause whilst the bill was before the House, in the hope (unrealised, of course) that by so doing he would facilitate the passing of the rest of the bill.

It is difficult to say exactly which statute first imposed a rate, since the earlier statutes order a duty to be performed, but are disappointingly vague as to exactly how the funds were to be raised for carrying it out. Probably the first reference to rates is an act of 1427[10] which empowered the king to appoint commissioners for sea defence works. These were to compel the repair of banks, etc. by the persons responsible, 'either by the number of acres or their ploughlands, for the rate of the portion of their tenure'. Rates for bridges were authorised by an act of 1530–1[11] and those for gaols by one of 1531–2.[12]

The next year was passed the act elsewhere referred to,[13] ordering by implication a rate for the destruction of vermin.[14] The 'rate in aid' principle first appears in 1555,[15] in an act empowering wealthy parishes in corporate towns to help their poorer neighbours. The highway act, passed the same year,[16] approved no rate, but depended on the old principle of unpaid service by local residents. In 1584–5[17] and 1592–3[18] other rates were ordained for the compensation of those who had lost goods by highway robbery, and for the relief of soldiers. The first poor rate was imposed by the great act of 1597–8.[19] Previous poor laws, as we point out below,[20] had depended upon the principle of voluntary contributions, although the act of 1562–3 came very near recognising a rate when it enacted that when parishioners obstinately refused their alms they should be referred by the bishop to the magistrates, who should assess them compulsorily and commit them to prison if they still declined to pay. When the 1597–8 act was re-enacted in an extended form in the poor law of 1601,[21] little difference was made in the rating provisions. In the history of rates it is notable as leaving the definition of persons rateable as 'inhabitants, parsons, vicars, and others', so introducing confusion and dispute concerning the rating of the clergy which took two and a half centuries to clear up. Other smaller rates were legalised by acts of 1605–6 and 1609–10[22] for conveying malefactors to gaol, and for building houses of correction. In 1654 was passed the Commonwealth ordinance elsewhere alluded to,[23] the only statutory authorisation of a compulsory church rate. This lapsed, of course, at the Restoration, and, unlike some other Commonwealth measures, it was not re-enacted. In 1654, too, was passed a highway ordinance authorising the levy of a highway rate in addition to the imposition of statute labour under the 1555 act. This gave power to rate both real estate and movable goods. Unlike its fellow it was re-enacted, almost *verbatim*, in 1662.[24] One important difference between the 1654 ordinance and the 1662 act is that in the former the rate is to be levied at a meeting of parishioners, in the latter the surveyors are to levy it with the assent of one or two principal parishioners; there is no mention of the inhabitants at large. The rating provisions were altered somewhat in the next highway act, that of 1670,[25] ordering that justices *might* approve a rate if other means of repairing the roads were insufficient, but they appear again, authorising the levy of a highway rate upon the same basis as the poor rate, in the act of 1691.[26] Meanwhile constables' rates for the cost of removing vagabonds were approved in 1662,[27] a rate for providing goods 'for setting prisoners on work' was ordered in 1666,[28] county gaol rates appear again in 1698–9,[29] and again rates for the removal of vagabonds to gaol in 1714.[30]

So there grew up the inconvenient and wasteful practice of levying a whole host of special rates, some of which were so small as to amount to only a fraction of a farthing in the pound, so that the cost of collection absorbed most of the sum received. This was abolished by an act of 1738–9,[31] when a host of such rates were amalgamated with the poor rate.

The justices were given jurisdiction to deal with rating appeals in 1743.[32] In 1815[33] an act abolished the levying of county rates upon the parishes in traditional and stereotyped proportions, and ordered that the true annual value should be taken as between parish and parish, as well as between individual occupiers in the same parish. Differential rating between houses and agricultural land was introduced by the Lighting and Watching Act of 1833.[34] In 1868 the ancient compulsory church rate was abolished.[35] The long drawn out controversy as to the inclusion of goods in assessment was finally set at rest by an act of 1874,[36] the last step in applying the poor rate to all immovable and to no movable property. By it all woods and mines were made rateable to the poor. The rating laws were again consolidated in 1925[37] and in 1929.[38] It is understood that they are due for other drastic reform in the near future.

The actual business of assessment in each parish was normally in the hands of the overseer, subject to the overriding decision of the vestry. The vestry, too, successfully claimed the right to determine which, if any, of the inhabitants should be excused the payment of rates. It was not until 1801[39] that the justices were given power not only to annul a poor rate, but alternatively, if they wished, to amend it, and to alter particular names and assessments. Assessments and surveys of the parish, made for rating purposes, are not uncommonly found among parish records. Flitton, Beds., has one of 1598 (most interesting as earlier than the 1601 poor law).

Monye to be collected for the town stocks of theise persones hereunder named.

Dundry, Som., has one:

made and agreed on by and between the inhabitants the 16th day of December in the first year of King James II's reign, 1685.

In 1790 the vestry of Gnosall, Staffs., agreed that since the poor rates appeared 'to be very irregular and disproportionate' Samuel Wyatt of Burton-on-Trent, a well-known land surveyor, should be employed to make a fresh valuation and assessment, a work which he completed at a cost of £100. The same vestry had in previous years experienced great difficulty in dealing with applications for the reduction of assessments, especially since, a levy having been agreed upon, any reduction of one person's share must involve a corresponding raising of someone else's. It seems that appellant *A* by whipping up his friends succeeded in getting part of his assessment transferred to ratepayer *B*. *B* then appealed, and if *he* canvassed his friends could pack the vestry, and get the increase transferred back again to *A*. Then *A* appealed again and so on, e.g.

April 17th 1682   Ralph Wild abated 1d. layd upon Philip Baker.
July 26th 1682   Philip Baker abated 1d. layd upon Ralph Wild.
Nov. 2nd 1682   Ralph Wild abated 1d. layd upon Philip Baker.

After this it seems that Philip Baker accepted the increase.

THE OFFICERS OF THE PARISH

In the parish there developed the ancient and honourable office of Churchwarden,[1] originating at some unknown date in connection with the maintenance and repair of the church fabric and definitely known to have existed in the fourteenth century. When the central government began to take a serious interest in matters of population, it was to the incumbents that Thomas Cromwell, in 1538, addressed his mandate,[2] appointing them as local registrars of baptisms, marriages and burials, an office which, with some modifications, they retain to this day. As we have already indicated,[3] the vestry or customary governing body of the parish began, according to some authorities, towards the end of the fifteenth century, but according to others derived in unbroken continuity from the purely democratic 'moots' and 'things' of an earlier era. This, with the officers it helped to choose, carried out, or was expected to carry out, in respectful subordination to the justices in quarter or petty sessions, almost the whole of local government, from the decay of the seignorial jurisdictions to the strangulation of the parish after 1834.

The overseers of the poor[4] in the parish probably originated as collectors of parochial alms, and were established more formally by the act of 1572 as alms collectors and supervisors of the labour of rogues and vagabonds. Finally they had these offices combined by the more famous statute of 1597. They were almost entirely responsible for the management of the poor for more than two centuries, and eventually became in fact, though not in legal theory, the principal executive servants of the vestry. Their functions, albeit in a somewhat attenuated (almost a vestigial) form, persisted until as late a period as 1925.

The constable[5] of the parish held an office evidently manorial in origin (legally a constable was chosen *by* the manor, but *for* the township), but perhaps bearing in it some traces of survivals even from pre-manorial times. Constables are known to have existed since the thirteenth century, and are, perhaps, first mentioned in the statutes in 1285. Like the overseers they were legally the subordinates of the justices, but in actual fact they were rather less than the overseers the nominees and servants of the vestry. The constables were almost wholly responsible for the maintenance of law and order in the parishes during many centuries of English history, and their remote descendant still bears a much restricted sway in a few out-of-the-way villages where the county police forces have not thought it worth while to station an officer.

Such local government as was not under the control of the churchwardens, the vestry, the overseers, or the constable, was in the hands of two more rural officials, one, the waywarden or surveyor of highways,[6] holding an office established like that of overseer by Tudor legislation, the other, the fieldmaster or field reeve. This latter was the descendant of the manorial hayward,[7] and, perhaps with subordinates such as pinder, common keeper, hedge looker, or more often by himself, carried out the instructions of the vestry concerning such management and regulation as was essential to the maintenance of open-field agriculture.

The principal parish records, then, which one may expect to find still surviving, are those left by this odd hierarchy of parochial dignitaries. Not that incumbent, churchwardens, overseers, constable, waywarden and fieldmaster by any means exhaust the list of township, manorial, or parochial officers. Probably the nearest approach to a complete list is that of Sir G. L. Gomme in his *Index of Municipal Officers*.[8] He calculates that the 285 municipal corporations existing at the time of the great report of 1835 had 635 different offices, a list of which he prints, besides a great many more which for various reasons the reports upon which he worked do not mention. And though, of course, those offices which were entirely municipal or burghal or which were purely manorial in no way concern us here, there are few of those given under Gomme's remaining heads, 'Township Officers', 'Agricultural Officers' and 'Curious Officers', which could not be paralleled from the records of rural parishes. Since to but 286 cities and boroughs (including London) there are approximately 10,000 of these,[9] or perhaps 13,000, if separate townships and constablewicks be included, it is certain that a complete list of parish officials would contain many hundreds of titles, so that even with full allowance for overlapping and for synonymous terms, there is ample scope for the curious inquirer.

We have dealt elsewhere with the part played by the vestry in the election of the churchwardens, and we shall later have something to say of the extent to which the vestry exercised real powers in the choice of the other parish officers. First, however, there are one or two points of general interest concerning the parish officers as a whole, to which it will be well to devote some attention.

For the principal office in the parish hierarchy—that of churchwarden—there is now and has always been no property qualification whatever. The same statement with little modification applies to the positions of constable and fieldmaster. The modest qualification fixed for the constable by the 1842 act (the occupation of lands or tenements assessed to poor rate or county rate at £4 or more) occurs, of course, after the time of which we are speaking. There was, however, a vague property qualification for the office of overseer—he was required to be a 'substantial householder', and the wider phrase 'Any person assessed to the relief of the poor' does not occur until 1819.[10] The waywarden had, however, a property qualification of a more specific kind, since he was required to be the owner of an estate of £10 within the parish or an occupier to the yearly value of £30 (in 1772–3,[11] later reduced to £20 in 1835),[12] and it was usual to appoint persons of some property. Probably the motive was largely one of prudence. By the act of 1691[13] the filling of an annual office gave a settlement in the parish.[14]

Mr Cutlack, who has examined in great detail the poor-law records of Gnosall, Staffs., covering a couple of centuries, has found not a single case of an outsider gaining a settlement by serving a parish office for a year, and his experience is confirmed by that of Mr F. G. Emmison, who in the study of some 20,000 settlement papers deposited in the Bedfordshire and Essex County Record Offices has found no instances also. Mr Cutlack suggests[15] that if such a case had occurred the facts would have been so well known that there would have been no attempt at removal. It seems likelier that such cases did not occur, and that except when a stranger of very considerable substance immigrated into the village, the parishioners were careful to elect as parish officers only those persons who already had settlements. It seems probable that here may be another reason for the fact alluded to elsewhere—that one person was often appointed to discharge two or more offices. I owe to the kindness of Mr Emmison these instances of such an arrangement in several small parishes in Bedfordshire. At Whipsnade the overseers and constables were the same men 1800–4, and the offices of constable and surveyor were filled by one man 1805–6. At Upper Stondon the overseer's and constable's offices were filled by a succession of individuals 1768–1821. At Melchbourne the offices of constable and surveyor went together 1740–1800.

I am obliged to Mr E. B. Hassell for the information that in the interesting Derbyshire parish of Horsley the list of constables is extant for the period 1761–90. 'Look' Abbott, constable 1776, was also overseer of the poor for this year, and John Woodward was constable and overseer in 1789. John Woodward was headborough in 1769, also overseer and 'Colector Lantax', John Walthall in 1772 was headborough, overseer and overseer of the highways, and William Whilton, John Whilton and John Tirpin, constables (or headboroughs—the terms were here used synonymously) in 1785, 1787 and 1788, occupied also the offices of church-warden and overseer of the poor. In the Lincolnshire parish of Long Bennington the offices of constable and surveyor of the high-ways were usually held together.

The officer's burden of liability for service became still heavier because of this restriction of the number of persons among whom the offices could be shared, and this made those who could by some means escape office all the more anxious to do so. A 'Tyburn Ticket' gave its holder exemption from parochial office and was transferable. Accordingly in some parishes such certificates became regular articles of commerce and fetched prices up to £20 each.

An instance of unwillingness to serve parish office is thus re-corded in the books of Cowden, Kent, where the list of officers elected in March 1758 is crossed out:

There was a fresh choice made April ye 3rd 1758 because they could not make Nichs. Firminger serve offices.

In many parishes the system elsewhere referred to in treating of churchwardens was applied to the election of other parish officers. They were taken in rotation or by house row from the owners or occupiers of certain specified houses or lands. Lists of estates liable to serve parochial offices often occur in registers and other parish records. To take but one or two instances: Ditcheat, Som., has in its overseers' accounts 1775–1824 a list of estates liable to serve the office of overseer, and Clutton, Som., has, in a volume of miscellaneous records, a

List of Estates which do serve the Office of Tithing Men for Clutton, according to Ancient Custom, 1740.

At Roseash, Devon, the custom is known to have existed from 1689, and the scheme is entered in the register under 1716, when the rota was fixed 'for ever'. It did not last for ever, but survived until 1784. The rector owned two of the forty-nine tenements which were liable, so twice served as warden (by deputy of course), in 1699 and 1707. Women were liable to serve if they owned or occupied tenements which were on the rota. At Kilmington, Devon, there were twelve woman wardens between 1556 and 1606. The observance of a similar rota is recorded in the register of Wolstanton, Staffs., from 1638, where one year's churchwardens were usually the next year's overseers. Both series of offices were often served by deputy.

Presumably it was because of the restrictions referred to upon

the parishioners' free choice, and the inconvenient obligation imposed upon a small proportion of the ratepayers in some parishes,
that persons sometimes accepted office and then endeavoured to
serve it, quite illegally, by deputy. An early instance of this, quoted
by Mr Emmison, is recorded in what he truly terms this delightful
agreement:

1716. April 14.   Agrement made between John Ashborn and Frances
Gurny to sarve in his rome for the yeare insuing for seven shillings and
six pence—which Re cants first to forfit ten shillings to the other.

Witness.   Thos. Stonbanks.

At Gnosall, Staffs., in 1747, Roger Fowke, being elected overseer for Gnosall Quarter, hired Richard Bernard to act for him.
In this same parish later instances of the same kind of thing are
very common. In 1777, Mrs Jane Barrett, elected overseer for the
same quarter, hired William Startin to act for her. There are
several other instances of the election of a woman officer. Almost
without exception she engaged a man to serve the office for her.
The election of a Mrs Margaret Reynolds, who served the
office personally in 1782, is an isolated instance to the contrary. A
woman served as surveyor of the highways at Sutton Bonington,
in 1750, and one as overseer at Barningham, Suffolk, in 1780.

During the eighteenth century the overseer became more and
more important in the parish organisation. The history of his office
is dealt with in some detail in a later chapter. One of its few features
which need mention here is the custom of appointing a salaried or
standing overseer, elected annually by the vestry and serving as
executive officer to the representative or 'regular' overseers. This
plan had been in operation in many parishes extra-legally, and it was
recognised statutorily by the Vestries Act of 1819.[16] The office of
overseer continued until our own time, though with greatly diminished powers after 1834, and it was not until after one of the
latest alleged 'reforms' of local government in 1925 that it finally
disappeared, after three and a half centuries of, on the whole, very
useful existence.[17] The duties had long been a miscellany; the
preparation of valuation lists and the levying of rates, the registration of electors (a duty retained until 1918),[18] the making of jury
lists, the giving of poor relief in sudden emergencies, the apprehension of wandering lunatics, the burial of dead bodies cast on
shore, the provision of mortuaries, the acceptance of notice of
certain proposed public works in the parish, the publication of

certain notices concerning schools and the militia, the perambulation of parish boundaries, the giving out of nomination papers for local elections, and a few heterogeneous obligations connected with brothels, pawnbrokers, alehouses, censuses and fire engines.

SURVIVING LISTS OF PARISH OFFICERS. Lists of parish officers are quite commonly found in parochial records of all kinds. Such lists of churchwardens and/or overseers occur, e.g. at Capel and Cobham, Surrey, 1686–1851 and 1676–1839 respectively, at Bramley in the same county, 1600–1780, at Arnold, Notts., where the registers contain lists of overseers from 1627 and of churchwardens from 1600, at Lympne, Kent, where a charity account book contains a list 1612–1717, and at Milton, Hants., which possesses a more or less complete list from 1712.

Annual lists of parish officers appear in the records of Great Dunmow, Essex, 1679–1768 in the churchwardens' account book, and several remain in the parish chests of Somerset: Axbridge, churchwardens 1671–1896, Banwell, constables 1669–1845 and waywardens 1739–1834, Chew Magna, tithingmen 1680–1838, and Farmborough, overseers 1681–1894.

The churchwardens' accounts of Pulloxhill, Beds., 1651, include a note as to the continuance in office of all the parish officers for another year, because 'very few appeared' at the vestry meeting.

The Chest Itself

Early injunctions as to the provision of chests. Later statutory requirements as to chests and boxes. VARIETIES AND STYLES OF CHEST. Early chests. Late mediaeval chests. Tudor chests. Later chests. Mention of chests in various records. Neglect and ill-usage of chests.

Church chests existed, of course, long before the Tudor injunctions as to their provision and use. Mediaeval churchwardens' accounts and the inventories of Edwardian days prove clearly that the ordinary parish church contained a wealth of metal work and rich fabrics almost inconceivable to a modern churchman, and for the custody of all this the incumbent and churchwardens were responsible. Sometimes the church records and treasures seem to have been stored in the house of the parish priest or in that of one of the wardens (very few ordinary parish churches had a proper sacristy) but usually the church's treasures as well as its records seem to have been kept in the church itself. Probably every church and nearly every chantry or gild had its chest, 'ark', 'coffer', or 'hutch'. Howard and Crossley[1] suggest that the main chest stood usually by the north wall of the sanctuary, where, if it was of a low type, it may have served occasionally as a convenient seat for the acolytes, while the chantry chests stood in convenient positions by their respective altars. There are still some churches which possess two or three chests all of mediaeval date. Ruislip, Middlesex, e.g. has two; Hadleigh, Suff., formerly had three. It was quite usual for a chest to be presented to the church by some parochial benefactor, e.g. that at Beckingham, Notts., was bequeathed by John de Manthorp, vicar of Hayton in 1434; one at Saffron Walden, Essex, was provided in accordance with the will of Katherine Sennar in 1514. And, of course, chests innumerable have been given by benefactors in much later years. A fine secular chest now in the abbey church of Waltham, Essex, was purchased by the vicar at a local sale, and given to the church c. 1850.

It may well be, as suggested by that distinguished antiquary the late Dr Cox, that a few of the earliest surviving chests are of Norman or even Saxon date, but the attribution of chests to such early periods as these must be very largely a matter of mere conjecture. Most of these are of the 'dug out' type described below. There is, however, at Hindringham, Norf., a carved chest with interlacing Norman arches lightly incised on the front. If it is safe to assume that this is more or less contemporary with stone work decorated after the same fashion, then certainly it cannot be much later than the year 1200, and it may be considerably earlier than this. Many of the early chests have money slots pierced in their lids (commonly, though quite erroneously, alleged to be for the reception of Peter's Pence), but it is certain that in by no means all of these was the slot made at the time when the chest was first constructed. It may be that some of these belong to the time of King Henry II,[2] when a royal mandate was issued ordering chests to be placed in all churches for the use of the faithful, who were to deposit therein their alms towards the prosecution of a crusade, or from that of King John, when Pope Innocent III issued a similar order.[3] The injunction was that in every church there should be provided 'a hollow trunk, fastened with three keys, the latter to be kept severally by the bishop, the priest, and a religious layman'. A further order as to the provision of chests was issued by the Synod of Exeter in 1287, when it was ordained that each church should have its chest for books and vestments (*cistam ad libros et vestimenta*). It is likely that some of these early chests were intended to serve a dual purpose. Others again may have been intended to hold general parish alms, or those given towards some other special fund, or they may have belonged to some special gild, and been intended at once to hold its communal property, and to receive its members' periodical dues.

The poor law of 1552[4] directed the parishioners in every parish to provide a strong chest with a hole in the upper part thereof, and having three keys, for holding the alms for the poor. This order was repeated in the Elizabethan legislation, and made still more definite in the canons of 1603.[5] Meanwhile, of course, quite separate legislation, dealt with elsewhere in the chapter on 'Parish Registers',[6] had enjoined the provision of suitable chests to hold the newly ordered registers. It is certain that while in some parishes separate coffers were provided for these two purposes, in others economically minded parishioners contrived to kill two birds with one stone. Often, indeed, no new chest was provided, and the old mediaeval one was adapted to serve both purposes.

VARIETIES AND STYLES OF CHEST. The oldest and most primitive form of chest is, of course, the clumsy 'dug-out', consisting simply of a substantial log, having its centre hollowed out, and its sides roughly squared with the axe. Whatever may be the date of chests of this kind, it is clearly prior to the development of the joiner's art in the thirteenth century. The method of construction, as Howard and Crossley point out, is plainly analogous to that adopted by the stone-mason in making a stone coffin. The wood chosen for such chests is generally oak, but two or three instances are known of the use of elm (e.g. Eckington, Worcs.), and one each of cedar and cypress (Swaffham Bulbeck and Cheveley, Cambs.).[7] Chests of this type are occasionally decorated with iron studs and bands, as well as having strap hinges and hasps. Sometimes they have lifting handles at the ends. They rarely bear any sort of carved decoration. They are clumsy and weighty in the extreme, and their storage capacity is very small in proportion to their size. One at Wimborne, Dorset, is 6 feet long, but the cavity in it is only 22 inches by 9 inches by 6 inches. One such chest at Curdworth, Warws., said to be the largest in the country (apart from a couple of giants in Westminster Abbey), is 10 feet long. Another at Shustoke in the same county is 9 feet long, and is said to weigh half a ton. Although this dug-out type is the most primitive of all it seems in some districts to have been popular until a surprisingly late period. Mr Roe,[8] e.g., quotes with scepticism an example dated 1684, but says: 'excavated coffers are known to have been made in the early part of the seventeenth century'. Fine examples of chests of this sort occur at Sutton cum Lound, Notts., Hatfield, Yorks., Hanningfield, Essex, Aldenham, Herts., Cheadle, Staffs., etc.

Another early form of chest is a primitive box type, made of substantial boards fastened with great wrought-iron nails. The ends are generally of much thicker material than the front and back, no doubt as a survival of dug-out structure, and the bottom is grooved into the ends and sides, additional security being given by nailing. Chests of this description seem to be common from the early part of the thirteenth century, as indicated by the iron scroll work characteristic of the period, and the decorated hinges and straps. A well-known example of a chest almost covered with scroll work is to be seen at Malpas, Cheshire.

Towards the end of the thirteenth century there was a great advance in the art of the carpenter. A typical late thirteenth-century chest has, according to Dr Cox, a front formed of a great solid slab of wood, or in some few cases of two such slabs joined longitudinally. The slab is flanked by two front uprights or stiles, often of considerable width, and is tenoned into them. The stiles are generally prolonged downwards to form feet (in order to raise the chest and its contents from the damp floor of the church). The ends are housed into the front and back, and are often sloped inwards slightly so as to permit the use of the hinging method mentioned below. The boards forming the lid are clamped together with wooden battens, and these are slotted into the front and back stiles. Sometimes the stiles themselves have semicircular ends which fit into semicircular hollows cut in the under side of the lid. To strengthen such chests they were sometimes fitted with plain iron bands, or chains were fixed round them, the chains being fastened to staples driven through the back, and to iron bands crossing the lid. Occasionally for still further security the chains were passed round a pillar in the church, as e.g. at North Scarle, Lincs. At Worth Climping, Sussex, two of the three chains still survive. The lower ends of the stiles which form the feet are sometimes pierced to make semicircular or quadrantal openings near the feet, as e.g. at Little Canfield, Essex, or Bloxham, Oxon. In lieu of iron-work decoration such chests have sometimes chip carved roundels, as e.g. at Stoke d'Abernon, Surrey. As the century advanced the custom developed of decorating the horizontal boards differently from the vertical stiles, e.g. with chip carved roundels on the stiles, and an arcading on the boards, as at Climping, Sussex. The shafts of the arcade were usually made separately and superimposed on the flat surface; so often, of course, these shafts have disappeared in subsequent centuries, as at St Mary Magdalen's, Oxford.

In the fourteenth century the arcading developed naturally into a band of tracery, and chests so ornamented may be dated with some accuracy if one is safe in assuming that the carvers followed the style of window tracery of the period. Usually the front and ends alone were carved, but there are exceptional instances (e.g. at Huttoft, Lincs.) of chests carved on all four sides. Very often the front of the chest is divided into three panels.

Another fourteenth-century type of chest has carved figures in each stile, and a scene, generally of a military or chivalrous nature, carved on the large front panel. St George and the dragon appear on a fourteenth-century panelled chest at York Minster, and a fine tilting scene on the well-known late fourteenth- or early fifteenth-century chest at Harty, Isle of Sheppey, Kent.

With the fourteenth century begins a further change in the method of construction of chests; after this time most of them take a form based upon the construction of a frame with corner posts and top and bottom rails, and the filling of the sides with panels of one sort or another. Applied buttresses serve the function fulfilled by the stout stiles in chests of earlier periods, that of stiffening the whole construction. True panelled construction is quite common from the fifteenth century onwards, the panels often bearing wonderfully rich tracery, and the chests being further decorated with richly fretted lock and scutcheon plates. Sometimes the fronts are in as many as five panels. There is a close resemblance between church chests of this period and the secular 'Flanders Kists'. Some of them seem to have been imported from the Continent, so much so that the native craftsmen raised a storm of protest, but it is certain that others of this same flamboyant type were made by native workers in imitation of the foreign product. It is a curious fact that English chests of true Perpendicular type are much rarer than those of any of the other classical periods of Gothic style.

While dealing with these imported chests one may spare a passing reference to the iron strong boxes of so-called 'Armada' type which appear as parish chests in many places, e.g. at Watford and Hitchin, Herts., Mortlake, Surrey, Hythe, Kent, Oxenton and Icomb (formerly Worcs. now Gloucs.), etc. They have a dummy keyhole on the front, but their real keyhole is concealed in the lid. On the under side of the lid there is a most complicated lock, with eight, ten, or even sixteen bolts, fastening the lid to all four sides of the chest. Actually chests of this sort have not the slightest connection with the Armada. They were made in Flanders, Germany and Austria during the sixteenth and seventeenth centuries, and were imported into this country in large numbers at a fixed rate of duty.

Towards the end of the fifteenth century the characteristic linen fold panelling, common in secular furniture, appears also in church chests. There is a fine example of a credence so decorated at Thaxted, Essex.

From the Tudor period onwards the identification and dating of chests presents comparatively little difficulty. Both in the wood chosen, and in the style adopted, these are more or less characteristic of their time, and they may be dated by reference to secular furniture of the same period. In Tudor times especially the Tudor rose is not uncommon as a decorative *motif*. At this time and later too it is quite common to find references in extant churchwardens' accounts to the purchase of the chest, e.g. at Mortlake, Surrey, where in 1610–11:

Payment for a cheist for the Register Books x^s iij^d.

The chests themselves are quite commonly dated, while mediaeval chests are very rarely so. With the exaltation of the office of churchwarden in Tudor times a custom developed of the reigning wardens having their names or initials inscribed when a new chest was provided. There is a good example at St Oswald's, Chester. There are numerous others, probably some in every county in England.

In the early post-Renaissance period the chests become more and more ornate, and of course the characteristic Gothic ornaments are seen no more, but are replaced by classical or semi-classical details, including even such inappropriate ornaments as plump cherubs. A very well-known chest of c. 1616 is that of Croscombe, Som., completely covered with a design of rosettes and interlacing bands in low relief. Woods other than oak begin to appear, rarely as the main material used in the construction of the chest, more usually as inlays, overlays and similar decorations. Well-known examples of inlaid work of this period are at Baldock,

Herts., and Loughton, Essex, and there is a very fine one in the cathedral church of St Saviour, Southwark. As the seventeenth century advanced the design becomes more restrained and much less exuberant, and one sees the beginning of the eighteenth-century sense of dignity and good taste. The seventeenth-century coffer at Frodsham, Ches., well illustrates this point, as do many of the chests in the City of London churches.

From about 1680 onwards one finds occasional instances of the prevalent rage for walnut affecting church chests of the period, the comparatively soft wood lending itself well to the elaborate carving then in vogue. Cabriole legs and ball feet are found occasionally even in church chests of the period. With the removal of the mahogany duty in 1753 mahogany began to take the place of the woods formerly in fashion, but only in a few wealthy city churches. Right through the century the traditional oak and the traditional methods of construction still held sway in the villages remote from urban centres. After the middle of the eighteenth century, however, one finds few chests which are in any sense of the term works of art. The utilitarian aspect of things was too much to the front, and the desire of the parish officials was not so much for the provision of a magnificent piece of furniture which would at once ornament their own church and be the envy of neighbouring parishes, as for a plain substantial box to give ample storage space for the holding of the vast masses of poor-law papers which they began to accumulate. Accordingly there were provided plain boxes, sometimes even deal ones, made after much the same fashion as those favoured until half a century ago by country girls going away to domestic service, and many of these survive to this day. A good example of such a deal box is to be seen at Thaxted, Essex, with the incised date 1789. An account of it appears in Mr Roe's book.[9] A kind of chest, too, is the cubical iron box provided in accordance with the registration act of 1812[10] for the safe custody of the registers. Such chests with the date 1813 set in relief on the lid are very common objects in our parish churches. They are not particularly beautiful affairs, and are best described in the words of the act: 'dry, well painted iron chests'.

We refer elsewhere to the mention of chests in churchwardens' accounts. Returns to visitation articles often present the failure of the parish to provide or maintain the chest, e.g. in Nottinghamshire in 1639 one chest was found to have no lock, at Gringley, where the parish clerk had assumed the right to hold the keys, 'whereof the minister hath been abridged of the due keeping of the same', the 'strong Chist' at Hawton 'wanted both locks and keys', and at Edwinstowe for lack of locks thieves had broken in and stolen goods to the value of £10 from the chest in which 'laye certaine writings' and other things belonging to that church. In another church, the wardens used the chest as a receptacle for bell ropes. In 1548 the wardens of Stonehouse, Gloucs., presented 'That their commin boxe lackethe hoop locks'. They were ordered to have it attended to, and in due course certified that this had been done.

Even to-day incumbents and churchwardens are not always free from blame in these matters.

In recent years a magnificent linenfold credence in an Essex church has been pickled with chemicals, every scrap of its patina has been removed, and the piece literally skinned to the bone through the efforts of a too enthusiastic custodian. A unique chest in Kent stood for some considerable time in a shallow pool of water. A fine mediaeval chest in Nottinghamshire had been allowed to stand for years on the floor of an abandoned church until it was now almost in pieces (its contents when last we examined it were the discarded toys of the vicarage children, who apparently used the church as playroom on wet days). A Staffordshire parish with a much restored and almost valueless church has a couple of fine chests, one of mediaeval and one (initialled) of Tudor date. Both when we visited the place were in an unlocked damp and dirty lumber room annexed to the church. The locks of both had been prized off, and the contents might be removed by anyone who cared to purloin them.

They comprise apparently the entire records of the parish for two centuries at least. The woodworms in a wonderful seventeenth-century chest in Derbyshire were left undisturbed for so long that they had entirely devoured the internal partitions. When last we saw it the sides were mere shells, and the worms having exhausted the nourishment to be found in the chest had transferred their attention to the contents, and were devouring a fine collection of seventeenth- and eighteenth-century parchments stored in the coffer, and apparently not aired or sorted since the eighteen-thirties. The reader who pursues the matter will probably find for himself examples of other chests which should be honoured residents in church chancels, but which have been relegated to damp and dirty belfries and cellars, or even to rectory and vicarage coach-houses and stables.

PART I

Records Mainly Ecclesiastical

I. PARISH REGISTERS

THE HISTORY OF THE REGISTERS. Cromwell's injunction. Early registers. Canon 70 and register transcription. Other register transcripts. The 1644 ordinance. The 1653 ordinance. The 'Registers' and their real or supposed misdeeds. The 1654 ordinance. Register references to the Interregnum. Parish registers and taxation. Eighteenth-century neglect of laws and canons as to registration. Lord Hardwicke's Act. Further attempts to use the registers for fiscal purposes. Rose's Act. Civil registration. MISSING REGISTERS AND REGISTER TRANSCRIPTS. The use of diocesan transcripts to supply gaps in registers. Transcripts of the registers of 'Peculiars'. Changes in diocesan boundaries. Published lists of register transcripts. THE PRINTING OF PARISH REGISTERS. ACCESS TO REGISTERS AND TRANSCRIPTS. REGISTER ENTRIES OF HISTORICAL INTEREST. Register entries concerning the Civil War. Register entries after the Restoration.
REGISTER ENTRIES. BAPTISMAL REGISTERS. Lay baptism and private baptism. Chrisom children. Foundlings and bastards. MARRIAGE REGISTERS. The law of marriage. The close seasons. Anglican marriages during the Interregnum. Marriage by banns and by licence. Irregular but valid marriages. Marriages in 'peculiars'. BURIAL REGISTERS. The reasons for the incompleteness of the entries. Burials of papists, dissenters and excommunicates. Remarks, laudatory and otherwise, in burial entries. Burials in woollen. Mortuaries. MISCELLANEOUS ENTRIES. Forged entries. Notes as to the purchase of registers. The 'Protestation' and similar documents. Notes of peculiars and donatives. Other sundry entries. Records of tithe and boundary disputes. Parochial boundary perambulations. Poor-law records in parish registers. Literary works in parish registers. 'Reading in' records. VARIOUS OTHER ENTRIES OF HISTORICAL INTEREST. Royal visits. The qualifications requisite in a model parson's wife. Medical recipes. The special value of the historical entries in the registers of the Chapels Royal. A NOTE UPON REGISTERS AND POPULATION STATISTICS.

THE HISTORY OF THE REGISTERS. When Hume included, in a well-known passage,[1] the 'irregular' keeping of parish registers in the twelfth century as amongst its most barbarous deficiencies, he was being over generous to the middle ages. In mediaeval times, properly so called, there were no parish registers. For some years before the Reformation monastic houses, especially the smaller ones, and parish priests had been developing the custom of noting in an album, or on the margins of the service books, the births and deaths in the leading local families. In 1497 Cardinal Ximenes exerted all his influence to secure that, firstly, throughout his own province of Toledo, then through all Western Europe, there should be a proper registration of baptisms. No doubt his aim was to check the growing scandal of wholesale divorces, disguised as decrees of nullity, based upon the alleged spiritual affinity contracted at baptism between the baptised and his relatives, and the sponsors and their relatives. How far this notion of affinity had gone may be seen from such instances as that of John Hawthorn of Tunbridge, who in 1463 was sentenced to be whipped thrice round church and market tor incest, i.e. for marrying as a second wife the god-daughter of his first.

In 1535 and 1536 a notion gained ground in England that the Vice-Gerent, Thomas Cromwell, intended to introduce some such registration system here. There was popular suspicion that any scheme of the sort would be found to have fiscal connections,[2] and it was not until 5 September 1538,[3] after the final suppression of the Pilgrimage of Grace and the Lincolnshire rising, which this rumour had helped to foment,[4] that Cromwell ventured to issue his mandate.[5] This ordered every parson, vicar or curate to enter in a book every wedding, christening and burial in his parish, with the names of the parties. The parish was to provide a 'sure coffer' with two locks, the parson having the custody of one key, the wardens that of the other. The entries were to be made each Sunday after service, in the presence of one of the wardens. The mandate was enforced under a penalty of 3s. 4d. for the repair of the church.

These entries were generally made upon paper, sometimes upon loose sheets, and sixty years later these registers were ordered to be copied upon parchment in books,[6] so that the registers which still survive dating back to 1538–9—perhaps about 1400 or 1500 in number—rarely contain original entries of this date. This may be seen in the fact that the entries 1538–98, when there are any, are almost invariably throughout in the hands of the incumbents of 1598 or, in some populous parishes, of the professional scriveners who transcribed data from the old paper registers. Sometimes the earliest paper registers had disappeared even before the transcription was ordered in 1598, e.g. at Kirton in Lindsey, Lincs.—according to a note in the earliest extant register, the register is missing since one 'Vicare was maryed and deprived and ye next incumbent kep one that non can fynd'.

In other cases the parishes were more fortunate, as e.g. at SS. Cosmas and Damian, Blean, Kent, where the register is headed:

The Register Book of the Parish of St. Cosmus and Damian in the Bleane within ye Diocese of Canterburie, bearing date from the beginning of ye queens Maties Rayne, viz, the 17th day of November 1558 of Christenings, Marriages, and Burialls...the which said Register booke is truly collected and gathered out of the Register bookes of ye Parish of Cosmus Damian in the Bleane.

Cromwell's injunction was repeated by Edward VI in 1547,

when an order was issued that the fine should be given to the poor. Edward's order was re-enacted the same year in the Canterbury visitation articles. In 1555 and 1557 Cardinal Pole required the bishops in their visitations to see that the names of sponsors were duly entered in the registers of baptisms. In 1559, soon after her accession, Queen Elizabeth repeated Cromwell's edict in more rigorous terms.

Abortive registration bills were introduced in Parliament in 1563 and 1590, and on 25 October 1597 a provincial constitution of Canterbury, approved by the Queen in 1598, ordered that parchment registers should be purchased by each parish, and that all names from the older (usually paper) registers should be copied therein from the beginning, 'but especially since the first year of her Majesty's reign'. It is for this reason that so many registers begin in 1558, the transcriber indolently complying with only the last part of the injunction, and omitting to copy the first twenty years of the original register. This time it was ordered that entries should be made as before, on Sundays, but in the presence of *both* wardens. Every page was to be subscribed by them as well as by the minister, and it was ordered that the coffer should have a third lock, the minister and each warden to have a key. The entries of the past week were to be read out each Sunday after service. Finally, it was provided that the churchwardens of each parish should, within a month after Easter each year, hand over to the diocesan registry a transcript of the register entries for the preceding year.

Luddenham, Kent, has this entry in its first register:

This register following is truly copied of the old Register Booke of Luddenham, and conferred together, nothing added or left out that concerneth the Record of Baptysings, buryalls, marriages or other thing pertayning to the church or parish. By me, Peter Jackson, Clerke, Rect. Eccl. Lud., 1598.

On 11 November 1563 the Roman Catholic Church ordered the general keeping of baptismal and marriage registers.

The canons of 1603 include an order based on the constitution of 1598, with the modification that the period during which the churchwardens were ordered to send in their transcripts was altered to within a month of Lady Day. The order as to public reading of entries was not repeated, but the injunction as to the three locks of the coffer was reiterated in the canon.

A great many transcripts seem to have been made following the constitution of 1597–8 and many more were made, for a variety of reasons, in later years. The Surrey Record Society volume above noted contains several entries as to the transcription of registers. At Albury, e.g. the first register, 1559–1728, notes that the early entries were taken from the ancient book by Robert Cowper, rector of the church aforesaid:

April 4th A.D. 1602
(*ex veteri libro per Robertum Cowper Rectorem Ecclesiae predictae* 4 *die Aprilis anno domini* 1602.)

At High and Low Ham, Som., is the note:

Let it be remembered that this register was transcribed 1679 31 Chas. II

(*Memorandum quod hoc Registrum transcriptum est anno* 1679 *trigesimo primo Caroli II.*)

The first register of Great Dunmow, Essex, has in a hand of c. 1625–50 an

appendix or extract of suche as were baptized...from...1538...as appeareth in a most ancient Register eaten out with tyme almost

The next important dates in the history of parish registers are 6 Dec. 1644 / 4 Jan. 1645, when the same ordinance which substituted the 'Directory' for the Prayer Book[7] required that each parish or chapelry in the country should provide a 'fair Register Book of Velim' wherein were to be recorded the dates of baptisms as before, plus the dates of births and the parents' names. The regulations as to marriage entries remained unchanged, but it was ordered that each burial entry was to record also the date of death. The Civil War being then in progress, there are very few parish registers in which these directions were observed.

Much more important changes were introduced by an act (of Barebones's Parliament), 24 Aug. 1653, taking effect 29 Sept. (Michaelmas Day) 1653.[8] By this the Government took away from the ministers not only the custody of the registers, but even the solemnisation of the marriage ceremony itself. The latter of these functions was entrusted to the justices, the former to a new secular official, the 'Parish Register' (not 'Registrar'), elected by all the ratepayers in a parish, and sworn before, and approved by, a magistrate.

At Ampthill, Beds., the appointment of the 'Register' is thus recorded in 1654 on p. 1 of Register II:

Bedd: By vertue of an Act of Parliament for the Regesteringe of Births and Burialls and allsoe touching Marriges and the Regestering

V. Three Parish chests: A, Uffington (Lincs.); B, Dersingham (Norf.);
C, Boston (Lincs.). (*See pp.* 37–40.)

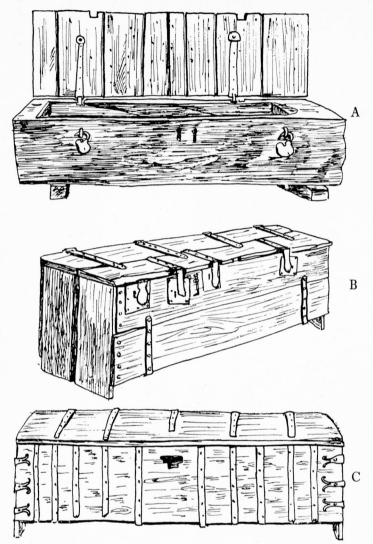

VI. The evolution of the chest: A, Cheadle (Staffs.); B, Stoak (Cheshire);
C, Astbury (Cheshire). (*Note:* the matchboarding lid of the Cheadle chest is
not, of course, original.) (*See pp.* 37–40.)

thereof we the inhabitants of Ampthill in the County aforesaid have made choyce of Robert Clearke of our said Towne to be Regester and is approved by us whose names are hereunto subscribed Justices of the peace for the County aforesaid....

All registration functions were entrusted to these officials at a fee of 12*d*. per birth and baptism, and 4*d*. per death and burial. One may occasionally find traces of the supposed reforms of the period in the amalgamation for registration purposes of two contiguous or intermixed parishes.[9] Sometimes the minister of the parish was elected 'Register'. In other parishes the parish clerk was chosen. At Chislet, Kent, according to Register II:

1654. Peter Randall the p'sh clerke of Chislett was chosen Register of Maryages, byrths, and buryalls, accordinge to an Act of Parliam^t to that purpose, by us the Minister and p'shyoners, whose names are hereunto subscribed.

A human note is struck by one of these Parliamentarian 'Registers', at Edwinstowe, Notts., when on 8 March 1653 he records the burial of

Anne, wife of Tho. Hallam deceased (She) was my first Masters wife, which taught me to spell and read in my childhood.

Generally, however, throughout much of England, the outstanding feature of the registers during the Interregnum is the haphazard and half-hearted fasion in which they were kept at any rate until 1653, and sometimes throughout the whole period. Archdeacon Fearon[10] notes, however, that in Hampshire the 'Registers' generally did their work well. Another common feature of the registers at this time is the entry of dates of birth and publication of marriages, as well as, or instead of, those of baptism and marriage.

The ordinance of 24 Aug./29 Sept. 1653 legalised civil marriage, such marriages being confirmed later by statute[11] after the Restoration.

In and after 1660 it is quite usual to find entries explaining the *lacunae* in the registers, especially those from about 1642 to the beginning of civil registration in 1653.

The rector of Keston, Kent, notes the strange goings on in a memorandum with a queer effect of anti-climax:

1643 on the 23 of Aprill our church was defaced our font thrown downe and new formes of prayer appointed.

Meanwhile, tactful churchmen kept quiet. The rector of Luddenham, Kent, e.g. enters in his register:

E

When a war, more than a civil one, was raging most grimly between Royalists and Parliamentarians throughout the greatest part of England I lived well because I lay low.

(*Bello plusquam civili inter Regios et Parliamentarios per plurimam partem Angliae horribiliter grassante Bene Vixi quia bene Latui.*)

Sometimes the critics of the work of their predecessors were almost equally culpable in matters of registration, e.g. at Flamstead, Herts., Christopher Cowyn, who 'came to officiate' in 1647, explains a gap 1644–7 as due either to 'the carelessness and neglect of the then present ministers, or the distraction and violence of the times'. But Christopher's handwriting becomes progressively less and less legible, and at the bottom of the next page he has upset his ink pot.

When the marriage ordinance was confirmed in 1657, the declaration that other marriages were illegal was omitted,[12] and in many places, from then until the end of the Commonwealth, marriages were celebrated by magistrate and 'Register' jointly. Since the intruders and 'Registers' could be guilty of such deplorable neglect, we may rejoice at any rate from the point of view of the parish historian that they disappeared together at the Restoration.

The next important act concerning parish registers is the celebrated order (dealt with below) as to burial in woollen.[13]

A few years later still the forebodings expressed when the registration system was first introduced—that the registers would be used to levy taxation—were at last fulfilled. Two acts were passed in connection with this. In 1694[14] Parliament granted the Crown, for a quinquennial period 'for carrying on the war against France with vigour', a duty of 2s. per birth, 2s. 6d. per marriage, and 4s. per burial of all non-paupers, with a sliding scale rising to £30 for the birth of the eldest son of a Duke, £50 for a Duke's marriage, and £50 for his burial. All births were to be notified to the rector or vicar within five days, under a penalty of 40s., and he was to record them for a fee of 6d., under a like penalty. It was specially provided that a birth should not be exempt from tax merely because the parents failed to have the child christened, but nevertheless it seems likely that in many parishes such births were not registered, and presumably no tax was paid. In other parishes, however, there is clear evidence that the parson in his capacity of tax-collector looked up the neglectful parishioner and collected the tax, plus, one hopes, his sixpenny fee.

How little regard was paid to the acts may be judged from the fact that in 1705[15] it was thought necessary to pass an act of indemnity on behalf of the clergy who had neglected to obey their provisions, and who, in consequence, were liable to colossal fines.

In 1702–3,[16] a committee of Convocation drew up a list of ecclesiastical offences notoriously requiring remedy, in which irregularity in keeping the registers is prominent in the list of *gravamina*. Another act was passed in 1711[17] ordering the provision of proper register books with ruled and numbered pages. The next incident in the history of the registers occurred in 1753, when a bill for the registration of births, marriages and deaths passed the Commons but was rejected by the Lords. Especially as to marriage, the laxity of the law lent itself to gross abuse, and when in 1755 Lord Hardwicke's famous Marriage Act[18] began to be enforced it introduced many long overdue reforms.

It ordered that records should be kept both of banns and of marriages, that these should be 'in proper books of vellum or good and durable paper' to be provided by the churchwardens. The entries were to be signed by the parties and to follow a prescribed form, and the registers were to be 'carefully kept and preserved for public use'. This is the origin of the Hardwicke Marriage Registers which are to be found in almost every chest, and which are the first registers consisting of bound volumes of printed forms.

An interesting mistake in connection with these Hardwicke Registers occurs in Wilkie Collins' *The Woman in White*.[19] The forged marriage entry in the registers of Old Welmingham upon which the whole plot hangs is so described that it is clear that Wilkie Collins had never seen a Hardwicke Register—composed of printed forms, four to the page.

According to Archdeacon Fearon's book,[20] the passing of the Hardwicke Act was followed by a total cessation of marriages in the Hampshire churches of Pear Tree, Greywell, and Winchester Cathedral, which were not licensed for marriages at all, and at Empshott, Newtown, Rowner, Sherborne St John and Tichborne the numbers fell to a remarkable extent. At Empshott, 1728–40, there had been seventy-two marriages of 'Outlanders'; at Newtown, 1731–44, twenty-six marriages out of thirty-three had been irregular; and at Rowner, 1655–1754, there had been 390 marriages of which 225 were irregular, since neither party lived in the parish. In this last-named parish, 1743–53, there were eighty-three marriages, of which forty-seven were irregular, while from 1753 to 1773 there were but twenty-eight in all.

The Stamp Act of 1783 [21] granted to the Crown a stamp duty of threepence upon every register entry of a burial, marriage, birth or christening, the officiating minister who collected the duty being allowed a commission of 10 per cent for his trouble. Two years later this act was extended to cover nonconformists.[22] This legislation—the second attempt to use the registers for fiscal purposes—remained in force only until 1794, when it was repealed.[23]

At Hawstead All Saints, Suff., the incumbent thus recorded the imposition of the tax:

1783, An Act takes place 1 October that imposes a tax of 3d. upon the entry of every christening, marriage and burial, except those of some poor persons, particularly circumstanced—a tax most vexatious to the Clergy, and which, it is thought, will be unproductive to the State.

About the end of the eighteenth century, questions of population came very much to the fore,[24] and there were discussions as to the use of the registers in obtaining statistical information for the benefit of the statesmen and economists of the time. The Public Records Committee of 1800 dealt in some detail with both registers and transcripts, and stated[25] that the transcripts ordered by the canons were sent forward regularly each year in but eighteen of the twenty-six dioceses, and triennially in two or three others, but that in a great proportion of the parishes in the remaining dioceses the provisions of the canon had been habitually ignored.

A few years later, despite the fact that proposals for systematising registration were denounced as hostile to the Church, and designed for governmental jobbery, the third major enactment as to registers was put on the statute book, after endless delay, and a vast deal of amendment: George Rose's Act of 1812.[26] The act was badly drafted, and contained the clause that in case of failure to observe its provisions, the informer should receive as reward half the penalty imposed upon the defaulter, one of the penalties so dealt with being a sentence of transportation for fourteen years!

The act contained a host of safeguards for the registration system. In future the transcripts were to be made by the incumbent on parchment, within two months of the end of each year, and to be forwarded regularly to the registrar, who was to have proper indexes made. Future entries were to be made in three separate registers, to be prepared by the King's Printers upon a uniform system. Each baptismal entry was to include the names, abodes and descriptions of the parents, and each burial entry, the age and place of abode of the deceased. Finally, the registers were in future to be kept in a 'dry well painted iron chest, in some dry and secure place, either at the parsonage or in the church'.

As noted above, the chests so provided, with the date 1813 set in relief on the lids, are very common indeed in our parish churches, and there must be thousands of them remaining to this day.

In 1831 a parliamentary return[27] gave details how far these provisions had been complied with. A select committee reported on the question again in 1833,[28] and on its report further legislation was passed in 1837.[29] By this registration of *some* baptisms, marriages and burials (those according to the rites of the Established church) remained in the hands of its clergy, that of births, marriages and deaths became the concern of the civil authorities.

Church marriage registers are now kept in duplicate, the incumbent sending each quarter a copy of all marriage entries to the district superintendent registrar, who sends it to the Registrar-General, together with the records of births, marriages and deaths he has collected through his secular registrars. When the marriage registers are filled, one copy is retained in the parish, and the other goes to the secular registrar.

The diary of the Rev. J. P. Chambers, rector of Hedenham, Norf., has an interesting example of the clerical opposition to the introduction of this civil registration:

1837. 15th Jan. Notice Sheet up at the Church door relative to the provisions of the Act for registering births, deaths, and marriages where Dissenters are concerned, but as I have no doubt some alteration must be made before they can work well, I forbear making further mention of what I consider a sop thrown by the present government to secure the dissenting interests on their side.

MISSING REGISTERS AND REGISTER TRANSCRIPTS. In Elizabeth's reign, Lord Treasurer Burghley endeavoured to establish a General Register Office for England and Wales, where 'there should be yearly delivered a summary...whereby it should appear how many christenings, weddings, and burials were every year within England and Wales, and every county particularly by itself, and how many men-children and women-children were born in all of them, severally set down by themselves'. This proposition, recommended by him to the Queen and the Archbishop of Canterbury, failed to secure adoption. The Constitution of 1597, however, established a system whereby copies of the parish registers were to be supplied to the diocesan registry.[30] We have mentioned above the canon as to furnishing these transcripts of parish register entries. It was frequently ignored, perhaps because no fee was payable upon the receipt of the copies.

The files of transcripts were described in 1883[31] as 'a lamentable picture of episcopal negligence, parochial parsimony, and official rapacity'. Because of their incompleteness, their relative inaccessibility, and the fear that further losses might occur, numerous proposals have been made for collecting the original registers in the Public Record Office, the diocesan registries, the Lambeth Library, Somerset House, the county record offices, etc., but all these have failed before the solid clerical opposition with which they were greeted, partly, perhaps, because of the fees legally payable[32] upon the consultation of registers (but in practice rarely demanded).

Few of the original paper registers are extant.[33] According to a ruling of 1604 they ought all to be in the diocesan registries.[34] An estimate of 1831 for the 11,000 parishes in England and Wales, gives 722 registers beginning in 1538 (i.e. the parchment copies made in 1597–8). A calculation of 1910 puts their number at 656. Probably most of the losses have occurred either by fire, by gross negligence upon the part of the custodian, or by lack of proper control during the vacancy of benefices.[35]

When registers have so disappeared, in whole or in part, the bishop's transcripts may be invaluable to the inquirer. Sometimes, forged entries in original registers have been checked by reference to transcripts. Unfortunately the transcripts are often far less complete than the originals, but, of course, it often happens that gaps in one series are filled in, by entries in the other. It is by no means unusual for the transcripts to go back to an earlier period than the existing originals.[36] Usually, when transcripts were handed in to the archdeacon at the visitation, the intention was that he should transmit them to the diocesan registry. Often they never found their way there, but remained till late years with the records of the archdeaconry, perhaps because the same person held the offices of commissary to the bishop and official to the archdeacon. This explains why the Leicestershire transcripts are, and the bulk of them always have been, at Leicester, how the bulk of the Archdeaconry of Richmond transcripts come to be at Leeds, and so on.

It should be borne in mind that until comparatively recent years many parishes, known as 'Peculiars', were not like their neighbours subject to the jurisdiction of the Ordinary. Other parishes, including most that had been properties of the Knights Templar or the Hospitallers, and others which were the sites of Religious Houses, were 'Donatives'—such as Winkburn and Ossington, Notts., and Kirkstead, Lincs.—and were chaplaincies of the squire, quite exempt from diocesan jurisdiction, yet possessing registers. Of these no transcripts need be remitted anywhere. Otherwise the incumbents of peculiars transmitted to their ecclesiastical superior, who was not the diocesan, the same records which a normal parish sent forward to its bishop, so both probates of wills and parish register transcripts for such parishes may well be found not in the diocesan registry or diocesan or county record office,[37] but among the records of the peculiar, which the inquirer must run to earth for himself.

Mediaevally there were seventeen English dioceses.[38] In the sixteenth century there were, excluding Sodor and Man but including Henry VIII's five new (permanent) foundations of 1542, Bristol, Chester, Gloucester, Oxford and Peterborough, twenty-two; there are now forty-two. But we must bear in mind that the boundaries of the present dioceses have been subject to a great deal of alteration.[38] Many of the dioceses bore little relation to the areas now covered by the same titles. Lincoln included half the Midlands, Lichfield covered Derbyshire and Cheshire as well as Staffordshire, North Shropshire and North Warwickshire, and so on. Consequently, e.g., the old transcripts of Derbyshire may be (in fact they actually are) at Lichfield, not at Derby; those of Nottinghamshire, now at Southwell, were until a short time ago at York, and so on. And the position is further complicated by the fact that, apart from peculiars, parishes might often be geographically in one diocese, but ecclesiastically in another, and therefore their records are most likely to be found amongst those of the latter, e.g. Rossington, in the West Riding of Yorkshire, was an outlying parish in the archdeaconry of Nottingham, so that its ecclesiastical records, including parish register transcripts, are with those of that archdeaconry. The archdeaconries were in as confused a state as the dioceses. The county of Huntingdon, e.g., lay in four different archdeaconries (though mainly in that of Huntingdon).

In earlier texts of this book we gave here, over endnote numbers 39–40, references to various works giving dates and other particulars of register transcripts. Most such references are now or will, in the very near future, become quite obsolete, with the appearance of Mr D. J. Steel's survey[39–40] to which the reader is referred.

THE PRINTING OF PARISH REGISTERS. Societies and private

persons have from time to time from 1834 onwards printed parish registers in whole or in part. The Society of Genealogists, 37 Harrington Gardens, S.W.7, has a vast collection of printed registers and transcripts and manuscript copies, covering at the time it was last catalogued (1963) over 5000 parishes. The society has the very sound plan of typing out all manuscript register copies lent to it, and giving the lender the carbon copy of the typescript.

The principal county parish register societies,[41] *active or defunct,* are for Bedfordshire (Beds. County Council), Buckinghamshire, Cambridgeshire, Cornwall and Devon, Cumberland and Westmorland, Derbyshire, Dorset, Gloucestershire (in *Gloucestershire Notes and Queries,* below), Hampshire, Hertfordshire, Lancashire, Lincolnshire, Norfolk, Northumberland and Durham, Shropshire, Somerset, Staffordshire, Surrey, Warwickshire, Worcestershire, and Yorkshire.

The principal societies, other than parish register societies, which print or have printed parish registers are the Harleian Society, Cambridge Antiquarian Society, Derbyshire Archaeological and Natural History Society, Devon and Cornwall Record Society,[42] Dorset Record Society, Lancashire and Cheshire Historical Society, Lancashire and Cheshire Record Society, Leicestershire Archaeological Society, Norfolk Archaeological Society, Shropshire Archaeological Society, (Leeds) Thoresby Society, and the Society of Antiquaries of Newcastle-upon-Tyne.[43] Messrs Phillimore, lately of Chancery Lane, printed many hundred registers, and had many more ready for publication when the necessary finance was available. It does not appear whether these gentlemen are now officially represented by Messrs Phillimore, of 38 Finsbury Square, E.C.2, or by Messrs Phillimore, of Bridge Place, near Canterbury. Anyhow, both concerns maintain the traditional Phillimore interest in genealogy and in parish registers.

ACCESS TO REGISTERS AND TRANSCRIPTS. Before discussing the registers in rather more detail it may be well to point out that parish registers are still legally in the custody of the incumbent. The fees payable for their consultation, laid down by statute in 1836, were a shilling for the first year consulted, plus sixpence for each subsequent year, with certified entries chargeable at 2s. 7d. extra.[44] Generally, however, the clergy are most generous in permitting access to the registers for bona fide students of history at much reduced or nominal rates, or even with no charge at all. But they are not bound to do anything of the sort, and it is at once gracious and prudent, when one has enjoyed such free access, to offer some small contribution to the poor-box, or to the funds for church expenses or fabric maintenance.

Since diocesan registrars were generally paid entirely by fees, and since they are, for the most part, solicitors, one could not expect them to afford free access to the transcripts in their charge. The rate of fee varied from diocese to diocese. Sometimes it might cover access to one bundle of transcripts (i.e. for all parishes in the diocese, one annual or triennial bundle), or, if the transcripts had been sorted into parishes, the fee would probably cover one complete parish bundle. Now that the transcripts, in the main, have been or are being transferred to diocesan or county record offices, it will be only in a minority of dioceses, and to a professional ' record-searcher ', that any fee will be chargeable.˙ This is a great improvement on the position when access to an annual or triennial bundle for the diocese, or a complete bundle for the parish, might cost anywhere from half a crown to as much as three guineas!

REGISTER ENTRIES OF HISTORICAL INTEREST. The clergy were actually encouraged to enter in the registers very much more than the minimum record of facts. Dr White Kennett, Bishop of Peterborough 1718–28, in his first visitation charge[45] took occasion to enjoin this duty upon his clergy. By way of contrast we may quote a note by a rector of Cheam, Surrey, in the earliest register, 1538–1728, that he desired all entries to be 'sine commentario'.

Where the register is old,[46] one may often find curious alterations in the formulae of entries, which, like the numerous historical notes entered in odd places, reflect the stirring events of the times. In the earliest of all, numerous references to the Mass are followed by a few mentioning the Communion Service: similarly the baptismal and burial entries bear the marks of the changes which were taking place. The register of Kirkburton, Yorks., contains a copy of the Bidding Prayer with a deletion. It runs:

1545. Yow shalt (*sic*) pray for the whole congregation of Xrystes churche wheresoever it be dyspersed throughout all the worlde. And espesyally for this churche of England and Hyreland wherein I commend unto your devout prayer (our most holie father and pope wyt all his true college of cardenalls) and for all archbyschopes, byschopes, parsons, vicars and curates who hayth care and charge of soulls and especyally for the vicar and curat of this churche, who also hayth care and charge of your soules.

The phrase in brackets has been deleted, probably by Archbishop Holgate at his visitation of 1546.

In 1547 the change is very marked. The introduction of the English Prayer Book is often mentioned, and in 1553 one may find entries relating to the reintroduction of the Latin service.

No doubt it was a parson or clerk puritanically inclined who entered in Register 1 of Landbeach, Cambs.:

Loke, the fox Will eate no grapes, and Whi, ·he can not git y^m; so at this towne thei loue inglish seruis, because thei can haue no Other, as apperith bi the candilbeme & rodlofte, as I think: iudge you by me.

Nicolas Nemo. A.D. 1594.[47]

Thenceforward from 1553 the entries take a more stable form. Except in a few out-of-the-way parishes, there is no more mention of sponsors in baptism (though here and there the 'squire's god-children are so honoured'). At Birchington, Kent, the custom lasted until 1606, and at Holy Trinity, Chester and Mansfield, Notts., to 1624 and 1625 respectively. References to communion at marriage are much scarcer, and the burial entries no longer contain the pious wish ' *Cujus animae propitietur Deus!* ' Since the death of a monarch might have a very important effect upon the affairs of the church, it is intelligible enough that the deaths of Henry VIII, Edward VI, Mary and Elizabeth should be recorded, as they often are, with notes of the proclamations of their successors, and the rejoicings at their coronations. The Armada naturally receives much attention, so do the Essex Conspiracy, the alleged Gowrie Plot, the Gunpowder Plot, and the alarms and excursions of the Civil War, from the raising of the royal standard at Nottingham on 22 August 1642 to the last scene in the tragedy —that enacted at Whitehall on 30 January 1649. The register of Reigate, Surrey, notes that the execution of the King was by 'separating his royall head from his shoulders'.

This note appears in the register of High and Low Ham, Som.:

The most deplorable beheading of Charles I was on Jan. 30th, from which day the reign of Charles II was inaugurated, and I pray long may he reign! 1648. 24 Chas. I, a year at once fatal to the aforesaid King and unhappy for us.

(*Infelicissima Caroli I decollatio Jan. 30 a quo die regnum auspicatum est Car. II, diuque regnet precor. Anon 1648 R. Regni Carl. I, 24, qui et eidem regi fatalis nobisque infelix.*)

We have referred above [48] to the entries explaining *lacunae* of this period. Puttenham, Surrey, 1641, has a note:

About this tyme began yᵉ warre and therwith began disorders, this Register not being carefully kept till yᵉ happy corona͡con of King Charles yᵉ II....

At Brotherton, Yorks.:

the redgesters for 1642, 43, 44, 45 were taken away out of the church when souldiers that were taken by yᵉ Commission of Array for the King's service were put in there to be kept.

A note in the earliest register of Fetcham, Surrey (1559–1712), which has lengthy gaps from 1653 onwards, explains that the volume is

very defective especially during the unnatural Rebellion begun in 1641, till the happy restoration of our sacred and civil liberties in the year 1660.

A later note points out with some justification that

the memory of the Restoration was so powerful in the reverend minister's mind that he forgot to enter in the register any marriages from 1660 to 1685, nor more than 23 baptisms from 1660 to 1683...and no burials from 1660–1684/5.

Notes of subscription to the Protestation of 1641 occur rarely, apparently only when 'squire or parson was puritanically inclined'. References to a few such appear below. Sometimes following such an entry is the record of the introduction in 1645 of the Presbyterian 'Directory' which replaced the Prayer Book.

So after the Restoration of 1660–1 the reinstated clergy most joyfully recorded that, like the king himself, they 'enjoyed their own again', and occasionally they or their parish clerks offered unflattering comment upon the character, conduct and scholarship of their supplanters, the 'intruding' ministers of the usurpation. Typical entries are these:

Moreton Corbet, Salop, 1660:

Most p'te of yᵉ war time before theyr was an uzerper in yᵉ place one p'son Gower put in by Traytors and Rebbells....

At St Margaret's, East Lavant, Sussex, the intruder, Richard Batsworth, is described as

a man of low stature, very violent for the rebels, and a plunderer of the royalists, particularly of the Morley family. He had some learning, a great deal of chicanery, though seldom more than one coat, which for some time he wore the wrong side out,—its right side was seen only on Sundays—till it was almost worn out, and then he had a new one which he used in the same manner.

At Keston, Kent, in the burial entry of Robert Low, the minister, someone has inserted *Pretended* before the style 'rector of Keston', and someone else has added *N.B. One of Cromwell's Parsons.*

Similarly records appear of the 'Black Bartholomew' of 1662, when those intruders who would not conform were finally ejected.

At Newport, Salop, e.g. the entry appears:

Aug. 1662. Honest Mr. Maldon forced from his ministry for Nonconformity this month the 24 day.

The Rye House Plot, the Monmouth Rebellion, the acquittal of the Seven Bishops, the coming of the Prince of Orange, the bitter ecclesiastical feuds of Queen Anne's reign, and the Jacobite rebellions of 1715 and 1745, are all duly recorded, but after the middle of the eighteenth century general historical notes become much rarer, while after 1800 there are hardly any. The registers of the Chapels Royal [49] of St James's, Whitehall, and Windsor, are, of course, not parish records at all. They are, as one would expect, very rich in entries of historical interest.[50] An account of them with facsimiles appears in the Registrar-General's booklet above noted.

REGISTER ENTRIES

BAPTISMAL REGISTERS. We have referred above to Cardinal Pole's mandate that the names of sponsors should be entered in the baptismal register. Apart from the introduction of entries of this sort in Mary's time and their general cessation when Elizabeth succeeded to the throne,[1] there is little of outstanding interest in the baptismal entries until the time of the Commonwealth. From 1645[2] entries occur of baptisms with the mutilated rite of 'pouring or sprinckling of water' in church, but not in one of 'the places where Fonts in the time of Popery were unfitly and superstitiously placed'.

And so after the Restoration,[3] when wholesale adult baptisms were made in the endeavour to convert a nation largely unbaptised, so far as its younger members were concerned, into a properly baptised people, there are records of adult baptism, and one finds again entries of baptisms in fonts instead of basins. At St Dunstan's, Canterbury, in 1660, is a note of a child the first to be baptised since the font was 'anabaptistically abused'. Perhaps the entries of baptism or conditional baptism of the children of non-conforming parents which are especially common in Queen Anne's reign may be connected with the sincere and devout churchmanship of one of our few genuinely Anglican monarchs. They may well be the signs of an effort to deal with slackness in baptismal matters following the acts of 1693–5.[4] Only for two periods are dates of birth regularly entered, as well as those of baptism—in the Commonwealth,[5] and in some parishes for several years after 1783.[6] A vicar of Betley, Staffs., regularly entered among his baptisms the births of children to anabaptists, although, of course, these were not baptised; thus:

BAPTISMS

1705 Aug. 28　Lydia d. of Mark Tomkin anabaptist was born.

It has always been recognised in ecclesiastical law that a layman can baptise in an emergency. In fact, the midwife, bound by a sort of hippocratic oath, and duly licensed by the bishop, was specially enjoined in no wise to neglect baptism in the presence of witnesses if there was any chance of the child dying before the priest could arrive. The canons[7] are very emphatic that there shall be neither delay nor refusal by any minister in celebrating the rite. It was the priest's duty to instruct the midwife in the exact manner and form of celebrating the rite, so as to ensure its validity. After private baptism, whether by cleric or layman, the child, if it happened to survive, was duly received in church later on.

In the stress and excitement of a dangerous delivery a mistake might well occur as to the sex of the child, and incidents are recorded of girls being baptised by boys' names and *vice versa*. It was possibly to avoid awkward cases of this kind that midwives often baptised children as 'Creature' or 'Creatura Christi', which would serve equally well for either sex. This expression Christ's Creature occurs as early as Piers Plowman, but it has been suggested that its use in such cases was drawn from Tyndale's translation of II Cor. v. 17.

At Bishop Wearmouth, Durham, there was once another reason for a mistake as to sex:

Robert, daughter of William Thompson, bap. 15 Feb. 1730, the midwife mistaking the sex,—she was crazed with liquor (*ebrietas dementat*).

It was an old custom that the chrisom cloth (used at the christening) should be worn for a week or two until the mother's churching.

Then it was handed over to the church for use in ablutions, etc.[8]
There is a celebrated reference to a chrisom child (Falstaff!) in
King . Henry V,[9] and another in Bishop Jeremy Taylor's *Holy
Dying*.[10]

Registers and terriers sometimes specify, among the customs of
the church, what shall be the size and quality of the chrisom cloth.
If the child died 'in its innocency' before the mother's churching,
in general perhaps within a month or so of its birth, the offering
was not due, and the chrisom cloth served the sad purpose of a
shroud. The use of the chrisom cloth is provided for in the First
Prayer Book of Edward VI:[11]

*Then the Godfathers and Godmothers shall take and lay theyr handes
upon the childe, and the minister shall put vpon him his white vesture,
commonly called the Crisome; and saye.*

Take this white vesture for a tokē of the innocencie, whiche by God's
grace in this holy sacramente of Baptisme, is giuen vnto the: and for
a signe wherby thou art admonished, so long as thou lyuest, to geue
thyselfe to innocencie of liuing, that, after this transitory lyfe, thou
mayest be partaker of the lyfe euerlasting. Amen.

*The minister shall commaunde that the Crisomes be brought to the Churche,
and delyuered to the priestes after the accustomed maner, at the purification
of the mother of every chylde.*

This rubric was omitted from the Second Prayer Book, but some
faint trace of the usage may still be seen in the custom surviving,
in some localities, of the godmother covering the child's face with
a clean cambric handkerchief immediately after the actual baptism,
and while the rest of the rite is proceeding.

Something will be said later, in the section dealing with illegitimacy and the Poor Law,[12] as to the circumstances leading to
the prevalence of illegitimacy during the seventeenth century and
still more markedly at the end of the eighteenth. Here it is
sufficient to say that illegitimate children are invariably so described
in the registers, whether from moral indignation at their parents'
offence, or from concern as to the effect their births might have
upon the poor rate. A rather pathetic instance of the extent to
which this righteous indignation might be carried occurs in the
register of Stockton, Salop, where in 1784 the parish had to pay a
shilling from the poor rate to a person to induce him to stand god-
father to 'Mary Rowley's base childe'.

A more extravagant expenditure for a similar purpose is at
Birchington All Saints, Kent, where Register 3, 1676–1801, has:

1695 June 9 Paid for Gossipes for a poor travelling woman's child (probably though not certainly illegitimate) 3s. 0d.

Edgmond, Salop, has a special bastard register, 1797–1828. In the records of their very christenings these unfortunate children were treated with more obloquy than even the most bigoted high churchman used with reference to the children of dissenters.

On occasion the precise description of the status of such illegitimate children is wrapped in the decent obscurity of a dead language. A selection of the Latin terms most often met with will be found in the glossary.[13] Generally the English phrases used are brutally frank.

Often foundlings were christened by the name of the parish or that of some street in it, from the Saint's Day nearest to the date of their discovery, or from some other circumstance connected with their finding. Thus among the children admitted in 1716 to the Cripplegate charity school was a foundling, sponsored by the parish officer, John Olave of St Olave's. Crabbe[14] describes a vestry meeting held to deal with a foundling:

> Then by what name th'unwelcome guest to call
> Was long a question, and it posed them all;
> For he who lent it to a babe unknown,
> Censorious men might take it for his own:
> They look'd about, they gravely spoke to all,
> And not one *Richard* answered to the call.
> Next they inquired the day, when, passing by,
> Th' unlucky peasant heard the stranger's cry:
> This known,—how food and raiment they might give,
> Was next debated—for the rogue would live;
> At last, with all their words and work content,
> Back to their homes the prudent vestry went,
> And *Richard Monday* to the workhouse sent.

Dickensians will remember that Mr Bumble,[15] living in an age when ecclesiastical authority and Catholic tradition alike were at a low ebb, had invented a more prosaic system, and worked through the alphabet:

'And notwithstanding a offered reward of ten pound, which was afterwards increased to twenty pound, Notwithstanding the most superlative, and, I may say, supernat'ral exertions on the part of this parish', said Bumble, 'we have never been able to discover who is his father, or what was his mother's settlement, name, or con-dition.'

Mrs Mann raised her hands in astonishment; but added after a moment's reflection, 'How comes he to have any name at all, then?'

The beadle drew himself up with great pride, and said: 'I inwented it.'

'You, Mr Bumble!'

'I, Mrs Mann. We name our fondlings in alphabetical order. The last was S—Swubble I named him. This was a T—Twist, I named *him*. The next one as comes will be Unwin, and the next Vilkins....'

'Why, you're quite a literary character, sir!'... said Mrs Mann.... And as he finished the gin and water, the beadle, evidently gratified by the compliment, said: 'Perhaps I may be. Perhaps I may be, Mrs Mann!'

In other parishes misbegotten children were christened by names having some reference to their parents' offence. This example is from Edingley, Notts.:

1614. Frendelesse the sonne of Joane Robinsonne base gotten as she saythe by one John Longe was baptysed the first day of November.

A very odd baptismal entry is this from Brotherton, Yorks.:

1651. Roger ye sonne of I know-not-who was baptized I know not when.

One displaying better feeling on the part of the priest is this from Wolstanton, Staffs.:

12 June 1698. Baptized Providence, an infant whom her father and mother abandoned; but GOD will take care of her.

MARRIAGE REGISTERS. Before the Reformation, espousal could take place at seven years of age, the end of the period of infancy; marriage at twelve for the girl and fourteen for the boy. The custom of espousal hardly survived the break with the papacy, although traces of it are still to be seen in the marriage service, but the rule as to the age for marriage held until the Hardwicke Act of 1754, and even after this, when the parents' consent had been obtained. Most of the restrictive rules as to marriage date from pre-Reformation times. The restriction of marriage to the forenoon which held canonically until 1886 was, of course, due to the close connection of the marriage service with the nuptial mass.

The close seasons of the year, too, have very old canonical authority. There were anciently three of these:

> from Advent to S. Hilary's Day (January 13th);
> Septuagesima to Low Sunday;
> Rogation Sunday to Trinity Sunday.

The Council of Trent reduced these to two in the Roman Church.[16] They remained in the English Church after the Reformation.

A A O G Q T S C E F J ff

N N M V W V P P R B B

B D D I L K H H X Y Z Z

a b c d đ e e f f g h i k ll m n o p q r r ſt s t v u w x y z

VII. Seventeenth-century Secretary Hand. (See p. 301.)

To the Reverend the Minifter of *Luton*

Susannah Punter of the Parifh of *Luton* —— in the *County* of *Bedford* —— maketh Oath, That the Body of *Mary Kingham of this Parifh* ——

which was lately buried at *the Burial Ground of the Baptift Meeting Houſe* was not wrapped up, when buried, in any Suit, Sheet, or Shroud, but what was made of *Sheep's Wool* only; nor put into any Coffin, lined, faced, or covered with any kind of Cloth, or Stuff, but what was made of *Sheep's Wool* only, according to the Direction of an Act of Parliament, intituled, *An Act for burying in Woollen.*——

Taken and Sworn this *Second* Day of *December* —— 1795

Before me *Coriolanus Copleston.*

Curate.

N. B. Affidavits of Burial in Woollen muft be delivered in to the Minifter of the Parifh where the Deceafed was buried, in eight Days from the Time of Burial, on pain of the Penalty of Five Pounds for neglect thereof.

VIII. A Certificate of Burial in Woollen, from Luton, Beds., 1795. (See pp. 67–9.)

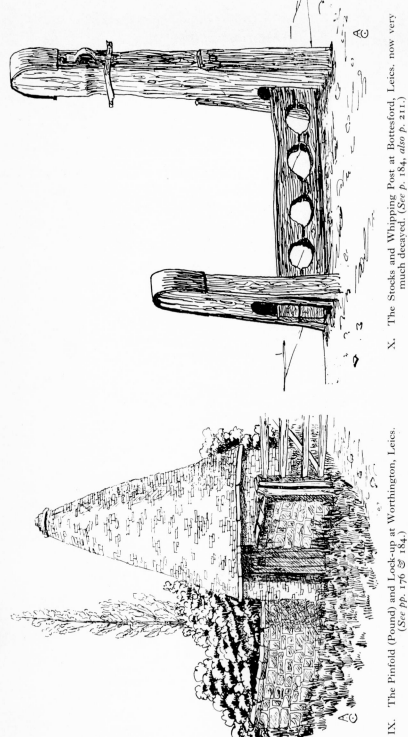

X. The Stocks and Whipping Post at Bottesford, Leics. now very much decayed. (*See* p. 184, *also* p. 211.)

IX. The Pinfold (Pound) and Lock-up at Worthington, Leics. (*See* pp. 176 & 184.)

In 1575 unsuccessful attempts were made both in Parliament and Convocation to make marriage lawful at all seasons of the year. The 1603 canons[17] forbid marriage 'at unseasonable times', but it has been disputed whether this rule applies to seasons of the year or hours of the day.

It seems that throughout the sixteenth century and a great part of the seventeenth these restrictions were generally observed. They lapsed, of course, during the Commonwealth, and attempts to reimpose them after the Restoration were not usually successful. Archdeacon Cosin mentioned the rule in his visitation articles in 1627, but apparently on its lapse during the Interregnum it is now virtually obsolete, and probably any attempt to put it in force would be held by the Privy Council as repugnant to common law. Verses embodying it are very often found entered on the fly-leaves of the older registers, e.g.

> Advent marriage doth thee deny,
> But Hilary gives thee liberty.
> Septuagesima says thee nay,
> Eight days from Easter says you may.
> Rogation bids thee to contain,
> But Trinity sets thee free again.[18]

or in more learned fashion:

> *Conjugium Adventus prohibet, Hilarius relaxat.*
> *Septuagena vetat, sed paschae octava remittit,*
> *Rogamen vetitat, concedit Trina potestas.*[19]

Similar rules in prose were entered in the register of Lympne, Kent, by the vicar, Richard Jaggard, who goes into great detail as to how he had received the rule and how it agreed with 'Linwood'. A successor a century later wrote:

We have no such rules as the foregoing in the Church of England, Marriage is lawful let Linwood and the Proctors say what they will about certain times prohibited.

During the Commonwealth it was quite usual for royalists in a parish having an 'intruded' minister to resort for marriages to the nearest Anglican clergyman who had managed to keep his living, and some parishes entirely ignored the new marriage legislation. An interesting entry illustrating this point occurs at Maid's Moreton, Bucks.:

A.D. 1653. By the Act before mentioned in the year 1653 marriages were not to be performed by the Minister, but the Justices of the Peace, yet none in this parish were bedded before they were solemnly wedded, in the Church, and that according to the orders of the Church of England.

F

Normally, of course, the English marriage took place, and still takes place, by banns, and until 1837 marriages (except those of Jews and Quakers) without banns could be lawfully celebrated only in virtue of licences issued by the bishop or archdeacon or his surrogate, or special licences issued by the archbishop.[20] In some particular archdeaconries the archdeacons too claimed the right to issue marriage licences. A great many indexes of such licences, and of the bonds which until 1823 were given in connection therewith, have been printed by various local record societies and by the British Record Society. The information given in these licences often supplements very materially the meagre information to be found in the parish registers. At some periods it was customary for all persons of any rank save the humblest to be married by licence. Such marriages are often marked in the registers *lic.* or *per licenciā*.

During the Commonwealth the registers often specify the name of the magistrate before whom the contract was made.

In the latter part of the seventeenth century and the first half of the eighteenth there was difficulty because of the ancient law that any marriage celebrated by a priest of the English Church, whether with banns or by licence or with neither, whether within or outside the canonical hours, whether in a parish church or elsewhere, however *irregular* it might be, was quite *valid*. The persons contracting such a marriage were liable to censure, and the priest celebrating it was subject to severe penalties involving the loss both of his liberty and of his benefice. In special areas, especially in the purlieus of such prisons as the Fleet,[21] there were, unhappily, many clergy who had neither benefice nor liberty, and who were quite prepared to marry applicants on demand. The subject is one of great interest, but hardly comes within our title, so the curious inquirer upon this point is referred for it to the works cited elsewhere.

Then there were the 'peculiars'[22] already mentioned, which claimed exemption from episcopal and archidiaconal visitation and control. After many dozen appalling scandals[23] the whole business was dealt with by the great Marriage Act of 1753, and since then, enterprising young men who felt disposed to elope with heiresses have had to cross the border into Scotland, where the marriage law was until 1939 less calculated to interfere with their schemes, or to the Channel Islands, vessels for which, specially designed for runaway couples, were until comparatively recent years always ready to set sail from Southampton.

BURIAL REGISTERS. Dr Burn[24] stresses that in point of accuracy and completeness the burial registers come after the marriage registers, and long before the records of baptism. Everyone must be born, but not everyone had Anglican parents. Although children of nonconformist families ought to have been entered in the registers, there is no doubt that many were not. There was no legal manner of marrying save in the parish church, and common prudence would suggest the desirability of making a proper record of all marriages in the interests of any future children. It is therefore natural to find the marriage registers best kept of all.

Probably the principal omissions in the burial registers are of data relating to unbaptised persons, whether children or adults, and of soldiers and sailors who died abroad. Moreover, from early times some papists and other dissenters were buried privately, sometimes at night in the churchyard by the connivance of an exceptionally tolerant incumbent, e.g. at Christchurch, Hants., 14 April 1604:

> Christian Steevens, the wife of Thomas Steevens, died in childbirth and was buried by women, for she was a papishe.[25]

A record of the burial of an excommunicate is this, from the register of High and Low Ham, Som., concerning the burial of Andreas Symock:

> This excommunicate was buried in the northern corner of the church-yard, but by what person or persons I know not.
>
> (*Excommunicatus sepultus est in septentrionale angulo coemeterii sed nescio per quem aut quos.*)

After the Toleration Act numerous cemeteries were opened for the benefit of nonconformists, including Roman Catholics and Jews. A few, especially some belonging to the Friends, had been opened half a century earlier.

Perhaps the most interesting of the burial entries are those in which the incumbent (or clerk) has recorded his opinion of the deceased. We have referred above to the Restoration clergy's notes upon their predecessors. Sometimes similar remarks were made as to other nonconformists. At Beeston, Notts., e.g., the burial entry of Ann Parrot on 18 June 1736 has the note: 'a dissembling canting Hollow presbiteriam'.

At Kingsworthy, Hants., Thomas Morrant, buried in 1695, is described as: 'A very constant comer to church, a widdow [*sic*].'

At Highclere, in the same county, when John Bond of Andover, 'a desirable young man of a comendable blameless and charitable disposition', was buried in 1718 the incumbent noted that he preached a funeral sermon on St John v. 24. At Cheriton, also in Hants., no less a person than Richard Cosen, churchwarden, is pronounced 'a Foole'. At Burghclere in 1816 John Potter is labelled as 'the egnorant'.

After the burial record of Frances Taylor, at St Maurice's, Winchester, in 1669, is the note: 'she was sunge to her grave by the Quire', and a later entry in another hand: 'Merry doings.'

At Rolleston, Notts., which is very rich in such entries,[26] the bare facts are given in English, and the comments in Latin, thus:

Margerie Deconsonne the wife of Bartholomew Deconsonne...fiftie yeares of age a tall slender womā, mighty thrifty, I should rather say stingy (*frugi admodū providene magis fuerit an parcior nescio*) shee leaving this life on Monday was buried on Tuesday the 30 of Aprill (1588).

Willm̄ Forrest about 60 years of age a cūninge fellow I will not say crafty, meagre in faith, extravagant in hope of eternal life, if one may make an inference from words, which are the index of the mind (*nō dicam versutū, fide pusillū, spe vitae aeternae, si ex verbis, mentis indicibus, cōiecturā facere liceret, nimium*), but in handie woorke as ditchinge, mowinge, sheip-clippinge & such like skilful: was buried December— xxviijth Tuesday.

Aug. 12. 1687. John Wise, Bachelor, a frequenter of taverns rather than of the Church and Sacrament, attacked by a raging fever, vomiting dreadful curses and blasphemies, died and was buried. In the hour of death Lord deliver us. (*Johanes Wise Caelebs, cauponularum magis quam Ecclesiae et Sacramenti frequentator, febre dementi accensus, diris execrationibus et blasphemijs evomens, mortem obijt: et sepultus fuit. In hora mortis libera nos Dñe.*)

At Newton Valence, Hants., in 1683:

Ann Baber Kinswoman of Cap. Farre (Regicide) was buried Feb. 5 1683, and that very day the moone was new and the snow thawed & the frost broke which had lasted from Nov. 26—the lands were frozen 2 feet and that little water which was, was not sweet. the very grave wherein she was buryed was frozen almost 2 feet. We and our cattel were in a bad case & we feared worse & just in our extremity God had pitty on us.

As Archdeacon Fearon remarks, the very elements seem to have felt the relief of the poor 'Regicide' lady's departure.

Title to a burial at the parish expense was given only by settlement. Hence such entries as this from the register of Appledore, Kent:

1722 July 2.   Elizabeth Bishop, brought from Great Chart to this parish.

N.B.   She died in 8 weeks time after she was brought here.

Among the most interesting of the burial entries are those relating to burials in woollen under the act of 1666 and its more famous successor of 1678,[27] which provided that:

no corpse of any person (except those who shall die of the plague), shall be buried in any shirt, shift, sheet, or shroud or anything whatsoever made or mingled with flax, hemp, silk, hair, gold or silver, or in any stuff or thing, other than what is made of sheep's wool only... or be put into any coffin lined or faced with...any other material but sheep's wool only.

The act was ordered to be given in charge at the sessions and assizes, and heavy penalties were ordered upon those neglecting to comply with it. Sometimes a new volume of the burial register begins in 1678,[28] as e.g. at Church Stretton, Salop, where it is entitled:

A Register Book for the parish of Church Stretton wherein is the names of all those that are interred according to a late Act of Parliament entituled 'An Act for burying in Woollen' (1679–1751);

at Newington next Hythe, Kent, where it contains the affidavits 1679–1766; at Warehorne, Kent, 1727–1813, and at Finedon, Northants, where.

on the first of August 1678, the Act of Parliament for burying in woollen came in force so that there is a New Book on purpose to enter Buryalls from that day.

Sometimes special books were provided for the affidavits, as e.g. at Cardington, Beds., where two separate volumes of affidavits cover the period 1678–1775. There is in the Lincoln Record Office a file of original affidavits, covering the eighteenth century, made at Stamford St Michael's.

In other parishes it was thought worth while to lay in a stock of printed forms for use in making the affidavit, and two such printed certificates, one of which is reproduced as fig. VIII, still survive at Luton, Beds. In some parishes it was the custom immediately after the conclusion of the burial service for the clerk to exclaim at the grave 'Who makes affidavit?' One of the relatives then came forward, and a note of the circumstance was made in the register or affidavit book.[29]

The act provided that within eight days of the funeral, affidavit must be made that the law had been complied with. The 1678 act authorised the making of the affidavit before a clergyman if no Justice was available. Penalties were ordered of £5 on the estate of every person not buried in woollen, on the householder in whose house he died, on the persons connected with the funeral, on ministers neglecting to certify the non-receipt of the affidavit, and on overseers neglecting to levy the penalty.

Typical entries made under the 1678 act are these from Cowden, Kent:

[1679] Feb 3d was buryed Margaret Underhill widow of that Parish the fifth day of the same month was made affidavit that she was not wrapt in anything nor the coffin lined with anything but what was made of Sheep's wool only by John Stacey farmer of Cowden before Mr. Farnaby.

Witness to the Affidavit

Elizabeth Stacey.   John Wickenden.

March 13 [1681] [Affidavit made] For Mr. Rich. Knight jun by Jane Botling before Mr. Boraston [rector of Hever]. witnesses Joh Eldred   Geo Boraston.

Half of each penalty went to the poor, half to the informer, so when persons had decided to defy the act it was usual for a member of the family to act as informer, and so in effect reduce the penalty from £5 to £2. 10*s*.

A clear instance of such a collusive arrangement is to be found in the register of Aldborough, Yorks. 1716, following the burial entry of Elizabeth Wilkinson:

The Information of Margaret Robinson, made on Oath before Mr. Thomas Wilkinson, her grand child that she, the said Mrs. Eliz. Wilkinson was buryed in Linning on the fifth day of Feb: 1717 contrary to the Act of Parliament for bureying in woolen.

(Thomas Wilkinson of Boroughbridge Hall was the local Justice.)

The act was not repealed until 1814,[30] but for many years it had been but partially obeyed. In some parishes, however, it was observed to the last, e.g. at Great Oakley, Essex, where the vestry minutes contain notes of burial in woollen up to 1813, and at Odell, Beds., where:

Lady Gertrude Alston, relict of the late Sir Rowland Alston was buried March 24th 1807. £2. 10. 0. was given to the poor in consequence of her not being buried in woollen.

The wealthier classes had long regarded it as imposing a tax to be paid rather than an injunction to be observed, and to judge by the register entries, for some years before its repeal the act had been generally disregarded. The Burial in Woollen Acts form one of the classical instances of protectionist legislation.

Pope's Narcissa (Nance Oldfield) objected very emphatically to the idea of burial in woollen:[31]

> Odious! in woollen! 'twould a Saint provoke
> (Were the last words that poor Narcissa spoke)
> No, let a charming Chintz, and Brussels lace
> Wrap my cold limbs, and shade my lifeless face:
> One would not, sure, be frightful when one's dead—
> And—Betty—give this Cheek a little Red.

Another topic connected with burial is that of mortuaries. The feudal rule was that, upon the decease of a tenant, the lord of the manor had the right to choose as heriot the best beast of the deceased. The parish priest might have the right to choose the second best,[32] in theory perhaps by way of making amends for any personal tithes the deceased might have omitted to pay during his lifetime. The system lent itself to gross abuse, and it was regulated by an act of Henry VIII[33] which enacted that strangers, non-residents and non-householders were not liable, and that such persons as were liable should pay at a fixed rate in cash on a sliding scale. All persons leaving goods less than £30 in worth were to be exempt, from £30 to £40 the rate was 3s. 4d. to 6s. 8d., over £40, 10s. 6d. The custom seems to have lapsed gradually. In many parishes it lasted well into the eighteenth century. At Eaton under Heywood, Salop, e.g. mortuaries are entered together with burials:

March 3rd 1717 [under the burial entry of Thomas Linley], A Mortuary 2s. was paid for Thos. Linley by Widow.

There are a great many more entries in subsequent years, the amounts ranging up to 10s. Ash, Surrey, has in Register III a list of mortuaries 1707–15. The registers of Wrestlingworth, Beds., contain among the burials in 1705 several entries of mortuaries.

The register of Ampthill, Beds., has, near the end of the fourth volume, notes of the mortuaries received by Edw. Rowse, rector 1713–22. The first entry is:

Mem. That on ye 1st of May 1713 I Recd of Mrs. Carleton widow ye full sum of Ten shillings for a Mortuary. becoming due upon ye

Death of Rowland Carleton Esq. her Husband: He dying possess'd of Goods to ye value of more than forty pounds:

witness my Hand. E. Rowse. Recr.

The enclosure acts of George III's reign, when authorising the commutation of tithe, nearly always contain a saving clause preserving the incumbent's right to other ecclesiastical dues. That for Yaxley, Hunts.,[34] e.g. has:

PROVIDED ALWAYS that nothing in this Act contained shall prejudice lessen or defeat the said Vicar and his Successors' Claim to all or any *Oblations*, *Mortuaries*, *Easter Offerings*, or *Surplice Fees* whatever.

The 1839 Tithe Act[35] was specially declared not to extend to offerings in these three classes, but provision was made for their voluntary commutation. There may be some remote parish where mortuaries are still paid, as they were at Boldon, Durham, and Tarvin, Cheshire, until a few years ago, but it seems likely that the latest to survive have lapsed during the last century.

MISCELLANEOUS ENTRIES. We have referred above to the celebrated forged entry of the marriage of Sir Felix Glyde in the register of Old Welmingham.[36] More veracious records of register forgeries are to be found. Such exist, e.g. with reference to the famous bigamy case of Elizabeth Chudleigh, Duchess of Kingston, in 1776, which hung upon the removal and replacement of a leaf in the register of Lainston, Hants. In 1718, the parish clerk of St Andrew's, Holborn, took a bribe of £5 to tear leaves from the marriage register so that a certain William Godyard might marry a second wife while his first was still alive. Both clerk and bridegroom eventually found themselves in the pillory for their pains.

A less culpable but still very reprehensible forgery is this chronicled in the register of Bromley, Kent:

1583. Memorand y^t Samson Calthrope & Thomas Johnson beinge examined did confesse y^t ye said Calthrope did rase ye last lyne of this page and instead of these words Thomas ye Bastard sonne of Joane Butler did falsify it as it now stands (as appeareth from the thing done and shown in this case in 1634 and the lord [bishop] hath decreed accordingly in these matters) (*prout apparet ex actis et exhibitis in hac caâ factis in anno 1634 et dñus decrevit prout in actis*).

Will Reynoldes, Regr̃i.

The entry is 'The 26th Thomas sonne of William Johnson'. How slack some of the clergy were in registration matters may be judged by this indignant note from the register of Bradley, Staffs.:

Thos. Tunnicliffs second marriage not put down—& more mistakes I imagine—and a Blank leaf cut out very Scandalous.

Entries of the types indicated by no means exhaust the variety of records which one may find entered in registers.

Often a register begins with a note as to where and for how much it was bought. Register I of Betley, Staffs. (1538–1652), begins:

This is the book and register of our lord the King, for baptisms, marriages and burials, concerning each of the faithful, written up by Hugh Tilston, curate of the same from Martinmas 1538, 30 Hen. VIII.
(*Hoc est volumen et Registerium Domini Regis ad Baptismat[a] matrimonii copulat[a] et sepulta cuiuscunque fidelis pertinens conscriptum per Hugonem Tilston curatum ibidem a festo Sancti Martini episcopi Anno Domini millessimo quingentesimo tricesimo octavo necnon Regis Henrici octavi tricesimo.*)

The register of Sutton-cum-Lound, Notts., commences:

This is the Register Booke of Sutton sup͡ Lounde bought at Retford Fayre being the twelft day of Marche A^d 1690 by George Hartshorne of Lo[und] and Ralph Halle of Sutto[n] Churchwardens & Coste in Pryce 24s.

Such other records as may be found often do not really relate to registration business at all, and have been entered in the registers largely for convenience, or perhaps from the notion that the recording of an agreement in the parish register gave it extra sanctity, or simply because the register was the book most readily at hand, e.g. the first register of Croxden, Staffs., 1681–1732, has several pages filled with the parish clerk's practice in handwriting, and with a record of his farming operations.

Betley, Staffs., has in Register 2 (among the burials of 1657) this composition written in a large childish hand:

Robert Stud and Tobey Dean born in nuting time. Sara dean his born in coucumber time. Joseph Dean his A very sober young man and mind the larming Bisnis. So that his father dotes him more thin all his Ribbis and sayes he will buy him a litel horse and he shall ride and up on doben tooe.

It was no doubt a farmer churchwarden who entered in the first register of Morley, Derbys., 'Breended Cow Bulld, June ye 6, 1739'.

In 1641 'The Knights, Citizens and Burgesses of the Commons house of Parliament finding to the great grief of their hearts that by the designs of priests and Jesuits there were plots and conspiracies to subvert the fundamental laws of the Kingdom and to introduce Arbitrarie and Tyrannicall government by the most pernicious Councels', etc., made a declaration of abhorrence of such designs, and entered into an oath to oppose them. All male parishioners over eighteen years old in every parish of England were invited to subscribe to the declaration: the original returns so far as they have survived are in the Victoria Tower of the House of Lords, but copies exist in a number of parish registers. To consider but one or two counties: Kedleston, South Wingfield and Pentrich, Derbys. have the declaration in Register I, each list being headed by the vicar, and in the second one, the next name being that of the (Presbyterian) minister, and at Ashover in the same county there is a similar list, with the original print of the parliamentary declaration pasted to the front cover of the earliest register. Appleby Magna, Leics., has one with 144 names, and there are others at Swineshead, Beds., at Aylestone, Bitteswell, Frolesworth, and Gaddesby, Leics., at East Rudham, Norf., at Hawton, Notts., and at Winsham, Som. Derbyshire, Leicestershire and Norfolk are among the counties whose original returns are not to be found in the Victoria Tower, so the parish register lists are the only ones extant. I have not found in any register a list of those who took the Association Oath of 1696, though no doubt there must be some register entries of this kind.[37]

Kent has at least five copies of the Vow and Covenant of 1643, at Eastwell, where there is also the Protestation of 1641, and at Great Doddington and East Haddon, Northants. (in the parish last-named it is recorded as the 'Prokylatiǫn'), and at Birchington, where there is also the Vow and Covenant of 1643; there are also loose copies at Ripple, Stourmouth and at Walmer. The copy in the last-named parish has this note in a later hand:

A league or bond of Iniquity. The number of the beast 166 (*sic*).

Cherry Burton, Yorks, has a list of fifty-six people who took the 'Scottish Covenant' in 1646.

This means, of course, that in these parishes we have almost a complete list of the adult male population in 1641–6, with a specimen of the signature of every resident who could write.

If there was the slightest evidence in favour of the benefice being a peculiar or a donative, the incumbent often stated it on a page in the register, explaining that in acquiescing in visitation or institution he was not surrendering any of the rights of his successors. At Northill, Beds., in a terrier of 1725, is:

The Living, being a Donative, is exempt from the Payment of First Fruits, & Tenths...it is exempt likewise from all Ecclesiastical Visitation, & the Payment of Procurations on that behalfe. However, for want of better evidence, the Rect^r hath of late years, Submitted thereto by constraint.

In a class by themselves are such entries as those at Bexley, Kent, recording frequent visits by John and Charles Wesley, and by George Whitefield.

In the days before ordnance maps, disputes often arose as to the position of parish boundaries, the extent to which distant hamlets in a parish were liable for the repair of the parish church, and the question which houses or lands were truly parochial, and therefore gave their occupier the right of sepulture in the churchyard. Questions of parish boundaries were regarded as falling within the jurisdiction of the courts Christian,[38] and it was specially appropriate that they should be recorded in ecclesiastical registers.

Agreements upon the points first named were sometimes entered in the registers, and when by agreement non-parishioners communicated or were christened or buried, it was usual to enter in the register a record of the circumstances, with a note that the concession was not to be treated as a precedent. Such a note of permission to communicate in 1634 appears in Register I (1560–1705) of Newdigate, Surrey, with reference to a certain John Butcher. The sanction was 'for this one time', as there was always a doubt whether his tenement was in Newdigate or Charlwood. At Davington, Kent, there are similar entries in Register I:

Margaret daughter of Jo. Brockwell and Ann his wife of ye parish of Preston near Faversham was in kindness and out of necessity baptised in ye parish church of Davington, November 25th, 1685.

At Kirkleatham St Cuthbert's, Yorks., a memorandum of 1 May 1622 records the vicar's efforts to compose a dispute between the different townships of his parish as to the liability for repairing the church, and the agreement which was finally effected in these terms:

y^t ye inhabitants of Wilton *cum mēbris*, shall hereafter...build, repaire, and uphold, and keep in reparations, the north side of ye Church and steeple of Kirkleatham, from the middle northward, with stone, lyme, glasse, iron, timber, and lead: and in consideration thereof, hereafter be exempted from whiting or painting of ye walls on ye inside and from paveing the ground, and building the stalls w^{t}in ye said Church.

But in 1651 the inhabitants of Wilton failed to carry out their share of the compact, and the inhabitants of Kirkleatham had to petition the North Riding justices for redress.

In one of the last pages in the register of Wrestlingworth, Beds., is this memorandum of a disputed parish boundary, not finally settled until the enclosure award of 1804:

Memorandum y^t Mr. Mawde parson of Hatley dyd. being denyed & forfended by me, Robert Reeve, parson of Wrestlingworth in ye Harvest tyme, viz: Anno Dni. 1601, and Anno Dni. 1603 intrude & thrust hymselfe into ye possession of ye tithe of a Stitch in...ye field of Wrestlingworth & into ye possession of the tithe of other lands, parcels alsoe of y^t land which is commonly called ye Quarter land.

The traditional manner of securing the maintenance of the ancient bounds of the parish was by the Rogationtide perambulations, or beating of the bounds. In Tudor and Stuart times when not only did common law confer on the parishioners as such very real rights and privileges, but also statute law came to impose upon them increasingly onerous financial duties and obligations, this was much more than an agreeable and picturesque old custom. George Herbert's model parson[39]—a lover of old customs—was particularly fond of 'procession'. The custom is referred to in the injunctions of Elizabeth, who ordered that at convenient places the curate should admonish the people to give thanks to God. Psalms 103 and 104 were to be recited and the minister should say such sentences as: 'Cursed is he that transgresseth the bounds or doles of his neighbour.' In 1758 Archbishop Secker endeavoured to induce his clergy to revive the practice.

At Turnworth, Dorset:

1747. On Ascension Day after morning prayer at Turnworth Church, was made a publick Perambulation of ye bounds of ye parish of Turnworth by me Richd. Cobbe, Vicar, Wm. Northover, Church-warden, Henry Sillers and Richard Mullen, Overseers and others with 4 boys; beginning at the Church Hatch and cutting a great T on the most principal parts of the bounds. Whipping ye boys by way of remembrance, and stopping their cry with some half-pence; we returned to church again, which Perambulation and Processioning had not been made for five years last past.

Perambulation records appear e.g. in the registers of the Hampshire parishes of Headley, 1723, Crondall, nine times in the first half of the eighteenth century, St Lawrence, Winchester, 1718, and Michelmersh, 1771; on separate sheets at Wells St Cuthbert's, Som., 1752, and at Berkswich, Staffs., eleven times between 1671 and 1805. Caddington, Beds., has perambulation records in its churchwardens' accounts, 1724, Little Barford, in the same county, has in its register four series, 1693–1724, and Ampthill, five, 1709–34. Cowden and Hever, Kent, have special bounds books, dated 1798 and 1805 respectively.

It is interesting to note that perambulation is still quite lawful, and that parish officers have the right to enter private property in carrying it out. Expenses properly incurred (including the cost of refreshments) may be paid from the rates, but perambulations may be only once in three years and the rates will not pay for music, banners, and 'other unnecessary adjuncts'.[40]

At Stone in Oxney, Kent, Register II contains a list of vagrants taken, whipped, and sent away, 1619–38. The first register of Bapchild, Kent, 1558–1641, has the order for the gathering of the smoke money or *burrowe* silver with the names of the persons assessed to the same.

That of Wrestlingworth, Beds., includes:

The names of ye monethly Contributions towd ye releife of ye poore of Wrestlingworth [apparently of some date before 1607].

The register of Stevington, Beds. has in its first volume notes of the whipping and passing of vagrants:

William Auckley and Susan his pretended wife taken up as sturdy beggars November 1687 whipt according to law and sent away with a passe to St. Margarets in ye Isle of Tenet in ye County of Kent . . . etc.

In the register of St Chad's, Saddleworth, W.R. Yorks., is a curious entry in an early shorthand. So far as it can be deciphered it appears to be an extract from an old ballad entitled 'The Gallow Tree Journey'. Less inappropriate to an ecclesiastical record are the literary entries in the register of Chiddingfold, Surrey, where Register I, 1573–1652, contains between the baptisms and the burials seven pages in a sixteenth- or early seventeenth-century hand with apparently part of a play entitled 'The old Tragedy of Henry VII or the Union of the White and Red Rose'.

Archdeacon Fearon has noted some interesting literary references in the Hampshire registers. At Romsey, in 1627, Anthony White, vicar, wrote on the cover of his register (I offer a rough translation):

> Here be those:
> Whom Water in Christ maketh holy:
> Whom Fire of Love bindeth duly:
> Whom Earth doth now cover truly.

> *Ecce:*
> *Aqua quos Christo sacrat:*
> *Quos Ignis amoris conciliat casti*
> *Quos quoque Terra tegit.*

At Monkton this couplet on a mother who died in childbirth is entered in 1778:

> Eve's debt this daughter doubly satisfied.
> In sorrow she brought forth, in sorrow died.
>
> (*Evae haec sustinuit geminatam foemina poenam,*
> *Cui dolor ex partu, mors et acerba fuit.*)

At Fordingbridge classical quotations are freely made, e.g. from Cato:

> Take time by the forelock.
>
> (*Fronte capillata post est occasio calva.*)

And in 1647 a loyal wish is boldly entered (again to translate):

> May the King live long,
> May the Law be strong,
> May his loyal flock
> Say 'Amen' to my song!
>
> *Vivat Rex,*
> *Vigeat Lex,*
> *'Amen' dicat*
> *pius Grex!*

Less dignified notes, presumably made by the parish clerk, appear at St Maurice's, Winchester:

> Because many leafes of this book wear toren in [twaine]
> I Thout hit good to wryt them nue againe.
>
> Henry Lurkyn.

And at Longparish in the seventeenth century appears the sound advice:

> Obsarve when you lok in a ragester and kep your stops.

At Wolstanton, Staffs., under 23 August 1766, there appears this not very clear instruction:

> Look forward in this Book & you'l find a mistake by Turning over the Leaves two far but follow the Number & you'l see. Turn over Ten Leaves. *Having turned over we find* Look back to the number that follows these five Marridges after this.

The title-page of the first register of Boxley, Kent, bought in 1598, contains between the heading and the usual note as to the price of the book, the names of the vicar and churchwardens, etc.,

a Latin inscription which we may perhaps venture to translate
thus:

> Long live Queen Elizabeth,
> Of England, France and Ireland Queen,
> Defendress (*sic*) of the Faith.
> A Virgin victorious through her manly mettle.
>
> (*Vivat Elyzabetha Regina*
> *Angliae, Franciae, et Hyberniae*
> *Regina, Fidei Defensatrix,*
> *Virgo virtute Victoriosa.*)

Sometimes the registers contain evidence that the parson has
tried his hand at a funeral elegy upon one of his parishioners, e.g.
at St Peter's, Cornhill, after the burial entry of David Powell,
Clothworker, 22 September 1601, is:

> This Powell was a plaine man and led an honest life
> He loved peace and amitie, and shun'd debate and strife.

The register of Eyeworth, Beds., has:

> Oct. 17 1624   The godly charitable and religious christian gentle-
> man Richard Gadburie departed this life one friday night being the
> 15th day of October 1624 about 3 of the clocke and was buried the
> 17th day Anno aetatis 63.

I have found it difficult to torture into anything approaching
English verse a reasonably close translation of the hexameters.

> If three more years you'd add, for sixty years he'd lived
> When all too soon by death he was cut off indeed.
> But Death is light for you, who darts of Fate repel.
> No more it pleaséd you earth's life to share. Farewell!
>
> (*Si modo tres addas sexdenos vixerat annos*
> *Cum prematura morte peremptus erat,*
> *Mors tibi levis erat qui Lethae tela repellis*
> *Non placet in terris cohabitare. Vale.*)[41]

At (Great) Carbrook, Norf., the burial entry of Mary Caudron, a
'woman rich in good works and almsdeeds', 23 October 1625, has:

> The Book of Life agrees with thy life's story,
> And by theise Bookes thou judged art to glory.

In the register of Great Easton, Essex, is an interesting farewell
by the parson to his parishioners, inserted by 'Matthew Rowlinson,
curate of this parish, left Feb. 1 1730':

To my parishioners.

Farewell, dear flock, my last kind wish receive
The only tribute that I now can give.
May my past labours claim a just regard
Great is the prize, and glorious the reward;
Transcendent joys, surpassing human thought
To meet in heaven, whom I on earth had taught.

Less flattering remarks concerning flock and pastor respectively are to be found at Newchurch, Kent, where Register II contains the note:

On Sunday 8th Nov. 1812, W. Webster officiated for the last time at Newchurch, and possesses a very easy mind on that subject.

At Sheldwich, Kent, there is the note:

Sept. yᵉ 29th 1696, Then Mr. Hollingworth left Sheldwich and Throwley for Stone in yᵉ Isle of Oxney,

with, in a later hand,

where I wish he may behave himself better than he did at Sheldwitch.

The rector of Boldre, Hants, entered in his register, 8 September 1756, the number of his lottery ticket, 6,454!!

Verse of a different kind from that noted above is found at St Peter's, Cornhill, where under the year 1593, after a summary account of the deaths by plague (totalling 15,000), there follow these entries:

In a thousand five hundred ninety and three
The Lord preserved my house and me
When of the pestilence theare died
Full maine a thousand els beeside.

(*Innumeros quantos consumpsit morbida pestis,
Seruauit dominus meque domumque meam.*)

Baschurch, Salop, Register I has this entry:

Memorandum yᵗ George Hudson were inducted into yᵉ Vicaridge and Parish Church of BasChurch yᵉ 29 day of November 1662.
    [four signatures]

Memorandum yᵗ George Hudson, Vicar, declared his assent and consent to all and everything contayned in yᵉ booke of Cõmon praier together with yᵉ abjuration of yᵉ oath called yᵉ Solemne League and Covēnt in yᵉ Parish Church of BasChurch yᵉ 21th day of December 1662 in yᵉ hearing of:
    [two signatures]

Memorandum yᵗ George Hudson Vicar, reade yᵉ 39 Articles and declared his assent and consent to yᵐ openly on yᵉ lord's day in yᵉ

Parish Church of BasChurch yᵉ 18 day of January 1662 in yᵉ hearing of [two signatures].

At Beelsby, Lincs., there is a similar record of the same year. Another record of 'reading in' is to be found in the first register of Barton-le-Clay, Beds. Later entries of the same sort occur in 1677, 1719, 1730 and 1757. Wendens Ambo, Essex, has in Register II similar memoranda of 1662 and 1665, Burnham-on-Sea and Monksilver, both in Somerset, have similar entries of 1668 and 1660 respectively.

VARIOUS OTHER ENTRIES OF HISTORICAL INTEREST. At Beckington, Som., are notes of two royal visits:

Charles the Second, King of England rode through Beckington, Sept. 10 1663, and Catherine his Queen whom God bless.

and

George III and Charlotte, King and Queen of England with three Princess', their daughters rode through Beckington, their road from Longleat where they had been on a visit to the Rt. Hon. Lord Viscount Weymouth, Marquis of Bath and one of H.M. most Honble. Privy Council, Sept. 15 1789. whom God preserve, Amen.

The register of Little Steeping, Lincs., records the fact that the rector kissed the hand of William III at Lincoln in 1695.

At Northill, Beds., the register contains this copy of a letter (apparently of c. 1570–82):

Right reverend father in god forasmuche as it is ordered and established by the quenes maᵗⁱᵉˢ Injunctions that no Minister or preacher of the worde of God shall mary any wiffe except prouffe (after examination had) [that] the woman be of honest and sober convers & lyveinge and without the consent of her Parents yf they be lyveinge or of her Mʳ or Mʳⁱˢ or for lacke of suche of two of the next of her frends: wherefor these shalbe to signifye unto your Lordeshippe that we Renolde Grey and Tho: Leyghe Esquiers & Justices of the queens maᵗⁱᵉˢ peace within the countie of Bedforde are credibly informed that one Marg: Gibson, servant to W[illiam] W[elles] clark Pars[on] of Sa[n]dy, is of honest and sober behaviour. So that we see no cause but that she may mary with one John Ha[veringe] Clark, Vicar of Roxton.
In Wytnes whereof...etc.

Quaint old medical recipes often appear in registers or on loose sheets preserved in the parish chest. Kingston Seymour, Som., has two, one from *The Gentleman's Magazine*, 1735, one from *The Bath Journal* of 1747/8, 'To cure yᵉ Bite of a Mad Dog'. Three similar recipes, two for the prevention of infection and one for curing the bite of a mad dog, appear at the beginning of the register (1754–90) of Axbridge, Somerset.

In a quite different class are the numerous historical entries in such registers as that of the Chapels Royal (not technically a parish register of course), of St James's, Whitehall, and Windsor. This book[42] contains entries of marriages, births or baptisms, and deaths from 1675 to 1709. They do not in all cases make it clear to which Chapel Royal the entry relates. These are, however, not strictly *parish* records, so can hardly be dealt with here. For information about them the inquirer is referred to the Registrar-General's pamphlet already cited.

A NOTE UPON REGISTERS AND POPULATION STATISTICS

Sometimes authorities, in other respects very reliable, have been inclined to minimise the importance of the registers as sources of historical information, and to regard them as the happy hunting ground of the antiquary, rather than that of the historian. It is clear, however, that on such questions as the stability or migration of population; the size of households and the influence thereon of periods of economic depression; occupations; mortality statistics; the effects of inbreeding; and the extent to which the population has been made up of families which may fairly be styled hereditary paupers, can often best be studied by use of the registers. (Register study is, however, one thing, mere register transcription another. There is some justice, e.g. in Dr Peyton's rather sweeping dismissal of the latter as 'a blameless occupation of dubious value—the first of a series of good works, and beyond all comparison the easiest'.)

At Cardington, Beds., the burial register 1783–94 is particularly valuable as distinguishing between paupers and other inhabitants. Unfortunately, however, the register ceases to make the distinction just when the information would be most valuable, at the period when economic depression was setting in more acutely, and when a vast flood of pauperism was beginning to engulf almost the whole of the labouring classes. In this parish an eighteenth-century vicar realised the value of the registers as sources of information on social and economic topics. For the period 1780–1800 he totalled the entries of baptisms and those of burials, then by subtraction he endeavoured to determine whether the population of his parish was increasing or declining. Like other amateur statisticians, he found unexpected difficulties:

Baptisms total 482. Burials total 503. Hence there appears a diminution of Population particularly if it be considered that some Dissenters from the Established Church are buried at the Meetinghouse & are not registered: but a Consideration must be had to the number of Children interred unbaptized, which increases the Proportion of Burials to that of Baptisms, in a greater ratio than that of Burials to Births. These two circumstances being considered, I doubt not but that there has been an increase in Population for the last 21 Years, tho' the average number of Burials exceeds that of Baptisms.

A very common endeavour of the local historian has been to estimate the population of his parish at various periods. There were, of course, no reliable general statistics until the decennial censuses from 1801 onwards. Numerous returns had been collected, however, for specified areas, generally by ecclesiastical authority. Archbishop Sheldon in 1676 gathered from his clergy parochial statistics of families, communicants, dissenters, etc. In 1781 there was concern as to the alleged depopulation of the country in the past century, and each incumbent was invited to complete a form giving the numbers of baptisms and of burials entered in his registers for three periods: 1688–97, 1741–50, 1771–80.

From time to time various schemes have been proposed by which the local historian might work out from the average annual number of baptisms, marriages or burials in any specific area what was the probable total population of the district concerned. In early days these methods were perhaps rather crude, thus (a) Cox's 'multiply by thirty the mean annual number of baptisms'; much better is (b) Razzell's proposal to multiply by 125 the mean annual number of marriages; probably not quite so sound as this (c) Brownlee's suggestion to multiply by thirty-one the mean annual number of burials.

Clearly any sound calculation of this kind must be based upon mean annual averages over a fairly lengthy period of time. Obviously also the method would be much more safely applicable to a whole group of neighbouring parishes than to any individual parish, especially any very small one. Even so it appears that any calculations made might be vitiated by unnoticed *lacunae* in the registers, (a) by deliberate under-registration caused by the views of such nonconformists as the Baptists, or (c) by non-recorded burials in their own burial grounds, instead of the churchyard, made by members of any of the historic Three Denominations. According to some authorities, notably Dr Eversley,[1] the marriage rate (*b*) seems to be the most reliable indicator of the three.

But even so one is beset with difficulties and problems in any attempt to base calculations upon the marriage entries, since special circumstances often caused a sort of concentration in one parish church of a great part of the marriages of the neighbourhood, e.g. in the early part of the Commonwealth[2] in a keenly Anglican and royalist neighbourhood the population often refrained from using the services of the 'intruded' puritan ministers, but resorted to some neighbouring parish church where the incumbent was a genuine churchman who had contrived to avoid ejection. This happened at Allington St Lawrence's, Kent, whither until the appointment of 'Registers' in 1653 churchpeople resorted from the neighbouring town of Maidstone, and from other places much farther afield.

Again some eighteenth-century incumbents, especially those in 'peculiars',[3] seem to have done a roaring trade in marriages in their little Gretna Greens. The tiny Trentside village of Fledborough, Notts., had from 1721 to 1751 an incumbent rejoicing in the name of the Rev. W. Sweetapple, who married couples from far and near. In this instance the parish was not a 'peculiar', but the incumbent prostituted his powers as surrogate.

At Bedford St John's, the disproportionate number of marriages of non-parishioners recorded in the registers between 1700 and 1753 is very remarkable. Nearly every parish in the county is represented among these 'foreign marriages'. It is quite usual for the registers of any market town to record a great many marriages between parishioners of the neighbouring villages (as e.g. in other Bedford parishes), but the excess in this parish is far too great to be explained in this way. At Old Warden, in the same county, of 115 marriages in the period 1658–66 only twelve of the parties subsequently had children baptised in the parish church, so it is clear that by far the greater part of the marriages were 'foreign' ones. The registers of Maperton, Som., in the latter part of the incumbency of the Rev. S. X. Collins and throughout that of his successor, the Rev. C. Michel, show that a similar state of affairs prevailed there.

In earlier texts of this book perhaps we minimised both the technical difficulties which must be overcome if the registers are to be used for serious demographic study, and the very real possibilities which the registers offer, once such difficulties are overcome, and work upon them becomes a matter of genuine historical scholarship may have been minimised. Work in the new field of historical demography has since been pioneered in France by M. Louis Henry, and in England by Drs P. Laslett, D. E. C. Eversley and E. A. Wrigley, and their fellows in the Cambridge Group for the History of Population and Social Structure. I am obliged to the editors of the Group's first publication, *An Introduction to English Historical Demography*, 1966, for permission to use their book in revising this part of the book.

II. CHURCHWARDENS' ACCOUNTS

THE OFFICE OF CHURCHWARDEN. The origin of churchwardens. The election of churchwardens. Custom and the churchwarden. Local customs as to the duties of churchwardens. The payment of churchwardens. CHURCHWARDENS' ACCOUNTS IN PRE-
REFORMATION TIMES. RECEIPTS. Church ales. The church flock. Sundry receipts.
EXPENSES. LATER ACCOUNTS. ECCLESIASTICAL BUSINESS. RECEIPTS. PEW-RENTS. Pew
scandals. The appropriation of pews. Faculty pews. Literary references to appropriated
pews. CHURCH RATES. The legal basis of church rates. Objections to the payment of
church rates. CHURCHWARDENS' EXPENSES CONSEQUENT UPON THEIR DUTIES. The duties
of churchwardens: (a) those deriving from the questmen, (b) those not deriving from
the questmen. The audit of churchwardens' accounts. The supervision of churchwardens. CHURCHWARDENS' RECORDS. THE CHURCH FABRIC. Church decoration. The
altar and its adjuncts. The pulpit. Sundry references to church furniture and equipment. Bells and bellringers. Various other articles of church equipment. THE CIVIL
DUTIES OF CHURCHWARDENS. Churchwardens and woollen caps. Churchwardens and
vermin. The dog-whipper. Other minor officials.

THE OFFICE OF CHURCHWARDEN. Although the churchwarden's
accounts *ought* to antedate the registers by several centuries, they
are still, despite Dr Cox's work,[1] so little known and so many
parishes have none,[2] that here they must take second place to the
registers.

The wardens are defined by an ecclesiastical authority as 'the
proper guardians or keepers of the parish church',[3] and they have
also certain additional civil duties which have been from time to
time imposed upon them.

Under such titles as stewards, guardians of the church, wardens
of church goods and ornaments (*Yconomi, guardiani ecclesiae,
custodes bonorum et ornamentorum ecclesiae*), they appear in the Year
Books, in monastic accounts, and in the earliest extant parish
records. Chaucer knows the churchwarden as church reeve.[4] It
was not altogether without reason that Toulmin Smith regarded
the wardens as the very foundation of democratic local government
in England.

According to Cripps[5] the office of churchwarden began in very
early times (perhaps originally in that of questman or sidesman
which latterly became merged in it), the bishop feeling the need
of reliable persons who could be summoned from each parish to
give information as to disorders of clergy and people. The wardens
were definitely appointed as officers of the church by the first canon
of the Council of London, 1127.[6]

Toulmin Smith equated the churchwardens with the '*custodes
bonorum ecclesiae*' found in fourteenth-century records, and also
with the 'sworn men' of such inquests as 'Nonarum Inquisitiones',
and discovered records as late as 21 Jac. I.,[7] which he interpreted

so. He even (an unkind cut this!) found references in Laud's famous Canons of 1640, which he understood in this sense.

Whatever may have been the origin of the office, it is certain that it was an important one in mediaeval times, and that a whole variety of duties attached to it. The fashion in which these duties were performed is illustrated by the records which mediaeval church-wardens have left behind, and which may still be found in the chests of a few fortunate parishes. Accounts continuous to the present day are rarest of all, but there are a few; e.g. Boughton-under-Blean, Kent, has a series, with but few breaks, from 1530 to the present.

In common usage there are two wardens to each parish, the people's warden and the vicar's warden. But this is a late develop-ment. Canon 89[8] provides that:

> All Churchwardens or Questmen in every parish shall be chosen by the joint consent of the Minister and the Parishioners,...but if they cannot agree...then the Minister shall choose one, and the Parishioners another.

According to Toulmin Smith the canon itself was a particularly glaring example of his bugbear, ecclesiastical usurpation. He alleged that the canon of 1603, being repugnant to common law, had and has no force whatever, save perhaps in a parish where the custom of the incumbent choosing one warden had existed time out of mind before 1603.

It is this idea of custom which rules many aspects of parish life connected with the wardens. Normally, as we have pointed out above, they are two, but in quite large areas the common custom has been to appoint four. A custom to choose but one was held good, and other customs provide for the choice of varying numbers up to eight, and even higher numbers, e.g. Kendal, Westmorland, has twelve, five nominated by the vicar, seven elected. Customs existed, and may still exist, for the election of separate wardens for the various townships in a large parish, or for the alternation of the office between two or more of the constituent areas. Service by rotation amongst all householders, or among the proprietors of specified houses or lands, is quite common, as indeed it is for the other offices in the parochial hierarchy. At Aisholt, Som., church-wardens were normally appointed by house row. At the end of the first register of this parish is a:

note of the yearly and orderly course concerning the office of Church-wardens and a list of tenures and tenements etc., in the Parish of Aisholt, 1581, Nov. 30.

At Feniton, Devon, the accounts of the wardens make it clear that service was exacted in respect of each tenement in turn. At Doveridge, Derbys., where there is a fine series of parish records for the whole of the eighteenth century, the name of the tenement for which each officer served normally follows his own name in the heading of the annual accounts, e.g. in the constable's accounts for 1720 the heading is:

The accounts of Francis Okey Serving Constable for Heywood's Farme for ye yeare 1720.

Nomination by the vicar or by the lord of the manor, and co-option by the retiring wardens, are all found, but the general use, in so far as one can speak of a general use, was election of the parish warden at Easter by the vestry meeting.[9] A most exceptional case occurred at Keston, Kent, where on 23 April 1655 church-wardens and overseers were elected like the constable at the court leet. At Petersfield, Hants., a wrangle as to the rector's right to appoint one of the wardens went on at the archdeacon's visitations for 125 years (from 1706 to 1830).

At Gnosall, Staffs., the settled poor were relieved by the over-seers, but vagrants, from the latter part of the seventeenth century until the early part of the eighteenth, were relieved by the church-wardens, as appears from the churchwardens' accounts:

(Overseers) 1690	Payd to Widow Dickin towards the keeping of her cow	00. 15. 00
(Churchwardens)	Given to a travelling woman yt had small pox	00. 01. 06
(Overseers) 1691	pd Thomas Stokes in hard weather	00. 01. 06
1694	Payd Widow Tyrer in her want & sicknesse	00. 11. 06
1697	Pd Mr. Samuel Fowke for fetching Thomas Lightwood to Church from Knightley he being dead in the snow	00. 01. 06

At Kettering Northants., the vestry, as noted above, apparently quite illegally drew a distinction between the two wardens, and resolved, naturally enough, to entrust as much authority as possible to the parish warden, whom they regarded as their special repre-sentative:

24 March 1818   Resolved unanimously that from this time the books and accounts belonging to the office of churchwardens shall be placed in the hands of the churchwarden chosen by the parish.

Dr Peyton, in his edition of the Kettering Vestry Minutes, points out that this resolution antedates by two months the act 58 Geo. III,

c. 69, which directs that parish books and papers, except the registers, shall be kept 'in such place and manner as the inhabitants in Vestry shall direct'.

Occasionally—very occasionally—the position of churchwarden carried a salary, but it is no wonder that, even in parishes wealthy enough to offer this inducement, nominees sometimes endeavoured to decline the office. If they did they were fined heavily, and until 1921 or, arguably, until 1964, common law compelled any parishioner[10] chosen as warden to serve the office. At St John's, Westminster, in later times, where serving the office involved the bearer in heavy expense, it was difficult to find parishioners willing to undertake it. Exemption by 'Tyburn Ticket' was often sought by likely candidates, but even so between 1768 and 1816 no less than £340 was credited to the parish by way of fines of £20 received from seventeen vestrymen who would rather pay than serve.

No doubt the warden often heaved a sigh of relief when he came to the end of his year of office, and felt that he thoroughly deserved the customary dinner which was provided by the vestry for the wardens and the other vestrymen, either on the election of the new wardens, or at the time of audit.

CHURCHWARDENS' ACCOUNTS IN PRE-REFORMATION TIMES. RECEIPTS. It is not intended here to give great details as to pre-Reformation accounts, since in any case there will be few readers who are fortunate enough to find them. Moreover, they are almost invariably in Latin, and to read them demands some knowledge of dog-Latin, and a fair acquaintance with palaeography. The reader who is lucky enough to find such accounts, and skilful enough to attempt to read them, cannot do better than refer to Dr Cox's book already cited, where a variety of transcripts and facsimiles will assist him in their elucidation.

Interesting features of the receipts side of such accounts are the enormous variety of occasions upon which the mediaeval church of England found it possible to base money-raising efforts. The modern bazaar-organising parson might profitably study the efforts of his mediaeval predecessors.

One of the most interesting methods was that of holding a 'Church ale', the wardens begging or buying the malt and brewing the liquor in the 'Church house' (the prototype of the parish hall). Aubrey describes every parish as having a 'Church house' to which belonged spits, crocks, and other utensils for dressing provisions. The parish of Wrington, Som., has still in its chest the conveyance

of the church house to the parishioners. It is dated 1447. A graphic
and highly critical account of church ale organisation is given in
Philip Stubbes' *Anatomie of Abuses*, 1583. More favourable
references are in ? Peter Mews' *Ex-ale-tation of Ale*, 1671:

> The churches much owe, as we all do knowe
> For when they be drooping and ready to fail.
> By a Whitsun or Church-Ale up again they shall go,
> And owe their repairing to a pot of good ale.

At Elvaston and Ockbrook, Derbys., four ales were brewed annually, 'and every inhabitant of Ockbrook shall be at the several
ales, and every husband and wife shall pay two pence, and every
cottager one penny to the use and behoof of the said church of
Elvaston'.

At Halesowen, Worcs., in 15 Eliz. (1572–3), regulations were
drawn up concerning the amount of ale brewed, restricting the
number of persons allowed to be present, and further ordaining
'that no unlawfull games on hys brydall daye' were to be permitted
by the groom 'on paine of 20 shillings'. Church ales in church,
chapel, or churchyard, were entirely (though vainly) forbidden in
1603. It seems likely that, in most parishes, they failed to survive
the Interregnum.

Then there were the profits from the church flock of sheep, or
herd of kine,[11] sometimes even from the church hive of bees, made
up of gifts and bequests, and generally lent out on bond to reputable parishioners. At All Hallows, Hoo (Kent), in 1577–99,
the stock was 'six score and iij shepe and two kine', let out at 3*d*.
a sheep and 2*s*. 4*d*. a cow, so producing £5. 2*s*. 0*d*. (*sic*) per
annum. The accounts are entered thus:

1557 Rec^d of Thomas Franke for farme of x shepe	ijs	vj^d
John Davy for farme of shepe	ijs	vj^d
John Smyth for farme of xxvj shepe	vjs	vj^d

Bees are mentioned at Cheswardine, Salop:

1558 It' xpr virges will geue a swarme of bies to mentene a leight
bifore sent Kateren.

Useful receipts also were the interest on cash loans from the
church stock (despite the mediaeval horror of usury!), as e.g. at
Kirton-in-Lindsey, Lincs., 1484, the rent of church houses and lands,
and such uncertain receipts as the balance in the hands of various
gilds and brotherhoods. At the year's end, after they had dis-

charged their duties of providing masses and lights, and suc-
couring members of the fellowship in distress, the gildwardens
seem to have handed these over towards general funds. There
were also gatherings during processions, and even from occasional
special collections in church. Most jollifications served as pretexts
for collections, from the genial horseplay at Hocktide to the primitive drama of mystery and miracle plays, and the traditional games
and dances of May Day and Plough Monday. Bequests to the
church were frequent, especially of such items as a 'brass pot' or
half a dozen spoons, and these were deposited in the sacristy until
the wardens saw an opportunity of disposing of them to advantage.
Fees were levied (apparently quite illegally) for the font tapers at
baptism, for such services as ringing the passing bell or hiring the
pall, cross, cope and censer, and for burial in church. This last
was very properly made extremely expensive, though, one fears,
rather from financial notions than upon hygienic considerations.
The hiring out of jewellery to brides for their weddings, the collection of rents and fees for the church bakehouse or brewhouse,
and those for the hiring out of the parish stock of properties for
miracle plays, must have made a heavy demand upon the wardens'
time and energies. At Chudleigh, Devon, in 1581, the wardens
made 1s. 2d. by lending out the church (cyder?) press. Probably
most mediaeval churches were landed proprietors, e.g. Frith Fen,
Landbeach, Cambs., was entirely grass land, and was allotted each
year among the proprietors, 'with a pale of xiij foot in length', the
allotments never beginning for two successive years at the same
spot. After each proprietor had had his share, the remnant left was
the 'Churche Lotte', and was let annually by the churchwardens
in aid of church expenses.[12]

EXPENSES. Some of the heaviest items in pre-Reformation accounts are those connected with the lights. Considerable sums
were spent on candles, beeswax, and tallow (this last consumed in
candles used solely for lighting, not for ceremonial purposes). The
maintenance of the multiplicity of service books also involved fairly
heavy expenditure, that of the bells and the clock commonly
occurs, there are numerous entries of profit-making items on
the other side of the balance sheet, and occasional references to
the cost of bonfires or feasts upon suitable occasions, salaries to
clerk and wardens, gifts to singers, rushes for the floor, and
boughs and flowers for the decoration of the church upon special
festivals. This custom last referred to survived the break with Rome,

for among the duties of the ideal country parson, as enumerated by George Herbert,[13] is the maintenance of the fabric in a condition

keeping in the middle way between superstition and slovenliness, swept clean without dust or cobwebs, and at great festivals strewed and stuck with boughs, and perfumed with incense.

We return to this point below.

LATER ACCOUNTS. ECCLESIASTICAL BUSINESS. RECEIPTS. The items found in post-Reformation accounts fall naturally into two classes (though in actual fact entries of these two classes are jumbled together indiscriminately). They are those following the tradition of earlier times, when the duties of the wardens were mainly connected with the church, its fabric, its services, and the manners and morals of the parishioners, and the quite dissimilar entries relating to a vast mass of civil duties which were thrown upon the wardens by legislation from Tudor times onwards, some of which duties were still retained by them until the final secularisation of parish administration by the Local Government Act of 1894.[14]

Perhaps the most striking feature of the accounts after the Reformation is that the raising of funds by such genial and attractive methods as those mentioned above—church ales, parish plays, and the rest—gradually disappears in the process of time. The church's stock, whether of cash or of live animals, too, is rarely found after, at the latest, Elizabethan times. Exactly what happened to the stock is not clear. It is not too much to say that the mediaeval methods were replaced by others much more open to objection.

PEW-RENTS. Since the church is a 'place dedicated and consecrated to the service of God, and is common to all the inhabitants of the parish', only in very exceptional circumstances could pews be appropriated. In fact, generally there were no pews to be appropriated. It was and is usual for the chief seat in the chancel to appertain to the rector, whether lay or ecclesiastical; apart from this, the seating of attendants is the duty of the wardens as ministers of the ordinary, and in no way concerns either incumbent or vestry. But in early times the wardens exercised a probably extralegal custom of allocating specified seats in return for substantial rents.[15] White's *Selborne*[16] refers to the curious effect this appropriation of pews had on the appearance of the inside of Selborne Church:

Nothing can be more irregular than the pews of this church, which are of all dimensions and heights, being patched up according to the fancy of the owners.

Perhaps there is some substance in Dr Cox's suggestion that the system of wholesale pew-renting following the Reformation developed naturally enough in a period when a tendency towards the exaltation of the pulpit accompanied the neglect of the altar, so that pew-rents led to the evolution of freehold pews, kept under lock and key by their purse-proud proprietors, while the unfortunate paupers were crammed into deal benches stuffed into odd corners. Borrovians will remember that in the early nineteenth century Mrs Petulengro[17] had a strong objection to sitting on the poor benches at the back of the church of Bushbury, Staffs.

The parish books of St Mary's, Dover, contain an interesting commission for seating parishioners in St Mary's Church, dated 2 May 1639:

forasmuch as there hath been lately a petition made unto me on behalf of yourselves and the rest of the said parish that I would grant unto you a comission to place and dispose of every parishioner respectively of yor said parish in the seates of yor. church according to their severall condition qualities, and estates....And for the preventing and taking away of all strife and contentions....

Originally a uniform fee per seat for every woman parishioner was agreed upon by the vestry, or a seat was allocated by name to every male householder, 'as well gentlemen as also husbandmen', at a reasonable uniform charge. Occasionally private seats are still met with on a large scale, either belonging to individual proprietors, or appertaining to special farm houses or lands, so that when the Church Building Society was founded in 1818 it thought it necessary to impose, as a condition of receipt of its grants, that a certain proportion of the seats in every church helped should be freed for ever.

A particularly gross pew scandal is thus recorded in the register of Woodmancote, Sussex:

On the 1st June Dr. Cooper Rector of the parish pulled down the great pew in the church in which the family of the Wests had nested themselves, by the permission of former parsons, so long that they would now have it to be their owne. The Dr. thinking there was no way to be rid of the birds, but by destroying their nest, notwithstanding their big looks and threats did downe with it....Jacob West hath declared how unwilling he is to part with it, by his boys bringing a chair after him, to sitt it on the bare earth, which he did the next day, being Sunday, after the chancel door was opened for the incomers, which made sport to the people in that he looked like one who would have been glad to be welcome, bringing his stooll with him.

In October West arrested Dr Cooper 'on an action of trespass,

God knows what', then West fell sick and hostilities were deferred until the Doctor nursed him to health. This 'beget terms of pacification between them', but on his recovery trouble began again and in March 1679 the matter was referred to the assizes, and we leave the Doctor 'waiting for what more Mr. Jacob West can and will do'.

Perhaps even more scandalous is the fact that at some places, e.g. Bury St Edmunds, until recent years, elections were held for the allocation of pews. Here every ratepayer had a vote, and the rival candidates issued election cards. It is said that on occasion public houses were opened and bribes given to poor electors in order to secure votes.

In early times allocation of seats by the wardens in return for cash payments was often confirmed by faculty. There is e.g. in the chest of Wilmington, Kent, a faculty of 1726, for the annexation of two pews to Wilmington House, and Hawkhurst, Kent, has a similar faculty of 1719. Nowadays such faculties are granted much more sparingly, for the good reason that once given they are valid against the ordinary himself. According to the ecclesiastical lawyers, even a faculty could not grant a pew to a non-parishioner, and for that matter could not grant to a parishioner 'in gross' but only in virtue of his occupation of house or land. The fact remains that such faculties were granted wholesale, even to non-parishioners, and that pews in very considerable numbers are held under them, e.g. in 1937 Mr W. E. Denchfield of Easington, Oxon., bequeathed his pew in St Mary's Church, Banbury, to his sister for life, and afterwards to the vicar of the said church to be used as a free pew for ever.

The register of Heptonstall, Yorks., contains a most interesting memorandum of 1641 concerning seats set up in that year at the public expense for general use, and it has also many memoranda for the 'sale' of appropriated sittings. That of Burslem St John, Staffs., contains many eighteenth- and early nineteenth-century memoranda of the same kind. Several records relating to pews and pew-rents are to be found in Somerset parish chests. Fitzhead has 'The ordering of seats in Fitzhead Church 1607', Bath St James a seat rent book of 1717. Aller has the 'Apportionment of Seats in Church, 1747', and Langport has records of the sales of seats for lives, 1812. Heswall, Ches., has a pew allocation of 1740.

There are one or two well-known literary references to appropriated pews. Pepys[18] was kept waiting by the (locked) door of his pew on Christmas Day 1661:

I was fain to stay because that the sexton had not opened the door.

Swift[19] in *Baucis and Philemon* has an unkind reference to them and the convenient privacy they afforded:

> A bedstead of the antique mode
> Compact of timbers many a load
> Such as our ancestors did use,
> Was metamorphosed into pews;
> Which still their ancient nature keep
> By lodging folks dispos'd to sleep.

CHURCH RATES. References to the levying of church rates are quite commonly found in churchwardens' accounts of late mediaeval and Tudor times. The accounts of Northill, Beds., e.g. give a list of the parishioners in arrear in the payment of the church 'sesmt' in 1582, and have several similar lists of later date.

There is an interesting analogy between church rates and the appropriation of pews. Like this other money-raising device last discussed, church rates in general have and have had no statutory basis whatsoever,[20] except, ironically enough, for a brief period during the Interregnum.[21] It is admitted that, by the general canon law of the church, the repair of the fabric, both chancel and nave, fell upon the owner of the tithe. But by the custom of the country, i.e. by the common law of England, the repair of the chancel only fell upon the rector, and that of the nave, where the parishioners sat, was the duty of these parishioners themselves.

The common law obligation had presumably existed from time immemorial. It was recognised by ecclesiastical authorities in the fourteenth century, when John of Athon, writing about 1340, says:

Every parishioner is bound to repair the church, according to the portion of land he possesses...and the number of animals he keeps and feeds there.[22]

And in a constitution issued by John Stratford, Archbishop of Canterbury, in 1342, occurs the ruling that all having any property in a parish except glebe, whether or not they are resident, shall pay with the other parishioners towards the charges incumbent by common right or by custom for the repair of the church, according to their possessions and revenues.[23]

Upon occasional emergencies, long before the Reformation, the parishioners exercised their ancient privilege of rating themselves, alleging that it had been' practised 'time out of mind',[24] but probably hoping that each case of necessity would be the last.[25]

Mr Toulmin Smith, in developing his theories already mentioned, proved to his own satisfaction that church rates were the very foundation of local democracy, and could be objected to only by 'slavish tools of an irresponsible functionarism', anxious to destroy representative institutions, and to degrade the national church to the level of a minor sect. It happened curiously enough, as indicated above, that, apart from one or two special parishes, church rates never received statutory recognition in the days when they were most common, except for the brief period 1647–60,[26] when they were imposed by ordinance of the Long Parliament. The parish books of St Mary's, Dover, contain an interesting correspondence of the vestry with the county magistrates in 1654 during the Commonwealth, in which the latter express their readiness to

earne effectual remedy, and such cause will be taken that men shall not be left loose to doe or pay what and when they please to your respective Godly Ministers.

A bill, introduced in the Restoration Parliament[27] to legalise church rates upon much the same arrangement as the poor rates, failed to pass the House. The last attempt to give them statutory authorisation, one made in 1692,[28] when the Commons added to a tithe bill a clause concerning the recovery of church rates, met with no better success, so that the first statutory recognition of their existence was in the act for their abolition,[29] or more properly for abolishing their compulsory nature.

There have always been those who wished to avoid paying rates. The Quakers, of course, were particularly hard to deal with, and one can see the reason why the rector of Bolnhurst, Beds., entered in Register I on the front cover and two paper leaves following (in the hand of Thomas Baker, rector 1711–49):

A Clause in ye Act for Exempting Their Majesties Protestant Subjects Dissenting from ye Ch. of England from ye Penalties of certain Laws,—Provided always yt nothing herein contain'd shall be construed to exempt any of ye Persons aforesd from paying of Tythes or other Parochial Duties....

According to the Nottingham archdeaconry records, in 1629, a certain Christopher Featherstone of Warsop, Notts., found himself before the archdeacon's court for

wishing the church steeple downe (and when he had paid his church laye with a very ill will) for saying the divell goe with it.

He escaped by pleading 'that he did but wish the church on t'other side of the water'. Church rates may still be levied, but their payment is quite voluntary, except in those parishes where a local act includes provision for levying church rates in return for some valuable consideration, and therefore confirms something in the nature of a contract.

CHURCHWARDENS' EXPENSES CONSEQUENT UPON THEIR DUTIES. The variety of ecclesiastical expenses upon which church rates might be and were quite properly spent in post-Reformation times is so great as almost to defy classification. Probably the first duty involving the expenditure of money was the wardens' attendance at the ordinary's visitation[30] to be sworn in. It is quite usual to find the first item in any year's accounts to be of expenses incurred in attendance at the visitation.

As soon as they were fully qualified, the newly fledged wardens found themselves plunged into the performance of a great mass of ecclesiastical duties. This is clear from copies of their present-ments preserved in the chest. As successors of the synodsmen or questmen the wardens must 'present' twice a year at the visitation of the ordinary whatever was amiss or irregular in their parish. Amissness and irregularity are defined in the canons[31] as schism, adultery, whoredom, incest, drunkenness, swearing, ribaldry, usury, and any other uncleannesses and wickednesses, hindering the Word of God to be read or sincerely preached, 'fauting' any usurped or foreign power, defending Popish or erroneous doctrine, disturbing divine service by behaving rudely and disorderly, or by untimely ringing of bells, walking, talking, or other noise, not communicating at Easter (being of the age of sixteen), or not attending church on Sundays or Holy Days. The wardens must repel loiterers from the neighbourhood of the church in service time,[32] witness the recantations of schismatics,[33] mark whether the parishioners communicated regularly, and repel strangers habitually resorting to another church to the neglect of their own,[34] keep a list of strange preachers,[35] report to the bishop public opposition between preachers,[36] and present persons declining to have children baptised by non-preaching ministers.[37] Their duties included keeping the peace in meetings of the congregation,[38] suffering no profane usage of the church,[39] seeing that all the parishioners resorted thither regularly,[40] and, except in parishes where customs existed for parish clerks to collect their wages from the parishioners, paying the parish clerks

H

their ancient wages without fraud or diminution.[41] So it seems that, however relatively virtuous our ancestors may have been, the wardens would find full scope for their energies. And they were carefully safeguarded in the performance of their duties, and declared to be guilty of the horrible crime of perjury, so liable to excommunication, if they neglected them.[42]

Their control over the parson was and is real, though rarely exercised now. Cripps[43] considers that they are still bound to present their parson if he is irregular in the performance of divine service, wilfully alters or omits parts thereof, introduces things not sanctioned by the rubric, refuses or neglects his parochial duties in visiting the sick, or administering the sacraments, is non-resident upon his benefice for more than three months in the year, or in any way is guilty of irregularity or immorality of life. Sometimes, of course, they have been disposed to take too lofty a view of their rights, as is shown by this note from the second register of Lower Halstow, Kent:

James Ayers, the Churchwarden of this parish, for having on Sunday the eleventh day of January 1784, locked the door of the Church and sent away the congregation therein assembled, did by Order of the Archdeacon publickly ask pardon in the Church, of Henry Friend the then Curate, for the above offence, on the sixteenth day of May following before a crowded audience.

The wardens' power of approach to the bishop is recognised by legislation as late as 1874.[44] It seems, too, that as successors of the questmen they have still to see that curates are properly licensed and approved, and that strange preachers are not admitted without evidence of their ordination. They must ensure that there is no irreverence of any kind among the congregation during service, and if necessary must eject disturbers from the building, though they must not refuse admission to parishioners.

In addition to this very considerable list of duties the wardens have others, which have always been appropriate to their own office and which do not derive from the questmen's. As the successors of the church ales' organisers they 'the Deacons or other fit persons' collect the alms.[45] If the alms are taken at a communion service, or in aid of general expenses, the wardens retain custody of them, and they are ultimately disposed of as the wardens and the incumbent shall agree.[46] Frequent collections in church except, of course, of the alms and oblations at the Communion Service, are of course a quite new-fangled notion, as is illustrated by this extract from the records of Hedenham, Norf., where in 1742

considering y^t we were used in pretty large numbers to meet twice a year at ye sacrament, without making any collection for ye poor, or for any other purpose (it having been customary to gather alms only at Easter) I resolv'd to apply myself to ye ordinary and accordingly obtain'd his leave to gather oblations from ye communicants at Xmas and Whitsuntide.

The wardens furnish the bread and wine for the Communion,[47] and they must provide the goods, utensils and ornaments required by the Prayer Book, the famous 'such ornaments of the church and of the minister thereof as were in this Church of England by authority of Parliament, in the second year of the reign of King Edward VI',[48] plus the table of Commandments ordered in 1550.[49] Cripps gives an authoritative list of these requisites.

They must still maintain the fabric of the church, and all contained therein, whether for use or ornament; they must see that it is kept orderly and decent, so that there is nothing noisome or unseemly; they must ensure that repairs are executed when needful, though, if the repairs or alterations are considerable ones, they must obtain a faculty for them. They must see that the rector maintains the chancel; they must arrange for the distribution of seats in the church. There has been some controversy as to their custody of the belfry keys—they certainly have not that of the church keys, and they must take care that the bells are not rung without due cause.[50] They must see the churchyard is kept clean, and its fences in repair. During the vacancy of a benefice they are appointed sequestrators. They must act together, since what one does alone has no force in law. And, at the end of their year, they must hand over, for delivery to their successors, whatever parish property they have, and must submit their accounts to the minister and parishioners.[51]

These last duties figure very prominently in the warden's oath, as noted in the registers of Pulverbatch, Salop, in 1661:

You shall duelie administer ye office of a Churchwarden for ye best benefit of ye Church and ye good governmt of ye parishoners, & take care espeacially y^t ye Church be sufficiently repaired in buildings, as likewise well provided wth ornamts. and preserve ye Church Goods & Deliver them up with a just accompt at ye end of yor. office to ye next Churchwardens & parishoneis.

At Moorlinch, Som., according to the churchwardens' accounts of 1594, it was agreed by the inhabitants that:

from henceforth the churchwardens of the parish aforesaid shall make their accompts to the parishioners at or upon the tombstone in the parish churchyard of Murlinch upon the Monday next after St. George his day about 12 of the clock of the same day yearly and that two persons of each village do appear at the same time and place and for default to forfeit the sum of five shillings and eight pence as hath been formerly accustomed....

That the passing (audit) of the wardens' accounts was not merely formal is shown by the overseers' and churchwardens' account book of Long Ditton, Surrey, where in 1794 the parishioners carried a resolution demanding that the parish books and accounts be more carefully kept.

The parishioners of Feniton, Devon, exercised a very careful supervision over their wardens. In 1689 they found their accounts 'soe fowle that the p'ishioners thought not fitt to have it ingrossed upon this book'; in 1689 when they paid their rector 6s. for keeping the registers they added the note: 'which we looke uppon as not due to him', and in 1693 their accounts include the item:

Spent uppon the ringers the 5th of November and at other reioyceing dayes 12s which yᵉ p'ishioners looks upon to be to muche and very extravigant and hardly alow it.

The sworn men (select vestry) of All Saints', Orton, Westmorland, in a series of resolutions drawn up and entered after a list of their names at the commencement of the register, include among their good resolves:

Secondlie to see that the Churchwardens be careful and diligent in executinge their office ioyne with thes in suppressinge of sinne and such as behave the'selves inordinatlie to reprove and rebuke those wh. be found offenders, and if they will not amend to pᵉsent the' to be punished.

The model parson beautifully described by holy George Herbert[52]

doth often, both publicly and privately, instruct his churchwardens what a great charge lies upon them...it being the greatest honour of this world to do God and His chosen service; or as David says 'to be even a doorkeeper in the house of God'.

In addition to their numerous and varied ecclesiastical duties, the wardens, from Tudor times onwards into comparatively recent years, had a host of civil duties, concerning which we shall have more to say later.[53]

CHURCHWARDENS' RECORDS. We consider below the references which may appear in churchwardens' accounts to the discharge of but a few of these multifarious duties. Generally, of course, their actual presentments are, or ought to be, among the records of the archdeaconries, and it is only by a fortunate accident that occasional odd copies have survived in the parish chests. A fairly typical presentment from the St Albans' archdeaconry records, of 10 Oct. 1616, is:

Redbourne (Herts)

(1) Touching the Church. We present one Feana French for striking of one William Countys in our Churchyard.
(2) Touching the Ministry, Service, and Sacraments, nothing.
(3) Touching Schoolmasters, nothing.
(4) (5) and (6) Nothing.

> John Hewar. Jerome Collyns, churchwardens;
> Nicholas Byrd, John Sibley (Mark).

Churchwardens' records, other than the accounts, with a few occasional presentments, are found much less frequently. A few survive, however, e.g. in Somerset, Bridgwater St Mary's had, until they were transferred to the borough archives, a great many records from 1260 onwards, including a quittance from the churchwardens for rent in Stour Eastover, 1492, and a quitclaim to them from a Bristol bell founder, 1521.

Pulloxhill churchwardens' accounts, Beds., include receipts by the churchwardens for church furniture and vestments, with brief inventories, 1612, 1616 and 1617.

THE CHURCH FABRIC. The maintenance of the church fabric, as perhaps the primary duty of the wardens, is very frequently mentioned in all extant accounts, from the earliest ones remaining to the current accounts of this present year. Mediaeval churches were constantly undergoing repair and extension, and it seems that the whole body of parishioners took it as a privilege to be allowed to support so necessary a work. After the Reformation, and especially during the Commonwealth, entries occur of the breaking of stained glass and the removal of 'crucifixes and scandalous pictures'. With a tendency towards the degeneration of the church into a preaching house, it became imperative to seat as many persons as possible, to enjoy the benefit of the sermons. It became usual to secure the extra accommodation by inserting galleries, many hundreds of which were built during the seventeenth and eighteenth centuries. Often at this time such structural alterations as were undertaken were carried out in a style which has enriched the vocabulary of architecture by a term of abuse: 'Churchwarden Gothic.' It was at this period, too, that great heights were reached in the churchwardens' mania for immortalising themselves by placing their names or initials prominently upon the work carried out during their year of office. In many churches it is hardly too much to say that the more unsightly the work, and the worse the taste in which it is executed, the more sure one is to find the wardens' names very prominently displayed upon it.

Two particularly hideous examples of enormous leaden slabs, erected by the wardens in the eighteenth century, apparently for no purpose on earth save that of commemorating their own period of office, are to be found in Nottinghamshire, in the parish churches of Markham Clinton and Normanton-on-Soar. It may well be, however, that some such *leaden* slabs are actually panels removed during re-roofing and preserved because of the historical interest of the names.

The accounts below (from Feniton, Devon) are quite characteristic in their quaint mixture of items for bread and wine, bricks, apparitor's fees, and washing:

The account of William Braddon (for his brother John Braddons tenement) & Will Stoaks (for that which was Mr. Mardoods ten'). Churchwardens for the p'ish of Feniton in the year 1690 (is as followeth).

Imprimis we doe charge our selves wth ye rent of ye Churchland	00. 17. 00
Item we charge our Selves with five shillings and a penny which we had from ye p^{r}ceding wardens	00. 05. 01
Lastly we doe charge our selves wth 4 Church rates	09. 00. 04
The Sume totall of our receipts is	10. 02. 05

Our Disbursements are as followeth (viz):

Laid out at the vissitation at Cullumton	00. 16. 08
Pd fr Bread & Wine at Whitesuntide	00. 05. 08
For Bricke for use about ye Churche	00. 01. 02
For Lime used about the Churche	00. 02. 00
For a man & a horse one daie to Fetche ye Brick & sande	00. 01. 06
Pd to John Stanlake for A peice of Timber to support the Lyerne & end wall over ye Kings Arms	00. 06. 00
For Leather made use of about ye Bels	00. 00. 06
Pd to ye Carpenters & Masons fr worke done about ye Churche	01. 10. 06
Pd to Asheford for keeping of the Clocke	01. 00. 00
Pd to John Asheford for clenseing of ye Churche ye Church yarde & doeing the Dogwhipers office	00. 06. 08
Pd to Asheford for Oyle used about ye Bels & Clocke	00. 01. 00
Pd for Bread & wine at Michaelmas	00. 04. 05

Pd to Parrator For 2 books brought by him	oo. 02. oo
Pd to ye Ringers ye 5th of 9br	oo. 09. oo
Pd to Mr. Woolcot	oo. 06. oo
Pd to Dorothy More for washing ye Surplice	oo. 03. oo
Pd for Bread & wine at Cristide	oo. 04. 02
For Bread and wine at Easter	oo. 06. 05
For makeing our books & p'fecting our accounts	oo. 04. oo

Soe the whole sume of our disbursements are as appears
by the aforsed account   06. 10. 08

Soe that we have received more than we have disburst
as appears by this our account   03. 11. 09

the which we acknoldg to be due to the present Wardens for the Year 1691.

Allied to the question of maintenance is that of decoration. The whitewashing of churches was not newly introduced at the Reformation,[54] but it was certainly in post-Reformation times that the least judicious applications of whitewash were made, often smothering old oak carving, or mediaeval wall paintings. The traditional seasonal decoration lasted, however, well into the eighteenth century; palm (flowering willow), box and yew were in demand throughout the year, especially upon Palm Sunday; holly, ivy, rosemary and 'bayes' (laurel or bay-laurel) were the traditional ornaments at Christmas. Birch was used on St John's Day, yew as an emblem of immortality at Easter, red roses in garlands and sweet woodruff on Corpus Christi and other major festivals. 'Garnishing' upon this last festival did not, of course, survive the Reformation, though it was revived in Mary's time. But the celebration of such feasts as All Saints by decorating the church lasted almost until modern times. In town churches full details appear in the accounts, since the materials had to be bought, but in country parishes the materials could be obtained freely, and the only record is that of paying a few coppers to the decorators, e.g. for 'sticking ye Church'.

Rushes, bentgrass, or even straw, were strewn upon church floors. It was usual to spread these by the seats of any important local dignitaries, or to use them more generally at the times of visitations, or sometimes upon 'Sacrament Sundays'.

In early accounts one often finds references to the cord and veil, and to the cord and pyx, with the canopy surmounting the pyx. Later, of course, these disappeared. And since the unhappy controversies of centuries have raged largely around the altar and its use, perhaps the altar entries are the most illuminating of all in the light they throw upon contemporary historical events. There is a very interesting series at All Hallows, Hoo, Kent.

1557	It^m for canvasse & payntyng of the roode clothe	vij^s vj^d
1576	Recevede of Mayster gladwell for one paynted clothe	xx^d
1557	To Burbyge for making the altar	ij^s iiij^d
1560	For takyng down the alter	vij^d
1571	Y^e forms for ye Communion Table	xj^d
1565	It^m paid for all manere of deuties as in retornying the chales into a cuppe for the church according to the lord Bysshope commandment	iiij^s v^d

Such entries relate, e.g. to the destruction of stone altars in Edward VI's time, their reintroduction in that of Mary, the setting of a wooden table in some 'convenient place', often not the eastern end of the chancel, in Elizabethan times, its restoration to the ancient position in Laudian days,[55] and the provision of panelling above it, frontals for its decoration, and the paving and railing of the sanctuary, or sometimes the removal of rails which had previously been in wrong positions, and their re-erection in a north-south line. Again in 1643, when Parliament was supreme, altars disappeared wholesale as 'monuments of superstition and idolatry'. The communion table references of the Commonwealth are a study in themselves.[56]

A remarkable feature of seventeenth- and eighteenth-century accounts is the enormous quantity of communion wine purchased.[57] At St Neot's, Cornwall, according to Dr Cox, ten gallons of sack were bought for Easter communion in 1664. Some notion of what happened to the surplus may perhaps be gathered from an entry which appears in the register of Clunbury, Salop:[58]

Mr. Parry has agreed with the Parishioners of Clunbury to take instead of the spare wine at the Sacrament ten quart Pottles of good Port wine annually to be delivered to him in every year at Easter—the Parish Clerk to have the Pottles.   Easter Day, 1808.

It is, of course, provided in the sixth rubric following the communion service, that 'if any of the Bread and Wine remain unconsecrated the Curate shall have it to his own use'.

In the same place[59] it is ordered that 'The Bread and Wine shall be provided at the charges of the Parish'. This seems to be the real origin of Easter offerings, and extant vestry books give several accounts of vestry meetings when the levy of paschal money was first agreed upon; generally at the rate of a halfpenny or a penny per head. Sometimes the paschal taper levy was continued after the disuse of the ceremony itself, to provide the materials for the celebration of the Holy Communion.

For the use of houseling cloths, and the technicalities of communion vestments, the inquirer is referred to more specialised works.

The idea that preaching too was an innovation of the Reformation is very far from the truth. Dr Owst's books[60] on mediaeval sermons are good enough evidence to the contrary, and so, for that matter, is the frequency with which entries relating to pulpits appear in mediaeval wardens' accounts.[61] As a matter of fact, immediately following the Reformation, popular unsettlement was such that the authorities dared not risk allowing any priest to preach upon any subject he chose.[62] Indeed the canons still draw a clear distinction between 'beneficed men" and 'allowed preachers', and clergy falling into the former class, but not the latter, are enjoined by the canons to confine themselves to 'reading the Homilies plainly and aptly, without glossing or adding'. This is, no doubt, why Elizabethan pulpits are so rarely found.

It is common knowledge that, during the seventeenth century, the pulpit became higher and more imposing, developing eventually into the stately three-decker. The pulpit cushion, as Bishop Stubbs said, 'seems to have been an object of special devotion', e.g. in the 1725 terrier of Northill, Beds. (in Register IV):

A Cushion for the Pulpit of Crimson Velvet with 4 Tassels of Silk Twist; and a Vailance of the Same Velvet, with a fringe of Gold and Silk Twist.

Wesley describes in his *Journal*[63] a pulpit mounted on wheels. It was shifted round each quarter so that all the parishioners, wherever they sat in church, might have a fair share of the benefits of the sermon. Occasionally in ordering a new pulpit the wardens seem to have thought it a good occasion for offering the incumbent a broad hint: 'Woe unto me if I preach not the gospel' is a great favourite, and is very often found carved on the structure. Perhaps the most interesting inscription upon a pulpit is that found in 1878 at Thrumpton, Notts., where it had been concealed since the pulpit was raised in the eighteenth century:

> A proud parson and a simple squire
> Bade me build this pulpit higher.

Neither the faldstool nor the surplice entries are likely to be of a great deal of interest. Those relating to the font, and to font locks, however, are often most interesting. (Font water, like consecrated wafers, could be used in witchcraft[64] and hence it was kept under lock and key.) Occasionally bills of costs of pre-Reformation fonts have been preserved among wardens' accounts. Odd references occur also to font covers, to chrismatories, and to christening cloths, generally of silk. During the Commonwealth, fonts suffered very badly, and in many parishes destruction took place immediately upon the issue of the Presbyterian 'Directory' of 1645. They were replaced by common pewter basins, bought for a few pence.[65] At the Restoration the ancient fonts were, as far as possible, restored, often with the ancient midwives' seats adjoining them, and the 'Presbyterian Fonts' relegated to the seventeenth-century equivalent of the dustbin.[66] At Newark, Notts., only the lower half of the original font survived the wreck of 1646, so a new top half was made in 1660, with figures in contemporary costume. Hence there is to be seen here the somewhat grotesque sight of saints whose legs are fourteenth-century, but whose lovelocks and moustaches are typically Caroline. Chalices appear often in mediaeval accounts and inventories, and, about the time of the Reformation, sales by wardens, anxious to anticipate the royal commissioners, occur in such years as 1538 and 1547.

Ringing on saints' eves and Saturdays, for matins and nones, with separate entries of ringing on the greater festivals, occurs very often. From at any rate the fifteenth century, it was usual also to ring the bells upon the entry to or departure from the parish of the reigning monarch (neglect to do this was finable by the royal almoner). Every king's coronation, the birth of every heir apparent, such battles as Flodden, Pinkie, Lepanto and Ivry, and the defeat of the Armada, were all celebrated in this truly English fashion, the ringers being encouraged by a plentiful supply of ale. The failures of the Wyatt Revolt, the Babington Plot, O'Neill's Rebellion, and the (alleged) Gowrie Plot, all received recognition. The failure of Gunpowder Treason was a favourite occasion for ringing. At Condover, Salop, it was celebrated as early as 1606. Later on, such happy events as the granting of the Petition of Right, the safe passing of the Triennial Bill, the bishops being 'voted down by Parliament', Edgehill, Worcester, the installation of the Lord Protector, and the proclamation of first his son, then his legitimate successor, were all celebrated in the traditional manner. One may imagine with what joy wardens and vicars would authorise the celebration of the last-named. But the activities of Charles II and James II were such as to put a strain even upon Anglican loyalty. Monmouth's and Argyle's captures were celebrated in the usual way, but so was the acquittal of the Bishops. Readers of Macaulay will remember his description of the very reeling of the church spires of London, upon the failure of James's attempt to snuff the Seven Candles of the Church of England.[67]

At Feniton, Devon, the usual fee to the ringers was a shilling a time, and both the proclamation and the coronation of William III and Mary carried only the customary fee. But according to the overseers' accounts of 1688:

Pd ye Ringers when ye Bishops were quitted and released   oo. o2. oo

Evidently the parishioners (whose own rector had refused to read the Declaration) thought the occasion warranted the payment of a double fee.

With the wars and rumours of wars of the eighteenth century, the occasions of rejoicing became still more numerous (and the expenditure upon ale still more profuse). The custom, as we have every reason to know, shows no signs of decay or permanent desuetude, and we may fairly hope that it never will. The wardens must provide a Bible, a *Book of Common Prayer*, and a *Book of Homilies*.[68] Concerning the registers and their 'sure coffer' a good deal has been said above.[69] The main feature of the Table of Prohibited Degrees is that it was designed to clear up all doubt what marriages were lawful and which forbidden.[70] As to the provision of the Ten Commandments there is little to observe save that apparently the canon embodied an instruction sent out by the Commissioners in Matters Ecclesiastical, in consequence of a complaint by the Queen in 1560 that the churches were desolate and unclean: and that the 'other chosen sentences', some of which still survive, are commonly, and very properly, the Lord's Prayer and the Creed.[71]

THE CIVIL DUTIES OF CHURCHWARDENS. Although it has been our general plan to confine the first part of this book to the ecclesiastical records of the parish, and to reserve the second part for the documents left by those parish officers whose duties were wholly or mainly secular, it has been impossible to follow this scheme consistently in dealing with the churchwardens. These almost invariably jumbled together in their accounts the items relating to their host of civil and ecclesiastical duties. Sometimes, especially in very small parishes, the wardens held also the office of constable; until a couple of generations ago[72] they were *ex officio* overseers of the poor, so the accounts of all these offices are often mixed together, quite indiscriminately, very often in the 'book kept for the poor's account' according to the act of 1691.[73] At Barnes, Surrey, the churchwardens' accounts, 1686–1760, included entries for sand and turf sold from the common: so apparently in some parishes the churchwardens carried out duties generally performed by the waywardens. In some parishes again, it was the custom that the wardens, having completed their year of office, should be overseers for the succeeding year. An old account book formerly in the parish chest of Pulverbatch, Salop, contains an interesting agreement that this custom should be established, apparently quite extra-legally, in the parish:

1654. It was agreed upon by Robert Milward Rector & Isaac Medlicot & Richard Peirs Churchwardens & ye rest of ye Parish y^t ye Churchwardens should be Overseers of ye Poore ye yeare following their Churchwardenship.

Most of the principal statutes imposing civil duties on the wardens are dealt with elsewhere in the text.

An odd function was given to them by a sumptuary and protectionist statute of 1571,[74] enjoining that all persons of common degree should wear English woollen caps on Sundays with a fine of 3s. 4d. a day for each transgression. The township, as well as the individual, was held liable, and for twenty or thirty years after this, one finds entries in churchwardens' accounts of payments 'for default of wearing of cappes etc.' One much more important series of duties remained with them until recent years. It was enacted in 1532–3[75] that, in consequence of the innumerable number of rooks, crows and choughs, every parish, township, or hamlet, was to provide itself with a net for their destruction. Two pence was to be paid for every twelve old crows, rooks, or choughs, by the owner or occupier of the manor or lands. In 1566[76] this act was renewed, with the proviso that the wardens with six more parishioners should assess holders of land or tithe for the destruction of 'Noyfull Fowles and Vermyn' to furnish a fund for paying a penny for every three heads of old 'Crowes, Chowes, Pyes, or Rockes', a penny for every six young owls, and a penny for every six unbroken eggs.

The heads of the animals and the eggs of the birds were to be shown to the wardens, and then cut in sunder or otherwise destroyed. The act was renewed in 1572[77] and in 1597–8.[78] At Warblington, Hants., in 1799, the wardens paid for 12 dozen sparrows' heads, 18s. 0d., and in other Hampshire parishes about the same time twice and thrice this number of sparrows were slaughtered annually. From the latter part of the eighteenth century to modern times, a number of Bedfordshire parishes accounted for nearly a hundred foxes each. At Eaton Socon, during this period, 1500 hedgehogs were paid for, and extant Bedfordshire records prove the destruction during the time when the system was in operation of at least ten thousand hedgehogs, with several million sparrows and hundreds of thousands of their eggs. At Rampton, Cambs., 1802–22, the vermin payments were made not from the church rate (there was none) but from the rents of the church lands, at least £32. 10s. being so spent. From the same fund sums were lent to fen-reeves, and even spent on special constables' staves.

At Feniton, Devon, if one may judge from the poor accounts of 1689, the wardens discharged this particular duty jointly with the overseers—at any rate the poor accounts (printed above, pp. 99–100) mix up payments for hedgehogs, owls, woodalls, fitches and jays with monthly payments to the parish paupers.

An important subordinate of the wardens was the dog-whipper, whose duty it was to preserve order amongst the canine attendants at church, and sometimes amongst the children too. Barclay's *Shyp of Folys*, 1508, refers to the iniquity of those who:

> Make of the church for their hawkes a mewe
> And canell for their dogges, which they shall after rewe.

Contemporary references show that towards the end of the eighteenth century it was usual not only for sheepdogs, but also for turnspits, to accompany their masters and mistresses to church.[79] Apparently, the dog-whipper's office has no statutory origin, but rests simply upon immemorial precedent. Among the manifestations of reforming zeal given by P. P. Clerk of this Parish in Pope's satire,[80] he

> was especially severe in whipping forth dogs from the Temple, all excepting the lap dog of the good widow, Howard, a sober Dog, which yelped not, nor was there offence in his mouth.

Philip Thicknesse mentions, in his *Bath New Guide*, 1778, how
William Warburton, Bishop of Gloucester, had declared:

that being at the *Abbey Church* one *Sunday*, when a certain Chapter
in *Ezekiel*[81] was read in which the Word *Wheel* is often mentioned,
that a great number of Turnspits, which had followed the Cooks to
Church, discovered a manifest Alarm, the first Time the Reader
uttered the Word *Wheel*: but upon its being repeated twice more, they
all clapt their Tails between their Legs, and ran out of the Church.

The accounts of Sutton Bonington St Michael's, Notts., contain
several references to dog-whipping in their first folio, the accounts
for 1731. They begin:

> 1731. For pases dog wip
> to pass for sweeping the reeds
> for Sticking ye Church
> for wiping ye dogs
> At ye visitation
> for candles backou and pips etc.

The 'dog-whipper' in Paules is mentioned in Nashe's *Pierce
Penilesse*, 1592.[82] The dog-whipper's business was not to expel
from the church all dogs, but to remove such as did not behave
themselves well. The wooden tongs which he used for gripping
the offenders by the neck are still to be found in churches here
and there. At East Leake, Notts., the officer was at work as late
as 1842, and at Southwell, in the old collegiate church, now the
cathedral, the position still exists as a sinecure. Its holder is col-
loquially known as the 'knocknobbler'. In many Welsh churches
the office survived during the eighteenth and nineteenth centuries,
and there are several pairs of dog tongs still to be seen in Wales.
A pair is preserved at Clodock, Herefs., a dog whip at Baslow,
Derbys. At Youlgreave in the same county the dog-whipper's
pew remained until 1868.[83]

There were a whole host of minor officials of the parish,[84] subordinate in some measure to the incumbent, the wardens, or the
vestry, or all three. Such information as may be needed concerning
most of these officials will be found in any of the old textbooks of
ecclesiastical law, and in the various handbooks published for the
use of parish officers.

III. CHARITY ACCOUNTS AND OTHER
CHARITY RECORDS. BRIEFS

ENGLAND'S WEALTH OF CHARITIES. Early charities—the Great Pillage. Tudor and Stuart charities legislation. Losses of charity funds. Early attempts to recover lost charities. Examples of lost charities in Nottinghamshire. Clerical protests upon the misappropriation of charity funds. Some early attempts at the safeguarding of charity funds. Sources of information as to local charities. SOME TYPICAL CHARITIES. Wealthy charities. Food charities. Clothing charities. Sermon charities. 'Windfall' charities. Conditional charities. Sporting charities. Educational charities. Bell charities. Loan charities. Dowry charities. 'Prenticing charities. Charities for public purposes. Cow and common charities. PARISH OFFICERS AND CHARITY FUNDS. CHARITY RECORDS IN PARISH CHESTS.
BRIEFS. The brief system. Typical references to briefs. The origin of briefs: papal briefs, episcopal briefs, royal briefs. The issuing of briefs. Early abuses in the brief system. The 'undertakers'. Brief scandals in the post-Restoration era. Statutory attempts to reform the system. The virtual abolition of briefs. The recording of briefs in parish archives. Literary references to the system.

ENGLAND'S WEALTH OF CHARITIES. It is usual to find in any old parish church a 'table of benefactors' giving the dates, donors and values of benefactions to the parish. Such gifts were in early times almost invariably entrusted for administration to the incumbent and churchwardens. On the passing of the Local Government Act of 1894, charities were divided into two classes, civil and ecclesiastical, and the ancient control of the incumbent and wardens was restricted to these latter, to which it still applies.

Charities of early mediaeval foundation still exist, but for all practical purposes it will be sufficient here to commence with the charities mentioned in the Chantry Certificates[1] of 1546 and 1548, made in pursuance of the acts of 1545[2] and 1547[3] respectively. Article A of the instructions to the commissioners enjoined them to inquire 'for what purposes and dedes of charitie anye of them were founded, and by whome', and 'Preacher Scolemaster or poore men (other than the said Chauntery preiste) that hathe ben Relieved by the said Chauntery'. It is perhaps significant that, while Article A of the first inquiry turned up a great deal of information, the corresponding item in the second inquiry, as to how far the benefactors' intention had been carried into effect, almost invariably has the brief response 'None'.[4]

But, after the emotions aroused by the Great Pillage had been softened by the passage of time, the philanthropic spirit again began to .manifest itself in good works. In Elizabethan times legislation was passed to protect charitable bequests, and this legislation was sympathetically interpreted by both common law and prerogative courts. The chest of Gedney Hill, formerly Gedney

Fen, Lincs., has a whole series of records connected with a suit concerning the misappropriation of the parish charities in 1604, with Coke's judgment in the King's Bench. Throughout the seventeenth century charities of one sort or another were established in almost every parish, and it is quite usual for the earliest item on the table of benefactions to be one of this period.

Losses, of course, have occurred wholesale, and all the efforts of the Charity Commissioners during their century of useful labour have not been able to recover more than a part of these. The Standfast Charity at Kilve, Som., was paid from 1643 to 1896 and has been lost since this last year! One source of loss has been the English law of mortmain. Another has been the custom, very prevalent until recent years, of handing the benefaction in a lump sum to some local tradesman upon whose bankruptcy or death it has been irretrievably lost. Other losses have occurred because it was a favourite plan to secure the income of the charity by imposing it as a rent charge, so that when once the rent charge had not been collected for a period of years the lapse of time prevented its recovery. Perhaps the meanest of all misappropriations of charity funds were those perpetrated by overseers and churchwardens, especially in the eighteenth century, when rents of charity lands vested in trustees were often calmly annexed and credited to the relief of the poor rate.

At Gnosall, Staffs., charities entrusted to the parish officers for administration were used to pay the rates of persons who were indigent, and, in the same parish, when the workhouse was built in 1733:

tis agreed upon by the Minister Churchwardens and other Inhabitance under written that ye trustees Belonging to Hencocke's liveing shall pay ye rents as they receive up into ye hands of ye Churchwardens or overseers or sum one of them and that ye said rent shall be Imployd to the maintanance of the workhouse.

After the act of 1601 [5] 'to redress the misemployment of landes, tenements, rentes, annuities, etc., heretofore given to charitable uses', *ad hoc* commissions might be appointed to inquire into the application of charities, and traces of such commissions' activities are sometimes found, e.g. the register of Stourmouth, Kent, contains an award of 1626 concerning the provisions of a will of 1587; that of Hawkhurst, Kent, has a commission of 14 Jac. 1, 1616–17.

To take a few instances of lost charities from but one county:

in Nottinghamshire (1616–17) 'The churchwardens and most auncient men of everie severall Parish' were summoned to give evidence to the commissioners appointed under the 1601 act, and the probate registers were searched for wills containing charitable bequests. At Tollerton, when the scare died down, the malpractices were quickly resumed—as they were elsewhere—and at the end of that century the churchwardens there had to appeal to the Crown for another inquiry. It was then found that the rental of certain land there, which had been devised to the use of the poor, had been pocketed for the last four years by a neighbouring owner, whilst a larger charity had been withheld by the village 'squire' for five years. It was ordered that these gentlemen should forthwith make full restitution to the churchwardens, and pay costs. In 1786 there had to be another inquiry, when it was ascertained that some of the charities guarded by the churchwardens of 1699 had been lost, and in 1844 it appeared that benefactions had disappeared which were being duly distributed twelve years before.

A legacy made in 1776 to the poor of Granby had been lost by the insolvency of a trustee; at Gedling, a comparatively recent bequest of 20s. a year for the poor had been lost owing to the carelessness of a trustee who had misplaced the deeds; the little charity of Rosamond Magson, in 1681, for the poor of Worksop, had 'long been lost'; the East Retford Corporation held much land and other properties in trust for charitable purposes, but had long been in the habit of misapplying such funds. The Municipal Corporations Act made numerous adjustments all over the country, and, although some of the Retford charity deeds had utterly vanished, some properties which had been diverted to the church were restored to Retford's ancient grammar school. George Wharton, when bequeathing property to that school in 1727, tried to guard against the loss of his bequest by leaving 5s. a year for the vicar of East Retford to announce the charity in church every Easter Sunday.

Nor was Retford the only place where school funds were questionably used. Mansfield was as bad or worse. Its grammar school had been founded in the time of Queen Elizabeth, but very soon the church and school accounts became confused, and the stage was set for a long series of disputes which lasted into the Victorian era. In Elizabethan times, the rival claims created unseemly wrangles in which the vicar, Brian Brittain, figured prominently, falling foul of the school representatives, churchwardens, and inhabitants. In 1595 judgment was given against the vicar. But the matter was by no means thereby settled. Altercations were recurrent, and in 1682 it was ordered that the church and charity incomes be lumped together, the vicar taking two-thirds and the school the remainder. As late as 1858 it was directed by Chancery that seven-ninths of this income be given to the school, whose endowment income was at once increased from £400 to £1200. But the vexed question was not solved, and in 1885 'most of the endowment of the Girls' Grammar School goes improperly to the vicar and various non-educational objects'.

Some diversions of charity funds were the result of sheer carelessness, but others were flagrantly dishonest, and, as an example of the latter, the case of Sir Robert Harding would be difficult to beat. Becoming possessed in some way of the title-deeds of the Handley Bequest for almshouses at Nottingham, he proceeded to stop their income, which he appropriated to himself. But this was too much! Ralph Edge, the Town Clerk, had the matter brought before the courts in 1679, and won the case.

Equally scandalous was the action of the surviving trustees of the Huntington charity at the little Trentside port of West Stockwith. In 1715, William Huntington, a shipwright there, had left £743 for the building in his shipyard of a chapel and ten small almshouses for widows and children of deceased sailors and shipwrights, and had endowed the charity with £30 a year in lands. By 1722 the premises had been erected, but within two decades malversation was rampant. Two or three (instead of ten) poor widows had been installed, but they received nothing of the maintenance provided for them, and the surviving trustees refused to render any account of income or expenditure. When the parson took up the case they spent the charity funds lavishly in opposing him. In the end, aided by the Archbishop of York, he seems to have secured some redress, as in 1883 the Charity Commissioners gave directions for the distribution of that and other benefactions there, and the charity still survives.

As it was left to the local inhabitants to check such abuses it is not surprising that so many charities have been lost. In the time of James I, two persons were thus sued by the churchwardens and overseers of Flintham for lands bequeathed for the repair of the church and relief of the poor. Later the inhabitants of Normanton-on-Soar acted similarly with respect to property in

Nottingham, Lenton and Radford, devised for the village poor. At Dunham there is a whole list of charities, all of which have been lost for lack of following up. In 1743 the Parkyns charity, for apprenticing poor boys of Bradmore, Bunny and Costock, was reported to be mismanaged. The Saltmarsh bequest of £50 in 1756, for the education of poor children at Retford, was unknown in 1827, and at Screveton a small bequest of 1748 was twice lost and twice restored by the parishioners.

Whilst numerous charities have been lost by sheer embezzlement, others may be accounted for as the result of equally wrong but less reprehensible ways of administration. Sometimes trust property was sold and the money realised was applied to church restorations or pressing parochial needs. At Dunham, for instance, the poor rate was thus reduced; at Upton such proceeds were diverted towards the cost of finding the statutory militiamen, and the Corporation of Newark, in 1773, obtained an act empowering it to apply a liberal part of the local charity income towards the erection of its town hall, street-making, church repairs, and other general public purposes, as well as providing for the support of its poor.

In Bolnhurst, Beds., parish register, vol. 1, is a note by the rector:

Mem: Part of the ancient legacies bequeathed to the Poor of this Parish having in April 1757 been given away by the Overseer to one particular Pauper without a lawful Vestry, I remonstrated at a lawful Vestry on Easter Monday....
What was given to y⁰ Pauper before mentioned, should have been charged to the Parish Rates and not taken out of that old Donation to save the Pockets of the present Farmers &c.

At Wadhurst St Peter's, Sussex, in 1633, is a similar entry.

To guard against abuses of various kinds an act of 1758[6] was passed, constituting a Board for the Recovery of Charitable Bequests. Towards the end of the century, too, a good many charity loans to tradespeople were called in by resolution of the vestries and the proceeds invested in land. Many such charity estates exist to this day.

According to the manuscript records of Sutton Bonington, Notts., in 1731 there were in the parish of Sutton Bonington St Michael's, Notts., no less than twelve charities—ten for the poor and two for the school. The funds of all were let out on note of hand to local tradespeople. In that year, by resolution of the vestry, they were all called in, realising a total of rather less than £100. A subscription was set on foot for raising this amount to £110, the price of a cottage with four acres of land at Hose in Leicestershire. The balance was raised, notice given in church as to the bargain proposed, and no objection raised, so the purchase was made, and until a few years ago the land remained vested in the parish. The rent of £15 was distributed by the parish council to poor persons except for £1—the schoolmaster's share—which was claimed by the County Education Committee.[7]

Where charity estates consisted of common-right houses, or land having right of common, the trustees, of course, like other proprietors, received an allotment of open land under the enclosure award. To this is due the common notion—a quite erroneous one—that charities were frequently endowed at the enclosures.[8]

Much useful information as to the earliest charities is to be found in the decrees relating to charities among the records of Chancery at the Public Record Office,[9] but still more useful, and a great deal more accessible, are the thirty-two huge volumes of printed *Reports* of the Charity Commissioners. An abstract arranged under parishes was published as a Blue Book in 1842, and these abstracts were abstracted again in the early directories of White and his rivals, from whence they have descended into the modern Kelly directories.

SOME TYPICAL CHARITIES. A good illustration of the difficulties arising from an unexpected increase in the value of the bequest is to be found at Stanton-on-Wye, Herefs. Here a handsome bequest of £30,000 for providing food, clothes and physic for the poor of three small rural parishes had increased threefold by the time the Charity Commissioners reported. Naturally enough, therefore, the total population entitled to benefit—some 1180 in all—was swollen by all the idlers and vagabonds of the countryside, who flocked to share the annual income of £3000.

Food charities are very common. St Mary Major, Exeter, had a bequest of £20 in 1729 for providing twenty pieces of beef for twenty poor families at Christmas. Piddle Hinton, Dorset, had a dole of mincepies, ale and bread to more than 300 people at Christmas. At Great Barr, Staffs., the rector gave to all comers, on Christmas Day, as much bread, beef, vinegar and mustard as they could eat. At Forebridge, Staffs., six shillings was charged on an estate, to be spent every Christmas on 'plums' for each person occupying one of a specified fifteen or sixteen houses, without reference to the need of these inhabitants. At Blithfield, Staffs., the pious founders of the school, Elizabeth Bagot and Jane Jones, provided in their foundation an endowment for small beer, bread and cheese for all the scholars who should come from a distance.

Clothes, too, are often provided for. At Minehead, Som., £100 was charged in 1669 on the rent of a 100-acre farm, for providing the poor with coats, clothes, blankets and money. Nor were clothing bequests made only for the benefit of the submerged. Robert Foster of Hatfield, Yorks., in 1619 showed a very proper sense of the dignity of two learned professions in bequeathing funds for a new gown every three years for the curate of Stainforth and one for the schoolmaster of Hatfield.

Spiritual food, too, received due recognition. Dorothy Parke in 1783 left £10 per annum for bread, Bibles and gowns for six poor women of Harborne, Staffs. Sermons, especially Armada and Royal Oak Day and Guy Fawkes Anniversary sermons, are quite common. A Lord Mayor of London who escaped from a lion in 1647 left funds for an annual thanksgiving sermon on 16 October. So bequests of charities to those 'known or reputed to be constant comers to church' are often found. A bequest of 1628 at Chippenham, Wilts., has grown so that the poor who listen to the sermon now receive half a crown each. At Grantham on the second Sunday in November a homily is read on the sin of drunkenness, the funds maintaining it being a rent charge of 40s. on a famous inn in the town. At Norton-le-Moors, Staffs., at some time in the eighteenth century:

Hugh Forde, of Forde Green, did in his life give the further-most pew situated in the north end of the gallery, and all the sitting in the arch in the wall in the middle part of the gallery, for the use of the poor inhabitants of this parish for ever.

Some parishes owe important charities to lucky windfalls accruing from sojourners who happened to die in the parish concerned. The Lambeth pedlar has passed into history, and he is not alone. At Holker, Lancs., five acres of poor land were bought with 185½ guineas found in the pocket of a beggar, and St Nicholas parish, Nottingham, received twelve acres of land and two cottages under the will of Anthony Walker, a traveller, who in 1714 bequeathed this estate 'to the poor of the parish wherein I may chance to breathe my last'.

Where people of family pride gave benefactions, they sometimes coupled them with conditions as to keeping their memory green. The widow of Captain Cook left £1000 in Consols to the parish of St Andrew the Great, Cambridge, the £27 interest whereon was to be spent in keeping clean her husband's monument, with £2 to the minister, and the balance to five poor women. At Hanbury, Staffs., there is an annual endowment of 10s. to the parish clerk, conditional upon his keeping clean some family monuments. Perhaps the most curious bequests of this nature are those of Melbourne, Derbys. Here, in 1691, Thomas Gray bequeathed £200 to be spent in the purchase of lands to provide six nobles, yearly, for six waistcoats and three coats of *gray* cloth, for poor men and widows of Castle Donington and Melbourne. Henry Greene of the same parish, fired by a spirit of emulation, charged on his lands payment for four *green* waistcoats with *green* lace, for four poor women, the waistcoats being distributed on 21 December ('Gooding Day') and worn on Christmas Day. A similar bequest to the parish of Barnes, Surrey, includes the condition that the churchwardens shall care for a *rose* tree to be grown on the grave of the benefactor, a certain Edward Rose.

Almost every conceivable philanthropic purpose has been attempted by one or more charitable benefactions somewhere in the country, from freeing a toll bridge, as at Clifton in Bristol, where in 1782 William Vick left money for redeeming the toll, to encouraging manly sports, as at Bunny, Notts., where Sir Thomas Parkyns in 1741 left an endowment for an annual wrestling match, or Princes Risborough, Bucks., where the lord of the manor up to 1813 gave the poor a bull, a boar, a sack of wheat, and a sack of malt every Christmas morning at 6 o'clock. Probably one should regard the curious charity of Thomas Tuke, of Wath, Yorks., founded in 1810, as essentially a sporting bequest rather than a food charity. Thomas evidently loved children and left a penny to every child who should attend his funeral, with the result that some six to seven hundred children duly arrived and collected their pence. He arranged also for forty dozen penny buns to be thrown from the church tower at noon on Christmas Day for ever. Eventually the scramble became so rough and noisy that only six or seven dozen were thrown out in accordance with the will, the rest being distributed in a more conventional fashion.

Nor were womanly occupations neglected: endowments for teaching poor girls stitchery are quite common. So at Clayworth, Notts., in 1818 Francis Otter left a rent charge of £4 to be shared annually among the two best ploughers and the two best female shearers in the parish.

Endowments for bell-ringing were naturally a great favourite in England—many of the 'bell closes' or 'bell-rope lands' still surviving from almost immemorial antiquity. In 1344 Margery Doubleday, a washerwoman of Nottingham, left her modest estate to pay for the ringing of the church bell at 6 o'clock in the morning to arouse the washerwomen of Nottingham to their labours. Even the church clock has been endowed. At Woolley, Yorks., there are sixteen half-acre doles taken at some unknown date from the common and applied to the use of sixteen poor people, subject only to an annual payment by each of a shilling to the parish clerk for winding the church clock.

As useful as any must have been the numerous charities providing for loans, either interest-free or at a very low rate of interest, to deserving young men anxious to set up in business. The Arneway Charity in Westminster is perhaps the best known of this class, and another famous endowment of the same kind is Sir Thomas White's gift, made to 24 towns, and still of great value to the burgesses of Coventry, Northampton, Leicester, Nottingham and Warwick. Allied to this are such charities as that of Rolleston, Staffs., where in 1672 William Roulstone charged his land with the payment of £52 to be lent upon security for four years to poor, young, newly-married people. Resembling this again are charities of the type found at Penkridge, Staffs., where in 1632 Sir Stephen Slaney left £40 'for the poor and for marrying poor maidens'. In 1814 Joseph Rennard left £300 in trust with the Corporation of Hull for the benefit of eight poor children of Reedness, Yorks., £2 to provide them with books, and £5 as rewards of good behaviour on leaving school or on marriage. In Hull, Cogan's Charity, founded 1753, gave its girl pupils marriage portions of £6:

to each of them who does not enter the matrimonial state until she has been six years in respectable servitude.

Of the same nature, too, are the endowments for paying for poor boys to be 'prenticed. At Eccleshall, Staffs., in 1688 Henry Bennett left £20 a year for apprenticing poor children; at Hooton Pagnell, Yorks., there was a benefaction of £100 for a similar purpose. At Hull, Cogan's Charity in 1787 paid the expense of binding each boy, plus £1 a year to his master throughout his apprenticeship for clothing, with, at the expiration of the apprenticeship, a payment of £2 to the master and £4 to the boy.

Charities for what would now be considered public purposes are found too. At Ackworth, Yorks., the parishioners bought the manorial rights in 1628, and applied the profits of the court, together with a fortunate windfall of 1803, when an illegitimate proprietor died intestate, and his estate escheated to the lords of the manor, in relieving the poor and in the reparation of highways. Again, an unknown benefactor left West Retford, Notts., a piece of land of area 3 a. o r. 30 p., which until fairly recent years was let rent-free to a person undertaking to maintain a bull for the free use of the parishioners.

Yet another class of benefactions, which can hardly have been open to the abuses alleged against schemes of purely eleemosynary character, are the cow and common charities. At Alresford, Essex, in 1558 Edmund Porter charged on a house, called Knapps, the morning milk of two beasts to be given to the poor each morning from Whitsun to Michaelmas, with a cash payment of 3s. 4d. on Christmas Day and Good Friday. At Marston, Oxon., twenty-six acres were set aside, twelve as cow common, the rest being let for a cash rent. The commons with payments of from 25s. to £2 a year were 'conferred by vote of the landowners and the vestry'.

Cheshire is particularly rich in cow charities. An interesting one of Bebington in that county, dating from the benefaction of William Hulme in 1620, provides for a cow to be let at three groats a year to three 'poor and godly parishioners'. By 1835 the cow had increased to a herd of eight, and the charge was 5s. per annum. Similar charities in the same county were at Woodchurch, where there were thirty-nine cows, and at West Kirby, where there were twenty-four.

PARISH OFFICERS AND CHARITY FUNDS. Sometimes parish officers seem to have had a very genuine care for the poor, as at Slindon, Sussex, where £15 found upon the person of a travelling beggar was applied to the use of the poor, and finally in 1824 banked for safety. In other instances, as noted above, far from using any windfall as a charity, unscrupulous overseers raided charity accounts and converted endowments for the poor into subsidies for the relief of the rate-payers. Often a condition—rarely laid down by the original donor—was imposed upon applicants for charity donations: 'never having been in the receipt of parochial assistance'. The 7 a. 3 r. 34 p. poor close of Auckley, Yorks. (formerly attached to Finningley parish, Notts.), for years had its rent 'placed to the poor rate account', while sometimes, as e.g. at Pontefract, Yorks., in 1811, with the ancient Bead House Hospital, the overseers added insult to injury by converting an almshouse into—of all places—a workhouse! Probably the most curious idea of charity is that found at Wolverhampton in 1555, where a list of church collections made for charitable purposes includes 'Charities to a gibbet beyond Bilston'! (apparently towards its repair!).

CHARITY RECORDS IN PARISH CHESTS.   In the parish chest may be found such charity records as e.g. lease counterparts relating to charity lands, deeds of charity estates as at St George's, Stamford, Lincs., where there is a series, 1338–1638: lists of beneficiaries, memoranda in vestry minute and other old parish books concerning the entrusting of endowments to local shopkeepers and farmers, and references in enclosure awards to the exchange of open lands for allotments in severalty.

A number of volumes of detailed and interesting charity accounts (from the sixteenth century) have recently been collected from the parish chests of Essex and Bedfordshire, and deposited with the county councils concerned. The two county record offices contain numerous charity deeds from c. 1280 and from c. 1200 respectively, which have been deposited there on loan. It is often impossible to distinguish between charity deeds, properly so called, and documents relating to 'town lands', a term often used to cover parish property the origin of which is lost. In the record offices mentioned above, documents of title relating to 'town lands' go back in some cases as far as the thirteenth century.

Lists of charitable donations may appear in almost any variety of parish records. At Everton,. Beds., e.g. there is a list of 1658 in the churchwardens' and overseers' account book, with additions 1659–83.

A few parishes have special 'charity registers', e.g. Cobham, Surrey, with 'A Register of Benefactors', and Ewell in the same county, which has a Charity Book, 1776–1894. Canterbury St Stephen's has a list of benefactors dating from 1691 'publickly to be read to the parishioners the week before Christmas'.

Evidently school records could appropriately be dealt with here, but since, unhappily we think, education is daily becoming more secularised, we propose to conform so far to the spirit of the times as to postpone what little further we shall have to say on them until our second part dealing with the civil records of the parish.

BRIEFS

Parish registers of the seventeenth and eighteenth centuries have very commonly lists of 'briefs', i.e. royal mandates for collections towards some supposedly deserving object. At the time mentioned the brief was so common as to be almost an early equivalent of the Mansion House Fund, or 'This week's good cause'. The brief was addressed to the minister and churchwardens, and it was read *in extenso* from the pulpit. At the close of the service the clerk stood by the church door to take the collection, saying as the congregation left, 'Please to remember the brief'. The funds were handed to a duly authorised travelling collector. Later, it became usual for the warden to hand the money to the chancellor of the diocese at the bishop's visitation.

Original briefs are rarely found, since the original was supposed to be returned with an endorsement of the amount contributed, but it was usual to list in the parish books the amounts raised. Eight original collection receipts have survived among the parish records of Maulden, Beds. They date 1658–69.

Briefs were issued for church repair, for the redemption of captives (especially those of the Barbary pirates of Algiers and Morocco), for persons who had suffered loss by fire or flood, and for a host of other purposes. It is curious that briefs in aid of church repair rarely produced very considerable receipts, except in the immediate neighbourhood. Sometimes one finds nowadays historically minded incumbents, anxious to restore their churches, who contrive to raise funds by approaching other churches named in the registers or the briefs book, perhaps two or three centuries ago, and which are glad to regard as a debt of honour the return of the help received.

A typical brief entry is this from the parish register of Norton-le-Moors, Staffs.:

Oct 20. 1678

Collected for the Building of Paull's Church	4s. 8d.
Collected for Uffington in Lincolnshire	3s. 11d.

(This is not asked for and it will be distributed among the poor.)
(*Haec non demandatur, et inter pauperes distribuetur.*)

Surprisingly large sums were given, however, for the relief of distressed or persecuted Protestants overseas, and for the redemption of Christian captives. When the purpose was such a popular one as these, sometimes small sums were given from the church rate, in addition to, or in lieu of, the collection.

At Stoke-on-Trent, Staffs., Register I has:

Collectiones 1686 May 16   Coll: upon a brief by His
Majestie for the Relief of the Distressed French Pro-   d
testants.   £3. 06s. 08½
          June 20. Coll: upon a brief for loss by   d
fire in Whitechapell, Middlesex.   £0. 07s. 06

The same register gives in 1673 a list of

The names of those who have given anything towards the ransoming
of Christians from Turkish slavery.

(*Nomina eorum qui aliquid contribuerunt ad redemptionem Chris-
tianorum ē servitute Turcica.*)

This includes fifty names, beginning with that of the rector, who
gave 5*s.*, and mentioning amounts ranging from this down to a
penny, a total of £2. 7*s.* 7*d.*

Briefs had existed long before this. No doubt they had their
origin in the papal or episcopal commendation of appeals of various
kinds. In fact the term 'brief' is properly part of the technical
vocabulary of the papal chancery. It refers to a document sealed
with the Fisherman Ring, not with the leaden *bulla*, in relatively
informal language, and on fine parchment. It differs considerably
then from the more formal document known as a bull. The brief
system in the middle ages was carried on by licensed *quaestores*, who
went round from church to church with indulgences for special
objects. Such licences are often noted in episcopal registers,
especially in the fifteenth century.

Mr Bewes found the first papal brief in very early times and
the first episcopal brief in one of 1247. Episcopal briefs he came
across at any rate as late as 1683. A still later one of 1742[1] is to be
found in the parish chest of Beaudesert, Warws.

At the Reformation the papal prerogative was vested in the
crown. In 1533–4 and again in 1536[2] 'bulls breves or other instruments or writings' from Rome were prohibited. Royal briefs existed,
however, before the Reformation. King John issued a brief for the
'Messengers of the House of St Thomas of Acon', and at some
time before 1533 Henry VIII issued one for the canons of Kirby
Bellars, Leics. These royal briefs were issued in the form of letters
patent, with an instruction that they were to be read in church
during divine service.

Such briefs are to be clearly distinguished from the licences to
beg which were issued under the acts of 1530–1 *et seq.*[3]

In Elizabeth's reign, briefs were issued sometimes under the Privy Seal, and occasionally included a commendatory letter from the Privy Council. From 1625 onwards, petitions for briefs were often supported by certificates from quarter sessions, testifying to the genuineness of the facts alleged. After the Restoration the whole process seems to have been regularised, and future royal briefs were issued by the Lord Chancellor. At Borough Green, Cambs, a parishioner, Francis Draper, was presented in 1618 'for that he useth commonly to depart out of the Church when any brief is to be read upon a Sabbath Day before Divine Service is done, to the great offence of Almighty God and the congregation'.[4]

The system early lent itself to abuse. There are·many references to complaints against it in the *Commons Journals*, 1624–5.[5] In 1642 the House adopted an order 'inhibiting any collections upon any Brief under the Great Seal' (no doubt to prevent the King from raising funds in this fashion), and again, on 10 January 1647, it was ordered that no collections should be made except under the Great Seal and with the concurrence of both Houses. During the Interregnum there were further allegations of abuse, e.g. in 1653. There is, however, no record of any action taken.

After the Restoration briefs were farmed out to professional 'undertakers', who contrived to pocket the lion's share of the proceeds. Enormous fees were paid to the Patent Officers, and to the King's Printers, so that in some instances much less than half the money raised was received by the supposed beneficiaries. The instance cited below gives a favourable view of the working of the system, since in this case rather more than half the money raised was applied to its proper purpose.

Montford, Salop, Register I (concerning the rebuilding of the church in 1738):

The number of Briefs laid were 9804 wch. brought in £619. 3s. 11¼d. Their Salary at 10d wthin. yᵉ Bills of Mortality at London, and 5d. all othr. places was £208. 0s. 5d. The Patent Fees were £85. 5s. 4d. Ballance £325. 18s. 4½d. [*sic*]....

Pepys refers to the abuse of the system 30 July 1661. The collection which aroused his indignation was one made

for several inhabitants of the parish of St. Dunstan in the West, towards their losse by fire.

and it raised 'xxs. viijd.' Contributions of one kind or another had been levied by brief at St Olave's for fourteen weeks in succession.

A particularly gross scandal arising from abuse of the whole process took place in Westminster about 1700. The sufferer was a certain Margaret Mortimer, for whose supposed benefit funds had been collected in 1697, and who petitioned the House for redress of her grievances in 1701.

Parliament inquired in 1704 into the misuse of the system, and an act was passed in 1705[6] 'For the better collecting Charity money on Briefs' and for preventing such abuses. However, the system was still seriously misapplied. Lengthy discussions on its rights and wrongs appeared in *The Gentleman's Magazine* in 1747, 1748 and 1749, and again in 1787.[7] Lord Hardwicke issued a regulating order in 1755[8] and another regulating circular was issued by the Secretary to the Lord Chancellor in 1804.[9] There was still more controversy in *The Gentleman's Magazine* in 1807.

The principal firm of 'undertakers' carrying out the work was in the middle of the eighteenth century an organisation managed by a certain Robert Hodgson. About 1754 they were supplanted by a new concern, Messrs Byrd, Hall and Stevenson of Stafford. This organisation, and its successors, the last being a John Stevenson Salt, retained control of the business until 1828. In 1816 there was renewed controversy, and the Staffordshire justices inquired into the management of the undertaking. The same year Lord Shaftesbury moved in the House of Lords for accounts.

The Church Building Society, which carried on much of the work which had formerly been financed by means of briefs, was founded in 1818. In the first few years of its existence it was granted briefs of its own, but in 1828 the act[10] incorporating the Society abolished in essentials the entire system. John Stevenson Salt, the principal undertaker, was ordered to hand to the Church Building Society all undistributed monies in his hands.

Briefs by the royal prerogative are apparently still lawful, and royal letters commendatory, which amount to much the same thing, have been issued in comparatively recent years in aid of one or two societies whose work was considered to be of national importance. The Church Building Society suffered particularly when the issue of the royal letters was discontinued in 1853, and its income fell from a maximum of £60,000 to £25,000, in 1861 it was £10,000, in 1896 £4,500, now (1957) it is £9,027.

Generally briefs were recorded upon a spare page of the parish registers, very often on the fly-leaf, but some churches kept special 'brief books'. Such are to be found, e.g. at Lissington, Lincs.,

1709–45, Culmington, Salop, 1706–33, and Hopton Castle in the same county, 1729–87. There are at least seven such books in the parish chests of Kent alone. There is an original brief of 1680 in the chest of St Clement's, Sandwich.

Occasionally the notes of collections include extracts from the briefs, e.g. in the register of Brotherton, Yorks.:

Aug. 5. 1666. Collected in the Parish Church of Brotherton for the relief of a distressed Minister, John Becket of Fryston, who had sustained great loss by fire by means of a carelesse maide who...carrying a Candle to bed with her, left it sticking on the bed's head; which, she falling asleepe, fell into the bed and burnt his house and goods to the amount of 40£ and himself since by a thorne fallen into his eyes hath lost his sight so...that he can neither see to preach nor teach schoole.

Literary references to the system, both in the days when it was flourishing, and in the later times when it had fallen into disrepute, are to be found in plenty. One of the earliest is in the Book of Common Prayer, which contains a rubric:

Then the Curate shall declare unto the people what Holy-days, or Fasting-days, are in the Week following to be observed. And then also (if occasion be) shall notice be given of the Communion; and Briefs, Citations, and Excommunications read.

George Herbert's *Country Parson*:[11]

if God hath sent any calamity, either by fire or famine, to any neighbouring parish...expects no brief; but taking his parish together the next Sunday, or holyday...he first gives himself liberally, and then incites them to give....

Pepys[12] has an interesting reference to the abuse of the system following the Great Fire of London in 1666. Charles Churchill refers to briefs incidentally in his satire *The Duellist*[13] written in 1764. Cowper has in *Charity*:[14]

> A conflagration or a wintry flood
> Has left some hundreds without home or food;...
> The brief proclaim'd, it visits every pew,
> But first the squire's, (a compliment but due):
> With slow deliberation he unties
> His glitt'ring purse—that envy of all eyes!
> And, while the clerk just puzzles out the psalm,
> Slides guinea behind guinea in his palm:
> Till, (finding as he might have found before;)
> A smaller piece amidst the precious store,
> Pinch'd close between his finger and his thumb,
> He half exhibits, and then drops the sum.
> Gold, to be sure! Throughout the town 'tis told
> How the good squire gives never less than gold.

Pope[15] in his ironical *Memoirs of P. P. Clerk of this Parish*, 1727, refers to the minute receipts upon some briefs:

The next chapter contains an account of the Briefs read in the church, and the sums collected upon each. For the reparation of nine churches, collected at nine several times 2s. and 7d.¾. For fifty families ruined by fire, 1s. ½d. For an inundation, a King Charles's groat given by Lady Frances, etc.

That this is not altogether a caricature is shown by such records as those of Burghclere, Hants., where of thirty-eight briefs, 1734–6, twenty-three produced nothing. At Bramley, in the same county, of fifty briefs for churches, 1761–9, forty-eight produced nothing whatever, the other two raising respectively sixpence and a shilling, and at Houghton, Hants., in August 1795, nine consecutive briefs produced nothing at all.

IV. GLEBE TERRIERS AND TITHE RECORDS

GLEBE TERRIERS. Canon 87. Early terriers. The historical value of glebe terriers. Terrier form and terrier entries. The church and the parsonage. The glebe. Other entries: customary payments. A typical Nottinghamshire terrier. Customary fees as set forth in a Shropshire terrier. A DISCURSION CONCERNING THE PARISH CLERK. Literary references to the parish clerk. The clerk's fees. Records left by the parish clerk. A DISCURSION CONCERNING THE 'CHURCHYARD RAILLES'.
TITHE RECORDS. The early history of tithe. The division of tithe. Classification of tithe. The Edwardian tithe legislation. The inconvenience of tithe. Tithe suits and controversies. The demand for tithe commutation. Tithe commutation before 1836. The Tithe Act of 1836. The later history of tithe. SOURCES OF INFORMATION AS TO TITHE. Tithe commutation under enclosure awards. Tithe apportionments. Tithe commutation by the imposition of corn-rents. Tithe plans—their value. Typical tithe records in parish chests.

GLEBE TERRIERS[1]

Canon 87 says: 'We ordain, that the Archbishops and all Bishops, within their several dioceses shall procure (as much as in them lieth) that a true note and terrier of all the glebes, lands, meadows, gardens, orchards, houses, stocks, implements, tenements, and portions of tithes...be taken by the view of honest men in every parish...and be laid up in the Bishop's Registry, there to be for a perpetual memory thereof.' But this injunction refers only to extra-parochial tithes and glebe. Presumably the custom of making a terrier of the church's possessions in the parish dates from immemorial antiquity. Terriers should properly be found in the registries of dioceses and archdeaconries, e.g. Lincoln has a file from 1577; it is said that Peterborough Diocesan Registry has a complete set for every parish in the diocese for the last three or four hundred years.

Terriers of date before 1604 are rarely to be met with in parish records, though Fordwich, Kent, has in its churchwarden's accounts one as early as 1501, but during the seventeenth and eighteenth centuries they seem to have been made with great regularity. In the province of Canterbury it is quite usual for the earliest terrier to be of date 1633-6, the time of Laud's energetic visitation. Probably incumbents and wardens were moved to industry, as they are still, by a wholesome awe of the archdeacon. A constitution of Archbishop Langton[2] (1222) enjoins archdeacons at visitations to

take account in writing of all the vestments and books; and they shall require them to be presented before them every year...

and apparently the terriers were included among the books.

Certainly terriers are very often found on loose parchment sheets in the chests, or on spare pages of the registers.

It will be seen that when terriers date back, as many do, to the seventeenth or early eighteenth centuries, when England was largely in a condition of open field,[3] they may be literally invaluable as giving almost detailed surveys of the agricultural activities of the countryside under the old primitive conditions.

Generally the terrier begins with an inventory, describing first the church itself, its fabric, furniture, plate, bells, and books. Then perhaps it covers the churchyard, with special notes as to customary obligations to repair its walls or fences.[4] Then the parsonage with its curtilage is minutely depicted, with a statement of how far it is made of brick, how far of 'stud and mud', how far thatched, how far tiled, how far 'plaistered', how far ceiled, and so on. Then the terrier states the number of yardlands, ploughlands, or oxgangs of glebe belonging to the benefice, with minute descriptions of the 'buttalls and boundings' of the dozens—perhaps almost hundreds—of scraps of which it was composed: specifies the allowance of meadow which accompanied the ploughland, and if the meadow was 'lot' or 'rotation' meadow may explain the method by which its (generally annual) re-allotment was determined:[5] and concludes the agricultural part of its contents by stating the number of cow- horse- or sheep-gates attached to the benefice, and exercisable upon the commons of the parish.

In the register of Little Abington St Mary, Cambs., after a most minute description of the 'rights of the Vicaridge' a Mr Colbatch, the compiler, concludes with a sort of colophon: 'Cursed is he that removeth his neighbour's landmark.'

After dealing with the landed property of the benefice the terrier usually goes on to describe its tithe revenue, with details of any tithe-free lands, and of any customary arrangements as to the collection of tithe, or as to the payments of moduses in lieu thereof.[6]

Finally it gives a note as to the use of the parish in such matters as Easter offerings, mortuaries and surplice fees, and other minor customary payments. Good examples of such terriers dated 1625 and 1749 are to be found in the register of Finchingfield, Essex. Then, in general, it concludes with a description of the methods adopted for the upkeep of those two most important ornaments of an eighteenth-century church, the church clock and the parish clerk.

K

A differentiation in burial fees is quite usual. At St Stephen's, Canterbury, e.g.:

1739. Mem^d...The accustomed fee when the service is read in ye Church at ye burial of a Parishioner is 6s. 8d. But when the service is read at ye burial of one brought from another parish the usual fee to the Minister is double viz: 13s. 4d.

At Brook St Mary's, Kent, the fee for a funeral sermon was 10s., or a guinea; at Lenham, in the same county, in the Hardwicke Marriage Register II, 1754, is:

Funeral Sermon if the Text is chose £1. 1s., if not 10s. 6d.

It was usual also to charge a fee 'for breaking the ground', for burial in church, as e.g. at Boughton Aluph All Saints' Kent.

By way of illustration we append below copies of and notes from unpublished terriers from the parish of Sutton Bonington, Notts., the first taken sixty years before the enclosure of 1774–5.

A True Terrier of the houses, out houses, lands, or gleab, belonging to the Rectory of St. Anne in Sutton Bonnington in the County of Nottingham, setting forth the buttings and boundings wth the manner of tything, and an account of all other matters relating to the said Rectory.

IMPRIMIS.   The house, containing six bays of building 2 barns containing five bays of barning, one stable containing one bay, a cowhouse containing three bays, wth a garden, close and yard, containing by estimation one Acre of land.

MIDSUMER GROUND.   One lay at [?]*East Gab.*, my Lord Ferrers on the North, one half acre butting on the Sore, my Lord Ferrers on both sides, one Rood in the *Middle Furlong*, my Lord Ferrers on both sides, One half acre butting on the *Far Meadow*, my Lord Ferrers on both sides.

MEADOW GROUND.   An acre of lays upon *Meadow Gore*, my Lord Ferrers on both sides, one half acre lying up at the top of *Meadow Gore Lays*, my Lord Ferrers on the South, one rood butting to *Coal Cart Way*, my Lord Ferrers on the East, one half acre butting on the *Dockey Hook*, John Wheatley lying on the East, one half acre on the *Over Latch Pool* Mr. Ross on the North, one half acre in the *Swathy*, the *Bull Hook* on the South, one half acre against the *Meadow Gate lays*, John Sarson on the North, one half acre next the *joyning acre*, John Sarson on the North side, one rood in the *Far Meadow*, Lord Ferrers on the South, one Rood in the *Knaves Acre*, John Bramley on the South, one half acre butting on the Soar, Mr. Draper on the South, one acre by the *Bridge Holme.*

LAND IN THE NEATHER FIELD.   Two half acres in the *Sandholm* butting upon the *Galls*, my Lord Ferrers on the North, Five roods on the *Short Oldings*, my Lord Ferrers on the West, one half acre in the *Long Oldings*, my Lord Ferrers on the East, the rood butting *on the furlong that goes to the Mill*, my Lord Ferrers on the West, one half rood on the *Mill-boards*, my Lord Ferrers on the West, one rood on the *Brisley Furlong*, Ld. Ferrers on the East, one rood butting on Millsick, Ld. Ferrers on the South, 2 half Acres *Willow Lays* Ld. Ferrers on both sides, a rood on *Little Hedge furlong*, my Lord Ferrers on the East, 2 roods on *Church Floors*, Ld. Ferrers on the North, one three rood in *Long ashes*, Ld. Ferrers on both sides. One rood on the top of *Short ashes*, Ld. Ferrers on the North, one half acre butting up to *Kirk Hill*, Ld. Ferrers on both sides, one half acre above the *Mear*, Butting to *Kirk Hill*, Lord Ferrers on the West, one rood butting up to *Kirk Hill* Ld. Ferrers on the East, One half acre on *Copilerow*, Lord Ferrers on the South, a half acre and rood together on the same Furlong. Ld. Ferrers on the North, one half acre on the *Cliffs*, butting to the *Thief's nook*, Mr. Draper on the West, 2 half acres more on the same Furlong, Ld. Ferrers on the West, 2 three roods upon the *over Water Falls*, Ld. Ferrers on the South, 2 half acres on acres on the *neather Water Falls*, Ld. Ferrers on both sides, one half acre on the same Furlong, my Lord Ferrers South, one half rood butting upon *Mr. Drapers Headland*, Ld. Ferrers on both sides, one rood on the same Furlong, Mr. Draper on both sides, one half acre butting upon the *Pasture*, Ld. Ferrers South, one rood near the *Causey*, Mr. Draper on both sides, a little half acre on *Clay Dales*, Ld. Ferrers on both sides, a rood and a [throng?] rood, butting upon *Street Mear*, Ld. Ferrers betwixt.

RUNDLE FIELD. One half acre butting to the *Little Causey*, Ld. Ferrers on both sides, a small land at *Evington Hedge*, Ld. Ferrers on both sides, one rood butting on the *Street Mear*, Ld. Ferrers North, a rood and a half at *Cart Saddles*, Ld. Ferrers West, a rood upon the same Furlong, Mr. Draper on the East, half a rood on *Clifford Nook*, Ld. Ferrers South, two roods butting upon *Thiefs Nook*, Ld. Ferres [*sic*] West, 2 roods more upon yᵉ same Furlong, Mr. Draper on the West, 2 half acres on *Thief's Nook*, Lord Ferrers West, one rood more of the same Furlong, my Lord on the East, one rood on the Furlong, below, Ld. Ferrers on the West, 3 lands by estimation one acre near [?], Ld. Ferrers West, one rood at [?].

RUNDLE FIELD. Four Roods at *Kitta Hedge*, Ld. Ferrers on both sides, 2 acres at *Blakelow*, Ld. Ferrers West. Two half acre upon *over Heath*, Ld. Ferrers on both sides, two roods on *long Breaches*, Will Osborn on the West, one half acre on the same Furlong, Ld. Ferrers East, 3 roods on *neather Heath*, Ld. Ferrers on both sides, half an acre on the same Furlong, Mr. Draper West, one rood in *Beaulands* [*sic* for *Beanlands*] Ld. Ferrers North, One half rood at *Gad's Bush*, Ld. Ferrers West, Half a rood at the end of that, Mr. Draper South, 2 more half roods on the same Furlong, Ld. Ferrers East, one rood at *Carters Slade*, Ld. Ferrers South, one rood more on the same Furlong, Mr. Draper North, one rood more on the same furlong, Lord Ferrers North, a half acre more on the same furlong, Ld. Ferrers North, one half acre on *Red Land*, Ld. Ferrers West, one rood next *Gotham Lay Hedge*, as also the Hedge, Ld. Ferrers South.

STANDARD FIELD. Six half acres lying about the Church Yard. One rood between the Charity, Ld. Ferrers South. Two roods at *Shooter's ditch*, Ld. Ferres [*sic*] West, Three lands containing an acre by the *Wind Mill*, Lord Ferrers both sides, One rood more on the same Furlong, Mr. Draper on the East, Two half acres on the *Standard*, Ld. Ferrers West, one rood upon the s^d Furlong, my Lord on the West, one rood more upon the same Furlong, Ld. Ferrers East, one rood butting against the *Dutchess of Newcastles Headland*, Ld. Ferrers on the South, one rood on the *Stony Way*, Ld. Ferrers on both sides, one rood on the *East Lands*, Ld. Ferrers South, one rood next *Trowell Close*, Ld. Ferrers East, 2 half acres below the *Trowell Close*, Ld. Ferrers East, one rood on the *high Bush furlong*, Ld. Ferrers West, one half acre on the same furlong, Ld. Ferrers on both sides, one acre at *Long Acre lands*, my Lord on the West, one half acre at *Causey Meadow*, Ld. Ferrers on both sides, one rood on *Willow Mear* furlong, Ld. Ferrers West, one half acre in the old *cross moate field*, Ld. Ferrers East, one half acre on *Bushell Wongs*, Ld. Ferrers West, one rood in the *Clay*, Ld. Ferrers north, one half rood more in the *Clay*, Ld. Ferres [*sic*] South, one rood on *Burley Hill*, Ld. Ferrers West, one rood more upon the same furlong, Mr. Draper West, one half acre on *Smith Stiles*, Ld. Ferrers South, one half acre more upon the same furlong, Mr. Draper North, One rood on *Pit House furlong*, Ld. Ferrers on both sides, one rood more on the same furlong, Ld. Ferrers East, one half acre in the . . . *leasure*, Ld. Ferrers North.

One ?(intake) and a croft containing half an acre of land, 12 Beast pastures, 6 Horse comons, Four Score and ten Sheep Comons, The Tythe of fifteen yard lands and one half lying in the Libertys of Sutton:

Dated the 9th day of July 1714.[7]

Other early terriers of the same benefice exist for 1726 and 1764. They follow the same general order, but the 1764 terrier gives in its last paragraph a few additional entries of some interest:

The Church Yard is Hedged round: no trees upon it but four or five young ones set by the Present Rector. The Garden rail'd, and a young quick set.

We have no Church Clock: two small bells. A small Silver Cup. The Parish repair the Church, The Rector the Chancel and Church-yard fence except the West side. The Clark's Wages paid by the Parish and half a Crown per annum given him by the Rector.

Dated the 7th Day of June 1764.

Several later terriers (after the enclosure of 1774–5) are pre-served, but these are naturally very much inferior in interest to those relating to the open-field conditions of the old village community.

We quote below the latter part of a terrier of Cheswardine, Salop, 14 July 1722, which gives a great deal of detail concerning tithes and methods of tithing and the payment of the parish clerk.

(After a description of the Vicarage, glebe, small tithes and moduses):

MORTUARYS:[8] Mortuaryes Due to ye Vicar at ye Death of householders. If any householder dye posest of ye Value of three hundred pounds of Free Estate or any sum between that & forty pounds pay ten shillings to ye Vicar & if it be thirty pounds or upwards pay six shillings 8d, If Twenty Nobles & under twenty Marks pays to ye Vicar three shillings 4 pence.

SURPLICE FEES IN CHESWARDINE PARISH: Weddings published in ye Church 3 times one shilling and for a certificat six pence & for Marriage one shilling two pence. The Register four pence belonging to the Vicar & for marring a Cupple w'th. a Licence five shillings, for Churching of a woman four pence and for burying a Corps 4d.—Note That if a woman live in ye parish ye fees are due to ye Vicar and Clark tho' she be married elsewhere.

CUSTOMERY FEES DUE TO YE CLARKE: The Clarke no sett or Standing Wages but only thirteen shillings & 4d. for looking to ye Clock. Likewise ye Clarke hath four pence for every plough land throughout the whole parish and for every cottage he hath two pence throughout ye old parish paid ann at Easter—Note. He gathers likewise at a Chrismass an antient customery payment of severall persons called Keech money some more some less whereby he is obliged to clean their seats and dress em against a good time.

EGGS: Their is likwise paid by Antient Custom to ye Clarke at Easter two Eggs for every Cock & for every Drake two throughout the whole parish, At ye churching of a woman he hath 2d. or 2 White loaves.

WEDDING: The Clark's Wages for a wedding asked in ye Church is 4d and as much more as he can gett but a Lycence more.

BURYING: For a Burying the Clarke hath foure pence for a Grave in ye Churchyard, and fourpence for his Office, and in ye Church or Chancell for a Grave he hath twelve pence—12d.

A DISCURSION CONCERNING THE PARISH CLERK. This functionary, often (in his own estimation) second in importance to no one in the parish, is a study in himself.[9] His desire for fees is very comically satirised in Pope's *Memoirs of P.P. Clerk of this Parish*. An example of an errant parish clerk appears in Crabbe's *Borough*: He withstood all save one of the crafts and assaults of the Devil, liquor, heresy, and even the temptation of St Anthony, but at last succumbed to the temptation to help himself from the alms box at the monthly communion service.[10]

A terrier of Betley, Staffs., in Register 2, 1658–1737, has appended to it, apparently in the hand of the parish clerk:

Dues belonging to the Clerk of the Parochial Chapel of Betley in the County of Stafford, 1735

Every plowgate	4d.
Every householder	2d.
For every burial and tolling the Bell	1s. 8d.
For every woman churched	4d.
For every corps brought out of another Parish to be buried & tolling the Bell	3s. 4d.
The same is due for a Corps taken out of this parish to be buried in another	3s. 4d.
The same has been given for a corps in church	
For every marriage by Banns	1s. 0d.
For every marriage by Licence	2s. 6d.

An interesting example of the modernisation of an existing custom occurs at Houghton-le-Spring, Durham, where on Lady Day 1611 'the gentlemen and most of the Four and Twenty' agreed that:

the clerk shall have from henceforth of every plough within the said parish in lieu and full satisfaction of his boon at Christmas 2d. in money, and for his eggs at Easter one penny.

According to Prynne: 'In poore Countrey Parishes, where the wages of the clerke is very small, the people, thinking it unfit that the clerke should duly attend at church, and lose by his office, were wont to send him in Provision, and then feast with him, and give him more liberallty than their quarterly payments (often a penny a house) would amount to in many years.'[11]

At Landbeach, Cambs., by vestry agreement of 1639, the clerk commuted his ancient wages and perquisites (here a feast at Easter and another at Christmas) in return for a regular salary to be paid quarterly from each house, the sums ranging from a penny to sixpence, and the total amount being 19s. 6d. 'Onely he shall retaine his accustomed Dueties at Churchings, Marriages, and Burialls.'[12]

At Old Warden, Beds., according to a terrier of 1727:

The Offices of Clerk & Sexton are in one Person appointed by ye Vicar, He hath for his Wages four shillings yearly from Gentlemen that have a Pew or Seat, & four pence yearly from every householder besides, as also the accustomed Fees, for Marriage by Licence two shillings, & six pence, by Banns, one shilling, For Burial in the Church or Chancel five shillings, In the Church Yard one shilling & four pence.

Often the parish clerk kept a draft register from which the proper parish register was posted up at intervals. At Barrow Gurney, Som., e.g. such a draft is still preserved. It covers the years 1755–1821.

Lists of parish clerks have been preserved even more often than those of the other parochial dignitaries. This is understandable enough from what we have said above as to the clerk's lofty view of the importance of his position, and from the fact that he must necessarily have been always more or less literate. Such a list at Mark, Som., e.g. gives the names of all the clerks from 1653 to 1781.

A DISCURSION CONCERNING THE 'CHURCHYARD RAILLES'. Either in glebe terriers or in separate documents it is quite usual to find notes of the customary obligation to repair the churchyard fence or walls, imposed proportionately upon all the lands or houses in the parish. The imposition of this liability upon tenants or freeholders seems perfectly logical if one considers that the freeholders especially often claimed special privileges in the church and in the churchyard, so in common fairness accepted special responsibilities as to their maintenance and protection. At Egmanton, Notts., according to a terrier of 1764, the churchyard fences were

charged upon ye Parish, 8 yards to a Farm House, and 4 yards to a cottage.

Lists of churchyard 'railles' appear also at Fledborough, Notts., and in a number of Hampshire registers and churchwardens' accounts, and in other parish books. They are known to exist at Baughurst, Bentworth, Botley, Ellisfield, Newnham, North Waltham, Weyhill, Wield, and Wonston. At Bentworth the liability lasted until 1892, and at Wield until 1900. At Combe there is a list of the persons liable for the repair of 'the New Stone Wall, 1682'. An early list at Wootton St Lawrence is headed

An ordinance by which the railings of the churchyard are to be set up.

(A: Dⁱ: 1600: *Ordo quo coemiterii repagula sunt struenda.*)

Speldhurst, Kent, has a list of 1666; Wickenby, Lincs., one of 1610; Moreton, Essex, has one of 1670; Cowden, Kent, lists of 1542, 1668, 1725 and 1829. Pavenham, Beds., has at the end of its first register: 'A Note how every man's dole lyeth in the Churchyard Wall', 1760, with similar entries of 1659 and 1661.. Streatley, Beds., has a similar note of 1708 in its register. Beercrocombe, Som., has such a record at the end of its churchwardens' accounts, 1687–1724, and Fitzhead in the same county has:

An accounts of yᵉ bounds Parrish and of yᵉ Churchyard as they belong 1755 to each Tenement and as it hath been maintained Reparied and kept up by yᵉ owners thereof Time out of Mind.

In Surrey there are such lists at: Alfold 1774, Ash 1793, Bisley 1685, 1705, Effingham 1788, Newdigate 1731, 1772, Stoke next Guildford in various years, and Walton on the Hill 1629.

For some reason, which is not apparent upon the surface, the custom of apportioning among the parishioners the repair of the churchyard fence seems to have been specially prevalent and long-lived in Sussex. In this county there is a list of 1772 at Chiddingly, (where the duty lasted until ?1924), one of 1636 at Lindfield. At Cowfold in 1636 eighty-one tenants shared the obligation, while at Chiddingly fifty-six owners or tenants repaired stretches of fence varying in length from 3 feet to 45 feet. At Cowfold the initials of the persons responsible for repair are deeply incised on the fence. Here lists of those subject to the liability survive from 1636 almost to the present day. There are similar records also at Ardingly and West Hoathly. The fact that they survive so largely in Sussex misled no less an authority than the late Dr Cox, who quoted, apparently with approval, a dictum that the custom 'though not confined to the parish [of Chiddingly] is peculiar to this part of the country'.

TITHE RECORDS

It is impossible in the space at our disposal to enter fully into the not very edifying history of tithes in England.

In apostolic times, no doubt, the clergy were supported solely by the alms of the faithful, but in the course of time the ecclesiastics of every European country established a claim to the receipt of a tenth part of the produce of the land, the proportion being based presumably upon that mentioned in the Old Testament,[1] or perhaps upon the tribute of a tenth levied upon estates in the later days of the Roman Empire. According to Selden,[2] during the first four centuries of the Christian era, tithes, even as voluntary offerings, were unknown, and it was not until the sixth century that the duty of tithe-paying was formally imposed by ecclesiastical authority. Gradually this duty came to be enforced by the excommunication of recalcitrants, and, if this failed, by the power of the secular arm. In England, where tithes are mentioned in a letter of St Boniface in 747, the duty was enforced by such councils as that of Chelsea (in 787).[3] As to the later history of tithe in Saxon times there is no need to say very much. It has been alleged that tithes were imposed by King Offa of Mercia, in penance for a murder. Tithes are mentioned in a treaty between King Alfred and Guthrum in 900,[4] King Athelstan in 925 directed his own reeves to pay tithe, and a national synod in King Edmund's reign, A.D. 944, authorized excommunication of recalcitrants if necessary as a sanction. Long before the Norman Conquest the tithe system was in operation. The very word 'tithe' is of old English origin.

A good deal of ink has been shed concerning the division of the tithe—the Levitical custom was a tripartite division for the priests, the Temple, and the poor; and upon this analogy, in England it was held that the thirds should go to the mother church, the clergy, and the poor.[5]

At first the custom was that tithe-payers paid their tithe where they chose, but by 970 the right of receipt was being vested in particular churches. By the third Lateran Council of 1179 this custom was forbidden, and the tithe system was fairly established for many centuries. The practice of laymen receiving tithe was forbidden by one of Anselm's canons in 1102. In 1342 one of Archbishop Stratford's constitutions enjoined the payment to the poor by religious houses of a proper proportion of the tithes they received as impropriators of benefices, and this, with the addition of regulations to ensure a proper maintenance to the vicar, was embodied in statute law in 1391.[6]

The technical classification of tithes is into predial (arising from the produce of land), mixed (coming from the stock on land), and personal (from the industry of the occupiers). Apart from the special instance of certain tithes in London,[7] these distinctions do not concern us, and the alternative classification into 'great' and 'small' tithes is more convenient. 'Great' tithes include those of corn, hay and wood: all other tithes are generally 'small'. The general though by no means invariable custom was that where there was both rector and vicar, whether the rector was a cleric or a layman, the rector took the former tithes, the vicar the latter ones. In such cases, of course, the rector was generally not an individual but a body corporate, though some sinecure rectories were held by individuals even before the Reformation.

Where the value of the small tithe was small in proportion to that of the great tithe, it might happen that a parish was denuded of produce paid to the not very useful absentee rector, while the provision made for the vicar in return for services rendered was quite insufficient. Acts were passed to deal with this scandal. In 1400–1 there was an act[8] forbidding the purchase of papal bulls for discharge of tithes, and two years later there was a statute[9] annulling many impropriations of vicarages.

At the Reformation a great deal of rectorial tithe held by the religious houses passed to the Crown, and from thence into the hands of laymen. There was a certain amount of legislation giving remedies for non-payment of tithes at this period,[10] and the Edwardian legislation postponed for seven years the liability to tithe upon barren land newly brought into cultivation. In the same way, when the commons of Pulverbatch (Salop) were enclosed c. 1655, it was agreed that half tithe only should be paid for the first three crops.

Anno 1655...it was agreed upon betwixt Robt. Milward Clarke Minister of ye parish of Pulverbatch on ye one party & ye inhabitants of ye township of Cuthercot on ye other party y^t there should be payed ye twentieth Sheffe or one halfe of ye teith due to be payd, for due teith for three Cropps....

Evidently here as elsewhere tithe was considered a hindrance to the improvement of agriculture. It was often a source of great irritation and endless bad blood to both payer and recipient. Even in mediaeval times endless difficulties had arisen, as the canons in Lyndwood plainly show.[11]

As instances of the kind of dispute engendered by tithe collection in kind we are privileged to quote from Dr Venn's book,[12] in which he embodies some of the facts elicited in his examination of all available reports of tithe cases in the law courts, from the fourteenth century to the nineteenth.

'A vicar in 1595 instituted a suit for the payment of tithe on turkeys and tame partridges; he failed, as it was held, naturally in the case of the latter, but surprisingly in that of the former bird, that both were *ferae naturae*. Next year saffron, much grown in East Anglia, was adjudged a small tithe. An attempt to secure payment as early as 1314 on colts born at the King's stud farm at Woodstock was successful, as was another seventeen years later, against the king's keeper, for underwood sold off a royal estate....A test case went against the vicar who demanded tithe of the "*germins*" or shoots growing from the roots of felled trees. A *confrère*, however, secured his tenth of acorns, as manifestly they were yearly

renewable, and as early as 1640 a nursery gardener was held liable
for payment on all young trees that he sold out of his orchard.
One hundred and sixty years later the rector of Elmsett, Suffolk,
proved his right to payment on wood converted into charcoal. In
1716 the rector of Hurstpierpoint, Sussex, went to law to secure
the grain that fell to the ground from the bottom of the tithe
cocks, and the Master of a Cambridge college as late as 1808
actually enforced payment on the stubble of wheat and rye. The
law courts had on another occasion to decree that tithe was not
due on the scraps of hay produced on the balks and headlands of
common fields. In the seventeenth century one vicar claimed successfully upon fallen apples; a few years earlier another had won
his case for tithing wild cherries...in 1681 a vicar confidently
claimed payment upon the wild ducks taken in an East Anglian
decoy, and naturally losing his case, then had the *sang froid* to enter
a plea for his tenth of the eggs laid by the tame ducks used in the
decoy....Tithe on livestock led to curious actions. Keen incumbents saw great possibilities in sheepfolds and grazing meadows,
and did not always rest content with their share at clipping time,
or with a modus on calves. They were, of course, entitled to the
"whole of the meal of milk every tenth morning and evening"
(as at Chigwell, Essex, 1678), but must the vicar fetch his pailful
himself, or must the cowkeeper deliver it? If the latter ruling
was given, whither should he take it—to the vicarage or to the church
porch? A majority of the bench decided that, this being a small
tithe, the cowkeeper should deliver the milk at the church porch.
Great tithes, of course, devolved on the owner to fetch and garner.
Cattle bred for "pail or plough" were exempted in cases tried
early in the seventeenth century, but cattle depastured in a parish
where they did not work at plough were tithable for agistment
there, though exempt in their own.'

Saddle-horses were exempt, 'but an innkeeper had to pay tithe
on the herbage eaten by the horses of his guests'. Turnips were a
fruitful source of contention; tobacco, hops, coleseed, saffron,
hemp, flax and potatoes all led to expensive litigation.

'Potatoes, although "grown in great quantities in common
fields", were yet small tithes, and turnips in similar circumstances
in Suffolk in 1718 had to be set out in heaps for the vicar to tithe,
but if they were grown on a small scale, he was entitled to each
tenth individual root. When turnips were fed to sheep the
position became hopelessly involved.'

An odd note in the first register of Old Warden, Beds., illustrates this point:

N.B.   T. Palmer, T. Rolf, and W. King pay too little,
N.B.   They never fat sheep with their Turneps but only sow yᵐ for their Ewes.

Such disputes as these related only to small tithes. Great tithes had not quite so many of their own. Market gardening raised a crop of difficulties, the tithes being adjudged to the rector if the land was tilled with a plough, to the vicar if it was tilled with a spade, and to the latter also (when the ground was hoed and managed by hand) 'if the soil had been tilled with a plough which did the work of a plough and a spade'. Minerals were not generally tithable, but it was argued that lead should be, since it 'grew' in the veins. 'Mills were tithable as representing personal profits, and there was a distinction drawn between new and "ancient" mills in favour of the former.' In theory, even profits of merchants and wages of labourers were tithable, though probably not those of farm labourers, and as late as 1832 there was an attempt to collect them by the rector of Lockington, Yorks.

One may well share Dr Venn's astonishment that agriculture could be carried on at all under such incessant friction as took place between the clergy and the farmers.

While farmers generally tried to pay as little tithe as possible the Quakers most resolutely declined to pay any at all.[13] George Fox had set forth that: 'They that take Tythes and they that pay Tythes according to the old covenant deny Jesus Christ, the everlasting Priest to be come in the flesh & here these Priests show themselves to be Antichrist.... All people that read these things, never come more at the Steeple-house, nor pay your Priest more Tythes, till they have answered them; for if ye do, ye uphold them in their sins, and must partake of their plagues.'

The parish clerk Paul Phillips, in Pope's *Memoirs of P.P. Clerk of this Parish*,[14] his celebrated parody upon Burnet's *History of My Own Time*, had:

full seventy chapters, containing an exact detail of the Law-suits *of the Parson and his Parishioners concerning tythes, and near an hundred pages left blank, with an earnest desire that the* history might be compleated by any of his successors, in whose time these suits should be ended.

From the seventeenth century onwards numerous agricultural propagandists had advocated a general commutation of tithe 'upon equitable terms'. By the end of the eighteenth century the demand for such commutation was both widely spread and highly vocal. The agricultural reporters of the Board of Agriculture, in their county volumes, published between 1793 and 1814, are almost unanimous in attributing most of the difficulties of practising farmers to commons and common fields,[15] or to the existence of tithing in kind. The only important opposition to general commutation came from a few clergy who feared that the tithe might be commuted at a valuation less than they wished, or that commutation would rob them of the increased value of tithe to which they looked forward, and from Cobbett, who with his usual wrong-headedness convinced himself that, as a general enclosure bill would pauperise the countryside, so a general commutation of tithe would inevitably lead to the disestablishment of the church, and the abolition of the monarchy.[16]

The Board of Agriculture attempted to kill the two birds of prey (open fields and tithing in kind) with one stone, in the general enclosure bills introduced in 1795, 1796, 1797 and 1800, all of which failed to pass because of clerical opposition to their tithe proposals. It was not until 1836 that the much desired commutation schemes were embodied in statute law.

A rector and a vicar, in the same parish, paid no tithe to one another. Non-payment of tithe was not, until 1836, recognised as giving a legal discharge from titheability, even if it could be proved over a course of centuries. Sometimes commutation was made for a fixed number of years, as e.g. at Wateringbury, Kent, where a document in the parish chest deals with a composition made in 1802 for a period of five years. Often tithes were extinguished by enclosure acts, ordering Commissioners to set out land in lieu thereof, 'for and in lieu and in full satisfaction of and for the Tithes, Tenths, and Ecclesiastical Dues by this Act extinguished and abolished'.[17]

A *modus decimandi*, generally called simply a modus, whether entirely pecuniary, or e.g. the agreement to take so many hens in lieu of tithe eggs, was held under certain conditions to be quite legal. It was supposed, like other prescriptive rights, to have originated before the time of legal memory,[18] to have been embodied in a deed, and confirmed by the patron and ordinary. Compositions of cash payment in lieu of tithe were very common, but before 1836 such compositions could be upset upon every change of incumbency.

A terrier of 1725, in Vol. 4 of the register of Northill, Beds., has a reference to such uncertain and terminable compositions:

The Rect^r hath the small Tythes throughout the whole Parish (except of the Say'd College of Northill). These Tythes have not been taken in Kind for Many Years tho the Minister hath all along been understood to have a Right so to do, as not being Limited by any Fix'd Modus or Prescription now Subsisting....

It was largely the inconvenience resulting from this state of affairs which led to the passing of Lord Tenterden's Act in 1832,[19] and after three unsuccessful attempts between 1833 and 1836 to that of the great Tithe Act of 1836.[20]

This gave facilities for the voluntary commutation of tithe, such commutation being confirmed by a body of Commissioners, or, if necessary, for compulsory commutation, whether or not the parties concerned desired it. By 1886, 11,787 tithe apportionments had been made under this act, and only in twenty-four parishes, where for some reason tithe commutation was impracticable, were tithes still payable in kind. Tithe had in general been replaced by tithe rent-charge, and this itself was a diminishing factor, falling from four million pounds at first to about three and a half millions by 1921.

Under the Tithe Act, 1935-6,[21] stock was created to provide compensation in respect of the extinguishment of tithe rent-charge. The tithe owner paid for the commutation of his tithe— a most ingenious example of the feeding of the ecclesiastical cat upon small sections of his own tail! The bulk of the stock was issued to Queen Anne's Bounty and the Ecclesiastical Commissioners (now the Church Commissioners), who distribute the income therefrom among incumbents and ecclesiastical corporations. The stock was not issuable to individual incumbents or corporations. Commencing in 1942, a sinking fund maintained by half-yearly payments, and sufficient to provide for the redemption of all outstanding stock on or before 1 October 1996, was established in the hands of the National Debt Commissioners.

SOURCES OF INFORMATION AS TO TITHE. The inquirer as to the history of tithe in any particular parish may obtain information from one or two quite distinct sources. Occasionally references in the registers, or more often mention in the oldest terriers, will furnish information as to early tithing customs and perhaps as to ancient moduses. 'Cases' submitted to counsel by new incumbents,[22] anxious to enjoy the full fruits of their benefices, are often found. It may be said in passing, that if lands in a parish are known to have been anciently held by a religious house, especially if the parish church was appropriated to the monastery, so as to make the abbot or prior rector, and the incumbent merely a vicar, it will generally be the case that such lands have never been titheable.

The MS.

Rights of yᵉ Vicarage of Oldwarden alias Adwarden in yᵉ Archdeaconry of Bedford, here inserted [in the second register of Old Warden, Beds.] by me M[atthew] Hanscombe, Vicar, 1727

has e.g.

All yᵉ small Tyths of...all yᵉ Cottages in yᵉ Parish except what are built on yᵉ Abbey lands....

To a less extent, too, this applies tó lands now or formerly belonging to a bishop, a capitular body, or sometimes to an ancient charity.

When the parish has had an enclosure of its open fields and/or commons under parliamentary authority,[23] it will often happen that the tithe or some part of it was redeemed by allotments of land. Sometimes even proprietors who had no property in the open lands had their tithe commuted under powers given in enclosure acts. In other places the old enclosures were left titheable, and the open lands only had their tithes redeemed. Often where both open lands and old enclosures were affected, the proportions of land allotted were different for the two classes. A usual rate was one-seventh of the acreage of open land, and one-tenth of the old enclosure, but the proportions vary considerably from act to act. Tithe-owners' allotments were almost invariably fenced at public expense, and allotted free from the other expenses of enclosure, which fell the more heavily on the remaining proprietors.

The tithe apportionments which exist for many thousands of parishes, and the revised apportionments, of which there must be hundreds, are most useful and interesting documents. They were executed in triplicate, the Tithe Commissioners (now, finally, the Tithe Redemption Commissioners) having the original, which may be consulted at the statutory fee of half a crown per document per diem.[24] A statutory copy was deposited in the diocesan registry. In some counties, Bedfordshire, Essex, Hertfordshire and Somerset, these have now been transferred to the County Record Offices, which are also the diocesan record offices. (In the Essex one there are e.g. 350 original awards and 2000 altered apportionments. From the parish chest there is also here an exceptionally detailed series of eighty volumes of tithe accounts for Ashdon, 1704–1824.) The second statutory copy[25] was originally handed to the incumbent and churchwardens, or some other local officer, to be kept in the parish chest. Later acts give power to quarter sessions[26] to require the deposit of this copy in a more convenient place, to any two justices[27] to order the return of a copy which had found its way into improper custody, and to the parish council[28] (with an overriding authority to the county council) to make proper arrangements for the safe custody of this parish copy of the apportionment. As a matter of fact, it is generally in the hands either of the incumbent, the churchwardens, or the parish council, though often the copy has been lent in the past to the solicitors or estate agents who collected the rent-charge. So it is clear that there was some danger of loss upon a change of incumbency, and thus a few awards have disappeared.

Tithe commutation before the general tithe acts was often arranged by the allotment of corn rents in lieu, and in fact the corn-rent principle was recognised in the 1836 act. The tithe was first estimated as a money payment, and this in turn was converted into a corn rent based on the prices of wheat, barley and oats over a septennial period.[29] Such corn rents in lieu of tithe as had been imposed under local acts of Parliament (largely under enclosure acts) were not affected by the acts either of 1836 or 1936, and they are still payable in accordance with the provisions of the acts under which they were first made.

The plans attached to the tithe awards are generally on a very large scale. They distinguish, of course, between titheable and non-titheable lands, they contain interesting references to ancient moduses, they may throw a great deal of light upon the history of land tenure, and they are invaluable sources of field names. The most detailed list of field names for any county, that compiled by the late W. C. Waller, and printed in the *Transactions* of the Essex Archaeological Society, was based entirely on the tithe maps of the county, and an admirable piece of work recently completed for the field names of Bedfordshire, the plotting of every one on the six-inch quarter sheet Ordnance plans, was rendered possible only by the deposit of all the tithe maps for the shire in the county (and archidiaconal) record office at Bedford Shire Hall.

Tithe books were kept by some incumbents, and a few have survived in the parish chests, e.g. at Mickleham, Surrey, where two volumes cover the periods 1727–44 and 1812–39; at Kingston, Kent, 1771–1801, and Charing, Kent, 1693–97 and 1698–1741; at Leverton Lincs., 1742–54; at St Nicholas, Stevenage, Herts., 1712–71 and 1737–73; at Brotherton, Yorks., 1732 and 1770; in Beds., at Milton Bryan, two volumes, 1742–61, Southill, 1773–97, and Houghton Conquest, 1767–9.

Early tithe maps are rarely met with, but there are a few, e.g. in the chest of Ashtead, Surrey, is one dated 1638. Tithe memoranda are often found in the registers, e.g. Wychling, Kent, has a memorandum of 1671, as to the division between the rectors of Wychling and Milstead of the tithe on Fendon Wood. The parish records of Houghton Conquest, Beds., include notes of an Exchequer suit of 1596–7 (in a copy of c. 1750) as to the tithe of Dame Ellenbury's pasture. The chest of Huntspill, Som., has a whole collection of tithe records, including loose papers, and a volume relating to tithe cases in Devon, 1677 and Surrey, 1752. The records of Sandy, Beds., include a copy (1500) of an agreement made in 1305, relating to the liability of certain lands in Northill to pay tithe to the rector of the neighbouring parish of Sandy.

V. OTHER ECCLESIASTICAL RECORDS

RECORDS OF CHURCH COURTS

THE CHURCH COURTS OF ENGLAND. The structure of the ancient ecclesiastical courts of England is likely to puzzle the inquirer, and fortunately there is no occasion to deal with it here in great detail. It will be sufficient to say that the old arrangement of England was, like the present one, a division into the two provinces of Canterbury and York. There were eighteen (we exclude the four Welsh sees)[1] dioceses in the former, and four (omitting Sodor and Man) in the latter. The dioceses were, and still are, divided into archdeaconries (of which in ancient times there were fifty-eight),[2] and these again were and are portioned out into rural deaneries.

The rural dean holds no court, and during the several centuries in which the office was in abeyance most of his functions lapsed to the archdeacon. The judge in the archdeacon's court is the archdeacon himself or his 'official'. In the bishop's (consistory) court, the judge is the chancellor. In the archbishop's (provincial) court the judge is the official principal—having jurisdiction over the archbishop's peculiars and in 'arduous cases' transmitted from inferior courts by letters of request. He has also an enormous appellate jurisdiction.[3] From each of these courts an appeal lies to the higher court, and the crown of the whole system is now the Judicial Committee of the Privy Council,[4] but was formerly the old Court of Delegates.[5] These ecclesiastical courts retained their jurisdiction over the laity until 1860.[6]

Such records of ecclesiastical courts as survive in parish chests generally relate to matters first brought to the notice of the authorities by churchwardens in their presentments,[7] or to similar business resulting from persistent refusal to pay tithe[8] or Easter offerings.[9] It was, in fact, the attempt to enforce the full penalties of excommunication for offences of this character that gradually brought the whole system into contempt, and secured its final disuse.[10]

Chaucer's archdeacon[11] took special interest in his punitive duties:

> Whilom ther was dwellinge in my contree
> An erchedeken, a man of heigh degree,
> That boldely dide execucioun
> In punisshinge of fornicacioun,
> Of wicchecraft, and eek of bauderye,
> Of diffamacioun and avoutrye,...

The archdeacon was not a popular figure in mediaeval England.[12] Piers Plowman has a scathing reference to him.[13]

It is not always realised that, apart from reforming one or two long-standing abuses, and securing that appeals in the final instance should be heard in England, not at Rome, the Reformation made very little difference to the government of the church and to its hierarchy of courts. A great many matters, now regarded as purely or mainly secular, remained in theory within the cognisance of the ecclesiastical courts until less than a century ago.

The canons of 1603 clearly visualise the Crown of England as that of a Christian monarchy, with church and state in friendly alliance for the punishment of wickedness and vice, and the maintenance of true religion and virtue. They take for granted the existence of a whole system of church courts,[14] to assist in attaining this happy end, with excommunication as the last and most dreadful weapon to be applied against the contumacious. More than a third of the canons are devoted to ecclesiastical courts and matters relating to them.[15] Canon 65 is particularly illuminating:

All ordinaries shall...see...that those who...stand lawfully excommunicate...be...by the Minister openly, in time of Divine Service, upon some Sunday, denounced and declared excommunicate.

Divorce jurisdiction (or more correctly jurisdiction relating to decrees of nullity) had always been in the hands of ecclesiastics.[16] Perhaps because the canons recognised only separation *a mensa et thoro*, and required the parties to give bonds not to re-marry during one another's lives, the courts were rarely resorted to. If persons of wealth and position desired divorce with power to re-marry, they had to proceed by way of private act of Parliament after obtaining a decree *a mensa et thoro* in the ecclesiastical court.

Incest and marriage within the prohibited degrees, like all sexual sins, were especially matters within the jurisdiction of the Courts Christian. Their rulings on marriage were based upon the Levitical law: 'None of you shall approach to any that is near of kin to him, to uncover their nakedness.'[17] Exactly what is meant by near of kin is a moot point, but there is general agreement that three degrees of relationship form a bar.[18] The Civil lawyers counted the degrees of relationship between two individuals from one up to the common stock, and then down again to the ôther individual. In this system first cousins are regarded as of the fourth degree,[19] and are therefore at liberty to marry. Pope Alexander II introduced a new system, in which the relationship was calculated by counting the steps only from the remoter individual to the common stock.

According to this calculation first cousins were related in the second degree, and not only they, but even second and third cousins, were forbidden to marry without a dispensation.[20] An additional complication (or according to unkind critics an extra source of revenue) was found in regarding the spiritual relationship between godparent and godchild as just as much an impediment to matrimony as was ordinary affinity or consanguinity; until 1918 illegitimate affinity also formed a bar, and so did sexual intercourse irrespective of issue. These also extended to the relatives of the parties. Precontract also invalidated a marriage. This state of affairs was dealt with by the statute of Henry VIII, enacting that the prohibition of marriage should affect only those within the prohibited degrees of Leviticus.[21] Blackstone summarises the whole business in scathing terms.[22]

A table showing the prohibited degrees (Archbishop Parker's Table) was published in 1563. This is to be found in the Prayer Book, and in most churches, since the canons[23] order every church to provide and display a copy. This has lately been revised.

Fornication and adultery were very appropriately entrusted to the spiritual courts for punishment; so was slander (as a moral offence). Below we give an extract from the registers of Sutton Valance, Kent:[24]

Nov. 25th 1717. On which day Eliz. Stace did public penance for ye foul sin of adultery committed with Tho: Hutchins junr in Sutton Vallence Church, as did Anne Hynds for ye foul sin of fornication committed with Tho: Daws.

Sa. Prat, Vicar.

Such offences as non-payment of tithe or Easter offerings, non-observance of Holy Days, and other less important offences[23] coming within the purview of the churchwardens were presented by them to the archdeacon at his visitation. The usual course was to admonish the offenders, to order amendment (and for adultery or fornication often public penances), and, when the court's order was complied with, to discharge the offender with the scriptural injunction to sin no more.[26]

But sometimes, especially in later years over such matters as tithe, in which the Quakers were particularly obstinate,[27] all the admonitions in the world were quite useless, and the practice was, after repeated adjournments, to excommunicate the culprit. Popish recusants, and in some cases other nonconformists, were treated as *ipso facto* excommunicate. When the penance imposed had been duly carried out, absolution was decreed and notice of this reconciliation made public. A pathetic record of such penance at Croydon, Surrey, records that a certain Margaret Sherioux

was enjoined to stand iij market days in the town and iij Sabeathe dayes in the Church, in a white sheete, with a paper on her back and bosom showing her sinne.... She stood one Saturday and one Sunday and died the nexte.

The process of excommunication and reconciliation after penance is thus recorded in the register of Wadhurst, Sussex:

1684 6 July Eleanor Woodgate and Sarah Moone in this parish church during divine service were publicly and solemnly declared excommunicate. 1685 5 Apr Eleanor Woodgate and Sarah Moone publicly and solemnly did their penance.

(*Eleanora Woodgate et Sarah Moone in Ecclesia Parochiali inter Divinorum solemnia palam publice et solemniter denunciatae et declaratae fuerunt pro excommunicatis.*) . . . (*palam publice et solemniter poenitentiam agebant.*)

After sentence had been delivered, the culprit was given six months to purge his offence and become reconciled. Then if he still proved obdurate the full penalties were imposed, after yet another waiting period of forty days. Some idea of their effect may be obtained from the final sentence reproduced below.

SURVIVING RECORDS OF THE ACTIVITIES OF CHURCH COURTS. Notes of excommunications, penances, and absolutions are often found in registers, and a few original sentences occur in parish chests.

Such a note occurs in the Register of Burials in Woollen, 1678–1737, at Holy Cross, Shrewsbury:

Hannah Julit was excommunicated on yᵉ 17 day of August 1707 by me Sam. Pearson. (*Hoc Mandat[um] Executu[m] fuit decimo Septimo die Sextilis* 1707 *pe[r]me* Sam Pearson Vic.)

By virtue of this mandate from the court of Lichfield

Hannah Julit of this parish for her contumacy and contempt to the said Court is to be excommunicated. Therefore by the Authority aforesaid I pronounce that the said Hannah Julit is excommunicated.

Died Oct. 14. 1712 entered in this book P.W.

At Brenzett, Kent, there is a similar note on a piece of leather stitched to the last page of Register 2. Lists of excommunicates appear at Aslackby, Lincs., 1629, 1633, 1637 and 1639.

A more cheerful entry appears on the cover of Register 1 at Sutton Bonington St Michael's, Notts.:

10 Sept. 1737. Relaxation of the Excommunication of Elizabeth Gadd.

A final sentence is reproduced below from the chest of Luccombe, Som.[28] It is dated 1628:

Samuel Ward doctor of divinity Archdeacon of the Archdeaconry of Taunton to our well-beloved the Parson Vicar or Curate of the parish church of Luccombe.... Whereas Walter Pugslie, Moses Pugslie, and John Anton of yᵉ parish aforesaid for their manifest contempte and disobedience have been longe time justlie excommunicated and for excommunicate persons openly denounced in the face of the Church at the time of divine service in which dangerous estate without feare of God or shame of yᵉ world they still remain in contempte of lawe and lawful magistrates. We therefore will and require yow that the next Sabbath day or holiday ensuinge the Receipt hereof in your said Parish Church at the time of divine service before the whole congregation assembled yow shall publiquely denounce those Walter Pugslie Moses Pugslie and John Anton for aggravated persons and also then and there yow shall admonish all Christian people by virtue hereof that they and any of them henceforth eschewe and avoide the society, fellowshippe and company of the said persons and neither eate, nor drink, buy, sell or otherwise by any other manner of Means communicate with them, being members cut off from all Christian Society under the payne of excommunication by lawe in this behalfe provided until they shall submit themselves to be reconciled...

At Middleham, Yorks., this appears in the burial register:

Burials, October 29th 1792.—I enter under the head of burials, as spiritually dead, the names of John Sadler, Clerk to Mr. John Breare,

Attorney-at-law of this place, and Christopher Felton, Clerk to Mr. Luke Yarker, Attorney-at-law of this place....

The burial of an excommunicate is thus chronicled at Thornton, Bucks., in 1696:

Francis Colman dyed March 3d but was not buryed in this paresh bec. he dyed excommunicate, and was fetcht by some Anabapt. brethren to a Burying place of theirs at Stony Stretford.

At Westbury-on-Severn, Gloucs., penance for incest was directed as late as 1835, but remitted on a medical certificate, and for defamation it was enjoined at least as late as 1846.

At Culworth, Northants., is this note of a penance:

1699 Memorandum.   Upon ye 25 of Febr. Margt. Tyler of this Parish did perform penance according to ye following order....

The s^d Margt. Tyler shall upon ye Sunday next after ye divine service stand before ye ministers Reading Desk appareld in a white sheet from head to foot and in ye presence of ye congregation there assembled make her confession as follows:—

Good People, I confess I have greviously offended Almighty God by falling into ye foul sin of Fornication and thereby given an evil example to my neighbours for wch I am most heartily sorry and do earnestly beg pardon of Almighty God and of all others that I have offended by this my evil example and I do promise (by ye grace of God) never to offend in ye like again. And I do also promise before God and this congregation to live hereafter more soberly and godly in all other respects as a good Christian ought to do. And that I may perform my good vows and promises made before this congregation I do most earnestly desire y^or prayers.

A submission and reconciliation is thus recorded in the register of Buxted, Sussex:

Memorandum.   Junii 20 Anno Dni. 1588

Whereas Walter Cushman hath these three years last past been presented divers tymes by the Churchwardens and Swornemen being honest men that favoured the laws of God and the Queen's Majesty's proceedings and also by Henry Monuques, minister of Buckstedde, and a preacher for divers sundry matters touched in Her Majesty's injunctions viz: that the said Walter Cushman mayntayned divers popish errors as of the Corporal Presence in the Sacrament which he confessed: also that he carried letters between papist and papist in the time of the Queen Majesty's danger by the 14 notorious trayters: that he led his horse up and down in the Church and about the Communion Table in the Chancel: that he was a contemner and abuser of ministers and especially now of late of Mr. Monuques by sundry malicious and opprobrious words against him; that he was a disturber of divine Service by talking and laughinge in the Church, and especially in the time of the Sermon; that he paid not to the poor, nor to the reparation of the Church, nor to the Clerke's wages as he ought, that he hath not receaved these three years at Buckstedd, and hath taken his oath lately that he durst not receave for fear of poysoning:—

The said Walter Cushman thereafter submitted and humbled himself to the Queen's Majesty's proceedings, and upon his reconciliation was receaved and admitted to the Lord's Supper.

June 2 1588 being Trinity Sunday.

Lists of excommunicates often appear about the time when Laud and his friends were trying to tighten up ecclesiastical discipline. Aslackby, Lincs., e.g. has such lists of 1629, 1633, 1637 and 1639.

VISITATION RECORDS

Since visitation by the ordinary has played and still plays so important a part in the disciplinary organisation of the Church of England, one would expect visitation records to turn up fairly frequently in parish chests. Our experience, however, has been that they rarely survive there. A few are to be found, for example Chaldon, Surrey, has printed injunctions to the archdeacons, 1694, and articles of visitation and enquiry, 1714, and Donington in Holland, Lincs., has a copy of returns to visitation articles c. 1563.

LISTS OF STRANGE PREACHERS

These generally appear upon odd pages of churchwardens' account books, or sometimes upon spare pages in the registers. The rather quaint title is to be taken quite literally—it was 'strangeness' of the preachers, not in the preaching, which the canons ordered the churchwardens to record.

That the Bishop may understand...what Sermons are made...the Churchwardens and Sidemen shall see that the names of all Preachers which come to their church...be noted in a Book which they shall have ready for that purpose.[1]

with the signature of the preacher, the date, and the name of the licensing bishop. Stamford St George's, Lincs., e.g. has such a list of 1634-5.

SPECIAL FORMS OF SERVICE

A Churchman who from time to time attends a variety of parish churches finds it difficult to believe that it is laid down by both canon and civil law that uniformity in order of worship shall be 'one of the leading and distinguishing principles of the Church of England'.[1] In former times severe penalties were imposed upon clerics who were guilty of irregularity in this respect. The spiritual courts can still take cognizance of such offences under the old laws, though generally, when indeed the matter is not merely ignored, the more expeditious and convenient procedure under the disciplinary legislation of Queen Victoria's reign is preferred.

The words of the canon are:

...I will use the form in the said book prescribed and none other, except so far as shall be ordered by lawful authority.

This term 'lawful authority' has only of late been authoritatively defined.[2] It is generally held to cover instructions given by the ordinary, or by the Queen in Council. Similarly such occasions as seemed to call for some special form of service—royal deaths and accessions, notable victories upon sea or land, or seasons of dearth and sickness—had and have very frequently such special forms of service duly authorised for use. Odd copies of these have often survived in parish chests, and here and there one may find a complete file for a couple of centuries.

Rempstone, Notts., has a very fine collection, nearly complete from the middle of the seventeenth century, and going down to the late Silver Jubilee, Coronation and Thanksgiving services. Several have survived in Somerset parish chests. Kewstoke has an assortment, 1740–95, West Bradley several of 1807–8–9–12–13, Rode has one 'for staying of the plague', 1625, Wembdon has one of 1708 for giving thanks for the battle of Oudenarde, one of 1715 for use on the anniversary of King George I's accession, one of 1720 for use during the plague. Allerton has one of 1817 ordering thanksgiving for that rather dubious blessing the 'preservation of the Prince Regent'.

NOTICES AND PROCLAMATIONS

One can understand that injunctions to the clergy were often entered on pages in the registers, e.g. Ansford, Som., has on a spare page of the register:

Instructions from our most gratious Kg. Charles to be observed by ye clergy.

1. That his majesties declaration for settling all questions in difference be strictly observed by all parties.

2. That in all parishes ye afternoone sermons be turned into catechizing by question and answere, where and whensoever there is not some great cause apparent to break this ancient and profittable order.

3. That every lecturer doe read divine Service, (according to ye Liturgy, printed by authority), in his surplis and hood before ye Lecture.

4. That noe Lecturer doe preach in a cloake but in gowne.

5. That they take especial care ye divine service be diligently frequented, as well for prayers and Catechisms as sermons and take particular note of all such as absent themselves, as recusants or otherwise.

Anno Dni. 1629.

Secular notices too were published through the ecclesiastical organisation.

Before the people of the countryside were generally literate, any notice, information, or advice which the central authorities thought well to bring to public attention, could best be published by reading in church. National events were so registered in proclamations; ecclesiastical decrees and citations were made public in the same way, and Parliament often, by express enactment, ordered notices affecting the parish generally to be read out in church, when all the parishioners were, or should have been, present.

From 1774 onwards the Commons' standing orders required that when an enclosure bill was proposed, notice of the scheme should be affixed to the door of the parish church for three successive Sundays in August or September. Similarly e.g. the Enclosure Act for Normanton-on-Soar, Notts.,[1] passed in 1770, orders

That the said Commissioners...shall...give publick Notice in the Parish Church of *Normanton upon Soar*, afore said upon some *Sunday* immediately after Divine Service, and also affix a like Notice in Writing upon the Door of the said Church of the Time and Place of their First and every other Meeting....

It was quite usual also to provide that on the execution of the award it should be proclaimed in the parish church, and one sometimes finds awards having a note of this proclamation endorsed upon them.

The modern usage of posting public notices upon the church door is, of course, a development of this. It had been growing for many years, partly because of the unseemliness of following morning service, or still worse interspersing a communion service, with a whole string of notices relating to secular affairs, but, one fears, probably largely because of the desire of the parishioners to return home for their dinners. The practice became general after 1837,[2] when the publication of such notices was forbidden and the minister's notices were ordered to be confined to those enjoined by the rubric,[3] the publication of banns of marriage, authorised by act of Parliament, and that of notices enjoined by the king or by the ordinary.

Proclamations after due reading in church sometimes found their way into the chest. Notable examples of such are the Declarations of Indulgence of Charles II and James II, notices as to national fast days and 'days of humiliation', and the long string of proclamations against vice and immorality, which eighteenth-century ministers had the effrontery to send down into the villages in order to warn the rustics from that primrose path which was strictly reserved for their betters.[4] Whaddon, Herts., has the 1830 proclamation against vice. Somerset seems particularly rich in documents of this kind. The principal varieties are those against blasphemy, for the reformation of manners, for the encouragement of piety and virtue; for the observance of certain anniversaries of national importance, of fasts in times of national crisis, of thanksgivings for national benefits; and those more formal proclamations for the alteration of references in the Prayer Book, in consequence of births, deaths, or marriages in the royal family. Kewstoke, in the county mentioned, as are all the parishes referred to in the next paragraph, has a varied collection, 1740–95, Selworthy has one 'as to God and the King', 1615, Goathurst has two of 1687 and 1699 for the suppression of immorality and profaneness, West Bradley has one 'as to piety and virtue, 1787', Selworthy has one of 1830 against blasphemy, and one of 1837 for the encouragement of piety and virtue.

Proclamations of fasts are found at Goathurst, 1680, on account of the 'popish plot', 1691–2, for a monthly fast on account of the war, and 1699, 1701, 1758 and 1793, general fasts. At Wembdon there is one of 1710–11 ordering a general fast, at Meare there is one of 1741 for a general fast in connection with the Spanish War, one of 1776 on account of the North American Rebellion, and one of 1810 for success in the war. Thanksgivings are found at Goathurst, 1688, 'for the prospect of an heir', 1691, for the conquest of Ireland, 1695–6, for the deliverance from assassination of King William III, 1695, for the taking of Namur (in which Uncle Toby distinguished himself), and at Meare, 1746, for the defeat of the Young Pretender, 1763, for peace with France and Spain. Goathurst has one of 1661 for observing 12 January and 30 January. Meare has an Order in Council of 1746 concerning distempered cattle; and proclamations, orders in council, or orders by the Lords of the Council for Prayer-Book alterations occur at Goathurst, 1694, on the death of Mary II, and 1702, on the death of William III, at Wembdon, 1714, on the death of Queen Anne, and at

Meare in 1801 and 1818. Other extensive collections are to be found at Rigsby and Stubton, Lincs.

FACULTIES AND LICENCES

FACULTIES. Roughly speaking, a faculty is a licence by the ordinary to the applicant to do something in matters relating to the church, which otherwise could not lawfully be done. Since the ordinary is rarely a lawyer, he delegates his authority to his chancellor. Faculties may be obtained either beforehand to authorise some proposed action, or afterwards to confirm something which has already been done.

We have dealt already with the suppositious faculties confirming exemption from tithe,[1] and with faculties for appropriating pews,[2] and we have had something to say of the creation of 'Select' vestry meetings by faculty.[3] Intending deacons may be dispensed by faculty from the requirement that they shall have attained the age of 23.[4] A compulsory church rate was supposed to be confirmed by faculty.[5] More usually, however, faculties relate to the church, its fabric, ornaments, goods and utensils, to vaults and graves, to glebe buildings, etc., and, in the last century, when controversy was very acute between churchmen of various schools, to the removal from churches of articles alleged to have been illegally introduced therein.

By far the most usual faculty is one authorising the improvement, alteration, or restoration of a church fabric. Faculties first appear in England in this connection in 1237.[6] The consent of the incumbent and wardens is not strictly necessary for the issue of a faculty, though, if a chancel is concerned, that of the rector is. Where faculty pews are concerned, the owner's consent is needful, and faculties relating to memorials of the dead are not granted if there is opposition from the owners, or from the representatives of the deceased.[7] Below we reproduce a typical petition for a faculty from Saleby, Lincs.[8] (from the Lincoln Episcopal Registry).

To the Right Revd Father in God John by divine Permission Lord Bishop of Lincoln...
The Humble Petition of Thomas Birch Vicar of the Vicarage and Parish Church of Saleby in the County and Diocese of Lincoln...and others Parishioners and Inhabitants thereof.

SHEWETH

That the West end and Steeple of the Church of Saleby being chiefly erected of Wood & Timber, and altho' they have been frequently repaired, yet by length of time, they are so ruinous & decayed, as that they can no longer be repaired but must be taken down and rebuilt. That your petitioners propose to rebuild the Steeple with Brick the Expence whereof is estimated at the Sum of forty pounds & upwards that your petitioners, being Farmers at rack rent cannot afford to raise so large a Sum amongst themselves without injury to themselves and Families. And whereas there are two crack'd Bells, which have laid by, entirely Useless for many Years, the weight whereof is about nine hundred pounds; they propose to sell those, and reserve a large one with a Saints Bell to assemble the parishioners at the usual times of divine Service, and by the Money arising by such Sale they will be the better enabled to rebuild their Steeple and put their Church into thorough repair;

Your Petitioners therefore humbly pray a Licence or Faculty to take down their said decayed and ruinous Steeple; and to sell their two cracked Bells, and useless old Materials, and with the Money arising therefrom to erect and build a new Steeple with brick and thoroughly repair their Church.

And your Petitioners, as in duty bound shall ever pray &c.

A similar faculty in the chest of Great Oakley, Essex, 1766, illustrates the same very common and most reprehensible eighteenth-century practice referred to above. In consequence of the fall of the tower it authorises the parishioners to sell four of the five bells, and to apply the receipts towards rebuilding the tower to accommodate the fifth bell.

Similar faculties survive elsewhere in Lincolnshire at Fiskerton, 1684, and St Michael's, Stamford, 1693. In the eighteenth century faculties were often obtained for the erection of the wooden galleries very popular at this time. Such a faculty (of 1726) still survives in the chest of Stogumber, Som.

Licences were, and are, granted by the bishop upon a great variety of matters in which his jurisdiction has not been completely delegated to his chancellor. The canons and statutes provide for such licences to a schoolmaster to teach;[9] to a curate to officiate, or to a minister to expound;[10] to an incumbent to reside elsewhere than upon his benefice,[11] to hold benefices in plurality,[12] to engage in trade, to occupy a farm of more than eighty acres (except upon his own glebe),[13] to appoint fasts or prophecies ('prophesyings'), or to exorcise devils;[14] to a layman to eat flesh in Lent[15], or to contract matrimony in the same forbidden season.[16]

In a rather different class are the marriage licences issued until 1836[17] solely by ecclesiastical authority, and many of which are so issued to this day, and the probates granted in church courts until 1857.[18] The surrogate who grants the former is, properly speaking, the deputy of the chancellor, while the commissaries who granted probate were each of them representatives of some ecclesiastical judge.

The old obligation to abstain from flesh eating during Lent was reimposed after the Reformation, from economic motives rather than those of religion. The idea was to encourage the home fishing fleet, that great reserve of seamen for national defence. An act of 1562–3[19] ordered abstinence during Lent and on Wednesdays, Fridays, Saturdays, and Ember Days, under a penalty of £3 or three months' imprisonment. Taylor, the 'water poet', has an interesting reference to this rigorous observance of Lent when:

> The Cut-throats Butchers wanting throats to cut
> At Lent's approach their bloody Shambles shut!

Dispensations could be obtained upon payment of fees, according to a tariff, based upon the rank of the applicant, but the minister of the parish was empowered to grant them, for a fee of fourpence, to persons whose health made the concession needful. It was provided, however, that he must make record of all such dispensations in the church book. The last act reinforcing the old obligation was one of Charles I's reign.[20] After the Restoration the injunctions were revived by royal proclamations, in 1660, 1667 and 1687. This time licences were sold freely to all and sundry, 'on condition of giving alms to the poor', so the licensing system came into popular odium, and the statutes became a dead letter after 1688. They remained on the statute book, however, until 1863.[21]

The parish register of Kempston, Beds., has on f. 1:

Mr. Tho. Fountaine his licence for eating of flesh during the tyme of his sicknes was entred y[e] 9th of March 1632 in the presence of [signature] John Crowly, churchwarden.

Below is a typical entry of the grant of a compassionate licence to eat meat, at the rate of fourpence.

Newington, Surrey, parish register:

March 8th. 1619. I, James Fludd, D.D., Parson of the Church of St. Mary, Newington, do give licence to Mrs. Anna Jones of Newington, the wyfe of Evan Jones, Gent., being notoriously sick, to eat flesh this time of Lent during the time of sickness only...provided alwaies that during the time of her sickness she eat no beef, veall, pork, mutton, or bacon...

RECORDS OF TOUCHING FOR THE KING'S EVIL

The picturesque custom of treating the king's evil (scrofula) with the divine power of the royal touch has left many traces in parish records. It was, of course, founded upon the doctrine of the king being the Lord's anointed: and curious as it seems to us, it was probably based upon quite as sound a principle as one or two modern methods of medical treatment popular in our own enlightened days.

The custom existed in France at least as early as 996–1031, and it is said to have been introduced into England by Edward the Confessor. It was regularly established by Henry II in 1163[1] after the canonisation of St Edward, perhaps as part of his policy of conciliating the conquered English. In early times there was a dole of a penny to each sufferer. From Edward I's time onwards there are numerous records of touching, and of the giving of the usual present. The ceremony continued throughout the reigns of Edward II and Edward III, then, so far as one may judge from the extant records, apart from a rather dubious entry of Richard II's time, it lapsed, or nearly lapsed until the reign of Henry VI. Henry VII developed it, established a set ceremonial, and instituted the custom of touching the sore with a gold angel noble, afterwards given to the sufferer, and worn on a ribbon round his neck. The legend on the angel

> Per Crucem Tua' Salva—Nos—Chr'—Redempt'.
> ('By thy Cross save us, Redeemer Christ', from the Sarum Breviary.)

made it particularly appropriate for the purpose.

Henry VIII continued the custom; it may have lapsed in the time of Edward VI; it was restored with a more elaborate ceremonial by Mary; and it burst into popularity in the reign of Elizabeth. James I in his early days in England, before he had shaken off the influence of the Scotch ministers, was, or seemed to be, unwilling to countenance the practice, but in his later years he carried it out frequently enough. One proclamation concerning it was issued in his reign. In his son's time it had become popular enough to make it worth while to mint special angels for use in the ceremony.

Ironically enough the legend on these 'healing angels' was

The Love of the Folk is the Bulwark of the King.

(*Amor Populi Praesidium Regis.*)

A proclamation of 18 June 1626 fixed times for healing and required each patient to bring with him the certificate of the minister and churchwardens of his parish that he had not already been touched. Altogether between 1626 and 1638 there were at least seventeen proclamations[2] regulating the observance of the ceremony. To Parliament's great indignation Charles practised the ceremony during his captivity: and during the Interregnum, while it lapsed, of course, in England, his son carried it out at various places on the continent. At the Restoration it became more popular than ever, and it is recorded that 90,798 persons were touched between 1660 and 1683. Charles II used a gold medalet, or touch-piece of the value of 10s. with the motto 'Glory be to God alone' (*Soli Deo Gloria*), and arranged to touch not more than two hundred patients every Friday.[3] To prevent the abuse of the custom it was again provided that sufferers should not enter the royal presence unless they could produce a certificate from the incumbent and wardens of their parish. Every minister was required to keep in his parish books a list of the certificates given. This proclamation is recorded in the register of Kempston, Beds., at the head of a list of certificates, 1684–1704. James II continued the practice, modifying the ceremony in a Romeward direction and using smaller and less expensive medalets than his spendthrift brother. Monmouth had observed it even in his father's lifetime, and his carrying out of the custom was one of the counts against him when he was tried for high treason. William III detested the whole business as a piece of popish mummery. Queen Anne practised it with some success, but after her death it seems to have lapsed entirely.

A typical record of the giving of the certificate referred to above is this, from the register of Stoke-on-Trent, Staffs.:

Mem: that the Minister and Ch.wardens of Stoke upon Trent in the County of Stafford gave unto Cathar: Fluit, yᵉ daughter of Arthur Fluit and Mary his wife of the parish aforesaid upon the third day of May in the year of our Lord God one thousand, six hundred eighty and Four a Certificate under their hands and seals in order to her obtaining of his Majestie's sacred touch for the healing of the Disease called the Kings Evill.

A much more laconic entry, perhaps made by a sceptical Whig parson, occurs on the title-page of the register of St Nicholas parish, Alfold, Surrey:[4]

27. 1710. I gave a certificate to be touched for the Evil in these words: Surrey S.S. These are to certify to whom it may concern that

James—son of Henry—Napper bearer hereof is a legal inhabitant of our parish of Alford in the County of Surrey aforesaid, and is supposed to have the disease commonly called the Evil, and hath desired this our certificate accordingly.

George Cavendish's *Life of Wolsey*,[5] written between 1554 and 1558, has an account of Wolsey's presence at the carrying out of this ceremony in France during the cardinal's embassy to Francis I in 1527. There is an interesting reference to the royal touch as a cure for the Evil in *Macbeth*:[6]

> *Macd.* What's the disease he means?
> *Mal.*   'Tis call'd the evil:
> A most miraculous work in this good king,
> Which often, since my here-remain in England,
> I have seen him do.   How he solicits heaven,
> Himself best knows; but strangely-visited people,
> All swoln and ulcerous, pitiful to the eye,
> The mere despair of surgery, he cures;
> Hanging a golden stamp about their necks,
> Put on with holy prayers; and 'tis spoken
> To the succeeding royalty he leaves
> The healing benediction.

Pepys[7] makes reference to the custom in 1660 and 1661.   Evelyn[8] has three mentions of the practice in 1660, and in 1684 when:

> There was so greate a concourse of people with their children to be touch'd for the Evil that six or seven were crush'd to death by pressing at the Chirurgeon's doore for tickets,

and in 1688 when almost the last action performed by James II as king, before he finally left London, was to touch for the Evil. Evelyn thus describes it:

> I saw his Majesty touch for the evil, Piten [? Petre] the Jesuit and Warner officiating.

Swift[9] refers to the custom in the *Journal to Stella* in 1711.

As indicated above, the custom was discountenanced by the Calvinist William III. It was restored again by Queen Anne. Probably one of the last persons to be touched was Samuel Johnson, whose visit to London in his infancy is thus described by Boswell:[10]

> Young Johnson had the misfortune to be afflicted with the scrophula, or king's-evil....His mother, yielding to the superstitious notion which, it is wonderful to think, prevailed so long in this country, as to the virtue of the regal touch...carried him to London, where he was actually touched by Queen Anne [c. *February or March* 1712]....This

touch, however, was without any effect. I ventured to say to him, in allusion to the political principles in which he was educated, and of which he ever retained some odour, that 'his mother had not carried him far enough; she should have taken him to ROME' [i.e. to the court of the Pretender].

Actually the Old Pretender touched frequently when he was on the continent and he is said to have touched successfully in Scotland in 1715. Prince Charles Edward touched during his occupation of Edinburgh, saying 'I touch but God heals'. Touch-pieces of Cardinal York are much more common than those of his brother, so presumably he carried out the ceremony fairly frequently. At his demise the magic was gone, and since his death no sovereign of England either *de jure* or *de facto* has carried on the ancient practice handed down from Saint Edward the Confessor.

The order for carrying out the ceremony, apparently first regularised by Henry VII, did not change appreciably for two centuries. James II, on pretext of reverting to the form used by Henry VII, again included Latin prayers, confession and absolution, and the invocation of Our Lady. Queen Anne, the last *de facto* monarch to touch, issued a briefer and more business-like order for the ceremony. Most of the forms include the reading of St John, chap. i, St Mark's Gospel, chap. xvi, the Kyrie and the Lord's Prayer. The gospels are those proper to Christmas Day and Ascension Day, and a good deal of the rest of the service is taken from the Communion, and the Office for the Visitation of the Sick. The English office appears in no less than four editions of the Prayer Book after the accession of George I, and in the Latin service as late as 1759.

Exactly how great a proportion of the patients were cured, to what extent such patients were genuinely scrofulous, and how far they suffered from other diseases readily curable by suggestion, it is difficult to say. As indicated above, it seems to us at least as likely that supra-normal powers should be exercised through the heirs of St Edward, as that they should form part of the stock-in-trade of the successors in business to Joseph Quimby. And on this last point a number of persons apparently quite honest, and fairly intelligent, seem to harbour not the least doubt!

Macaulay, as one would suppose, considered the whole business an absurd fraud, and his hero William III[11]

had too much sense to be duped and too much honesty to bear a part in what he knew to be an imposture. 'It is a silly superstition' he exclaimed, when he heard that, at the close of Lent, his palace was besieged by a crowd of the sick. 'Give the poor creatures some money and send them away.' On one single occasion he was importuned into laying his hand on a patient. 'God give you better health', he said, 'and more sense.'...William was not to be moved, and was accordingly set down by many High Churchmen as either an infidel or a puritan.

After all this Macaulay has some difficulty in explaining away the fact that indisputable cures were effected. The (Jacobite) Shirburns of Stonyhurst, Lancs., spent over £300 in sending their five-year-old daughter to St Germains to be touched in May 1698. She returned in December duly cured (and lived to become Duchess of Norfolk). The parents were so grateful for the cure that they spent £26. 12s. 6d. upon a gold watch for James's physician, Sir William Waldegrave, for the great care and kindness he had shown to the girl. William's solitary patient was healed, and it is said that Charles II

once handled a scrofulous Quaker and made him a healthy man and a sound Churchman in a moment.

So large a proportion of the population Macaulay thinks cannot have been really scrofulous: 'No doubt many persons who had slight and transient maladies were brought to the King' (actually as we have indicated this was most carefully guarded against) 'and the recovery of these persons kept up the vulgar belief.'

Despite Pepys' adverse criticism the service seems a particularly beautiful one, and against Macaulay's scepticism one may set the conclusion of Dr Wiseman[12], who as one of the leading surgeons of his day is quite as much as Macaulay entitled to express an opinion:

a mighty number of (his) Majestyes most loyall subjects and also many strangers borne are daily cured and healed, which otherwise would most miserably have perished.

Even so the compiler of the 1679 office as printed on a broadside[13] of that year was perhaps unduly sanguine when he concluded:

which, being ended, the healed persons depart, first giving thanks to God, and to His Majesty, and congratulating one another for their *recovery* [our italics].

PART II

Records Mainly Civil

VI. VESTRY MINUTES AND AGREEMENTS

THE VARIED NATURE OF VESTRY BUSINESS. AGREEMENTS UPON ECCLESIASTICAL MATTERS. Sabbath observance. Sermons and sacraments. Fees for burial in church. Agreements upon sundry matters. AGREEMENTS UPON SECULAR AFFAIRS. Agreements for discouraging the influx of strangers. Agreements concerning the giving of relief. Agreements concerning the boarding and lodging of the poor. Agreements as to medical treatment for the poor. Agreements as to the clothing of poor children. Bastardy agreements. THE WIDE RANGE OF VESTRY INTERESTS AS ILLUSTRATED BY THE MINUTES OF THE KETTERING VESTRY. References to literary, philanthropic, or educational institutions supported by the parish. Three discursions: (a) concerning psalm singers, (b) concerning the prosecution of felons, (c) concerning beer. Parish officers and beer.

THE VARIED NATURE OF VESTRY BUSINESS. We have dealt elsewhere with the origin and development of the parish parliament, the vestry meeting.

It will be understood that Vestry Minutes may contain orders upon almost any subject under the sun. We mentioned above e.g. vestry minutes concerning the allocation of pews in the parish church.[1] Many such orders and agreements are dealt with also under miscellaneous records. Here it may be sufficient to give one or two further instances of the vestry concerning itself with spiritual matters.

AGREEMENTS UPON ECCLESIASTICAL MATTERS. In the register of Buxted, Sussex, is this entry of 1613:

Because God hath commanded us to have a care, that the Sabbath daye be kept holy,...therefore, upon consideration that the Lord's day hath been by many and divers ways Prophaned by unlawful meetings and feastings for manie years past: we, whose names are under signed do give our consente that for the time to come the Parish feast...shall be kept on St. James his Day, except it fall on the Sabbath; and then it may, and must be kept, if it be kept at all, on the next day following.

There is a similar agreement of 1654 in the register of Spofforth, Yorks.

At Rainham, Essex, the vestry book of 1730 contains this entry:

Whereas att a Vestry in the Parish Church of Raynham on Sunday ye 24th of May last past, it was agreed by ye Parishioners then present to assess the Rev. Mr. Shove, Vicar of the sd Parish, att an £100 pr ann towards ye Poor Rates....Mr. Shove haveing engaged that two sermons shall be preached on Sundays both Summer and Winter; and that neither he nor his Curate shall or will expect any Surplice Fees for any Office relateing to ye Poor; we do unanimously agree that Mr. Shove shall not be charged or assessed anything to any Poor Rate whatever....

The vestry of St Mary's, Dover, not only appointed a minister, but on 26 August 1660 set up a Committee

to arrange with the Minister Mr. Nath: Berry, at what times, and in what manner he should administer the Sacrament of the Lord's Supper, and catechise the children.

Another example of a vestry by-law upon purely ecclesiastical matters is this from the parish register of Stoke-on-Trent, Staffs., in 1631:

That no person or persons whatsoever shall hereafter burie anie corps within the compasse of the Formes or seats in the Church of Stoke aforesaid nor shall break upp anie soyle within the same Church to b[urie] anie corps there unlesse hee she or they doe first paie to the minister or churchwardens of Stoke aforesaid (for the tyme beinge) Tenn Shillings currant money of England to the use of the parisheners of Stoke aforesaid to be ymployed upon the said Church.

In the time of Queen Mary I the vestry of South Littleton, Worcs., agreed with their vicar that they would allow him to keep pigeons in the church tower in consideration of his undertaking to supply the parish with new service books. A more conventional contract between incumbent and parishioners is found at Bick-noller, Som.: 'An Agreement between the Vicar of Stogumber and the Parish 1576.' The register of Longparish, Hants., contains an agreement of 1726 between the vicar and the vestry by which he acquired an extra seat in the church 'he covenanting to give fourteen sermons in the afternoon as full satisfaction'. The vestry of Cannington, Som., entered into an agreement with the incumbent, the Rev. Gregory Larkworthy, in 1734, as to a variety of matters including the payment of tithe and the hours at which divine service should be held.

At St Margaret's at Cliffe, Kent, the vestry in 1696 ordered the curfew to be rung as in years past for a quarter of an hour every night throughout the winter, and fined the holder of the curfew land twopence for every omission.

AGREEMENTS UPON SECULAR AFFAIRS. Of course, the eternal question of the rates, and the means to be adopted for keeping them as low as possible, was as near to the heart of a seventeenth- or eighteenth-century vestry as to that of a modern parish council. At Sebergham St Margaret's, Cumberland, in 1776, and at Gnosall,

Staffs., in 1686, it was ordered that any parishioner bringing cottagers or 'inmates' into the parish should execute a bond to cover any expense which the parish might be put to in relieving them.

The following extract is taken from the vestry minutes of Ardeley, Herts., in 1713:

Whereas it does appear by yᵉ poors rates...that yᵉ charge of yᵉ parish is much encreased by yᵉ undue practice of those owners and Inhabitants who have brought into the parish several strangers and have also converted several farm Houses into new erected cottages for their habitations;...We doe hereby order and ordaine, that if any Owner, Tenant or Inhabitant of this Parish shall hereafter take or receive into any of their Houses any strangers or persons whatsoever, who are likely to become a charge to this Parish, without yᵉ consent of yᵉ major part of yᵉ parishioners, every such offender shall be charged to yᵉ rates of yᵉ Poor, over and above his proportion to yᵉ neighbours, to such overgrowing charge when it shall happen, without respect to his ability or the land he occupies but according to yᵉ damage and danger he bringeth to the Parish by his own folly.

The principal owners of land in Nantwich, Ches., made a similar agreement in 1631 and for security had it entered in the burial register.

A similar by-law for Steeple Ashton, Wilts., on 13 March 1664, orders all offenders to be rated to the poor at 20s. *per mensem* in addition to the ordinary monthly rate. There is an agreement of 1654 to much the same effect at Pulverbatch, Salop.

In 1694, at Cowden, Kent, the overseers' books include the following memorandum, subscribed by the rector, wardens, and an unusually large number of other parishioners, but not by the overseers:

...That if any officer, Churchwarden or Overseer doe buy or allow to the buying of any clothes or give any Reliefe to any poor inhabitant of the said Parish or any otherwise Charge the said Parish without hee or they call a Vestry. That then such officers or officer shall beare the loss of such moneys as hee or they shall Lay Out or give away without Consent of A Vestry as aforesaid.

Notwithstanding the Bill of the Goods for Clothing of Goody Stace's two girls be allowed this time.

We have referred above to the abuse of 'briefs'[2]—probably it is in consequence of this that we find such entries as that at Bleasby, Notts., 1750:

The Parish has agreed that nothing shall be pade to letter of Request for losse by Fire.

Similarly at St Michael's, East Peckham, Kent, in 1822, it was agreed that no relief be given to persons who kept dogs. At East Leake, Notts., in 1772 an agreement was entered into that all the farmers, under a monetary penalty, should refrain from engaging labourers for any period longer than 364 days, so, of course, preventing the labourers from gaining a settlement.³ At Bleasby, Notts., a similar agreement was made in 1824, naming a 51-week period, and a £10 penalty.

At Bozeat, Northants., in 1722, it was agreed that in no circumstances should any relief be given to any vagrant or beggar by any succeeding churchwarden. A similar agreement was made at Harefield, Middlesex, in 1671. So in 1695 in the same parish the giving of relief was left to the churchwarden only, the constable merely to 'pass away criples'. The institution of select vestries is often bound up with campaigns for economy in parish expenditure. E.g. in the parish last-named, in 1710:

No overseer of the poor hereafter shall be allowed anything that is given to the poor besides monthly payments unlesse it is ordered by a Vestry....And [if] the overseer then neglects to see the order of the Vestry entered in the Book [he] shall not be allowed it when the accounts are passed not so much money to be spent at the rate making. But some of the most substantial inhabitants of the Parish shall make the rates and settle the expenses. And that the Churchwardens shall not pay for ringing except it be upon thanksgiving Days....

An entry of the next year makes the matter rather more clear:

Memorand: It is agreed by and between us...that some of the most substantial of the Parish for the future shall meet, make Rates and do the Parish business at their own general and sufficient charges.

The authentic voice of rural England speaks in the record given below, in explanation of which it may be remarked that, in 1709, swarms of Germans from the Palatinate, harried mercilessly by the soldiers both of Prince Eugene and of Louis XIV, emigrated *en masse* to England. An attempt was made to settle some in the villages of West Kent, the county magistrates appealing to the parishioners in each village to accept one or more families. Shoreham agreed to take 'a protestant Family yᵗ are laborers and not exceeding four in family...'. At Cowden⁴ the vestry answered:

Where as A Vesterey Has Bin called By The Churchwardens & overseares of the Parish of Cowden. We Hoose names are Heare Under subscribed Chiefs of The in Habitance of the Parish of Cowden Have no ocashun for any of the Pallatins, for wee Have more of ouer one Poor than we can imploy, nither Have we any Housing to Pott them in.

Agreements for boarding and lodging the poor are very common. At Pulverbatch, Salop, it was

Agreed between yᵉ parishioners at a parish meeting yᵉ 25 day of July 1701 yᵗ Tho: Ingle Senior, shall have from this time forward 6d. a week till Mich: next ensuing & from thence forward 9d. yᵉ week and yᵗ George Harris shall have 3s. 6d. a quarter for his housroom washing & supping during pleasure.

Sometimes the entries are very quaintly phrased. At Sutton Bonington, Notts., on 17 February 1769, there was

An Agreement then made by the Churchwardens and Overseers to Lodge and Wash Matthew Rower for one Year Ensueing the Date hereof for five Shillings and three pence per Quarter to be paid Quarterly.

A similar agreement of 1773 at Mainstone, Salop, makes one realise how incredibly inconsiderate our ancestors could be, especially when their motives included at once the sound parochial idea of keeping down the rates, and the indulgence of the national taste for a 'bit of a flutter' even in the unlikeliest connection. The unfortunate youngster must surely have found his hosts more and more grudging in their hospitality as their bargains became worse and worse. Presumably the mathematics of the agreement provide that after the first half-dozen, his hosts were to keep him for nothing at all, since they had drawn blanks in the lottery. Or perhaps the idea was that each year as the boy grew older he would be able to earn a greater proportion of the cost of his keep.

Agreed in publick Vestry held on this day in the Parish Church of Mainstone that John Jones a poor boy maintained by the parish is to be settled as here followeth, vizᵗ:—that every householder shall keep this boy for half a year according to Lott—first half year to be allowed fifteen shillings, second half year twelve shillings and sixpence and for every half year after two shillings and sixpence less till he shall be able to gett his living; only yᵉ Parish to keep him in whole clothing and reasonably to be alowd if yᵉ boy shall be sick.

References to medical treatment are very interesting. In the parish of Sutton Bonington, Notts., when a female pauper was confined the parish's contribution to the expenses of accouchement was usually 'a Qt. of Ginn'. The standard of the medical practitioners employed may be judged from this doctor's bill of 1781, in the same parish:

Janᵉy 12th 1781. Recᵈ of Mr. Clark overseer of yᵉ poor the sum of five shilling and Sixpence for Doctering pims Leg thirteen years ago and in full of all Demands by me.

Stephen X Dumleo.
Mark.

A typical example of a vestry contract as to medical attention for the poor from Cardington, Beds., in 1777 runs:

It is agreed at A Vestory Meeting This 7th Day of April 1777 That Mr. Edwd. Jackson of Bedford Surgeion Bone Setter & Apothacary & Man Midwife (If a woman Cant Do.) To Attend the Poor of the Parish of Cardington (The Small Pox Exsepted) For the sum of Ten pounds & Ten shillings to Easter 1778 The Overseers sending an Order.

At Bozeat, Northants., c. 1789, an agreement was made between the parish officers and Mr Lettice, surgeon and apothecary, by which Lettice engaged to furnish the parish poor with attendance and medicine for the year for five guineas. Smallpox inoculation was exempted from the agreement, and the wisdom of the exemption is shown by the fact that a note in the parish books shows a total expense during the year of £45. 2s. 6d. for inoculating the parish poor.

The references to clothing, especially of pauper apprentices,[5] may be quite entertaining. It was perhaps a bachelor overseer unacquainted with the mysteries of feminine attire who specified the boys' clothing in such detail as in the agreement given below, again from Sutton Bonington, Notts., but who modestly refrained from detail in his description of the girls':

1795. 3 poor Children put Town Apprentices and cloathed as follows:
    each boy one hat, one coat and waist, one p^r of Leathern Briches, Shirt, Stockings, Shoes, and new Buckles for Sundays. And each boy for every days Ware, one shirt, one waist coat, one Smock frock, one p^r of Leathern Breeches, one p^r of Stockings, and one p^r of new shoes. And the Girl Cloathed much after the same manner According to the fashion of girls Apperil viz: two of each sort. And each m^r rec with the boys 4£ and for the girl 5£.

The eternal bastardy problem,[6] to which we refer below, is illustrated by an agreement at Stockton, Salop:

April 14th 1800. It was agreed by the undermentioned occupiers of Land within the Parish of Stockton that from the date hereof. To indemnify the Father of a Bastard Child no smaller a sum shall be excepted than Eighteen pound eighteen shillings.

THE WIDE RANGE OF VESTRY INTERESTS AS ILLUSTRATED BY THE MINUTES OF THE KETTERING VESTRY. No subject was too great, and none too small, for the attention of a really keen vestry. A vestry particularly wide in its interests was that of Kettering, Northants., whose minutes are available for study in Dr Peyton's admirable volume. On 4 May 1815 we see it taking upon itself to ban horse-play from the streets, desiring the constables to apprehend all offenders, and ordering a copy of the printed resolution to be left at every house in the parish.

In 1818 it appointed a committee to inquire into the principles upon which the enclosure commissioners had allotted land to the church and town estates, and eventually succeeded in having the land re-allotted by agreement.

Most remarkable of all, when in 1830 it petitioned the House of Commons for a variety of remedies for the enormous burden of the poor rate, it even included in its suggestions something approaching a scheme for a capital levy:

that if every reduction which is in the power of your Hon. House to make, shall still be found insufficient to meet the distress of the country, the Fundholders be then required to bear their just proportion of the burthens which so heavily press upon the other parts of the community.

References to literary, philanthropic, or educational institutions supported by the parish are found, though, as one would expect, they are few in the extreme. Sometimes, however, one finds a contribution from the rates to one of the numerous infirmaries which began to spring up in the county towns towards the end of the eighteenth century. E.g. East Leake, Notts., in 1782 made an annual donation from its poor rate towards the maintenance of the Nottingham General Hospital, established in the previous year, no doubt receiving its due equivalent in 'letters of recommendation' for distribution to the deserving poor of the parish.

The Bedfordshire overseers' accounts contain numerous records of vestry resolutions to make annual donations to the Bedford Infirmary from 1803 onwards. In 1805 the Houghton Conquest records in chronicling such a decision term the establishment 'that noble institution', and those of Oakley, Beds., contain printed form notices given by patients to the minister to 'return thanks to Almighty God for their cures'.

The vestry of Gnosall, Staffs., subscribed from 1778 onwards to the Stafford Infirmary founded in 1766. In 1802 it raised its subscription to five guineas per annum, and in 1823, when the infirmary was in difficulties because of unpaid subscriptions, the vestry authorised the payment of £21, being four years' subscriptions overdue.

At Cobham, Kent, the Society of Psalm Singers received a grant of £1. 10s. 0d. given by the vestry from the rates in 1779 'wherewith to purchase books to their use'. These societies of psalm singers seem to have existed in many parishes. At Gnosall, Staffs., the vestry in 1775 passed a resolution authorising the expenditure of £5 'to keep up Psalm Singing in the Parish Church'. The rules and articles of association of the psalm singers of Wysall, Notts., 1773, are to be found in the parish chest there. Farmborough, Som., has a similar agreement of 1763. The chest of Stubton, Lincs., contains the parishioners' agreement of 1778 to form themselves into a society 'for the encouragement of piety and religion and the improvement of themselves in Psalmody'. Caddington, Beds., invited over the Luton psalm singers in 1779, rewarded them with 22½ quarts of beer for their labours (since evidently it considered that psalm singing was thirsty work), then, apparently fired by a spirit of emulation, it formed a band of its own in 1785, spending five shillings for a 'psalms pipe' to give the musicians their pitch.

In 1796 the churchwardens' accounts of Cowden, Kent, include a payment of two guineas to James Carpenter 'for Instructing the Psalm-Singers'. The overseers' accounts of the same parish include the 10s. cost of a 'singing feast' (choir supper?) in 1793, and payment to the psalm singers of Chiddingstone for some service unspecified. In 1831 £2. 3s. 0d. was paid for 'Malt Liquor etc., at the Singing Treat at the Crown'.

The Gentleman's Magazine for February 1741 has an article on 'The Abuse of Psalmody in Churches', which says a good deal of the conceit and incompetence of the psalm singers. Sometimes they could be quite as much a nuisance as the most cantankerous modern choir. At Hayes, Middlesex, they seem to have initiated a disturbance which lasted from 1748 to 1754. Some of the records of this which the rector entered in his register have been printed by Mr Thiselton Dyer. They ordered the carpenter to pull down part of the belfry 'without leave from the Minister and Churchwardens'; when the clerk 'gave out the 100th Psalm, the singers immediately opposed him and sung the 15th, and bred a disturbance. The clerk then ceased.' In the development of the quarrel the churchwardens ordered the breaking open of the belfry door for the benefit of a visiting party of ringers,

contrary to the Canon and without leave of the minister, the ringers and other inhabitants disturbed the service from the beginning of prayers to the end of the sermon, by ringing the bells, and by going into the gallery to spit below, and most scandalous of all,

a fellow came into Church with a pot of beer and a pipe, and remained smoking in his own pew until the end of the sermon.

Wimbledon, Surrey, has a (benevolent society) 'Clubb Book', 1776–87. At Gnosall, Staffs., the parish records include the minutes of another early friendly society, 'The Cowley Club' (Cowley is a hamlet in Gnosall parish). The club was formed at least as early as 1766. The society, as tending to relieve the poor rate, enjoyed the blessing of the parish authorities, so that the overseers occasionally paid from the poor rate the subscriptions of members who were in difficulties. It is interesting to note the expenditure of 6s. od. to the ringers, 12s. od. for 'musick', and half a guinea to the minister for a sermon. It is perhaps a sign of the degeneracy of the times that in 1773 a dinner was substituted for the sermon.

Chetton, Salop, has a very fine copy of

Articles of agreement made indented and fully agreed upon this eight day of May in the year of our Lord One thousand eight hundred and nineteen

for forming one of the Associations for the Prosecution of Felons which carried out a useful work in the century preceding the establishment of the county police, when the old parochial organisation of watch and ward was outgrown, but no satisfactory substitute had yet developed.

Many eighteenth-century acts of Parliament enacted that, in cases of breach of the statute, half the penalties should go, on the conviction of the offender, to the person who laid the information. Property owners clubbed together in societies to which they paid subscriptions to be used as a fund for the payment of additional rewards to informers. I am obliged to my friend Mr A. Cossons for notes upon some Nottinghamshire associations.

One of these societies was the 'Association of the Inhabitants of Beeston, Bramcote and Chilwell [Notts.] for prosecuting persons guilty of felony'. In common with its fellow societies, it issued an annual advertisement stating the scale of rewards to be paid, over and above the remuneration allowed by law. The scale of this society for 1814 was:

To persons who may be the Means of convicting Offenders—
For Burglary or Highway Robbery   £10. 10. 0
Horse stealing; wounding or maiming of Cattle; Beast
    stealing; Sheep stealing; or any Felony for which the
    Offender shall be transported   £5. 5. 0

For any other Felony for which less Punishment than
    Transportation is inflicted   £2. 2. 0

For breaking Hedges or Fences; damaging any Waggon or
    Cart, Plough, or other Implement of Husbandry; breaking
    any Gate, Stile, Pale, Fleak, Post or Rail; pulling up,
    stealing or destroying any turnips, Potatoes, Cabbages,
    Pease, Beans, or Carrots; robbing any Orchard or
    Garden; or wilfully and maliciously destroying or
    damaging the Property of the Subscribers   £1. 1. 0

The following advertisement is typical of the kind issued by
these associations, apart from those calling together the members for
the annual meetings and dinners. It appeared in *The Nottingham
Journal* for 25 April 1807 and was issued by the Beeston, Bramcote and Chilwell Association:

FELONY. Whereas in the Night between Saturday the 18th and
Sunday the 19th of April instant, Sixteen Hen Fowls of different
descriptions, chiefly of a mixing breed, between the Game and the
Barndoor Sorts, and two of them of the Brown Bantam Sort with
Rosy Combs: also one Game Cock, the Property of Mr. Robert Lacey,
of Beeston, near Nottingham, were feloniously stolen, taken and carried
away from off his Premises in Beeston aforesaid. Any Person giving
such Information as may be the Means of bringing the Offender or
Offenders to Justice shall on Conviction, receive a Reward of Five
Guineas, from the Treasurer of the Beeston, Bramcote and Chilwell
Association: and a further Reward of One Guinea from the said Robert
Lacey.

These associations were very active during the progress of the
movement for enclosing the common pastures and open fields. In
1811, the same society offered five guineas reward, to which the
owner added one of 50 guineas, for the discovery of the 'evil-
disposed Person or Persons', who did 'cut, break down, and
damage upwards of SEVENTY YOUNG TREES' growing in a newly
planted enclosure.

The 'Grantham and Neighbourhood Thereof Association' had,
in 1804, a membership of 240. At East Stoke (Notts.) met a society
with the typically Georgian title of the 'Association of the Tenants
of Sir George Pauncefote, Bart., and several Gentlemen, Farmers,
and others, of the County of Nottingham for the Prosecution of
Persons guilty of committing Felony, or any other Depredation,
against the Properties of the Subscribers, in the said County'.
Meeting in Newark was the 'Nottinghamshire New Friendly
Association for the Prosecution of Felons'. The Farnsfield, Notts.,
Association, with a membership of twenty-four, fined its sub-

scribers eighteenpence if they failed to attend the annual dinner 'to be applied towards defraying the Expenses of the Day'. A part of the Collingham (Notts.) Association's annual notice ran: 'Dinner on the Table at one o'clock. N.B. The Accounts will be audited before Dinner'! The inference seems fairly obvious.

These societies were not all rural. There was at least one in Nottingham town. This was called the 'Kingston's Arms Association for the Prosecution of Persons guilty of Felony and other Offences against the Persons and Property of the Subscribers', who consisted of twenty-five tradesmen. Another agreement of this kind in 1778, at Sutton-cum-Lound, Notts., is referred to above. Chilton Polden, Som., has one of 1805. The chest of Appleby, Lincs., contains a similar agreement of the landowners dated 1800. These associations are of considerable interest and would repay a detailed study. The minute book of the Sevenoaks [Kent] Association, 1836–76, is in the local museum. Arundel, Sussex, has an association, still active (in organising an annual dinner), which paid a reward for the apprehension of a felon (poacher) in 1912. There is one which held its annual dinner, at the *White Hart*, Newmarket, Suff., from the 1820's until the destruction of the house by a German bomb in 1940. Burslem, Staffs., has one which is now entirely a social organisation, so that in the Potteries one of the summits of local ambition is the being elected a 'felon'.

There is in England a traditional association between vestries and beer. Perhaps there may be food for the mind of the democratic theorist in the fact that an Englishman may become drunk 'as a lord', but dines 'like an alderman', or guzzles 'like a vestryman', and the reader may pardon a discursion concerning this same liquid.

At Kirton-in-Lindsey, Lincs., the letting of the 'church headland' or 'common headlands' was always accompanied by a certain amount of conviviality, e.g. in 1597 2s. was spent 'at the George at the common headlands selinge'. Here in 1678, a balance in hand at the Easter vestry, totalling 7s. 1d., since Edmond Short the innkeeper, who had leased the land for the last year, was 'considered to have had an hard bargain', was 'ordered to be drunk by yᵉ Neighbours then present at the said Edmond Short's house'. The parish book of Sutton Bonington, Notts., 1731, contains among a mass of parish accounts this, apparently the composition of some weary churchwarden during a particularly dull or lengthy vestry meeting:

Mault is the graine by which a Foxe we gaine
And ale is the liquor makes our tongue rune quick[r]
Let these tow boast but in the honour of a Toast
Then sit and tipple, 'twill your Senses crippl.

The accounts of the church levy here contain each year fairly
substantial amounts for 'ale, backou & pips'.

A seventeenth-century account book at East Malling, Kent,
has:

Paid for a drinking bout at J[n] Allchins when the Parish
    met to make a Sess but not made   £00. 02s. 6d.

The vestry book of Frampton, Lincs., records a meeting in 1716
where most of the persons attending left *en masse* to visit the local
alehouse. The vestry meetings of Landbeach, Cambs., were usually
held in a local inn. So were those of Tempsford, Beds. Here the
lady of the manor, Ann St John, was constantly present 1674–94,
and it appears that in the absence of the rector she sometimes
occupied the chair. Other female names occasionally appear in the
records of this vestry.[7]

At St Lawrence, Winchester, the annual election of the parish
officers in 1766 cost:

April 4   At choyce of New Officers at the Whit Hart:—
A Ham, Fowls, quarter of Lamb, Salets, Appel Pyes, Bread
    Butter and Chees all included £1. 5. 0, Beer £0. 8. 5,
    Punch £1. 4. 0, Rumbo £0. 2. 6. 3 Dozn and one Bottles
    of Wine £3. 14. 0. Fier £0. 4. 0. Tobacco £0. 2. 6.
    8 Glass Broke £0. 4. 0   £7. 4. 6

This interesting note appears in the wardens' account book for
St Julian's, Shrewsbury, under the date 8 April 1751:

It is a custom when Wardens are elected to adjourn to a public house.
    The Wardens elect pay each   0. 3. 6d.
    And—one shilling each to y[e] ringers   0. 1. 0
    and further pays equul with y[e] Company
    The Old Wardens pay each   0. 2. 6
    And pays equul with y[e] Company.

Similarly, half a century later, there is an entry at Gnosall,
Staffs., which seems to show the parish officers paying a proportion
of the cost of liquor, and the parish finding the balance.

At Eaton Socon, Beds., apparently in general a very well-
managed parish, there was less extravagance upon beer than in
many vestries at the same period. The records contain such
entries as:

1719 spent in victualle and drink when we went about
the parish taking an account of ye poors goods   3s. 10d.
1794 Spent at Month's night at the White Horse   £1. 1s. 0d.

At the same time the vestry seems to have approved the provision of a reasonable amount of beer for the workhouse inmates
too. The Eaton workhouse accounts include such entries as:

1719 3 bushell of malt   10s. 6d.
      for the brewing of it   2s. 0d.
1735 Pd for spigots and fossets (faucets)   3d.

but quite properly the only workhouse inmates to be frequently
regaled with beer were those who were engaged upon exceptionally
thirsty tasks, e.g. there are regular entries:

A quart of beer for ye brewer   3d.
and To ye washerwoman 6d. for a quart of beer at washing . 3d.

The Gnosall overseers, who evidently drank at least one and
sixpence worth of beer at a sitting, were not averse from giving
occasional treats to the poor, as witness the entry

1800 Matt. Tunnyclift allow 1 penny for Tobacco   0. 0. 1d.

but a few years later we find in the same set of accounts:

1822 Paid for Ale etc., at the meetings   1. 3. 1

followed by this note as to an applicant for relief:

William Bradbury no work & was Drunk yesterday & Day
before   Nothing

A century earlier, at Eaton, Beds., are a couple of entries rich
in human interest: one in

1725 For beer at Sarah Bellamy's child's christening   1s. 0d.

and a rather pathetic suggestion that one poor old soul needed
a little humouring before she would leave her cottage and enter
the workhouse:

Paid for a quart of beer for Mary Oliver before she came
into the house   3d.

At Pavenham, Beds., those doing statute labour on the roads
received an allowance of ale according to a scale drawn up by the
vestry in 1774. Cowden, Kent, shows in its parish records an
unpleasant contrast between the luxuries allowed to the paupers
and those thought necessary by the vestrymen for their own con-

sumption. In 1815 the Christmas treat of the old men in the work-house consisted of the division of a shilling among them, but when the vestry met at Easter 1816 £1. 10s. 0d. was spent: 'Towards the Feast Chusing officers.'

The provision of liquor for visiting clergy was quite usual. This is, of course, quite apart from the Communion wine perquisite referred to elsewhere, p. 101. The vestry of St Margaret's, West-minster, on 9 September 1697,

ordered that the churchwardens for the time to come allow but a pint of Canary to any bishop that shall preach in our church, and noe more than halfe a pint of Canary for our owne Ministers and others.

At Preston, Lancs., in 1731, the allowance of each preacher was fixed by resolution at two bottles of wine; at Haveringe atte Bower, Essex, on 9 November 1717, a more economical vestry stabilised the allowance at 'a pint of sack each Lords Day in winter'.

After what has been said above concerning the convivial habits of vestrymen, it is surprising to find a notion that a vestry held at an inn was not legally binding. At any rate the rector of Keston, Kent, entered in the minute Book:

1754, April 19. N.B. This was an illegal vestry because held at a publick Ale House.

The idea still survives, and legislation of 1933 prohibits a parish council from meeting in a public house except in special circum-stances.

VII. PETTY CONSTABLES' ACCOUNTS

THE PARISH CONSTABLE. THE ORIGIN OF THE OFFICE OF CONSTABLE. The constable's dual office—headborough and constable. The constable in the parish. Late survivals of the manorial appointment of the constable. Parish constables to-day. Constables' charges—a Bedfordshire example. Special local customs as to the appointment or non-appointment of constables. THE CONSTABLE'S DUTIES. Watch and ward. The parish armour. Other military duties. The militia. The constable as fiscal officer. The constable as pensions officer. The constable and saltpetre men. The constable and royal purveyors. A Derbyshire series of constable's accounts. The constable and popish recusants. The constable and the poor. The constable and the church bells. The constable and the parish bull. The constable as odd job man. A Nottinghamshire example of the constable's duties. Typical constables' records still surviving.

THE PARISH CONSTABLE

THE ORIGIN OF THE OFFICE OF CONSTABLE. The office of constable, often known under some such alternative title as that of headborough, thirdborough, borsholder, or tithing man,[1] may well be the most ancient of all the parochial positions. Blackstone[2] thought some portion of it 'as ancient as the time of King Alfred'. Perhaps the office may have originated in manorial days; possibly there may be some substance in Toulmin Smith's contention that it belongs to the more democratic organisation of society which the manorial system in part overlaid, and partly supplanted. The office proper began, according to Blackstone, about the reign of Edward III;[3] Toulmin Smith[4] saw the constable (provost) as the head of the parish, making provision for the king's service in 1332–3, and in 1348–9, in an order relating to purveyance, which says that provisions shall be taken for the king's service only upon a note in writing from the marshal to the constable of the parish. He found the title first given in 1299–1300, but the Webbs[5] have discovered it in a writ of 1252, on the statute book in 1285[6] and in literature in the *Vision of Piers Plowman* in 1362. Professor Helen Cam[7] regards the office as originating in 1242. For the function of the constable in the manorial economy the reader is referred to more specialised works.[8]

As indicated above, the constable united in himself two quite distinct offices, that of headborough, borsholder, or tithing man, concerning which we have spoken above, and a more modern one originating in the fourteenth-century legislation. There is a curious parallel here to the history of the office of churchwarden. In each case the more ancient office became merged in the less ancient position, while the title of the former eventually came to be applied to a sort of assistant to the latter. In some places the words constable and headborough are taken as quite synonymous, and are used indiscriminately of the same person.

And somehow or other the constable, originally an officer either of the manor or of the township or tithing, became by general consent the principal executive authority in the parish on which so many duties were laid by legislation in Tudor and Stuart times. His powers of arrest (for by common law he was a 'conservator of the peace') were very frequently exercised, and the staff of office sometimes affixed to the outside door of his house was a sign of real authority. References to this staff[9] appear in constables' and more often in overseers' accounts. At Walsoken, Norf., e.g. in 1785

> Mr. Ashton for constable staff   2s. od.
> Mr. Storr for painting ditto.   14s. od.

He could take in charge any who had committed a felony, and intervene, when he saw a minor offence committed or apprehended a breach of the peace, to detain the offender. The culprit might be held in the stocks, the roundhouse, or the cage, or even in the constable's own house, until it was possible to bring him before a magistrate.

The power of the manor court to appoint the constable was quite usually exercised until 1842, when the powers of the leet were transferred to the vestry. Traces of the ancient connection between the constable and the court baron are seen in such parish chests as that of Meare, Som., which includes presentments for Meare Tything, Glastonbury Twelve Hydes, at courts leet held at Glastonbury, 1721–74.

To this day a rural parish for which the County Police Act[10] has not been put in operation by the justices may have constables of its own by adopting the Lighting and Watching Act of 1833[11] or the Parish Constables' Acts of 1842 and 1872.[12] Under the Lighting and Watching Act the constables, until 1872, were to some extent controlled as well as paid by the vestry. Under the act of 1842, however, the vestry may decide that there shall be constables, and may pay their salaries, but the justices actually make the appointments, and decide whether or not the salaries are sufficient. The parish council or meeting compiles a list of qualified persons, and the justices make their choice from this list. So, in a great many parishes, e.g. in Leicestershire, and at Faldingworth, Lincs., the office survives to the present day.

Constables' charges, detailing all the numerous duties of the position, are often found in parish chests, e.g. at Stowmarket,

Suff., which has a very interesting one undated, and at Houghton Conquest, Beds., where there is one reproduced below:

1616 the 11 off June

Beds. To the Constables off Houghton Conqweste whiche nowe
Houghton Ayre And to the reste Succeding. heireafter. In their
Conqweste playsses

Theis Articles to Be Enqwyred. off And Seirtyffied From tyme to tyme: Especiallye Syxe Days beffore Everye generall Assyzes particulerlye: by the petie Constables unto the Cheeffe Constables. off the hondred off Readborn. stowke by A Commandemente From the Judgeis

1 In Prymus . what Fellonies ben Commytted within yowr parishe off what And Ageinste whome. And what pursute . hayve beine mayd For the Fellons. And what is become off theime

2 Item what Escapes off Fellones: Idle vagarond or suspicious persons hayth bein Suffered. without Apprehenshyon. And ponnishemente by the Constables or anny other peirson and in whose Deffawte any suchc Did ascape and whether yowr nyghts wattchinge be Dully keepte accordinge to the lawe

3 Item what Ryeotous owtregious or unllawffull. Assemblyes tendinge to the breache off his majessties pease

4 Item what recuzantes Popishe or sectary. that Com not to Churche to heare Devyn servise According to the law: by whom harbored. And how longe they beine recusantes

5 Item what Extorshyon or oppresshyon. haythe beine Commytid with in yowr Parishe by annye offycer whatsoever

6 Item what engrosseirs Foorstallers. Regrators. And bagdgers be with in yowr parishe lysensed or not lyssensed and who they bee

7 Item what Alhowsseis or Typplinge howsses be with in yowr parishe lyssensyd or not lyssensyd and who they bee and whether those lysensed Do observe the orders to them laytlye prescrybed yee or no And whatt ponnishemente hayth ben Don them unlysenced

8 Item what Commun Dronkeirdes or Commen hawnters off alhowses be with in yowr parishe

9 Item yow shall sertiffye iff annye be admytted to the offyese off a petie Constable Excepte shalbee subcidimen: and off Good undarstandinge

10 Item yow shall seirtiffie all masters that shall reteyn any servantes owt off the generall pettie seishens or geive Gretter waygeis then is or shalbe ratted and seitt Downe. accordinge to the lawe and non to reteyn any servantes but in the generall pettye sesheons Excepte it bee in Cayse off nessessittie. and the sayd reteinor to be mayd knowne unto the cheeffe Constable off the hondreth to be Entered Into theyr booke: and whether yowr pettye seshyons be keept att the tymes ackustomed yee or no

11 Item iff anny person shall goe abowgte anny new Cottige or small tenemente and ley or provid tymber ston or Clay For the builldîng Theyr off that yow pressently Geve notis ther off to the next Justices

12 Item iff anny lorde or Freeholders shall buildanny new Cottige or

Small Tenemente. not leyinge theire unto Foore ackeirs off land accordinge to the law. that yow pressently Geive nottis to the next Justyse off
the pease that shuche ordr may be tacken with the bulders heiroff as is
laytlie ordeyned by athorittye

13   Item yow shall Enqwyer. off all proviowrs and pollters whiche anny
vytualles and seill the sayme ageane at a nonrezoble raytte

14   Item yow shall Enqwyer. off Dove howzeese Ereckted or mentayned
by anny not beinge lord off the manor or peirson off the towne

Feall not the Due Execushyon off all theys articles From tyme to tyme
as yow and Every off yow will awnswere to the Contrayrie at yowr
peirells

And theis Articles see that yow Dow Delever From tyme to tyme unto
the nexte Constables succeidinge yowr plasseis as yow lykwyse awnswer
to the Contrayrie at yowr peirels

As indicated above, in some parishes the constable continued
until 1842 to be appointed at the manor courts. In others again the
functions of constable were largely discharged by the overseers or
the churchwardens or their deputies, so that the whole county of
Kent e.g. is said (but this is an exaggeration) to have no constable's
accounts whatever. In others again, as the leets gradually lapsed,
the vestries took their place, and the constable was appointed by
the vestry, though sworn before the justices. From this in some
districts the justices assumed the right of appointing constables,
though, if one may believe Toulmin Smith, this was a right never
given them by statute, and was pure usurpation.

THE CONSTABLE'S DUTIES. A great many of the constable's duties
will be discussed incidentally when we are speaking of the overseers. It is almost impossible to deal with them systematically. In
many places the duties, and therefore the accounts of constables,
wardens and overseers, were mixed together in a condition of in-
describable confusion. It may suffice to indicate here a few of them
not covered very fully elsewhere.

The primary duty of the constable[13] was to take charge of the
arrangements for keeping watch and ward in the parish. If one
may believe Lord Coke:[14] 'By the due execution of this Law such
peace was universally holden within this realm as no injuries,
homicides, robberies, thefts, riots, tumults, or other offences were
committed.' Perhaps this is a rather optimistic view of the effective-
ness of the system! Allied to this was the duty of providing and
maintaining the parish butts,[15] making sure they were properly
used, and taking charge of the parish armour.

Since this parish armour[16] was particularly valuable it was usual
for each year's constable to take a receipt upon handing it over to

his successor. This entry is from the Bozeat, Northants., constable's book:

Delivered the Traine Band Armes and Cloathes viz: one Pike, one Muskett, 2 bolts and bandoleers, 2 swords, 2 pairs of stockings, 2 hatts, 2 sashes, 2 coats, and iron armour for one man.

These are delivered to Thomas Estwick, Constable, by me Thomas Clayton, (*late constable*). November the 4th 1698.

Similar inventories survive at Repton, Derbys., 1590–1620, and Fulham, Mx., 1593. In one or two parishes relics of the parish armour are still preserved in the church, e.g. at Rushbrooke and at Woodbridge, Suff. At Baldock, Herts., where a porch room full of armour was discovered c. 1850, the rector, after allowing the workmen to take away as much as they pleased to sell for old iron, threw the residue down a well! At Mendlesham, Suff., there is a proper armoury over the church porch, and similar armouries exist or have existed at Chelmsford, Essex, and Repton, Derbys. The contents of such armouries are most varied, and suggest that the parish officers took the opportunity of making a bargain when any second-hand armour came into the market. The pieces still preserved at Mendlesham range in date from 1470 to 1600.[17]

The constable must collect the appointed men, take them to the musters with the parish arms and armour, and provide the stipulated amounts of money for the maintenance of the men at the muster. The parish records of Flitton, Beds., contain, *inter alia*, a precept of 1660 to collect money for the army and to raise armed horsemen.

Until recent years that old English institution, the Militia, was arranged on a county basis,[18] the raising of each county's quota being enforced by fine in 1761. No parliamentary vote was taken for the Militia between 1715 and 1757 except on two occasions, in 1734 and 1745. Under the 1662 Militia Act all owners of property were charged with horses, arms and men, in accordance with their property, but in 1757 the liability was removed from the individual to the parish. In every parish men were chosen by lot and compelled to serve for three years or each to provide £10 for a substitute. Small owners were discharged of their liabilities by a rate levied on the parish. The management of the parish's contribution to the Militia in both men and money was usually part of the constable's business.

What a very considerable mass of duties were imposed upon the parish officials in this matter may be seen from the surviving

records of such parishes as e.g. Meare, Som. They consist of the
orders for assembly and training of the Militia, 1766; orders to the
churchwardens and overseers for payments for substitutes, 1803
and 1808; enrolment papers, 1803; certificates as to allowances to
militia men's families, 1799, 1800 and 1804; orders for the charge
of families of substitutes, 1799 and 1805; orders for the transfer
of the charge of families of substitutes from one parish to another,
1798–1808; an application for discharge from service upon provision of a substitute, 1803; and certificates for payments in connection with the army of reserve, 1803. The parish register of
Renhold, Beds, contains a loose paper, the chief constable's precept
to the parish constable to attend the meeting for choosing militia
men by lot, 1796. The chest of Stamford St Michael's, Lincs., has
a series of militia papers, 1783–1810.

As a rule the collection of the 'quarter dues' (county rate) was
part of the petty constable's function: its transmission to the county
authorities was part of the high constable's. Most national levies
were made by the authorities through the agency of this same useful
personage. The chest of Kirton-in-Lindsey, Lincs., contains many
receipts to the constables for subsidies collected from 1581 onwards. The oldest register of Alton Barnes, Wilts., contains detailed assessments of the Ship Money of 1636–9, and the Parliamentary Levies of 1642–51. In this document from Hogsthorpe,
Lincs., concerning the Ship Money of 1634, the sheriff assesses on
the inhabitants and landholders:

...Hogstropp beinge a maritime towne within the County aforesaid upon
informacion that it is of the yearly vallew of 1000 li. the some of xxxij li.
x s. towards the charge of providinge the said Shipp for his Majesties
service. And I doe by virtue of his Majesties said writt charge you the
Constables and every of you that immediatly upon the Receipt hereof
you doe make an Assessment of the said somme soe charged upon y^e
said Towne. And that you conferr with the best sorte of the In-
habitantes of your said Towne soe to order and lay the Assessment that
the poorer sorte may not suffer therein, that the middle sorte may not
have cause to complaine and that amongest the better sorte an equallity
may be obserrved whereby the service may goe speedely on, and none
have anye cause of complaint....

> Walter Norton Vic(e Comes)
> [i.e. Sheriff].

Elizabethan legislation placed on the parish responsibility for
relieving maimed or sick pressed soldiers or mariners. The
churchwardens and constable gathered a rate to pay the pensions,
usually of twelvepence a week, granted by the county treasurer.

Apparently this same rate covered the relief paid by the parish to soldiers travelling through on their way home. Often its administration was left to the constable.

A standing grievance of Tudor and early Stuart times was the inconvenience caused by the constant visits of 'saltpetre men' claiming under royal patent the right of entering stables and even houses in search of nitrogenous refuse which they could use as raw material for the manufacture of nitre, and adding insult to injury by impressing the carts of the parishioners for conveying this material to their works. In 1624 patents for making saltpetre were expressly excluded from the statute against monopolies.[20] It was not until 1656 that it was enacted that no saltpetre man should dig within any houses or lands unless he had first obtained the consent of the owner. Levies made to free the parish from the activities of the saltpetre men were usually collected by the constable.

Even more irritating were the exactions of the royal servants exercising the ancient right of purveyance—the compulsory purchase of provisions for the use of the royal household at much less than the market price. The grievance was one of long standing. Piers Plowman[21] mentions it. At first the constables made up the difference between market price and the sum paid by the purveyors, and later the monarch permitted the counties to buy exemption from the exercise of this privilege. Levies for this purpose too were made by that useful *factotum*, the constable. A reference to improper use of ancient endowments to discharge the parishioners of liability for such expenses occurs in the register of Whittlesford, Cambs., under 1625:

Concerning the lands called Ciprious lands given to the towne of Whittlesford, we doe think it fitte that the profits coming of these lands shall not hereafter be employed towards the payment of the taske, nor any of the King's carriage, but for the comon town charges where most neede shall be....

Bishop Percy of the *Reliques* had the old registers of Wilby, Northants., rebound and entered up to date, and had bound up with them 'an ancient book of rates' which contains the constable's accounts of Wilby for the period in 1627 when King Charles I's court was at Wellingborough for the benefit of the queen, who wished to drink the chalybeate waters. This contains some most interesting entries on this point, many of which were printed by Dr Cox.

This series of unpublished constable's accounts from Doveridge, Derbys., is more typical. It brings out well the constable's poor-law duties:

The Accounts of Francis Okey, Serving Constable for Haywoods
Farme for ye year 1720.

			£	s.	d.
Nov. 2	p^d to a vagrant with a pass		00	00	04
5	p^d to three vagrants with a pass		00	00	06
13	p^d to two vagrants with a pass		00	00	04
20	p^d to six vagrants with a pass		00	00	08
21	p^d to two vagrants with a pass		00	00	04
26	p^d charges when ye old Constable gave up's Accounts		00	04	00
27	p^d to William Wood for carrying vagrants to Baslo & charges		00	16	00
Dec. 2	p^d to a vagrant with a pass		00	00	04
4	p^d to a vagrant with a pass		00	00	02
6	p^d to a vagrant with a pass		00	00	03
7	For serving a War^t on Dorothy Lee		00	00	04
	p^d charges attending her all Night		00	05	00
	p^d for a Warr^t and Mittimas (*sic*)		00	02	00
	p^d for carrying her to the House of correction		00	02	06
	For charges		00	01	06
18	p^d to Three vagrants with a pass		00	00	06
21	p^d to one vagrant with a pass		00	00	03
27	p^d to Three vagrants with a pass		00	00	06
29	p^d to two vagrants with a pass		00	00	04
	p^d to the Head Constable		00	14	09
	For my charges		00	02	06
Jan. 1	p^d to Two vagrants with a pass		00	00	04
4	p^d to Two vagrants		00	00	04
5	p^d for a p^{r}sentment for the Highways		00	04	00
	p^d the old Overseers charges		00	02	06
	For my selfe		00	02	06
8	p^d to Three vagrants with a pass		00	00	06
11	p^d to Two vagrants with a pass		00	00	04
11	p^d to Two vagrants with a pass		00	00	04
18	p^d to Two vagrants		00	00	04
23	p^d to one vagrant with a pass		00	00	02
29	p^d to Tho. Phillips what he was out of pocket	01	10	02
Feb. 4	p^d to Three vagrants with a pass		00	00	06
11	p^d to Two vagrants		00	00	04
13	p^d to a vagrant		00	00	02
	For serving a War^t upon Isaac Smith		00	00	04
	p^d for carrying a Huandcry to Uttoxeter		00	00	02
	p^d to the head Constable for a p^{r}sentm^t		00	00	08
	For my charges		00	02	06
Ap. 7	p^d to the Collect^r to make up the Land Tax		00	04	06½
8	p^d to Two vagrants		00	00	03

Ap. 10	p^d to a vagrant with a pass	00	00	02
11	p^d to Four vagrants with a pass	00	00	04
12	p^d to the head Constable	00	08	00
	For my Selfe and Mare	00	02	06
14	p^d to Two vagrants	00	00	04
17	p^d to Three vagrants	00	00	06
20	p^d to Two vagrants	00	00	04
21	p^d for Two warr^{ts} one for Supravisor and the other for the Constable	00	04	00
24	p^d for p^{r}sentm^t	00	00	08
	For my charges	00	02	06
26	p^d a Jurymens charge and my Selfe to ye Clarke Makett	00	06	08
27	p^d to Three vagrants with a pass	00	00	06
30	p^d the Clarke of the Market	00	00	06
May 5	p^d for Two warr^{ts} and a p^{r}sentm^t for the Sessions	00	02	06
7	p^d my charges to Langford	00	02	06
7	p^d to Two vagrants with a pass	00	00	04
8	p^d to Ed. Slater for scowring Dovebridge lane	00	06	08
	p^d Humphery Walls charges to make his p^{r}sentment to the Wayes	00	02	06
10	p^d for flitering Jeffery bridge	00	02	06
17	charges with The Men all Night taken on Suspition for Attendance & charges to Ashborne	00	09	00
19	p^d to a vagrant	00	00	02
20	p^d to a vagrant with a pass	00	00	02
	p^d gravelling the poundfould	00	03	04
22	p^d to Two vagrants with a pass	00	00	04
26	p^d for meate & drinke to the Highwayes	00	10	00
July 4	p^d to the head Constable	00	04	11
	For my selfe	00	02	06
5	p^d for Two p^{r}sentments	00	02	00
	For my selfe	00	02	06
8	p^d to Mr. Baxton to make up the Land Tax	00	02	03
15	p^d for carrying a Huandcry to Uttoxeter	00	00	02
Aug. 1	p^d for a p^{r}sentment for ye Assizes	00	00	08
	For my selfe	00	02	06
15	p^d to a vagrant	00	00	02
Sept. 6	p^d for a Warr^t to the Clarke of the Market	00	00	06
8	charges my selfe and Two Jury Men	00	06	08
10	charges with Jno Bell and his Son and Dorothy Lees before a Justice	00	02	06
	p^d for Two Warr^{ts}	00	00	08
	p^d to Tho: Phillips for attendance	00	00	06
14	p^d to Two vagrants with a pass	00	00	04
	p^d for mending Hookes Lane	00	03	00
26	p^d to the head Constable	01	00	03$\frac{1}{2}$
	my charges	00	02	06
Octo. 3	p^d for a warr^t for the Overseers of y^e wayes	00	01	00
	One for the Constable	00	01	00

8	p^d for a p^{r}sentm^t for the Overseers of y^e wayes		00 00 06
10	p^d for Swearing the new Constable		00 01 00
	my charges		00 02 06
	Mr. Baxtons charges		00 02 06
15	p^d for Gravelling Broxford bridge		00 02 06
	p^d Jno Wall for writeing		00 15 00
	my selfe for serving the office		00 05 00
	p^d for giveing notice in the Church		03 00 05$\frac{1}{2}$

Paid p. cost   12. 1. 5
Paid above   3. 0. 5$\frac{1}{2}$
                15 1 10$\frac{1}{2}$

Recd two Leveys *w* Mr. Cockain Deducted	19 01 05$\frac{1}{2}$
Disbursed	15 01 10$\frac{1}{2}$
So that it appears there is due to the Town to ballance the Accounts the Sum of	03 19 07
Recd. Two Leveys	19 10 5$\frac{1}{2}$
Deducted out of the sesm^t Mr. Cockain	00 09 00
So y^t y^e officer hath recd/but just	19 01 10$\frac{1}{2}$
Disbursed	15 01 10$\frac{1}{2}$
Soe y^t there is owing to the Town to ballance	03 19 07

These Accounts Seen and allowed by us the 10th Day of December 1720
    Fra Lomas for Mr. Cavendish, Geo. Cokayne, Jno Wall, Jno
    Savage, Will Allcock, John Buxton, Joseph Kerry, William
    Gilbert, Jhn Robotham, John Palemer, his X mark.

In 1605 it was the constable who was entrusted with the supervision of those dangerous persons the papists, and he shared with
the churchwardens the duty of presenting parishioners who persist-
ently abstained from attending the parish church. The stocks and
whipping-post in all parishes, and the pillory, ducking-stool and
cage in those which rejoiced in the possession of such amenities,
were under the constable's supervision. The whipping, which we
shall notice later as corrective treatment for vagrancy, was administered by the constable.

Until the latter part of the sixteenth century it was the constable
who was held responsible for the suppression of beggars, the
lodging of the impotent poor, the apprenticing of children, etc.;
and even after the Elizabethan poor laws he remained the principal
officer in such matters as the removal of vagrants, the supervision
of alehouses, and the convening of parish meetings.

The following entry seems to show a constable with more zeal than humanity at Little Chesterford, Essex:

September 4 1623 buryed a poore man brought by the Little Chesterford constables to be examined by the justice; the justice being a hunting the poore man died before his coming home from hunting.

It was often the constable who collected the fine payable in the circumstances above referred to, when the parish authorities failed to ring the church bells upon the passage through the parish of a reigning monarch, as at Wootton St Lawrence, Hants.:

1612   For not ringing when the Quene came by 4s.

Yet another important duty originally discharged by the manor and so falling to the constable or occasionally to the churchwardens, but in many parishes later transferred to the waywardens, was the charge of that most important personage, the parish bull, concerning whom we shall have more to say later.

The constable's records of Kirton-in-Lindsey,[22] Lincs., thus refer to him in 1582:

by me John laughton

I receav'd to bye a bull	xxvjs. viijd.
and he cost	xxvjs.
and it cost me on thursday at nyght at supper	vjd.
agayne it cost at Louth	vjd.
coming agayne homeward on fryday at nyght my supper	iiijd.
and meat for the bull	ijd.
and on setterday at home for my breakfast	iijd.
and meat for bull	jd.

In 1588, 28s. 3d. was received 'for the towne bull that was soulde', while a new one was bought for 26s. 8d. from a Mr Kent.

The constable must apprehend offenders taken in the act, or upon justifiable presumption, and must carry out the justices' warrants. He had powers of inspection of ale and beer houses, vagrants and unlicensed hawkers. He summoned the coroner's jury—though when the parish had a beadle, this duty was often delegated to him.[23] As noted above, where there was no poor rate, the constable levied the county rate on the warrant of the high constable of the hundred. He administered the sale to appraisers of goods taken for distress, he collected soldiers, prosecuted gaming and disorderly houses, and in a sea-coast parish rendered such help as he could in case of wreck. Parishes having beacons under the statutes of Richard II, Henry IV and Elizabeth generally left the supervision of them to the constable. It is hardly too much to say that in every branch of the parish business, from removing the indigent poor to their places of settlement[24] to pulling down the signs of suppressed alehouses;[25] from summoning meetings of inhabitants to put in operation his Majesty's latest proclamation concerning the alarming growth of vice and immorality[26] (amongst the lower orders of course!) to returning to the county authorities lists of freeholders (for jury lists), or duplicate returns of land tax payable, somehow or other the constable was concerned. It was perhaps natural that where so much was to be done that few men could carry out the whole of their duties, many made no attempt to discharge the half of them. They contented themselves with levying a modest rate, whipping an occasional vagrant, leaving rogues alone so long as they made no attempt to interfere with the constable, upon the principle laid down by the most distinguished member of their class—Dogberry,[27]—and submitted at quarter sessions the gratifying, but not wholly veracious presentment, which appears in the records as *omnia bene*.

At East Bridgford, Notts., where the office of constable has survived as a sinecure to the present day, its holder had to attend to parish legal matters, pay fees at quarter sessions, call meetings for the adjustment of the window tax and land tax, attend to take the oath at Bingham or other statute-hiring fairs, hire a neatherd for the parish, and see to the gates and fences of the common fields, meadows and footpaths. The pinfolds for stray beasts, and the village stocks for erring men and lads, were under his care, and he had charge of the parish gun, and spent above £1 a year on powder and shot. He also paid men for scaring the crows, and paid the pinder and two men for 'tenting' the fields. He gave gratuities at discretion to travellers in distress, and passed on—usually well whipped—the vagrants who entered the parish.

Constables' warrants will often be found amongst overseers' settlement papers. Presentments by constables as to absence from church, etc., will normally be not in parish chests but among assize files, which should normally be in the P.R.O., though Bedfordshire has a file of such, 1668–84, acquired by purchase. Constables' accounts will normally still be among parish records. It would be sheer guess-work to estimate for how many parishes they still survive. Early ones can hardly be very common, since Bedfordshire, almost a model county so far as local records are concerned, has gathered but eighteen sets, and the earliest of these goes no farther back than 1680. There are known to be several fairly early sets extant in Lincolnshire chests, especially at Kirton-in-Lindsey (accounts and other papers from 1590), Whitton from 1608, and Addlethorpe from 1637.

VIII. RECORDS OF POOR-LAW ADMINISTRATION

THE POOR LAW. THE INTIMATE CONNECTION BETWEEN THE PARISH AND THE POOR. The early history of poor relief. Early vagrancy acts. Tudor legislation. The creation of the office of overseer. The poor law of 1601. The poor law of 1662. Later poor laws, 1685–1743. Other poor laws, 1781–2–1792. The humanising of the poor law. The need for humanising measures. Inquiries as to poor-law administration. Poor-law reform. The New Poor Law of 1834. SIDELIGHTS UPON THE OPERATION OF THE OLD SYSTEM. Acts of Parliament and reported cases. A parochial dispute. The justices and the parish officers. Poor-law administration as revealed by parish records.

(a) SETTLEMENT AND REMOVAL. The early history of the law of settlement. Evasion of the law of settlement. Agreements for preventing the gaining of settlements. Settlement disputes. The expense of the settlement system. A Bedfordshire example of two exceptionally sensible parishes. A typical series of removal expenses from Nottinghamshire. The principal types of settlement records found in parish chests. The special interest and value of 'examinations'. The prizing of settlement records by parish and parishioners. A TYPICAL SERIES OF EXAMINATION AND REMOVAL RECORDS FROM NOTTINGHAMSHIRE. The examination. The order. The suspension and confirmation. Other minor settlement records.

(b) PAROCHIAL GENEROSITY, PAROCHIAL DETERRENT MEASURES AND PAROCHIAL EXPERIMENTS. Parochial generosity. Parochial deterrent measures. Badging the poor. Parochial experiments.

(c) OVERSEERS' ACCOUNTS AND THE INFORMATION TO BE OBTAINED FROM THEM. Graphical statements of poor-law expenditure. A typical series of overseers' accounts from Staffordshire.

(d) VAGRANTS AND VAGRANCY. The classification of vagrants. VAGRANCY RECORDS. Various early vagrancy records. A Suffolk example of register entries concerning a female vagrant. A typical eighteenth-century vagrant removal order from London.

(e) BASTARDS AND BASTARDY. Early references to bastardy. Bastardy and settlement. The rise in the illegitimate birth-rate in the eighteenth century. Suggested explanations. Parochial poor-law management and its influence upon the rise of bastardy. The early law of bastardy. Later bastardy laws. Parochial methods of dealing with the problem in early time. The increased seriousness of the question after the 1750's. Various methods attempted for its solution. Literary references to the question. The evidence of parish records. Types of parish record giving data in the matter. A typical bond of indemnification from Essex.

(f) APPRENTICES AND APPRENTICESHIP INDENTURES. Varieties of apprenticeship. The apprenticeship fiction in the eighteenth century. Methods of allocating apprentices. Ill-usage of apprentices. An apprenticeship bond from Staffordshire. An apprenticeship indenture from Bedfordshire. Sundry statutory references to apprenticeship. Types of apprenticeship record commonly found in parish chests.

(g) IN-RELIEF AND OUT-RELIEF—WORKHOUSES. Early proposals for workhouse building. Statutory authorisation of workhouse erection from 1695 onwards. The Workhouse Act of 1723. The Workhouse Test. Ameliorative legislation concerning workhouses from 1782 onwards. Parish record references to local workhouses. An unflattering picture of the parish workhouse. Gilbert's Act and the abolition of the Workhouse Test.

(h) THE LAST DAYS OF THE OLD SYSTEM. SPEENHAMLAND. WHITBREAD'S BILL AND THE 1797 ACT. FURTHER ILL-JUDGED DEVICES—ROUNDSMEN. A roundsman agreement from Bedfordshire. A Northamptonshire roundsman agreement. THE LABOUR RATE. A Northamptonshire agreement for its imposition. THE RESULTS OF THE EXPEDIENTS ADOPTED. THE REFORM OF THE POOR LAW.

(i) THE POOR AND THE POOR LAWS. RECORDS LEFT BY THE POOR THEMSELVES. A STAFFORDSHIRE APPLICATION FOR RELIEF. A POOR MAN'S OPINION OF A NORTHAMPTONSHIRE WORKHOUSE. A CAMBRIDGESHIRE PLEA FOR A SETTLEMENT CERTIFICATE. A SOMERSET MANIFESTO THREATENING ARMED REVOLT.

THE POOR LAW

THE INTIMATE CONNECTION BETWEEN THE PARISH AND THE POOR. The relation between the poor and the parish is a peculiarly close and intimate one. When the central government began to cast upon local authorities a whole host of statutory duties, almost the first of the delegated powers and responsibilities were those relating to the relief and government of the poor. Until comparatively recent years almost all rates could be said to form adaptations or modifications of the poor rate. In the great days of parochial self-government the amount of time, attention and money spent upon matters relating to the poor seems to have been (at any rate if the proportions in the records remaining are a fair criterion) quite as great as that devoted to all other matters of local concern together.

When the parish became a prison it was the poor-law settlement system which made it so; when the parish became a vast almshouse it was ill-advised relaxation of poor-law principles which pauperised the labourer and bankrupted the small farmer. Finally, when the parish was strangled in the red tape of a centralised officialdom in the years following 1834, it was almost entirely the heavy pressure of the poor rate which served as cause or pretext for the legislators and bureaucrats in their assault upon one of the most interesting and ancient of English institutions.

In mediaeval times, of course, the duty of relieving the poor, though legally incumbent upon the manor,[1] was generally recognised as morally falling especially upon the church. It has been alleged[2] that a specific proportion of tithes received was allocated for the sustenance of the poor, and though this has been disputed, there is abundant evidence of large-scale almsgiving by religious houses, by the parochial clergy, by such religious organisations as the gilds, and by the pious laity. So much was this so, that instances occurred of wholesale and indiscriminate charity being a positive harm to the population, deadening the sense of personal responsibility, sapping the moral fibre of the labouring population, and therefore tending towards an increase of the very evil it was intended to cure.

Fuller,[3] speaking of the charity of the religious houses, says:

Yea these abbeys did but maintain poor which they made....We may observe that generally such places wherein the great abbeys were seated swarm most with poor people at this day, as if beggary were entailed upon them.

In 1391 the second Statute of Mortmain ordered that upon the appropriation of a benefice a proportion of its fruits should be reserved for distribution among the poor of the parish. Despite such regulations, however, it was found even before the Reformation that ecclesiastical funds were wholly insufficient to deal with the problem. Beggars began to swarm, roaming about the country, and degenerating into 'rogues and vagabonds' who endangered public order. Then it became necessary for the state to intervene, in order to protect society at large. There were still, of course, Anglicans who held the view that the relief of the poor was primarily a matter for the church rather than the state. Thus, George Herbert, describing in 1632 the model parish priest, says:

He first considers his own parish, and takes care that there be not a beggar or idle person in his parish, but that all be in a competent way of getting their living.

The problem had grown too serious to be solved in this way, and it was not altogether without reason that a whole series of acts had been passed, each reciting that the previous legislation had been ineffective, and each therefore increasing the penalties imposed upon vagrants. The foundation of the whole system was an act of 1388,[4] forbidding vagrancy, and ordering all 'beggars impotent to serve' to remain where they are at the passing of the act. If they could not be maintained there they were to be sent back to their birthplaces.[5] Severe penalties were then ordained for 'sturdy vagabonds' and 'valiant beggars'. By subsequent legislation a scale of penalties was imposed, ranging from whipping for the first offence, to loss of ears for the second, and hanging for the third. Such legislation was of course impossibly severe even for that age, and it was, to say the least of it, inconsistent for the church to preach the duty of alms-giving as one of the highest Christian virtues, while the state punished alms-asking as a capital crime.[6]

A new type of provision appears in the act of 1530–1.[7] This introduces the distinction between those found begging, though able to labour, and those incapable of work. The latter are to be given licences by the magistrates, authorising them to beg within strictly defined limits.

In 1536–9 the English monasteries were suppressed, and in the former year[8] a new poor law was found necessary. This reinforces the distinction between the 'can't works' and the 'won't works', and imposes upon the individual parishes the duty of caring for the impotent poor. The clergy and churchwardens are to 'gather and procure voluntary alms with boxes every Sunday and holiday'. Private alms are forbidden under the penalty of forfeiting ten times the amount given.

The poor-law legislation of Edward VI need not detain us here, though we may spare a passing reference to the atrocious measure of 1547[9] with its imposition of branding and slavery as the punishment for persistent vagrancy and the condemnation in its preamble of 'foolish pity and mercy'. A more humane but no more effective act two years later, in 1549–50,[10] still upholds the principle of maintaining the poor by voluntary alms but gives the collectors the power of calling in the bishop's aid if their gentle exhortations prove inefficacious. Two years later still[11] an act imposes on the parson of the parish the duty of exhorting his parishioners to show charity to their neighbours. Legislation of Philip and Mary[12] and the early acts of Elizabeth's reign still depend on the voluntary principle, but gradually reinforce the moral obligation with definite legal sanctions. One of 1562–3[13] gives power to bring in the civil magistrate if the bishop's exhortations prove as unavailing as the parson's.

Another, in 1572,[14] allows the magistrate to assess recalcitrants without the bishop's intervention. It renews the penalty upon almsgiving (20s.), and orders beggars to be branded on the shoulder. No more licences to beg are to be issued.

This act creates the office of overseer. It is followed by a still more important act in 1597–8.[15] This orders the appointment of overseers by the justices, and lays down their rights and duties. It is part of a body of social legislation drafted by a committee of the Commons. The next act is the great poor law of 1601.[16]

The 1601 act was the very foundation of local poor-law administration for over two centuries. It was intended as a temporary measure—lasting to the end of the current Parliament, but it was prolonged in 1603–4 and made permanent in 1640.[17] This is the great poor law of Elizabeth, *the* poor law *par excellence*, and its twenty sections deserve careful study. The most important of all is s. 1, ordering the churchwardens and four, three, or two substantial householders to be nominated each year as overseers of the poor, and imposing on them the duty of maintaining and setting to work the poor, the funds being provided by taxation of 'every inhabitant, parson, vicar, and other and every occupier of lands, houses, tithes impropriate and propriations of tithes, coal-

o

mines, or saleable underwood'. Two acts of 1609–10[18] are designed
to prevent the misuse of apprenticing charities, and to ensure that
all the poor laws not put in execution shall be so put in operation
forthwith. They order that houses of correction shall be built,
that the constables shall search out rogues in each parish, and
apprehend vagrants and shall take them before the justices who
shall commit them to the house of correction. 'Lewd women who
have bastards' and parents leaving their children chargeable to the
parish are to be committed to the same establishment. Such acts
are, however, of minor importance compared with that of 1662.[19]

This is the most important poor law between 1601 and 1834. It
is the foundation of the law of settlement and removal, containing
the outrageous provision that any stranger settling in a parish may
be removed forthwith by the justices, unless he rents a tenement
of £10 or finds security to discharge the parish of his adoption
from all expense it may incur upon his behalf. Where the stranger
expects only a temporary stay, e.g. at harvest, he must bring a
certificate from his own parish, agreeing to take him back. It also
authorises the justices to transport to the plantations incorrigible
rogues, vagabonds and sturdy beggars, and contains in s. 21 the
provisions already mentioned for dividing large parishes in the
northern counties.

An act of 1685[20] continues in part the act of 1662 and 'forasmuch
as such poor persons coming to a parish do commonly conceal themselves' orders that the forty days' residence giving a settlement
shall be reckoned from the incomers' giving written notice of
arrival to one of the churchwardens or overseers.

Further steps in the establishment of the settlement system were
taken in 1691, when there was passed an act[21] which makes
permanent the act of 1662 above, but 'forasmuch as the said
acts are somewhat defective' orders that the notice shall be
registered in the parish book, and read aloud in church after service
on Sunday. It provides also that serving a parish office, paying the
parish rate, residing in the parish, being bound apprentice by indenture to a parishioner, or (if unmarried) serving a year in service
in the parish, shall give a settlement, even if no written notice has
been given. There are other provisions as to settlement and removal, which the inquirer may turn up for himself. By now the
poor were almost immobilised, so the next act[22] orders that from
1 May 1697 poor persons may enter any parish upon bringing from
their parish of settlement a certificate, guaranteeing to receive

them back again if they prove chargeable (the famous settlement certificates). It contains also the iniquitous provision that in future every pauper and his wife and children

shall wear upon the shoulder of the right sleeve of the uppermost garment...in an open and visible manner...a large Roman P together with the first letter of the name of the parish...in red or blue cloth.

Any pauper refusing to wear such a badge shall either lose his relief or be sent to the house of correction, there whipped, and set to hard labour for three weeks. In the next twenty-five years there were half a dozen poor acts of minor importance.[23] A rather more important act in 1722-3[24] prohibits justices from interfering in the giving of relief until they are assured that proper application has been made to the overseers or to a vestry. It also authorises the parish officers to buy or rent workhouses and to contract with enterprising business men to 'lodge, keep, maintain, and employ' the poor. Persons declining to enter the workhouse are to receive no more relief. Parishes too small to establish a workhouse may unite for the purpose, or may contract with another parish having its own workhouse.

An act of 1729-30 tightens up the regulations as to the issue of settlement certificates and orders that costs of removal shall be paid by the parish of settlement. Another in 1732-3[25] takes measures to ensure that any person after 24 June 1733 charged on oath with being the father of a bastard child shall be apprehended and committed to gaol until he gives security to indemnify the parish from expense. An act of 1743-4, dealt with more fully below,[26] orders a reward of five shillings for the apprehension of any vagrant, and the removal of such, after whipping or confinement, to his place of settlement under a pass. Incorrigible rogues after six months' imprisonment, with whipping at the justices' discretion, may be either sent home or impressed into naval or military service. The route of return and the rate of payment to the constable are to be appointed by the justices. Persons sheltering vagabonds are to be fined a sum from 10s. to 40s. Vagrants' children may be apprenticed by the justices, and bastard children of vagrant women are not to gain a settlement in the parish of their birth.

Probably the reader will think it quite sufficient if we summarise very briefly the remaining poor-law legislation up to the great act of 1834. It seems to have been designed in general to deal with abuses in the existing system, and to ensure that some regard was paid to the claims of humanity in its administration. In 1781-2[27] because of the 'incapacity, negligence or misconduct' of overseers 'the sufferings and distresses of the poor are very grievous', so provisions were made for the inspection of workhouses, and for no poor being sent into a workhouse more than ten miles from their own parish. No persons except the indigent were to be sent to the workhouse. Orphan children and children with their parents might be sent, but other children might be boarded out, with a preference given to their parents or other relatives. No children of less than seven years were to be forcibly separated from their parents! The parish officers were authorised to give relief in augmentation of wages to deserving persons. Persons might be excused wearing the badge ordered by the act of 1696–7 above 'upon proof of very decent and orderly behaviour'. Persons enticing or removing pregnant women without a justice's order were made liable to a fine of twenty pounds. There is a schedule of sixteen forms and an appendix of 'rules, orders, bye-laws and regulations to be observed at every poor-house...'.

An act of 1792[28] dealt with abuses in the removal of vagrants. In future no reward was to be paid for the apprehension of a vagrant until he had been punished, but no female vagrant was to be whipped for any reason whatever. A most valuable measure of reform was enacted in 1794–5.[29] This prohibited the removal of poor persons upon the mere apprehension of their becoming chargeable. In future they were not to be removed until they were actually chargeable, and the justices were authorised to suspend at their discretion orders of removal upon sick and infirm people. The next year another act[30] authorised overseers, with the approval of the vestry, to give out-relief without imposing the 'workhouse test', and this power was further extended by an act of 1815.[31]

The need of exercising some control over the activities of the parish officers began to be more clearly realised. In 1743–4[32] they had been ordered to keep proper poor accounts. In 1786 they were to send in a statement of their expenses under various heads. Parish file copies of this return sometimes turn up amongst other poor-law papers, e.g. at St Paul's, Bedford. In 1790[33] the justices were empowered to inspect and report on workhouses. An act of 1792–3[34] authorised, *inter alia*, the punishment of overseers and constables for neglect of duty. Special measures were taken for the protection of parish apprentices. Halfway through the century an act had sanctioned the cancellation of indentures of those apprentices 'whose masters use them ill'.[35] Later still[36] the law had been amended to make the upward age limit for male apprentices twenty-one instead of twenty-four, apprenticeship at the later age having been found to 'disturb the peace of domestic life, check marriage, and discourage industry', and the lowering of the age being to 'avoid the hardships brought on such apprentices by the length of their apprenticeship', and 'to maintain the good harmony between master and apprentice'. Another act concerning the welfare of apprentices was passed in 1792.[37] This ordered that in general after the death of any master an apprentice should have his indentures cancelled. The act of 1793,[38] which authorised the punishment of constables and overseers for neglect of duty, also provided for punishing masters of apprentices for ill usage. Still another act in 1801–2[39] ordered the overseers to keep a register of parish apprentices according to a prescribed form.

An act of 1802–3, consolidating the militia laws, ordered the relief of destitute families of militia men and substitutes; others of the same year[40] conditionally exempted discharged soldiers and sailors from the penalties attaching to vagrancy.

Apart from the vestry acts of 1818, 1819 and 1831, already dealt with, the only other poor-law measure of importance before the great act of 1834 was the Vagrants Act of 1824.[41] This adopted the classification of vagrants in the act of 1743–4 and imposed penalties upon those falling into each class. To some extent it still holds force among the laws relating to vagrancy.

In 1817 a committee of the House reported that largely through maladministration the poor rates were increasing, so that eventually they seemed likely to swallow up the entire rent of the land. The only important result of this report was the passing of the vestry acts of 1818 and 1819. Following a flood of propaganda against the mismanagement of the business, from 1817 to 1832, and a royal commission of inquiry, which reported, with a scathing indictment of the entire system, giving chapter and verse for its allegations of such abuses by the score, the old parochial system was wound up by the act of 1834, the parishes being compulsorily amalgamated unto 'unions'. The governing bodies of the unions were 'guardians' having a property qualification, and elected by voters upon a system of plural voting depending on other property qualifications. The whole system was centralised under the control of a body of Poor Law Commissioners, virtually autocrats in charge of the entire management of the poor throughout England and Wales. The major events in the subsequent history of the poor law have been the transfer of its administration from the guardians to the county authorities in 1929, and, last of all, the assumption by the central government in 1948 and 1966 of responsibility not only for the broad lines of ' public assistance ' and now ' social security ' policy, but also for much the greater part of its detailed administration.[42]

SIDELIGHTS UPON THE OPERATION OF THE OLD SYSTEM. Most interesting sidelights on the old system are to be found in the preambles of the numerous acts, and among the many references in reported cases. Any of the numerous legal text-books with lists of statutes will give a good deal of insight into the working of the old poor law, the endless frauds, abuses and collusive actions to which it gave rise, and the colossal volume of litigation between parishes resulting from it. It will give also instances of frequent stony inhumanity, with occasional bestial cruelty to the poor by parish officers, against which the justices waged constant though not very effective warfare.

The act of 1662 gives a graphic picture of the poor who were

not restrained from going from one parish to another, and therefore do endeavour to settle themselves in those parishes where there is the best stock, the largest commons or wastes to build cottages, and the most woods for them to burn and destroy; and when they have consumed it, then to another parish, and at last become rogues and vagabonds....

The act of 1666 informs us that the poor, living 'idly and un-imployed' in gaol, become debauched, and come forth 'instructed in the practice of thievery and lewdness'. That of 1723 deals with the excessive relief ordered by tender-hearted justices, from whom paupers

without the knowledge of any officers of the parish...upon untrue suggestions, and sometimes upon false or frivolous pretences, have obtained relief, which hath greatly contributed to the increase of the parish rates...;

and so on.

An interesting picture of a parochial dispute is given by this record from Crondall,[43] Hants.:

Memorandum—That the aforesaid Margaret Hyller was sent eight times by the officers and inhabitants of Crondall to the overseers and inhabitants of Haslemere, who did refuse to receive and retain her for one of their poor, and seven times by them brought again to Crondall, and there left contrary to her Majesty's laws in such cases made and provided, but the eighth time, being sent, they returned her not.

Even the justices were not always impeccable, since it was found necessary to enact in 1732-3[44] that 'it shall not be lawful for any justice or justices to send for any woman whatsoever before she shall be delivered, and one month after, in order to her being examined concerning her pregnancy'. Some idea of the attitude of the worst parish officers may be gathered from the act of 1743-4 (above), which declares that churchwardens and overseers 'frequently, on frivolous pretences, and for private ends, make unjust and illegal rates in a secret and clandestine manner', or that of 1781-2, which refers to the 'incapacity, negligence, or misconduct of overseers'. Until 1792 it was not only within the power—but definitely also the duty—of the justices to have female vagabonds publicly whipped according to the barbarous legislation of Elizabeth I.

Reference to the information to be obtained from reported cases will appear later when we are discussing the thorny problem of settlement. Burn in his *History of the Poor Law*[45] says:

The office of an overseer seems to be understood to be this: to keep an extraordinary look-out to prevent persons coming to inhabit without certificates, and to fly to the justices to remove them; and if a man brings a certificate...to take care to keep him out of all parish offices, to warn them, if they will hire servants to hire them half-yearly...and so to get rid of them. To bind out poor children apprentices, no matter to whom, or to what trade, but to take special care that the master live in another parish.

In many parishes it would no doubt have gone still harder with the poor but for the fact that the local magistrates retained their supervising powers, and were available as a sort of court of appeal against the refusal of relief by some stony-hearted parish officer. An example of a justice's order in a case of refusal is reproduced elsewhere. Unless there was prompt and wholehearted compliance with the justices' orders the parish officials found themselves in serious trouble, as e.g. at Sutton Bonington, Notts., where in 1775 Hart Buck, farmer, constable, was

presented for contemptuously neglecting to cause the Overseers of the Poor to come before Sir Gervas Clifton, Bart., to answer for refusing to give Relief to Richard James and his family, Paupers.

There were, of course, some magistrates as inhuman as the worst of the parish officers, and it must have been one of these, under a quite mistaken notion that baptism in the parish church gave a settlement in the parish, of whom we find in the register of Wimbledon, Surrey, 1723, this memorandum:

Susannah, daughter of Moses and Mary Cooper, Travellers, born in Martin (Merton), and the poor woman being desirous to have it baptised, though she had lain in but a week, carried it in her own arms to Martin Church....But Justice Meriton being informed by the Constable of her being in the Porch with that intention, went out of his seat in time of service to her, and took hold of her, and led her to the Court of his house, and...made the man's mittimus to send him to the house of correction if he would not cary his wife and child out of the parish without being Baptized...she brought up her child to me, to my house on this day being Tuesday, July 2nd, complaining of her hard usage, and passionately desiring me to Baptize it, which I did....

An interesting sidelight on the system appears in the register of Wootton St Lawrence, Hants., where there is this record of re-marriage:

It having appeared after 26 March, that Geo. Wyatt had not attained the age of twenty-one years by two days, the officers of the parish of Preston Candover, where he had gained a settlement, and to which he was removed, objected to the marriage, the ceremony was therefore performed again at the request of the said George Wyatt and Elizabeth Lavey, on 4 April 1792, by me....

SOME SPECIAL FEATURES OF POOR-LAW ADMINISTRATION

(a) *SETTLEMENT AND REMOVAL*

The key to an understanding of a great deal that occurred is that 'in manorial days it was essential to control the outflow of labour from the district; under the parochial system to control its influx'.[1] Until 1662 the poor could seek employment wherever it was to be found, and only persons unable or unwilling to work had to abide in their parish of settlement. But with the more stringent clauses of the 1662 act difficulties began to arise at once.[2] A settlement could be gained by clandestine residence, so the act of 1685 was passed. Evidently then the parish officers entered into private arrangements with paupers wishing to gain settlements, so these were prevented by the act of 1691.

Arrangements to evade the law occurred even before 1662. These were later forbidden by statute. At Cheswardine, Salop, the churchwardens' accounts for 1619 include this entry:

given to a woman y^t had a child borne at Hunters of
   gouldston for to dischardg the parishe for ever of the
   said child   vjs. 8d.

Then persons entered into engagements to serve a year, but
actually served only a few weeks and so gained a settlement. This
was put a stop to by the 1696–7 act. Next the favourite device was
for the settler to purchase a fictitious estate or one of small value,
and measures were taken in the 1722–3 act to prohibit this.

Meanwhile it had become almost impossible for the poor working
labourer to move at all, so in the 1696–7 act the issue of settlement
certificates was allowed, the holders of these gaining no settlement
unless they rented a £10 tenement or served a parish office, and
the parish of settlement agreeing to receive back the holders if they
should fall chargeable to the parish of residence. To discourage
paupers still further the act contained the abominable provision
which is referred to above as to badging the poor. Even so paupers
swarmed, and when refused relief by the parish officers they went
with a plausible tale to the neighbouring justice who was known
to be most susceptible. This had to be checked by the act of 1723.
There was then no substantial change until the act of 1795, which
forbade removal until the person was actually chargeable, and
which therefore authorised the English labourer to remain in
whatever parish he chose, so long as he remained solvent. Even
the 1834 New Poor Law made very little difference as to settlement; the law of settlement was not substantially altered until
1876.[3] On this question of settlement Blackstone[4] says:

This [out-relief to the deserving poor and to these only] appears
to have been the plan of the statute of queen Elizabeth...the laborious
poor were then at liberty to seek employment wherever it was to be
had: none being obliged to reside in the places of their settlement, but
such as were unable or unwilling to work; and those places of settlement
being only such where they were *born* or had made their abode....
After the restoration a very different plan was adopted, which has
rendered the employment of the poor more difficult...has greatly
increased their number...has given birth to the intricacy of our poor
laws...and in consequence has created an infinity of expensive law
suits between contending neighbourhoods, concerning those settlements
and removals.

We refer elsewhere[5] to the agreements adopted in many parishes
for preventing outsiders from gaining settlements. As late as 1830
the vestry of Caddington, Beds., executed such an agreement, viz.
that no outside labourer be hired for a whole year. Another Bed-

fordshire parish, Potton, forty years earlier in 1788, had resolved that every resident having no settlement, and being uncertificated, be forthwith removed.

During the currency of the old law, endless time and vast amounts of public money were spent upon contested settlement cases: e.g. when a £10 tenement gave a settlement, what of a man who rented a tenement situated in two parishes? This was decided as giving a settlement in the parish where his bed was.[6] In one case where the parish boundary ran through a house it was ruled that the master's settlement was in one parish, the servant's in another. Settlement was given by paying to the parish rates: what of a person who had been rated by the *parish* officers towards a *county* bridge? He was adjudged to gain no settlement. Where a father had no known settlement before a child became chargeable, the child took the maiden settlement of the mother:

but as the father's settlement where he has one must always fix that of the child, it is obvious that recourse should be had to the settlement of the father's mother, prior to that of the pauper's own mother...and upon the same principle that of the father's grandfather's mother precedes that of his own mother and so on.[7]

Despite such protests as that of Sir Josiah Child in 1668[8] concerning the useless cruelty of whipping vagrants about the country for them to wander out again as soon as they had reached their place of settlement, and the scathing denunciation by Adam Smith[9] of the 'violation of natural liberty and justice', in putting it in the power of a parish officer to imprison a man as it were for life the system developed apace.

From 1776 to 1815 the annual expense of litigation grew from £35,000 to £287,000. Constables in parishes on main roads sometimes spent the whole of their time transporting paupers, counties and parishes entered into pauper removal contracts with business men who specialised in the work,[10] unhappy families were removed by vigilant parish officers from Cornwall to Westmorland, only for the officers of other parishes to remove them again back into Cornwall. Half the business of every quarter sessions consisted in deciding appeals on orders of removal, at an expense which, so it was alleged, would in many cases have covered the entire cost of the pauper's maintenance several times over and still left the contesting parishes a handsome profit.

At Kettering, Northants., where the vestry in 1817 petitioned Parliament for the amendment of the poor laws, the petitioners represented that the expenses attending the removal of paupers and the lawsuits respecting settlements form no inconsiderable items in the annual expenditure of the parish.

Sometimes abstracts of parish expenditure classified under various heads are met with, e.g. at Albury, Surrey, there is such an abstract, 1800–17, of all sums spent each year in Albury under detailed heads. It is noteworthy that study of these, and of such accounts as are available, hardly bears out the view that the expenses incurred solely in removals were as heavy as is generally supposed, though even so they were far *too* heavy.

Not many parishes had as much common sense as Keysoe and Riseley, Beds., which entered into this agreement in 1743:

WHEREAS Elizabeth Dickens Widow was...removed...from the Parish of Keysoe...to the...Parish of Risely,...AND WHEREAS the Inhabitants of the said two parishes of Keysoe and Risely are of the Opinion that it is a Matter of great doubt whether the said Elizabeth Dickens was last legally Settled in the said Parish of Risely or in the Parish of Keysoe aforesaid and being apprehensive that it may be much more Expensive to both the said Parishes to try and determine the Meritts of the said Settlement at Law than to keep maintain and cloath her at their joint & equal expence inasmuch as she is grown very old Therefore to avoid an Appeal and all Proceedings & Expences thereon or in Consequence thereof The Inhabitants of the said Two Parishes have respectively Agreed that the said Elizabeth Dickens shall be kept maintain'd & Cloathed as often as need shall require at the Joynt & Equal Expence of the Inhabitants of both the said Parishes unless she the said Elizabeth Dickens shall by any future Act or Means Acquire any Subsequent legal Settlement in Either of the said Parishes or elsewhere.

Below we reproduce (from the chest of Bleasby, Notts.) a fairly typical record of the costs incurred in removal. Its date is c. 1750. This particular removal was relatively very economically done and was to a neighbouring parish.

A Bill of Chearges for the Removall of Elizabeth Low
to her Setement

Mar. 19	Paid at Newark	o.	2.	2
	My chearges at Elton	o.	1.	1
	Paid for warrant and examination	o.	3.	o
	Chearges at Southwell	o.	1.	2
	John Hanes for going to Newark	o.	o.	6
	For going to Newark & Elton		2.	6
	Paid John Hanes	o.	o.	6
	For serving the Warrants	o.	2.	o
	Paid George Hodgkinson for going to Southwell 3 times and chearges	o.	2.	6
	For going to Nottingham	o.	2.	o

	And my chearges	0.	2.	3
	Paid for the wagin	0.	8.	0
	Chearges at Richard Horsepools	0.	3.	10½
Mar. 22	Servt of the waginer	0.	0.	6
June 15	Paid to Wm Ward	2.	3.	0
	Spent at Heselford	0.	17.	10
		0.	1.	6
	Paid John Haynes	0.	0.	6
	For serving the warrants	0.	2.	0 £4. 14. 4½

The principal records to be found in a parish chest bearing upon this matter of settlement and removal are the notes of expenses incurred by the overseers in ascertaining a pauper's place of legal settlement, or in correspondence with the officers of other parishes; and those of removal itself, which generally appear in constables' accounts. Then there are the settlement certificates (*see* Fig. 15), examinations, removal orders, appeals, counsels' opinions and a whole host of allied documents. Bedfordshire has collected some 5000, and multiplying this by eighty for the country as a whole gives us a rough estimate of 400,000 still surviving in England and Wales. It is clear then what an enormous field they offer to the social historian.

For the wandering poor the records include vagrant examinations, warrants to the constables to whip vagrants, passes of these last to their parishes of legal settlement, and commitments of such undesirables to the house of correction.

The chest of Rode, Som., has no less than thirty-two counsels' opinions and appeals to quarter sessions, 1689–1817, almost wholly as to settlement questions. Settlement certificates, examinations as to settlement, and removal orders generally make up the bulk of the poor-law records in the chest, and often are the only such records to have survived. The earlier documents of each class are generally handwritten, but by about the seventeen-forties printed forms came into use, the stationers in each country town evidently finding it worth while to keep a stock, from which parish officers replenished their smaller stocks as occasion arose.

The examinations (*see* Fig. 11) are particularly interesting since they are virtually autobiographies of persons in a class of which other biographical records are rarely found.[11] They give the place of birth of the person concerned and often his whole history over a long period of years, especially with reference to apprenticeship, the length of time for which he has been hired, the rental value of any property he has occupied, and, in short, anything bearing upon the question whether or not he has acquired a settlement. At Gnosall, Staffs., a pauper examined in 1788 deposed that:

at the time of the hiring he was very much in liquor and therefore does not remember the exact time for which he was hired, but remembers that he was to have six pounds ten shillings for the service.

Documents relating to settlement were, of course, highly prized. A labourer's family would treasure up for years any scrap of evidence that he had rented a £10 tenement, served an annual office, been apprenticed in the parish, or even paid a shilling to the poor rate. Similarly, the parish officers carefully preserved any evidence that a parishioner was legally settled in another parish. This letter is entered in the books of this same parish of Gnosall, Staffs., whither a John Low and family immigrated from Eccleshall, though legally settled in Ashley. The Eccleshall officers readily sent Gnosall a copy of the settlement certificate, but firmly declined to part with the original:

If any of the parishioners of Gnoshall have a mind to see the Certificate let them come to me & I will show it them, (for the Gen:men of Eccleshall parish will not part wth it).

A TYPICAL SERIES OF EXAMINATION AND REMOVAL RECORDS FROM NOTTINGHAMSHIRE. The process of examination and removal is well illustrated by the documents printed below from the chest of Shelford, Notts. The only feature of the set not typical is the suspension of the order because of the man's illness.

The Examination

County of Nottingham.⎫   THE Examination of Humphrey Foulds
              ⎬ taken upon Oath before me, one of HIS
    (TO WIT). ⎭ MAJESTY's Justices of the Peace in and for
the said County, this seventh Day of April 1809 touching the Place of his Settlement. This Examinant, upon Oath, saith, That he is about the Age of Thirty Eight Years, and that he was born, as he hath been informed, and verily believes, in the Parish of Old Daulbey in the County of Leicester of Parents legally settled at Shelford in the County of Nottingham, That when about seventeen years of Age he was hired to Mr. Simpson of Saxelby in the County of Leicester aforesaid for one year and served him Two years, That at Martinmas following he was hired to Henry Ellis of Shelford in the County of Nottingham for one year and served him accordingly. That at Martinmas following was hired to Mr. John Cooper of Shelford aforesaid and served him Eighteen Months. That in the Month of December following he went to Work at Grantham Canal. That in the year 1800 he went to Great Grimsby in Lincolnshire and Married Fanny his now Wife which gave him a

Vote for great Grimsby aforesaid, and there Rented a House, at one Pound ten shillings a year and paid Rates or Assessments about five Shillings a year, and lived there about five or six years. That he afterwards went to live at Boston, and Rented a Room and Paid Three Shillings a week for Thirty Nine Weeks, and remainder of the year Paid 2s. 6d. per week, and was then Removed by a Warrant of Removal to the Parish of Shelford aforesaid....

The Order (*see* Fig. 12)

The Borough and Parish of Boston ⎫
    In the County of Lincoln ⎭

UPON the Complaint of the Churchwardens and Overseers of the Poor of the Parish of Boston aforesaid...in the said County of Lincoln unto us...that Humphrey Foulds and Frances his Wife and their three children namely Humphrey aged about six Years, Mary Ann aged about five years and Sarah aged about two years have come to inhabit in the said Parish of Boston, not having gained a legal Settlement there, nor produced any Certificate owning them to be settled elsewhere, and that the said Humphrey Foulds and Frances his Wife and their said three children have become chargeable to the said Parish of Boston; we the said Justices...do therefore require you the said Churchwardens and Overseers of the Poor of the said Parish of Boston, or some, or one of you to convey the said Humphrey Foulds and Frances his Wife and their said three children from and out of the said Parish of Boston to the said Parish of Shelford and them to deliver to the Churchwardens and Overseers of the Poor there, or to some or one of them together with our Order or a true Copy thereof, at the same Time shewing to them the Original; and we do also hereby require you the said Churchwardens and Overseers of the Poor of the said Parish of Shelford to receive and provide for them as Inhabitants of your said Parish....

The Suspension and Confirmation

To the Overseers of the Poor of the within mentioned
Parish of Boston and to each and every of them

WHEREAS it appears to us the within named Justices that the within named Humphrey Foulds is unable to travel by Reason of Sickness and that it would be dangerous for him so to do We do hereby require and authorise you the said overseers and each and every of you to suspend the Execution of the within written order of Removal until we are satisfied that it may be safely executed GIVEN under our Hands this twentieth Day of January one thousand eight hundred and nine....

WHEREAS it is now made appear unto us the within named Justices and we are fully satisfied that the within Order of Removal may be executed without danger. We do therefore hereby Order the same to be forthwith put in Execution accordingly. And we do therefore order and direct the Churchwardens or Overseers of the Poor of the Parish of Shelford in the County of Nottingham, to which Parish the within named Humphrey Foulds is ordered to be removed to pay the sum of Six pounds and ten shillings to John Harwood Overseer of the Parish of Boston upon demand. Given our Hands the thirtieth day of March 1809.

Other similar documents which sometimes turn up in parish records are summonses to the parish of settlement to show cause against the order of removal applied for, and notices given by the parish of residence to the parish of settlement of an intention to apply for a removal order. Burn strongly recommends[12] that such should be issued in every settlement case, but they are much rarer than the other settlement papers. Probably these were issued only when justices or parish officers were either particularly fair-minded or somewhat nervous as to the legality of their proceedings.

(b) PAROCHIAL GENEROSITY, PAROCHIAL DETERRENT MEASURES AND PAROCHIAL EXPERIMENTS

Sometimes the parish acted really generously in paying for medical relief or clothing for a settled pauper. At Gnosall, Staffs., e.g. where the parish had four 'quarters', the accounts of Cowley Quarter for 1703 have:

Pd towards the cure of Robt. Gost 02 - 08 - 07

those of Knightley:

pd towards the cure of Robt. Gost 02 - 01 - 06

In 1705 this resolution was passed:

December ye 21st 1705
A Lewne was then agreed upon to be Levyed for the necessary Releife of the poore of the Parish of GNOSALL after the usual way of a double Leawne and at the same time it was agreed that another double poors Leawne be Levyed for and towards the paying of Mr. Key for the Cure of Robt. Gosts Leg.

The rate raised £9. 15s. 8d. and the bill was settled for £7. 12s. od. And even then further entries occur from time to time for 'salve for Robt. Gosts Leg'.

So it seems that from 1703 to 1715 nearly a quarter of the whole poor-rate expenditure in one particular parish was devoted to medical treatment for one pauper. Probably few Public Assistance authorities of late years spent twenty-five per cent of their incomes on medical treatment for the whole of the sick poor in their areas.

A rather pathetic series of entries from Kirton-in-Lindsey, Lincs.,[1] runs:

1677 a paire of bodies for Dorithy Routh	3s. 4d.
two shifts cloth and makeing and a yeard of cloth for white clothing for Dori: Routh	3s. 11d.
A paire of stokings and sum meddisonne for her	1s. 0d.
A sute of clothing for her	5s. 6d.
A pair of shows for Dor. Routh	2s. 0d.
Dorithy Routh buriing	2s. 10d.

Mr Emmison found that in the exceptionally interesting parish of Eaton Socon, Beds., the overseers dealt in second-hand clothing, as well as new, and that for thirteen years, 1706–18, more than six hundred entries concern the provision or mending of clothes or materials for making them, involving in all well over one thousand articles. The Gnosall, Staffs., overseer even did a little pawnbroking:

1823 Saml. Stanley to be advanced £3 upon his clock, which if he claims it again in 12 months shall be returned to him for £2.

The records of Eaton Socon have one or two entries in the early part of the eighteenth century suggesting that this parish was not ungenerous in the treatment of its pauper children:

1724 For bread & beer at ye children's breaking up at Christmas	9d.
1738 Pd for 12 pound of cherries for ye children in ye house	6d.
1744 Gave to ye children at Fair	2s. 8d.

In this same parish, after a record of beer for a pauper's child's christening, is this entry concerning its mother:

| 1717 For money for her churching | 6d. |

At Walsoken, Norf., the overseer's accounts of 1787 show the official claiming not only for his Christmas box to the constable, but also for Christmas presents to the workhouse inmates:

| Gave the children & old people in the work house Christmas presents | 7s. 6d. |

There is, however, plenty of evidence of the operation of a quite contrary tendency. Perhaps the meanest example of this was the refusal of one parish to relieve disabled ex-soldiers unless they hypothecated in favour of the overseers their quarterly 'penchens' from Chelsea Hospital. Less open to objection was the action of the vestry of Horsley, Gloucs., which in 1815 printed and circulated

Essex –

The Examination of Robert Bond late of Coggeshall but now a prisoner in the House of Correction at Chelmsford taken before us two of His Majesty's Justices of the Peace in and for the said County this 23d day of November 1821 touching the place of his last legal settlement

Who on his oath saith that he is about twenty seven years of age and was born at Braxtead in the County of Suffolk as he hath been informed and believes that about seven years ago at old Michaelmas he let himself to Mr William Greenwood of Withering near Dedham in the said County of Suffolk to serve for a year at the sum of Ten pounds Board and Lodging that he entered upon such service the old Michaelmas day and served the said year and continued in the service of the said Mr William Greenwood until the old Michaelmas day following and received his full wages and has not done any act whereby to gain a subsequent settlement. Except saith he

entered and Examinate further saith that about five years ago he went into the service of Mr William Bacon at the Black Boy Inn at Chelmsford being engaged there as Boot Cate ler by George Wilson the Head Waiter for the ... Examinate agreed with Wilson to serve Mr Bacon for what he could get of the Customers for cleaning their Boots & Shoes and to Board and Lodge in Mr Bacon's House that he served all Mr Bacon under such agreement with Wilson for the term fifteen or sixteen Months and was absent with Mr Bacon's team only four days during the whole of that period and with that about a year ago in consequence within this parish Church of Great Coggeshall so forward to certain that his present life

Sworn before us this day and year first above written at Chelmsford

the mark of
X
Robert Bond

[signatures]

XI. An Examination from Chelmsford, Essex, 1821. (See p. 202.)

G   **R**

R.B.

Suffolk⎰ To the Church Wardens and Overseers of the Poor of the
parish - - - - - - of *Hadleigh* - - - - - - - - - in the
said *County* - - and to the Church Wardens and Overseers of the Poor of the parish - of *Coggeshall*
- - - - - - - - - in the *County of Essex*
- - - - - - and to each and every of them. - - -

Tanner

UPON the Complaint of the Church Wardens and Overseers of the
Poor of the *parish* - - - - - of *Hadleigh* - - aforesaid
in the said *County* - of *Suffolk* - - - - unto us whose Names
are hereunto set and Seals affixed, being two of his Majesty's Justices
of the Peace in and for the said *County* - of *Suffolk* - - - -
and one of us of the Quorum, that - - - - - - - -

Ellen Trowls - - - -

ha*th* - - come to inhabit in the said *parish* of *Hadleigh*
- - - - - - - - - not having gained a legal Settlement there, nor
produced any Certificate owning *Her* - - - - to be settled elsewhere, and that the said *Ellen Trowls* - - - - - -
- - - - - - - - is likely to be chargeable to the said
parish - - - - of *Hadleigh* - - - - - - We the said
Justices upon due Proof made hereof, as well upon the Examination
of the said *Ellen Trowls* - - - - - - - - upon Oath,
as otherwise, and likewise upon due Consideration had of the Premises, do adjudge the same to be true ; and we do likewise adjudge,
that the lawful Settlement of *Her* the said *Ellen Trowls* - -
is in the said *parish* - - - of *Coggeshall* - - - in the said
County - - - - - of *Essex* - - - - We do therefore
require you the said Churchwardens and Overseers of the Poor of the
said *parish* - - - - of *Hadleigh* - - - - - or some, or
one of you, to convey the said *Ellen Trowls* - - - -
from and out of your said *parish* - - of *Hadleigh*
to the said *parish* - of *Coggeshall* - - - - - and *Her*
to deliver to the Churchwardens and Overseers of the Poor there, or
to some, or one of them, together with this our Order, or a true Copy
thereof : And we do also hereby require you the said Churchwardens
and Overseers of the Poor of the said *parish* of *Coggeshall*
to receive and provide for *Her* - - - - - as Inhabitants of your
parish - - - Given under our Hands and Seals the *Seventh*
Day of *December* - in the Year of our Lord One Thousand
Seven Hundred and Sixty *Seven* - - - - - - - -

Wm. B. Brand

XII. A Removal Order from Coggeshall, Essex, 1767. (*See p. 203.*)

a list of all paupers drawing relief. Based on the same principle was the inventorying and seizure of a pauper's goods at his death and their sale by the parish officers in order to reimburse the parish for as much as possible of its expenditure.

Mr Emmison prints[2] three such inventories from Eaton Socon, Beds., all about 1737–41. The goods in the lengthiest one fetched £2. 18s. 2d., those in the shortest 7s. 0d. A fairly typical one runs:

Widow Peaks Goods.

In her Fire-room in the chimney,—1 paire of hooks, 1 paire of tongs, 1 paire of bellows, 1 middling brass kettle, 1 small brass porrage pott, 1 little kettle, 1 brass skillett, 2 pewter dishes, 1 pretty large firr table, 1 square brown table, 4 bass bottom chairs, 1 press cubberd. In her Chamber—1 bedstead matt cord, 1 flock bed, 1 red rugg, 1 blankett, 1 paire of sheets, 2 bass bottom chairs, 1 small coffer, 1 box, 1 small tubb.

Towards the end of the eighteenth century, it was quite usual for vestries to instruct the parish officers to go round the parish taking inventories of paupers' goods, so that the parish should not be cheated when they died and the goods fell to the parish. At Gnosall, Staffs., e.g. in 1776:

the Overseers in every Quarter to take an account of all Paupers goods which may require weekly pay.

Towards the end of the seventeenth century a suggestion was made by a certain Thomas Firmin[3] that, to prevent the poor who were 'on the parish' from augmenting their income by begging, the old Tudor plan of badging the poor should be adopted. The badge wearers were not, however, to be duly licensed beggars, but poor in receipt of relief, who were strictly forbidden to beg generally upon pain of losing their parish allowance. They were, however, to be allowed to beg broken victuals from their neighbours at certain fixed hours, and these wealthier neighbours were to pledge themselves to give nothing to unbadged applicants. In 1683 the scheme, or some part of it, was in operation in Tonbridge, Kent; it was adopted by the Middlesex justices in 1694[4] and in 1696–7 the provision was included in an act[5] with a clause authorising the punishment of recalcitrant paupers.

Nevertheless the paupers continued to object. Vestries legislated vainly that relief should be refused to all who declined to wear the badges. At Barnet, Herts.,[6] a certain T. Omitt was committed

for assaulting Ed. Hughes the churchwarden and not wearing the badge as act of Parliament directs.

P

Overseers' accounts often contain references to the provision of
the badges ordered by the act of 1697. At Eaton Socon, Beds.,
there are such entries as:

1706   For 12 badges yᵉ cloth 1s., and yᵉ makeing of them 2s.
1727   Pd Mr. Hockley for 1 yard of red duffel and a yard of blue
       searge for yᵉ badges.

A reference to 'baging yᵉ poor' at Sutton Bonington, Notts.,
appears in the churchwardens' accounts of 1731, referred to elsewhere.[7] At Harefield, Mdx., in 1695, appears an entry:

pd. for the brasse bages for the poor and carraige from London.

In 1699 the parish followed the more economical plan of having
the badges made in cloth by the local tailor:

pd. for redd cloath to make the pees and to John Hill for
  makeing of them   1s. 9d.
pd. Jo. Hill, Taylor, for 24 pees   4s. 0d.
spent when the pore had theire pees set on   3s. 0d.
given to Spakman to give the poor notice to wear pees   6d.

The chest of Marston Bigot, Som., contains a justice's warrant
of 1757 directing the overseers to ensure that all in receipt of relief
wear a badge.

At Gnosall, Staffs., the practice had lapsed during the eighteenth
century, but was revived by order of the vestry in 1800:

It is Concluded upon that every Poor Person or Persons obtaining
relief from the aforesaid Parish shl wear the Badge (Viz.) two Roman
Letters P.G.

This part of the act was repealed in 1810,[8] although in many
parishes its provisions had been ignored before this. And even after
the repeal stout conservatives felt inclined to use its powers—no
longer existent. At Toddington, Beds., the overseers' accounts in
1819 record the provision of two hundred and ten badges, and
the withholding of relief from one obstreperous pauper nine years
after the provision had been repealed.

The expedients adopted at Eaton Socon, Beds., have been
described in detail in Mr Emmison's[9] admirable work:

1706–19   Direct relief (outdoor): weekly pensions and extraordinary
          disbursements.
1719–27   Workhouse (direct maintenance, i.e. food bought by over-
          seers). Very little supervision by a caretaker.
1728–30   Reversion to outdoor relief (paupers still retained in house
          but providing own food etc.).

1731–44 Workhouse (direct maintenance, i.e. food bought by overseers). A governor in strict charge.

1745–49 First contract (£13. 6s. 8d. a month).

1749 Feb.–Oct. Temporary reversion to direct maintenance in workhouse.

1749–62 Series of contracts (all £13. 6s. 8d. a month). Five or six different small contractors.

1762–88 Accounts missing.

1789 Apparently direct maintenance with food and pensions provided by the overseers in first month. But change in second month.

1789–91 Contract for £36 a month.

1791–99 Reversion to direct maintenance of workhouse by overseers with food and pensions provided by them.

1799–1807 Contract on *per capita* basis (3s. a week).

1807–09 Contract for two years. Total £1850.

1809 Feb.–May Temporary reversion to direct maintenance.

1809–13 Contract for fixed sum (£83 a month, but increased to £106 at end of period).

1813–14 Contract on *per capita* basis (4s. 6d. a week), but numerous direct payments, allowances in aid of wages, etc., in addition).

1814–34 Final reversion to direct maintenance by overseers (weekly pensions, and food bought for poorhouse inmates).

We have referred elsewhere to the experiment of contracting with a speculative business man for the entire maintenance of the paupers for a year. This is a contract from Walsoken, Norf.:

March 8 1787. At a vestry then met the Churchwardens and Overseers and Chief Inhabitants of the parish of Walsoken has agreed with Richard Carter for one hundred pounds of lawfull money of Grate brittin for the Maintenance and Clothing of the poore of the said parish that becomes chargeable for one hole yeare

his
Richard X Carter.
mark

The experiment of obeying the law strictly and providing *work* or maintenance seems rarely to have been made towards the end of our period, though commonly (almost invariably with disappointing results) in earlier years. But despite common sense there were administrators who were convinced that with business management the poor-law organisation could be made more or less self-supporting. The vestry minutes of Hinton Charterhouse, Som., contain a resolution of 1830 that

the paupers of the parish be taught to knit stockings, especially the women and old men.

And in the same year

that the pay of Thomas Smith and Joseph Francis be stopped for not attending at the Church to knit.

(c) OVERSEERS' ACCOUNTS AND THE INFORMATION TO BE OBTAINED FROM THEM

Overseers' expenses seem to lend themselves to graphical state-ment. Among the first published diagrams of such with which we are acquainted are those of the Bedfordshire parishes: Eaton Socon, 1789–1819; Lidlington, Pavenham, Roxton, Wootton, 1789–1805; Haynes, Northill, Roxton, 1805–19; printed on the same chart as Appendix IV to Mr Emmison's book, and the chart of churchwardens' and other rates in Sutton Bonington, Notts. 1731–1803, drawn up by the present author.[1]

The overseers' accounts of Gnosall, Staffs., illustrate at once the wide variety of the overseers' expenses in the seventeenth century and their small total amount. This is the same parish which we refer to later as having in 1816 a total expenditure of £2727. 18s. 3d. £726. 3s. 2d. of this was for Gnosall Quarter, apparently identical with the Holding Quarter mentioned below.

The Acc:ts of Thomas Heeley one of the Overseers of the poore for the parish of Gnoshall in the Holding Quarter Anno Domi 1682.

I charge my selfe with 4 double Lewnes to 10. 16. 08
Disbst as followeth:

Payd to Robert Mosse for 51 weekes at 6d. ye weeke	01. 05. 06
Payd to Margaret Davies de Gnoshall at 4d. ye weeke to	00. 17. 00
Payd to Mary Taylor at 5d. ye weeke	01. 01. 03
Payd to Margaret Davies de Hollies at 4d. ye weeke for 44 weekes & 6d. for seaven weekes	00. 18. 02
Spent in distributing 50/- being forfeited for burying Mary Meeson in Linen	00. 00. 06
Payd for writing my Assessment	00. 00. 06
Given towards the cure of Sarah Coopers shoulder	00. 02. 00
Spent when we mett to sett forth poor children	00. 00. 06
Payd for two pair of shoes for John Stafford	00. 10. 00
Given to John Venables	00. 14. 00
Spent when we layd a Lewne for the poore	00. 00. 06
Payd for Leather to make John Stafford's clothes	00. 08. 00
Payd for thred and buttons	00. 02. 08
Payd for makeing his Clothes	00. 02. 08
Spent at laying a Lewne for the poore	00. 00. 06
Payd to Margaret Davies for washing John Stafford's clothes	00. 00. 04
Payd John Adderley charges at the monthly meeteing & sessions about Joane Brodbury	00. 03. 00
Payd to the Church Wardens their charge upon the same Acc:t	00. 02. 00
Payd to Thomas Foster the Rent for Margaret Davies	00. 10. 00

Spent at the laying of a Lewne upon St: Thomas day	00. 01. 00
Payd John Lees which he was out of purse the last yeare	00. 14. 05½
Given to John Eccleshall in his sicknesse	00. 05. 03
Payd Mary Burrows for washing Staffords Linens	00. 02. 00
Payd Charles Burrows for keepeing Thomas Hundling	00. 03. 04
Spent upon Ash-Wednesday when we distributed Mr Fyges gift	00. 00. 06
Given to William Bradshaw	00. 05. 00
Given to Margery Taylor	00. 05. 00
Given to Cicely Bromley	00. 03. 00
Given to Humphrey Davies	00. 02. 00
For writeing & keepeing my Acc^{ts}	00. 01. 00
For ingrosseing them & my Assessment	00. 00. 06
Payd to Thomas Ward	01. 12. 00
Spent upon Good-Friday when we distributed money to the poore	00. 00. 06
	10. 14. 01½
recd [by four 'double Lewnes'] the sum of	10. 16. 08
Disburst the sum of	10. 14. 01½
The rest in my hand is	00. 02. 06½
which was payd to William Hill	

An exceptionally interesting series of accounts actually going back before the creation of the office of overseer by the act of 1572 is to be found in the chest of Leverton, Lincs., (Collectors' and) Overseers' accounts, 1563–98.

(d) *VAGRANTS AND VAGRANCY*

By the 1743–4 act[1] vagrants were classified into three sections, 'idle and disorderly persons', 'rogues and vagabonds', and 'incorrigible rogues'. The first class was made up of persons threatening to run away and leave their dependants, those returning to a parish from which they had been removed, and persons living idle lives, and then begging in their own parishes. All persons were authorised to apprehend such, a reward of five shillings[2] being payable for their apprehension.

The second class was made up of two divisions—those wandering about as patent gatherers or gatherers of alms,[3] persons collecting for prisons and hospitals, fencers, bearwards, 'common players of interludes', minstrels, jugglers, 'persons pretending to be Egyptians', 'those pretending to have skill in physiognomy etc.', or 'using any subtil craft to deceive her majesty's subjects', 'playing at any unlawful game of chance', 'leaving[4] their dependents chargeable to the parish', unlicensed pedlars and chapmen, persons lodging in barns, etc. or in the open air 'not giving a good account of themselves', pretending to be soldiers or mariners,[5] or to go to work in harvest, and, most comprehensively, 'all other persons wandering abroad and begging'.

Rogues in the incorrigible class were of four groups: persons 'end gathering' contrary to the statute of 1726–7,[6] persons in class two escaping from custody, or refusing to be examined, those lying at their examinations, or escaping from the house of correction, and rogues and vagabonds who repeated the offence.

VAGRANCY RECORDS. Forms of such documents as the order upon the overseer to pay five shillings for apprehending a person begging in his own parish (an idle and disorderly person), or upon the high constable to pay from the county funds the ten shillings due upon the apprehension of a rogue and vagabond, will be found in Burn.[7] Documents of this last class should be among the county archives; commitments presumably were retained at the house of correction. The principal vagrant papers surviving in the chests are the orders upon the overseers, licences to mariners, etc. to pass unapprehended, and passes (*see* Fig. 14) each ordering the conveyance of a vagabond, every constable in turn taking him to the next county boundary, until he reached eventually his place of settlement. The route of the journey was generally entered on the pass, each magistrate planning the route across his own county, and approving the charge to be made by the constable, and the number of days allowed for the journey. Finally there are the warrants to constables authorising the whipping of rogues (*see* Fig. 10).

Parish records of almost any sort may contain references to this problem of vagrancy, e.g. Cerne Abbas, Dorset, has a register labelled:

1661 a registered book of all such rogues & vagabonds as have been punished according at Cerne Abbas in Dorsetshire.

More typical are these entries in the poor accounts of Harefield, Middlesex, in 1701–11:

pd the 25th of Feb. for passing away vagrants   1. 2. 3
gave to a woman that was redy to cry out and to 2 women
    to have her away to a nother Parish   3. 0

In early times the execution of the vagrancy laws is often recorded in the parish registers, e.g. at Godalming, Surrey:

April 26. 1658. Here was taken a vagrant, one Mary Parker, widow with a child, and she was whipped according to law, about the age of thirty years, proper of personage; and she was to go to the place of her birth that is Gravesend, in Kent, and she is limited to iiij days, and to be carried from tithing to Tything till she comes to the end of the said journey.

A similar entry from the register of Bacton, Suff., 1633, is:

WHEREAS upon Saturday the 22 March last past between the hours of 9 and 10 of ye clock at night Magdalen Payne had secretly conveyed herself into ye barne of Robert Cooper dwelling in ye outmost skirts of ye towne of Backeton in Suffolk and whereas further in ye night time ye sayde Magdalen Payne in ye extremity of pains of childe bearing cryed out in ye night time by which ye sayde Robert Cooper was enforced to runne and to implore for aide and assistance of ye neighbouring wives by whose good assistance (God so blessing their endeavours) the sayde Magdalen Payne was then and there delivered of a woman childe since christened and named Katherine.

AND WHEREAS yet further ye sayde Magdalen Payne was upon Monday the (?) day of this instant April convented and conveyed before ye right worshipfull Sir Henry Beckenham, Knight one of ye King's Majesty's Justices of the Peace for this countie of Suffolk and thereupon being examined by oath taken did confess that she had been a long time a vagrant....That therefore...the sayde Sir Henry Beckenham did order that the sayde Magdalen Payne should be whipped untill her bodie was bloodie....These therefore are to certify that the sayde Magdalen Payne was accordingly whipped and these presents are to require all Constables (whom it may concern) to be carefull in the conveying of the sayde Magdalen Payne and Katherine her daughter from Constable to Constable by direct way to ye towne of Hitcham aforesaid there to be provided for according to his Majesties lawes on that behalf made and provided....

How very zealously this removal was carried out may be judged from the note below from the register of Staplehurst, Kent:

1578 There was comytted to the earth the body of one Johan Longley who died in the highway as she was carried on horseback to have been conveyed from officer to officer, till she should have come to the parish Rayershe [Ryarsh].

A typical vagrant order is this:

City of London to wit   Order for the removal of a
                                         vagrant May 20 1709

WHEREAS Phebe Hood, widow, and her two children [seven and six years old respectively] were on the day of the date of these presents brought before me, one of her Majesty's Justices of the Peace of the City aforesaid next residing to the Parish of St. Sepulchre, where the said Phebe Hood and her children were taken and in pursuance of a late act of Parliament....I have carefully examined her, the said Phebe Hood: and it appears to me That her late Husband, William Hood had served his apprenticeship to his Father John Hood of Attenborough in the County of Nottingham about twelve years ago, and I did not find that since that time he obtained any legall settlement elsewhere. And I have exeused the correction of the Aforesaid Phebe for good reasons to me appearing.

These are therefore in her Majesty's name to Will and Require you upon sight hereof to Remove the said Phebe Hood and her two children from the said Parish of St. Sepulchre London, and to conduct her out of the said City to the Parish of St. Sepulchre in the County of Middlesex which I think the most direct and proper way to the said Parish of Attenborough...to be from thence conveyed thither as the law directs.

Given under my hand and seal the 20th day of May Ano Dni 1709. To the Constable of St. Sepulchre, London, and to the Constable of St. Sepulchre in the County of Middlesex and to each of them and all others whom it may concern.

With endorsements instructing the Constable of St. Sepulchre's, Mx. to convey the persons to Barnet, Herts.

· · · · · ·

St. Albans, Herts., to Studham, Beds.,
Studham, Beds., to Little Brickhill, Bucks.,
Little Brickhill, Bucks., to Passenham, Northants.

· · · · · ·

Other endorsements are lacking, but it is clear that on 27 June Phœbe was reconveyed from Attenborough to Nottingham and the order for her removal there was confirmed July 1709.

So a month was spent in conveying this poor woman and her children across country, keeping her at the public expense meanwhile, hauling her before at least six justices and entrusting her to the hands of at least six constables, finally depositing her in a parish where she had no title to remain, and from whence she was promptly deported again.

(e) BASTARDS AND BASTARDY

We are obliged to our friend Mr J. Meeds of Kirklington, Notts., for much help in writing the following notes upon bastardy and bastardy records, which are based upon a chapter in his forthcoming book, *The Operation of the Poor Law in Nottinghamshire*.

Anyone spending much study upon parish records cannot fail to notice the numerous records of illegitimacy which appear in them. The earliest references are those occurring in the registers[1] where the records of baptisms of such children have generally some note of the child's condition,[2] or in the records of penances inflicted by the ecclesiastical court for the incontinency of the parents. But in the sixteenth and seventeenth centuries the birth of an illegitimate child in the average country parish seems to have been an unusual event,[3] such an occurrence perhaps becoming rather commoner with the seventeenth century, still more common with the eighteenth, and so common as to create little surprise, though a great deal of consternation, in the years from 1750 onwards.[4] At this time the parishioners' concern in the matter was not solely or mainly a moral one.

As we have pointed out above, normally a legitimate child took its father's settlement—failing that, its mother's. Now legally the bastard, having no privity of blood between it and its parents, could not take their settlement, and hence was settled in the parish of its birth, very much to that parish's indignation.

It may be interesting, though perhaps not very profitable, to speculate as to the cause of this enormous increase in the illegitimate birthrate referred to above. The fact itself is indisputable. It is generally held that before enclosure[5] became general the standard of living among the peasantry was in general quite high. It is fairly certain too that in the first half of the century housing of a sort was readily available to the labourer. With the developments in agricultural technique however, squatters upon the commons were more rudely discouraged, and upon the growth of the poor rate manorial lords began to destroy cottages at the same time that the population was showing a rapid increase. The labourer then found it impossible to secure accommodation for himself and his intended bride, almost impossible to leave the parish because of the settlement system, and quite out of the question to secure a scrap of land and set up as a small farmer. He was compelled to live where he could, often among conditions of overcrowding. The old moral restraints had gone, and naturally enough he and his like sometimes drifted into conditions approaching sexual promiscuity.[6]

A host of contemporary references might be cited to this effect. Roger North[7] e.g. in the seventeenth century wrote:

Gentlemen of late years have taken up an Humour of Destroying their Tenements and Cottages.... This is done sometimes bare faced, because they harbour the Poor that are a charge to the Parish.

A century later Arthur Young[8] has a celebrated passage in *Political Arithmetic* attacking the settlement laws:

If they marry therefore, where are they to live? No cottage is empty—they must live with their fathers and mothers or lodge: the poor abhor both as much as their betters and certainly in many cases run into licentious amours mainly for want of a cottage or a certificate.

The tendency was encouraged by the custom which sprung up about the early part of the century whereby the parish officers used their considerable powers almost to compel the marriage of any woman found pregnant (the infamous 'knobstick weddings', so called from the staves which were and are the churchwardens' insignia of office). Certainly this is true of the beginning of the nineteenth century, when pregnancy was valid title at least to increased relief, and with any luck to the possession of a husband provided by the parish. The reforms in individual parishes in the eighteen-twenties, and throughout the country after 1834, were very much overdue:[9]

In the Year 1817, there were fifteen Bastard Children supported entirely by the Parish of Bingham, at a weekly expense of £1. 14. 6. Now, the sum of 2s. only is paid weekly by the Parish towards the support of Two Bastard Children.

In dealing with this very real problem the parish officers had to work principally under the acts of 1575–6, 1609–10, 1627, 1732–3 and 1743–4. There are, however, a number of other acts also relating to bastardy. The principal legislative enactments are dealt with below.

In early statutes bastardy is considered as affecting questions of inheritance; there is no question of bastardy among the populace[10] until 1575–6,[11] when a vagrant act makes provision, *inter alia*, for punishing the mothers and fathers of bastards. Two justices, one of the quorum, are given power to deal with it as an 'offence against God and man'. They are to make an order, and if it is not performed to commit the offender to jail until the next sessions unless he gives security to appear, when a fresh order shall be made or the old one confirmed. This act remained the basis of the law until 1834. This act also orders that in every shire shall be at least one house of correction.

By an act of the next reign, passed in 1609–10,[12] any lewd woman having had a bastard chargeable *may* be sent to the house of correction for a year. If she offends again she *shall* be sent to the house of correction until she gives securities for good behaviour. These acts had much the effect one would have supposed in encouraging abortion and infanticide. By an act of 1623–4,[13] to kill a bastard is murder, and one witness at least is necessary to prove a still birth. The preamble 'that many lewd women do...' suggests that the murder of unwanted children must have been fairly common.

In 1627[14] the powers of the justices are extended, so that hence-forward all justices may carry out the provisions of the act of 1576. Evidently the tightened administration of the law causes offenders to abscond, so it is ordered in 1662[15] that when the mother and father of a bastard run away the overseers on the order of two justices may seize their goods. It seems that women then keep quiet about their condition, hoping to dispose of the child quietly, and fathers often dispute paternity, so a law of 1732–3[16] ordains that a woman pregnant with a bastard child is to declare herself so, and to name the father. Next, apparently the parish of settlement uses every means to secure that in future bastards shall be born in someone else's parish. The next act, one of 1743–4,[17] lays down the rule that a bastard born in a place where the mother is not settled is to have its mother's settlement. The mother is to be punished by public whipping.

Later acts relate principally to bastards born in hospitals and workhouses, etc., and do not affect the main principles of the law.

Until about 1750 it seems that the parish officers dealt with the problem without much fuss. It seems that few cases were brought before quarter sessions.[18] The most general method was that of making the father responsible by bond for the keep of his child: another similar practice was to allow him to pay a lump sum in discharge of all responsibility.

With the sudden rise in the illegitimate birth rate after the 1750's the problem thrust itself forcefully upon the overseer and his fellow-members of the village community, through the increased and increasing demands it caused upon their pockets.[19] This problem and the financial stress it caused were equally general in agricultural and in industrial districts.

The methods of dealing with it in the countryside varied very considerably, perhaps with the views of the overseer, or the tradition of the village. The problem to decide was whether it would be better to force the putative father to marry the woman before the child's birth,[20] leaving it to the father to provide for his offspring, or whether to force the father to pay for the child's keep under an order from justices or quarter sessions. The advantage of the former method was a saving in court fees, transport, meals, and accommodation at an inn for at least three people, but the disadvantage was that the whole family might eventually 'come on the parish'. The advantage of the latter was that the putative father could be imprisoned or frightened by the threat of imprisonment, or punished by having his recognisances estreated.[21]

The indemnity offered might be either a lump sum paid down, a lump sum in instalments, an agreement to pay a regular contribution to the mother through the parish officers, or one, enforced by bond, to undertake the maintenance of the child himself. Another option was available when the father came from a different parish—a hasty wedding to secure the legitimacy of the child (since all children born more than a month after marriage were legitimate). This would ensure its settlement in the father's parish, and then in due course could follow the deportation of the family.[22] So some parishes appear regularly as suitors at quarter sessions, others not at all. There is indisputable evidence in the Poor Law Report of 1834 of 'a vast number of marriages in which the woman is obviously pregnant'. There is also some contemporary literary evidence, particularly in the works of Crabbe:[23]

> Next at our altar stood a luckless pair,
> Brought by strong passions and a warrant there;
> By long rent cloak, hung loosely, strove the bride,
> From every eye, what all perceived, to hide.
> While the boy-bridegroom, shuffling in his pace,
> Now hid awhile and then exposed his face;

By far the most entertaining reference to this not very edifying topic is one made by *P. P. Clerk of this Parish* in Pope's parody of Bishop Burnet. He describes his own experience in this matter, and the providential way in which it turned out to his benefit after all:

A week after I had a base-born child laid unto me;...Thus was I led into sin by the comeliness of Susanna Smith, who first tempted me and then put me to shame....I humbled myself before the Justice, I acknowledged my crime to our curate; and to do away mine offences and make her some atonement, was joined to her in holy wedlock....

How often do those things which seem unto us misfortunes, redound to our advantage! For the Minister (who had long look'd on Susanna as the most lovely of his parishioners) liked so well of my demeanour, that he recommended me to the honour of being his Clerk....

Clear evidence of pressure being brought upon the man or a bribe being offered to persuade him to marry the woman concerned is found in such entries as these from Gnosall, Staffs.:

1740 Nov. 4th.   It is also agreed at the said Vestry to allow Hannah Parton £3. 8s. od. provided she solemnizes marriage with Richd Worrall.

Again in 1780 a putative father succeeded in extorting £5. 5s. od. from the parish officers as his price for taking the woman off their hands:

1780. A Journey with Ann fox to Father her Childe her examination a Warrant and Expenses	o.	5.	o
for tacking Jn Edge in to Custerty is Expences & a Journey to Justice pd a man for tacking Care of him all night	o.	8.	o
A Journey to Eccleshall with Jn Edge & expences	1.	18.	6
Jn Edge for a porshun	5.	5.	o
Mr. Low for Marring Edge	o.	5.	o
pd Sam Adderley	o.	2.	6
pd Misses Adderley for our expences & hale for the Ringers	o.	9.	o

If one supplements the information in parish records by reference to the proceedings of quarter sessions it is clear that in the majority of cases an order was made, a few men were 'discharged having married the woman',[24] a few 'discharged' with no reason given, or 'discharged, not being the father', and a very few 'discharged, the woman not proving to be with child'.[25] It seems strange that in the majority of such cases the unfortunate person named as putative father, if he was unable to find securities, had to spend a month or so in gaol waiting for the sessions. When a child was born, the overseers usually paid the amount of the order, whether or not they succeeded in extracting it from the father. Men were, as a general rule, forced to find securities after the order had been made, but women were seldom bound over to perform their share, i.e. to pay sixpence a week if they did not nurse the child.[26] Again, only rarely were women punished for lewdness as the law directed if they had a second illegitimate child chargeable to the parish,[27] and such instances as do occur were almost all before 1750. Occasionally a case was dismissed on the ground that the woman was too lewd to be trustworthy in her evidence.

But the vast majority of bastard births have no record save an entry in the baptismal register. What happened in these cases one can but conjecture. Did the father rather sheepishly but without protest either make a regular payment or pay a lump sum to the parish authorities?[28] Did a gentleman's agreement between father and overseer suffice, or did the girl's father keep the child in order to avoid advertising his daughter's shame? As to shame it seems that bastardy was looked upon very much as a matter of course towards the end of the eighteenth century. According to the Report of 1832–4, among the evil effects of the Speenhamland System[29] was that

the daughters of some farmers and even landowners have bastard children, who keep their daughters and children with them, and regularly keep back their poor rate to meet the parish allowance for their daughters' bastards.[30]

Did the mother often refuse to filiate the child? If so, may one judge that when the mother did filiate pressure had been brought upon her to induce her to do so? How far are records lacking because the question was settled quietly before two justices? All these and a great many other questions arise, and not even examination of parish and quarter session records can determine them.

From our own inquiries in Nottinghamshire alone it seems that there was a good deal of sympathy shown by the overseers. It is noticeable that, when parishes took advantage of the powers given[31] to appoint paid assistant overseers, the system was markedly tightened up, and more cases appeared before the bench, whether because of the efficiency of the professional parish officers, or by reason of the increasing pressure of the rates, it is impossible to say.

Beyond this there is a tantalising mass of disconnected references well worth following up. Such are settlement certificates for

...singlewoman and the child or children wherewith she is now pregnant,

removal orders or settlement examinations of women mentioning that they have with them their bastard(s), orders for the apprehension of putative fathers, etc., and above all, bonds of indemnification[32] given by them to the parish. Such volumes as the registers, churchwardens', constables' and overseers' accounts are especially informative. The vestry minutes often contain agreements for the care of bastards, and the lists of apprentices and lists of newcomers to the parish are useful too.[33]

Settlement certificates, examinations, and removal orders in bastardy cases do not differ a great deal from the usual formulae. Bonds of indemnification take some such form as the following:

July 21st 1747. KNOW ALL MEN BY THESE PRESENTS that I Abraham Atkinson of Cambridge in the County of Cambridge apothecary am held and firmly bound unto William Smith and Francis Tipping Churchwardens of the Parish of Littlebury in the County of Essex and William Kent and George Buck Overseers of the Poor of the said Parish in the Sum of fifty Pounds of good and lawfull money of Great Britain....

The Condition of this Obligation is such that Whereas Mary Russell of the parish of Littlebury aforesaid Singlewoman was lately gotten with Child by John Atkinson Son of the above bounden Abraham Atkinson as she the said Mary Russell hath upon her Oath affirmed which Child when Born will be a Bastard and Likely to become Chargeable to the said Parish of Littlebury. If Therefore the above bounden Abraham Atkinson his heirs Executors or Administrators Do and shall from time to time and at all Times hereafter fully and clearly acquit Discharge Save harmless and indemnified as well the above named William Smith and Francis Tipping Churchwardens of the said Parish of Littlebury and William Kent and George Buck Overseers of the Poor of the said Parish and their Successers for the time being and every of them...of and from all and all manner of Costs Charges and Expences whatsoever which shall or may in any wise at any time hereafter arise happen come grow or be imposed upon them or any of them or they or any of them be Compelled to Lay out Disburse or expend for or by reason or means of the Birth Maintenance or bringing up of the said Bastard Child....Then this Obligation to be Void.

(f) APPRENTICES AND APPRENTICESHIP INDENTURES

Apprentices were of two classes, those apprenticed by voluntary consent without the intervention of parish officers,[1] and parish apprentices bound by the parish authorities.[2] Apprenticeship of either sort was recognised as giving a legal settlement.[3] Here, of course, we are mainly concerned with apprentices in the second class. Until 1757 it was required that apprentices should be bound by deed indented (indenture), but in 1757–8 binding by any deed properly stamped was recognised as legally binding. Sometimes before this date, and often after, a great many poor children were bound by agreement entered in the vestry minute books or the parish register.

By the eighteenth century the old rules as to apprenticeship were disappearing, and the 'apprenticeship' often consisted solely of a fiction convenient in disposing of a pauper child, generally in someone else's parish so that he might gain a settlement there. A girl e.g. could be bound apprentice to a day labourer 'to learn the art and mystery of a housewife', or a boy to a clergyman 'to learn the art and science of husbandry'. Mr Cutlack's[4] admirable work gives an analysis of the 216 apprenticeship bonds executed at Gnosall, Staffs., from 1691 to 1816. Of the 178 children apprenticed within the parish seven were to tailors, three to shoemakers, two to cordwainers, one each to masters of nine other trades, and 157 to 'husbandry' and 'housewifery'. Similarly, from 1817 to 1835, 240 children were apprenticed, but only ten to trades properly so called.

We are obliged to our friend, Mr H. E. Poole, with whom we

conducted an investigation on this point into the unpublished
records of the parish of Doveridge, Derbys., for permission to
quote here our joint findings. The Doveridge chest contains
ninety-two indentures, 1699–1818. Sixty-five of these are for
males, twenty-seven for females. Particulars of the parish in
which the master was domiciled are available for eighty-six of the
indentures, and details of the master's trade are included in
ninety. Sixty-four of the children were apprenticed in their own
parish, and twenty-two in twelve other (generally neighbouring)
parishes. Most of the children apprenticed in their own parish
were indentured to learn husbandry or housewifery (i.e. presumably, they were used as farm labourers or domestic servants),
but those apprenticed elsewhere were indentured to a variety of
trades, mostly, it appears, fairly skilled. The trades chosen
include 'chape filing', bucklemaking, tailoring, cordwaining,
weaving and framework knitting, breeches making, the making
of hats, etc. One child was even apprenticed to a surgeon. If the
Doveridge documents are really typical, which we very much
doubt, it appears that the apprenticeship system of the eighteenth
century was by no means so black as it is sometimes painted.

When the parish wanted to bind a poor child within its own
limits the master was compellable[5] to receive him, quite irrespective of his own wishes. In some parishes fines paid for excusal
furnished a regular and substantial revenue. In some parishes,
again, apprentices were allocated to the householders in rotation,
or by 'house row'.

This method is illustrated by the following extract from the
title of a volume in the parish chest of Meare, Som.:

...with an account of all the lands in the Parish of Meare annexed
together in Lots to the value of £50 each for the purpose of taking
Poor Children Apprentices. 1813.

In other parishes apprentices were drawn for in a kind of
parochial raffle, unlike other lotteries in that the winners were
those who drew the blanks. This method was in vogue at Gnosall,
Staffs., in 1739:

It is also agreed at this time that Rich[d] Beckitt and John Williams
of Gnosall Quarter Thomas Haines and Joseph Podmore of Cowley
Quarter Edward Bates and William Davies of Moreton Quarter John
Tomkisson and Richard Hardin of Knightley Quarter within the Parish
of Gnosall to draw ticketts for two Parish Apprentices being accos-
tomery in the said Parish.

XIII. An Apprenticeship Indenture of a pauper child of seven to a Lancashire millowner, from Chelmsford, Essex, 1799.

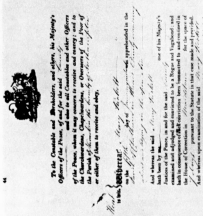

44

XIV. A Vagrant Pass from Chatham, Kent, to Newark, Notts., 1819. (See p. 212.)

XV. A Settlement Certificate from Basford, Notts. to Arnold, Notts., 1760. (See p. 201.)

The only requirements were that the indentures should be executed by the child, his parents, the master, and the parish officers, and allowed by two justices. Sometimes the parents objected and the records of this same parish give a good idea of the method which was adopted in dealing with such recalcitrants:

Aug. 5th, 1754. Ordered at this time that William Botts pay be taken of he refusing to let his son go out as an apprentice.

Sept. 29th 1754 agreed then with John Williams of Wolverhampton Locksmith to take John Bott son of William Bott apprentice till he shall attain the age of one and twenty.

Oct. 2nd 1754. William Bott to be allowed sixpence per week towards the maintenance of his Children.

Later records are particularly illuminating as to the manner in which apprentices were allocated. In 1800 it was ordered that

Every Substantial Householder to have an Apprentice or two according to the Extent of their premises.

Again it seems the householders were selected by ballot. In 1801 the vestry meeting

unanimously Agreed to Dispose of the remaining part of the Apprentices which Incumber the Parish.

Yet again in 1829 it was agreed that householders should be excused taking apprentices upon a uniform levy of two shillings in the pound of their assessment.

Evidently the apprentices were not wanted, and one cannot be surprised that occasional instances of ill-usage of apprentices are met with. But in the parish referred to Mr Cutlack has found but few cases of ill-treatment among the 418 children apprenticed 1691–1835: in only one instance was the case so clearly proved that the justices cancelled the indentures.

Probably parental allegations of ill-usage were often made, but rarely substantiated. E.g. at Sutton Bonington, Notts., the overseers' accounts for 1800 have the entry:

1800 May 12. Going to Quorndon about Baxter Bosworth
when he said he was not used ill 3s. 6d.

Dr Marshall[6] points out: 'Our actual knowledge of the pauper apprentices is scanty because an ignorant child of twelve, separated from its friends, and absolutely at the mercy of its master, had no real chance of making its wrongs known.' It is fairly certain that pauper children bound out at the cheapest rate to unwilling masters would assuredly be no better treated than children bound out by their friends upon the payment of substantial premiums. And the records of ill-usage among ordinary apprentices are horrifying in the extreme. For details of the abuses of pauper apprenticeship at its worst one must consult the records of the mills in manufacturing towns and villages which imported pauper children by the wagon load from London, contracting to take 'one idiot in every twenty', where the conditions were indescribably horrible, and where the graveyards are crammed with scores of the bodies of these unfortunates who were literally worked to death. No less a person than Karl Marx[7] said with some justice:

A great deal of capital...was yesterday in England the capitalised blood of children.

The due performance of all the covenants in the indenture was enforced by the execution of a bond. Such an agreement of 1675 from Gnosall, Staffs., runs (after a Latin bond proper of very much the same style as that in the bastardy undertaking quoted above):

The Condition of this obligation is such that if the above bounden George Podmore his heirs executors & Administrators shall observe performe fulfill & keepe all & singular the covenants and Agreements as they are specified & contayned in a paire of Indentures betwixt Thomas Forster & Abraham Swanne of the one parte and George Podmore on the other and beareing coequall date with these presents, as they ought to be observed performed fulfilled and kept, that then this obligation to be void and of none effect, or els to stand and continue in full force power and vertue.

Entries in the vestry books generally take some such form as these from Harefield, Middlesex:

November the 11th 1717 for binding out Mary Winfield apprentice to Uxbridge and Elizabeth Stanley apprentice to Robert Trunly of Harrefield   £1. 0. 0
spent at thomas Loids when the agreement was made to put Milton prentes   2
1722 pd when Margaret Iley was bound prentes Charges and indentures 19s. 1d. gave her in money   £5. 0. 0

We refer elsewhere[8] to the provision of an outfit of clothes with each apprentice, and the solemn entering up in the parish book of an inventory of the clothes supplied. Another later inventory is this from Buxted, Sussex:

1790   A gown for Sundays. A pair of Stais, a Chatt Apron A Sunday Handkerchief too pair of Stockings a pair of pattens a Linsusy Coat and some Stuf for Caps. A tuct apron.

Apprentices gained a settlement after forty days' service. The desire of the parish officers to use this fact is illustrated by this agreement of 1787 from the parish book of Gnosall, Staffs.:

Ordered that Mary Dudson be placed out as an apprentice to John Carter of Walsall-Wood, and that Mr. Reynolds Overseer of Gnosall Quarter do pay him when the said Mary Dudson shall have gained a settlement under her indentures of Apprenticeship the sum of Fifty shill^{gs} and Sixpence.

Before about the middle of the seventeenth century indentures often follow the archaic wording handed down from another form of apprenticeship, and from much earlier times (cards, dice or other unlawful games he shall not play; taverns or alehouses he shall not haunt or frequent; fornication he shall not commit; matrimony he shall not contract . . . etc. Later equally stereotyped and meaningless (but much less picturesque) phraseology is adopted (see Fig. XIII). Mr Emmison[9] prints for comparison two indentures from Eaton Socon, Beds., of 1618 and 1635 respectively, the earlier of which is reproduced below:

This Indenture Witnesseth that Willyam Gore and Gawin Wright Churchwardens of Eaton Soocon in the Countie of Bedd' and Richard Gery Esquire Andrew Spencer gent and Clement Day yeoman Overseers chosen and appoynted for the poore of Eaton Soocon aforesaid Have put Agnes Parson the daughter of Michael Parson of Eaton Soocon aforesaid in the said Countie of Bedd' Whitt tawer to Henry Cooper of Eaton aforesaid in the said Countie of Bedd' Bricklayer and Elen Cooper his now wife to learne to Sowe And with them after the manner of Apprentice to serve from the Second day of Februarij last past before the date hereof unto the full end and terme of Nyne yeares from thence next following fully to be compleate and ended. During which terme the said Apprentice hir said Maister and Dame faithfully shall serve their secrettes keepe their lawfull Comandementes every where gladly doe, And in all thinges as a faithfull Apprentice she shall behave hirselfe towardes hir said Mr. and Dame, and all theirs. During the said terme AND the said Maister and Dame, their said Apprentice in the same Art of Sowing which she the said Elen nowe useth by the best meanes she can shall teach, or cause to be taught, And in due manner to Chastice hir, fynding to their said Apprentice meate Drinck Apparrell, lodging, and all other necessaries, as well in sicknes as in health during the said terme And at the end of the said terme to give and Deliver or cause to be given and Delivered unto their said Apprentice Double or two sutes of Apparrell, as well in lynnen woollen hose and shooes....
IN witnes whereof the parties above named to theis Indentures interchangeably have put their handes and seales the Fift day of March Anno Domini 1617

Other odd references to parish apprentices occur in an act of 1765–6,[10] which authorises the apprehension and imprisonment of runaway apprentices. The act of 1766–7[11] referring to London only, which we have already quoted concerning the apprenticing which 'disturbs the peace of domestic life, checks marriage, and discourages industry', also says that the fees usually paid 'are by no means adequate to the procuring such masters and mistresses as are fit and proper', and raises the rate to not less than £4. 2s. 0d. It also orders the keeping of a register of parish apprentices according to a set form.[12] Similar regulations for the country at large were made in 1778, 1782 and 1802.[13] Provisions for protecting apprentices from ill-usage are to be found in acts of 1746–7, 1792 and 1792–3.[14]

The principal apprenticeship records one may expect to find are, of course, the indentures and the bonds. These last occur both as loose documents and as copies entered in parish registers, overseers' account books, or vestry minute books. Claverley, Salop, has a 'list of parishioners liable to take [i.e. to be saddled with] parish apprentices', 1773. Edgmond, Salop, has a list of apprentices, 1783–1820, in the vestry minute book, 1802–1848. Registers of apprentices, mostly under the 1802 act, are more rarely met with. Billinghay, Lincs., has one, 1813–33, and they are found e.g. at Crowhurst, Surrey, Shifnal, c. 1798–1824, Albrighton, 1811–35, Hodnet, 1802–29, and Great Wollaston, 1818–36 (all in Salop). Gnosall, Staffs., has two, 1804–21 and 1821–35, and Hartlip, Kent, one of 1822. Tolland, Som., has one of 1802–34, and in this last county there are others at Bath St Michael, 1802–15, Bishop's Lydeard, 1741–65, Bleadon, 1809–32, Chilton Polden, 1803–33, and Meare, 1792–1810, with a Memorandum: That none are bound out since.

(g) IN-RELIEF AND OUT-RELIEF—WORKHOUSES

According to Blackstone[1] the Elizabethan poor law imposed upon the overseers a dual duty—that of supporting those who were unable to work, and that of providing work for such as were unable to find it for themselves. This latter was, in his view, 'most shamefully neglected'. He expounds the duty and discourses upon the excellent results which would follow from its proper performance:

To find employment for such as are able to work...by providing stocks of raw materials to be worked up at home...might perhaps be more beneficial than accumulating all the poor in one common work-house;

a practice which tends to destroy all domestic connexions, (the only felicity of the honest and industrious labourer)...whereas (if the statute were applied as originally intended)...the most indigent peasant would go through his task without a murmur, if assured that he and his children, (when incapable of work through infancy, age, or infirmity), would then, and then only, be entitled to support from his opulent neighbours.

In the act of 1601 the only reference to buildings was that in s. 5 to 'convenient houses of habitation or dwelling' and 'necessary places of habitation' for the impotent poor. The section provided that more families than one might be placed in one cottage or house, but made no provision whatever for the erection of a building solely for the use of those who were to be set to work. This was presumably the reason why the employment provisions of the 1601 act were so much less observed than were its eleemosynary clauses. The inconsistency was pointed out as early as 1646, where an author complained[2] that although the poor were punished as beggars for not working, there were actually no places where they could be employed. He suggested as a remedy the erection of workhouses in suitable places. After the act of 1662,[3] which allowed the division of parishes into townships, and so made it more difficult for these smaller areas to provide employment for their able-bodied poor, the proposal was made again. In 1663 it was put forward by Sir Matthew Hale in his *Discourse touching provision for the Poor*. Hale's work is most well worth consultation by all who are interested in the history of the poor law. We quote below from the reprint issued in 1927:[4]

That the Justices of the Peace at the Quarter Sessions do set out and distribute the Parishes in their several Counties into several Divisions, in Each of which there may be a Work-house for the common use of the respective Divisions, wherein they are respectively placed, *viz*: one, two, three, four, five, or six Parishes to a Work-House, according to the greatness or smallness, and accommodation of the several Parishes.

In 1687 it was suggested again by Thomas Firmin in *Some proposals for the employing of the Poor*. In 1704 Defoe attacked all such proposals in his celebrated pamphlet *Giving Alms no Charity*, in which he pointed out quite reasonably that the products of workhouse industry would compete unfairly with those of free labour. However, the move towards workhouse erection continued. Probably it was based very largely on the same punitive and deterrent motions which led to the passing of the 1696–7 act.

In 1695–6 a special act of Parliament was passed authorising the building of a workhouse in Bristol, and this was followed by similar acts for Exeter, Hereford, Colchester, Hull, Shaftesbury, Sudbury, Gloucester etc., and King's Lynn, for Worcester, 1703, Plymouth, 1706–7, Norwich, 1711, and so on.[5] Rural parishes began to set up workhouses of their own. Thaxted, Essex, had one in 1711, and the overseers' accounts, still extant, give a good deal of information about it. Eaton Socon, Beds., had one in 1719; and by the seventeen-thirties workhouses were quite general even in rural districts, and traces of them belonging to this period are often met with. Blagdon, Som., has e.g. in its chest its original workhouse conveyance of 1732.

After these experimental measures, which were said to have had a most excellent result, if not in setting the poor at work, at any rate in deterring persons from applying for relief except in cases of the direst necessity, a general act was passed in 1722–3.[6] Other special acts incorporating for workhouse purposes special hundreds, cities, or groups of parishes continued to be passed for a great many years. The 1722–3 act provided that the overseers and churchwardens with the consent of the majority of the inhabitants might purchase or hire buildings, and contract with any person for lodging, keeping, maintaining, and employing the poor. Persons refusing to enter the workhouse were to lose all their title to relief. There were also provisions for the voluntary union of parishes which were too small to support their own workhouses, and for the parish officers of one parish to contract with those of another for the management of the poor. According to Sir Frederick Morton Eden this led to a great improvement in poor-law administration. At any rate the expenditure upon poor relief fell markedly, despite a considerable increase in the population.[7]

With the reign of George III, there begins a series of measures designed by philanthropists to mitigate the harshness of the existing laws. Several of these acts have been referred to elsewhere. By far the most important of them was the famous Gilbert's Act of 1781–2, the foundation of many important items in modern poor-law administration, including especially provisions for the reformed workhouse.

Before considering Gilbert's Act in some little detail we may consider one or two typical series of parish records concerning workhouses before and after 1782, and deal with the one outstanding literary reference.

Child's Ercall, Salop, has the articles of association of several parishes for the maintenance of a workhouse (1735). Chiddingstone, Kent, has the workhouse rules of 1740. At Cleobury Mortimer, Salop, is a list of the parish stock in a book (1770–1819) containing

an inventory of the goods, cattle, and chattels, and also the stock at the Workhouse belonging to the parish of Cleobury Mortimer.

Crofton, in the same county, has its workhouse accounts, 1787–1836. Detailed dietaries of the workhouse inmates are sometimes met with, e.g. at Clifton, Beds., 1821. The parish books of Sutton Bonington, Notts., contain bills for showing the purchases made for the paupers' Christmas dinner in the little workhouse in 1800. (During the rest of the year the accounts record purchases of 'turnopes', 'taters', etc., with occasionally a cheese. For the Christmas festivities, an extra item appears in a sheep's head.) The first five overseers' account books of St Paul's, Bedford, contain numerous inventories of workhouse furniture and goods. From 1774 a 'lace room' is mentioned. Other Bedfordshire inventories reveal that it was usual to employ the poor in pillow lacemaking. Nevertheless it is not safe to assume that any building described in the parish accounts as a 'workhouse' was properly so called. A great many were poorhouses pure and simple.

The first edition of Crabbe's *Village* appeared in 1783, the year after Gilbert's Act. Presumably it describes some village workhouse near his cure of Aldeburgh, Suff., about the time when Gilbert's scheme was being widely discussed. Crabbe's strongest criticisms are directed at the horrible, higgledy-piggledy conglomeration of idiots, children, sick poor, senile cases, unmarried mothers, and unemployed which prevailed in the smaller houses, where the small scale of the establishments made proper classification utterly impossible:[8]

> Theirs is yon house that holds the parish poor—
> Where walls of mud scarce bear the broken door;
> There, where the putrid vapours, flagging, play,
> And the dull wheel hums doleful through the day;
> There children dwell who know no parents' care;
> Parents, who know no children's love, dwell there!
> Heartbroken matrons on their joyless bed,
> Forsaken wives, and mothers never wed;
> Dejected widows with unheeded tears,
> And crippled age with more than childhood fears;
> The lame, the blind, and, far the happiest they!
> The moping idiot and the madman gay.

To appreciate the full horror of the position it is necessary to remember that the 1722–3 act authorised the overseers to apply the workhouse test, i.e. to refuse any relief to those poor who declined to enter such an institution as that described above. Fortunately the justices continued to discharge their duties perhaps with more humanity than efficiency, and they were generally ready to hear appeals against the refusal of out-relief by the overseers, as the following mandate (Burton Joyce, Notts., 4 May 1719) shows. This is dated before the 1722–3 act, but it could easily be matched from the period following it:

To the Constable and Churchwarden and others, the Overseers
of the poor of the Parish of Burton Joyce.

Greeting:

Whereas complaint hath been made unto me Sir Thos. Parkyns Bart., one of his Majesty's Justices of the Peace...that Geo. Merston of your town who appears to Me to be an Inhabitant legally settled in your s^d Parish is in Great need and Poverty and likely to perish for want of Employment to maintain himself and family.

These are therefore in His Majesty's Name to command you the Ch. Warden etc.,...to set ye said George Merston on work or pay unto him Two shillings weekly forth and out of your Publick Levey for ye use of ye Poor made...etc....otherwise to come before me and show cause to the contrary. Hereof faill not at your peril.

From the purely legal point of view there was little improvement in the condition of the poor until Gilbert's Act.[9] The member for Lichfield had a genuine love of the poor and concern for their welfare. His act was an adoptive one, requiring the consent of two-thirds of the ratepayers in number and value. Parishes were allowed to unite for carrying out its provisions (so forming the 'Gilbert Unions', some of which acted as the bases of unions under the 1834 act, and therefore lasted into our own time). Parishes adopting its provisions were incorporated, they were allowed to employ paid guardians, and the justices were given more extensive powers of supervising the whole system. So far the act was certainly in the direction of efficiency as well as humanity. At Smalley, Derbys., however, the vicar entered in his register in 1785 a note that the standing overseer appointed was 'the meanest and most hard-hearted wretch in the parish', and if such men were appointed it was well that they should be subject to some control. The establishment in which the poor were to be maintained was however to be a poorhouse, not a workhouse; the sick, the infirm, the aged, and young children were to be its occupants.

There were, however, provisions for 'boarding out' young children with 'reputable persons' in or near the parish, and 'poor persons able and willing to work' were not to be brought into the poorhouse. The guardian was to agree with an employer to find them employment, making up from the rates the deficiency of their wages. This was the first enactment authorising monetary assistance to the able-bodied.[10]

(h) THE LAST DAYS OF THE OLD SYSTEM

SPEENHAMLAND. This provision and the later developments which followed from it had a very serious effect upon the morals of the labourers. 'They considered themselves as pensioners on the rates, upon which they believed they had a legal claim, irrespective of the amount and the value of their work.'[1] Naturally the rates rose apace. In 1795 the act already noted[2] modified the settlement law in the labourer's favour, and in 1795, too, occurred the celebrated meeting of the Berkshire justices at the George-and-Pelican Inn at Speenhamland, which gave its name to the ill-advised Speenhamland System. Following the lines suggested by Gilbert's Act the magistrates, touched by the distress prevalent in their area, devised a scale of relief based upon the size of the family and the price of bread. The first and last only of thirteen sets of figures are:[3]

INCOME SHALL BE FOR:	MAN	SINGLE WOMAN	MAN AND WIFE
When the gallon loaf is 1s.	3s.	2s.	4s. 6d.
When the gallon loaf is 2s.	5s.	3s.	7s. 6d.

MAN, WIFE AND

1 CHILD	2 CH.	3 CH.	4 CH.	5 CH.	6 CH.	7 CH.
6s.	7s. 6d.	9s.	10s. 6d.	12s.	13s. 6d.	15s.
10s.	12s. 6d.	15s.	17s. 6d.	20s.	22s. 6d.	25s.

i.e. 'so in proportion as the price of bread rises or falls (that is to say) 3d. to the man and 1d. to every other of the family, on every penny which the loaf rises above a shilling'.

The meeting was originally intended to issue an Assize of Wages. The first resolution stated that it was unanimously agreed 'that the state of the poor does require further assistance than has been generally given them'. But when the remedy was discussed, it was decided that it was 'not expedient for the Magistrates to...grant assistance by regulating the wages of Day Labourers according to the Statutes...'. The justices 'recommended' farmers and others to increase labourers' wages 'in proportion to the price of provisions' and unanimously resolved 'That they will in their several divisions make the following calculations and allowances...for the relief of poor and industrious men and their families'. (Then follows a statement which is summarised in the table above.)

It will be seen that the basis of the calculation was that a man could not live upon less than the equivalent of two and a half or three loaves a week, and that his wife and each of his other dependents were estimated to consume a loaf and a quarter or a loaf and a half.[4] The arrangement was felt to be just, in a period of low wages and enormous corn-prices, and the Berkshire example was followed throughout the country. It never received statutory recognition, though there was a popular notion that it had done, and tables showing the provisions of the 'Speenhamland Act of Parliament' were displayed in alehouses from one end of the country to the other for the edification of their clientèle. At Drayton, Som., a printed copy of the scale is pasted on the cover of the overseers' accounts, 1819–31, at North Perrott and at Preston Plucknett in the same county the scale is copied inside the cover of the overseers' book.

WHITBREAD'S BILL AND THE 1794–5 ACT. Whitbread in 1796 brought in a bill based upon the Speenhamland arrangement 'for regulating wages according to the price of provisions', but this was thrown out by the House. Pitt objected to any method savouring of the mediaeval assize of bread and assize of wages as departing too far from the reigning principles of *laissez faire*. Instead he brought in a scheme of his own in an enormous measure of one hundred and thirty clauses, providing, *inter alia*, for the provision of a gift to each poor person of 'a cow, a pig, or some other useful domestic animal'. This, however, was fiercely attacked, and was subsequently withdrawn.

In 1796 the principle of outdoor relief to the able-bodied, already applied in limited areas by Gilbert's Act, was allowed for the whole country.[5] The old laws were said to have been found inconvenient and oppressive. Either the overseers, with the assent of the vestry, or the justices at their own discretion, were empowered to order outdoor relief without imposing the workhouse test. The net result of the resolution of 1795 and the act of 1796 was that by 1834 the Speenhamland System was at work pauperising the labourers and corrupting their employers in every county in England except Northumberland and Durham.

FURTHER ILL-JUDGED DEVICES—ROUNDSMEN. As if this were not bad enough, further complications were introduced by the roundsman system, sometimes known as 'house row'. It will be remembered that Gilbert's Act had contemplated the reserving of the poorhouse for the sick and infirm, and the finding of work outside for the able-bodied unemployed. The parish was to receive the wages and provide maintenance, handing the surplus, if any (of course there never was any!), to the pauper concerned. This system of subsidising wages spread to many parishes where the Gilbert Act had not been adopted. The pauper applied to the overseer, who sent him from house to house. On an average perhaps half his wages came from the employer, the other half from the parish. Sometimes every house in turn took a pauper for a week, sometimes farmers took one per hundred acres, or one per £20 rent. In some places the labourers were put up to auction. The dubious honour of inventing the system has been attributed[6] to Sir William Young, c. 1788, but it is quite incorrect to regard the roundsman system as originating towards the end of the eighteenth century. There are instances at Turvey, Beds. (eleven names in the account), in 1734,[7] and at Toddington, Beds., in 1758. At Caddington, Beds., in 1781, the vestry agreed to adopt the system, and the minute is worth quotation:

Memarandom Of An Agreement At A Vesstrey on the 26 Day of October 1781; for the Purpose of Imploying the Poor By Rotation; or what is Comanly Called Going the Rounds; it ware then Agreed on that when Aney Poor Person Could Not Gett imployment to mounetaine him sellf, & famely; he shall Apply to the overseer for the time Being & he shall send him to Be Imployed As follows; Evrey Person who shall Be Taxed at 10 Pounds in the Poors Rate shall Be Obliged to Imploy such Labourer one Day or Pay him for one Day According to the Directions Under written; & so Evrey Renter Respectivly for Evrey 10 Pounds so Charged in the Oversseers Tax Book; And the Payment of such Labourers shall Be As follows

To Evrey Labourer having 3 Children or more Not fit for Labour	1s	0d par Day
Evrey Labourer having one or two Children	0	10d par Day
Evry Labourer having No Child	0	8d par Day
Evrey Single Person Not a widower	0	6 par Day

Actually, of course, the system was an atrociously bad one, but its worst effects came after 1795 when the Speenhamland System was grafted upon it.

The Bedfordshire quarter sessions at Epiphany 1819[8] came to the conclusion that the system was essentially an evil one and incorporated their decision in certain *Resolutions about Roundsmen*, setting forth very truly:

That the System of Roundsmen or of paying Labourers a certain portion of the wages of their Labor out of the Parish Poor Rates, which has too long prevailed in this County, is destructive of the Moral Energies of the Laborer, and equally injurious to the Interests of the Farmer, who has a right to expect a fair and adequate portion of Labour from the Hands employed on his farm...etc....

For years after this, however, desperate parishes were adopting the system, since, bad as it was, it offered some faint hope of a reduction in the poor rate. There is a note of despair in the minute of the vestry at Kettering,[9] Northants., 2 February 1826:

That for want of a better the Round System be continued.

At Bozeat, Northants., on 12 June 1826, it was decided

1.   That every occupier of land shall employ one labourer as a Constant man for every £50 rate.
2.   Every one who employs his right number of Constant men, shall be entitled to one extra man called Roundsman for two weeks in the month (which will be equal to half the Constant men employed). These Roundsmen are to be paid 6d. per day from the Parish Book, and the remainder of his money from his employer.
3.   If any one will not employ his right number of Constant men he shall not be entitled to a Roundsman....

(Six signatures.)

THE LABOUR RATE.   Less open to objection than the round system was the Labour Rate.   Details of the operation of this in Kettering, Northants., are to be found in Dr Peyton's book. The vestry minutes contain this entry:

AT A VESTRY legally called & held this day, Wednesday, the 3rd of January 1821....

Resolved that it is the opinion of this Vestry that a labour rate for the employment of the poor who are & may be out of work during the ensuing six weeks, is expedient.

Resolved that any person employing men or boys who are upon the parish & out of work shall be exempted from the rate in the proportion of 9s./o per week for an effective, or 4/o for a non-effective man or 2/o per week for boys....

at the next vestry it was, *inter alia*...

Resolved that the Vestry do recommend to the Select Vestry to fix a price upon the men between the sum of four shillgs & nine shillings in proportion to their worth.

The method of operation is fairly clear. The parish officers calculated the cost of relieving the able-bodied unemployed for a period. Then a rate was levied to cover the amount. Each man's services had a price set on them and every ratepayer had the option of paying the rate or employing the man at the appropriate wage. His certified wage bill was compared with his assessment—if he had paid his full share of wages he was excused payment of the rate. If he had paid less, he must hand to the overseer the difference. If he had employed no pauper labour at all then he must pay the rate in full. Any surplus labourers were divided among the ratepayers in proportion to the rates paid.[10] The system, bad as it was, was better than that of roundsmen, since it was easy to ensure that every ratepayer must either employ or pay; the employer could choose his employees, and competition amongst employers would mean a fair price for the best men; while a 'non-effective' if willing and honest could be engaged at an appropriate rate for odd jobs, running errands, etc.

THE RESULTS OF THE EXPEDIENTS ADOPTED. It is still a matter of controversy how far it was the net result of all this that families grew enormously, since early and improvident marriage was encouraged. Certainly the self-respecting, independent labourer suffered unfair competition from the parish-subsidised pauper. The decent employer was heavily mulcted in rates to pay a proportion of his neighbours' wages. This was one of the final blows to the small proprietor who had not enough land to employ any labour save that of himself and his family. The masters complained that the labourers grew daily more lazy and insubordinate, since they regarded themselves as possessing a vested interest in the rates, and considered that since the employers paid only half their week's wage they were entitled to but half a week's work. In return the labourers accused the employers of harshness and injustice, and the exaction of an unreasonable amount of work. Crabbe[11] evidently thought there was some substance in the men's complaints, at any rate so far as the older labourers were concerned:

> Alternate masters now their slave command,
> Urge the weak efforts of his feeble hand,
> And, when his age attempts its task in vain,
> With ruthless taunts, of lazy poor complain.

Cottages were pulled down wholesale in order that landlords and farmers could employ the labour of men settled in neighbouring parishes. Wives of independent labourers grieved that their husbands were so unprincipled as to decline to better themselves by becoming paupers.[12] Village shopkeepers were driven out of existence by the pressure of the rates, unless they were fortunate enough to manœuvre themselves into the vestry contracts, when they might recoup themselves at the expense of ratepayers and labourers upon being chosen as the suppliers of relief in kind.[13] In many parishes the rates levied greatly exceeded the rental, and in one celebrated instance, that of Cholesbury,[14] Bucks., of ninety-eight persons settled in the parish, sixty-four were in receipt of relief. The rates exceeded twenty-four shillings in the pound, and only sixteen acres in the parish were cultivated. Paupers who were offered land rent-free refused it since they 'preferred their present situation'.

At Eaton Socon, Beds., a well-administered parish where the total population in 1831 was 2490, there were, in 1830, 135 able-bodied men in receipt of relief, and from 1821 to 1834 there were never less than 100. One can understand the exasperation of such vestries as the 'select' organisation of Gnosall, Staffs., who entered in their order book in 1826, after a long list of undeserving poor who claimed relief but were refused it because they were 'seen drunk', or 'frequent public houses', this record:

> William Owen. Wants everything. Allowed nothing.

THE REFORM OF THE POOR LAW. A whole flood of pamphleteers encouraged the ratepayers in this line of thought and in this mode of action:

> The readiest and most obvious mode of discouraging such applications, will be to lessen the Wages of those persons for whom the Parish may still be obliged to find employment...in short, let the Poor see and feel, that their Parish, although it will not allow them to perish through absolute want, is yet the hardest Taskmaster, the closest Paymaster, and the most harsh and unkind Friend that they can apply to; ...If this be not done...the labouring Classes throughout the country ...will gradually, but too surely be broken down into a fearful host of discontented Paupers, grovelling in Vice and Misery...and ever ready to trample on the Government and Institutions of their Country, and to prey on the Property of their richer Neighbours.[15]

Here and there efforts were made to deal with this state of affairs, and keen local administrators in such parishes as Southwell and Bingham, Notts., Uley, Glos., and Llangattock, Mon., adopted the workhouse test.[16] In some sixty other parishes allowances were done away with, but throughout the country at large things tended to go from bad to worse. The reformed Parliament of 1832 set up a commission to inquire into the practical operation of the poor laws. Its report dealt with scandals innumerable, and in consequence of its famous Report in 1834 the old poor-law system was abolished lock, stock and barrel.[17] The independence of the parish was taken entirely away, parishes were united into unions by order of the commissioners established by the 1834 act,[18] 'the Three Bashaws (i.e. Pashas—tyrants) of Somerset House', and the whole system was centralised under the nearly absolute control of these commissioners.

How necessary it was that some change should be made may be judged from the figures below. The first series relates to one Staffordshire parish,[19] the second to the country at large:

Poor Rate at Gnosall, Staffs.				Poor Rate in England	
	£	s.	d.		£
1681	31	18	5½	1776	1,530,800
1731	109	19	6	1785	1,912,000
1781	380	13	10½	1803	4,077,891
1816	2,727	18	3	1817	7,870,801
1818	2,576	8	1½	1824	5,736,900
1835	1,375	14	6	1832	7,036,969
				1837	4,044,741

(i) THE POOR AND THE POOR LAWS

RECORDS LEFT BY THE POOR THEMSELVES. What the poor themselves thought of the operation of the elaborate system designed for their benefit it is difficult to say. Probably very few of them were sufficiently literate to make written records, and a great proportion of such records as were made must have perished. Here and there, however, records of this type have survived—perhaps the richest of all in human interest and appeal.

We reproduce three below. Each of the first two seems to call for a little comment; it appears not unreasonable to read into the former, which dates from the time of the old poor law, a confidence that provided the applicant is respectful and willing to eat humble pie the parish will stand by him in his time of need—in very marked contrast to the tone of the second letter, which expresses in every line the fierce hatred felt by the labouring classes for the New Poor Law of 1834 and everything and everyone connected with it.

A STAFFORDSHIRE APPLICATION FOR RELIEF. This has been preserved among the parish records of Gnosall, Staffs.:

Dec. 12 1822

Jeantlemen at this time I ham In grate distress my youngest son is dad and I have another doughter vury bad and I my sealfe am hill

Sir the cofin will be 12s. and the ground with the fees will be 5s. 6d. and the shoud 3s. 6d. Sir threaugh stoping my trifle of pay I have 14s. in det for seame and if not paid by christmas I must be trioublead.

Jeantlemen I hope you will not stop my trifle of pay at this time your humble sarvant

THOS. BANNISTER.

(endorsed)

Mr. Haynes. It appears by this letter that one of Bannister's Child[n] are dead (*sic*), I think it will be necessary to allow him something towards burying it about one pound and take care of this Note

Yrs

etc

JOS. TAYLOR

14th Dec. 1822.

The Child's name is—Enoch—[and, in another hand] Gave him a Pound Note.

A POOR MAN'S OPINION OF A NORTHAMPTONSHIRE WORKHOUSE. The following most interesting document[1] is a letter addressed to John Gotch, a leading member of the old Kettering vestry, and apparently the first guardian elected by the division when the New Poor Law came into force.

March 26—1838

Sir,

After much anxiety and labor you have now nearly completed the new workhouse, and I understand that so great was your anxiety to see this place that you rose early this morning and went before Brekfast to admire the beautiful spot, in which is to be deposited the poor and needy...here are not only large and small sleeping rooms but water closets,...and a *Chappell* i think they call it, for to promote their *spiritual* as well as their temporal welfare...but when i entered the Building and saw the rooms with the closets, and beheld how you had provided for them every way, I thought why,—this building is fit for a nobleman to dwell in...there is everything that is nessecary for the inmates, and a beautiful prospect on which they can gaze, and see all the beauties of Creation putting forth their *grandeur* to charm the eye and please the heart....

Then the writer, 'Honest Jack', changes his tone and continues:

but upon enquiry I found that these were not for different characters, but for the seperating of single familyes into 4 parts and thus cruelly tearing asunder man and wife, parents and children, thus breaking those bonds that nought but death should break. Can you after so much profession of sympathy for the poor now join with the tyrannical Commissioner to tear the suckling infant from the mother's breast and seperate those who are united like David & Jonathan and whose life was bound up in each other life. . . . But how High Professors of the religion of him who went about doing good, can act like those brutal beings in the West Indies and tear asunder Fathers, Mothers, and Children the same time they read the command to love one another . . .

with a great deal more in the same strain and of some literary merit, and the ironical subscription:

Adieu for the present, when I have an opportunity I shall resume the subject

> Yours affect^ly
> HONEST JACK.

A CAMBRIDGESHIRE PLEA FOR A SETTLEMENT CERTIFICATE. To appreciate the next document, one of 1764 from the chest of St Bene't's, Cambridge,[2] it is necessary to enter into some detail concerning the man to whom it relates. Argent Keemish was born in Hants. in the seventeen-thirties. He was never apprenticed, but at the age of thirteen went into service at Winchester, where his wage eventually rose to seven guineas a year. When he left this parish for employment in Houghton, Hants., his master engaged him for a period of eight months only. Next he entered the service of Lord 'Mazarene' (the II Earl of Massareene), then a boy in his last term at Harrow, at a salary of twelve guineas a year, and accompanied his young master to Cambridge. The last forty days of his service he spent in St Bene't's parish. When his master left for foreign travel Keemish took service in Berkshire, but left before a year, after he had married a fellow-servant.

He seems to have been a man of some prudence and foresight, and to have desired to begin married life with some measure of security for his dependants. He came to the conclusion that his service in Cambridge having been with a minor, and his terms of employment elsewhere having all been less than a year, he was legally settled in Winchester. Accordingly since he had friends there he removed thither and secured employment.

After the birth of his second child the overseer swooped upon him, declared that his place of settlement was St Bene't's and demanded for their security that he obtain from the parish officers there a settlement certificate. His letter to the overseers has a good deal of pathos:

Gentlemen,

I am very Sorry to trouble you But am oblig'd by the officers of the Parish of St. Thomas which I live in at winchester. I Come here Expecting my Parish had been In the Close at winton, but they have taken my Examination & Says they have had Councell & that I Belong to your Parish by Serving Ld. Massereene. I Canot See how that Can be as he was under age & I at Boardwages, I have Sent a Coppy of the Examination [copy in Keemish's hand enclosed] that you may be Certified & I Beg of you to write to me at least in a week for if not the Parish are Determ'd to Remove me to you. I am in no fear of main-taining my family if I was where I Belong'd, for there is But 2 Children & no likelyhood of any more & my wife & all well. I once more Beg you will write as the Expense of So Long a Journy if I am oblig'd to Come must Certainly fall on the Parish whereunto I Belong.

I am Gentlemen
your Obedt & oblig'd Humble Servt.
ARGENT KEEMISH

Winton., Novr. the 20:1764

I wrote to Mr Adams bout a week ago & hoped he would have been So Good mention it to you as I Didnot Know who to write to.

St Bene't's declined to grant a certificate, Keemish was obliged to sell his effects to save the cost of transport, and to help him to face a probable period of unemployment after removal. He next appears in the books of St Bene't's in receipt of the loan of some of the workhouse belongings. In short, a respectable and self-supporting working man, of education, thrift and foresight, had been manufactured by the law of settlement into a parish pauper. No doubt numerous similar cases occurred until at last the 1795 act prohibited the removal of a pauper until he had actually become chargeable.

A SOMERSET MANIFESTO THREATENING ARMED REVOLT. Perhaps most significant of all is an anonymous document until lately preserved in the chest of Stogursey, Som.[3] It was found posted on the church door in April 1795. In plain terms it threatened the armed revolt of the labourers unless their reasonable demands were met. It was perhaps a fortunate thing for the propertied classes, if it was a great misfortune for the poor, that at this very time the Speenhamland expedient had been suggested and that it shortly came into operation over the length and breadth of the country. The Speenhamland Scale was first adopted in Berkshire in May 1795.

IX. RECORDS OF HIGHWAY MAINTENANCE

EARLY HIGHWAY RECORDS. The breakdown of the old system of highway maintenance in Tudor times. A Bedfordshire highway in 1549. The Highway Act of 1555. SURVEYORS OF HIGHWAYS. The appointment of surveyors. The duties of the surveyors. The justices' work of supervision. The highways ordinance of 1654. Highway rates. The standard of highway maintenance in the seventeenth and eighteenth centuries. The unfairness in operation of the old system. A Nottinghamshire instance of the inequity of the old system. The highways surveyor and the parish bull. Extant records of the old system. A typical series of highways accounts from Bedfordshire. THE HIGHWAYS IN LATER TIMES. Highway maintenance by pauper labour. The last attempt at preserving parochial autonomy in highway management. Surviving traces of parochial responsibility for highway maintenance.

EARLY HIGHWAY RECORDS. It appears that originally liability for the maintenance of the highways in each manor lay upon the holders of land. In mediaeval times it was indeed recognised as one of the three fundamental obligations attaching to land holding —the *trinoda necessitas*. The lord naturally cast this obligation as largely as possible upon his tenants, and enforced it through his court baron.

Long after unpaid labour upon the roads had been enforced by statute there were manors where the court baron supervised this, and amerced defaulters, e.g. on 11 September 1625 the court baron of Tunstall, Staffs., amerced John Twamlow 4s. 'because he has not worked in the high road with his wagon' (*carrus*).[1]

The first road act upon the statute book—the Statute of Winchester[2] of 1285—clearly recognises the manorial obligation and by implication imposes upon the constable, who was originally a manorial officer, the extra duties it orders. The Webbs[3] plainly consider that until perhaps 1350 or thereabouts the manorial management of highway worked not very badly, and it is clear enough from the *Canterbury Tales* and from such works as Jusserand's[4] that in the early part of the Middle Ages there was a tremendous amount of travelling about the country, on foot, on horseback, and even locally in primitive wheeled vehicles.

But in the fourteenth, fifteenth and sixteenth centuries the amount of travelling may very well have diminished. The great fairs declined in importance, and local markets were affected by the growth of towns. Landed estates were not so scattered as they had been, since proprietors had taken the opportunity to consolidate their estates afforded by the Wars of the Roses and the redistribution of property which followed them, and by the first agricultural revolution and the Great Pillage. Pilgrimages came to an end with the Reformation, and so did the perpetual journeying backwards and forwards to Rome. So though much heavy use of the roads finished it was simultaneously with the abolition of the bodies which had done something for road maintenance. Therefore the roads suffered.[5]

How bad was the condition of the roads at their worst is well illustrated by a Bedfordshire document, the depositions in a suit between the inhabitants of Upper Gravenhurst and the vicar of Shillington, in 1549, six years before the highway act of 1555. In quaint phrases one of the inhabitants insists that in refusing to attend Shillington church they might be risking their souls, but they were avoiding as great a risk to their bodies, for between the two villages

there ys twoo severall waters betwene the seyd towne of Gravenhurste and the parishe Churche of Shytlyngton and that the same waters At dyvers and manye tymes of the yeare doo vse to ryse with lande fludes soe highe that the people cannot passe over the same to theyre parisshe Churche without daunger of drownyng and cannot passe by the highe waye in the wynter season for dyrte and myre.

Various piecemeal measures were adopted in the reign of Henry VIII[6] and in that of Philip and Mary. Finally, in 1555[7], was passed the great highway act which remained the foundation of highway law for nearly three centuries. By this the manorial duty was cast upon that administrative unit rapidly growing into favour with the central authorities, the parish.[8] Every parishioner for every ploughland in tillage or pasture that he occupied within the parish, and every person keeping a draught (of horses) or plough in the parish, had to provide for four days[9] in the year 'one wain or cart furnished after the custom of the country...and also two able men with the same'. Every other householder, cottager and labourer, able to labour and being no hired servant by the year, had either to put in four days' labour or to send 'one sufficient labourer in his stead'. This figure four was changed to six by Elizabethan legislation.

SURVEYORS OF HIGHWAYS. The supervision of this 'Statute Labour' was entrusted to an unpaid surveyor of highways, nominated by the parishioners and at first set in office by the parishioners themselves, but after 1691 appointed by the justices at their special 'Highways Sessions'. These officials, sometimes known as boonmasters, overseers or supervisors of the highways, stonemen, stone-wardens, or waywardens, remained, subject to the justices' over-riding authority, in charge of highways until the general highway act of 1835.[10] In some areas they survived, with modified powers, until the last year of the nineteenth century.[11] According to another authority the last set disappeared in 1894.

The only important change made in the law relating to them for almost three hundred years was in reference to the method of their appointment. The 1555 act orders the constables and church-wardens to nominate them 'after calling together a number of the parishioners', on the Tuesday or Wednesday in Easter week; in 1662[12] the power was given to

the Churchwardens and Constables or Tythingmen with the advice and consent of the major part of the inhabitants

present in the church at the close of morning prayer on the Monday or Tuesday in Easter week. Possibly the 1662 act expired in 1670 (as a matter of fact it was to continue at any rate until the next Parliament); in this year there was a new act[13] with the original phrasing, but with the rule that surveyors should be chosen in Christmas week. In 1691[14] the function of the inhabitants and officers was restricted to furnishing to the local justices a list of holders of land and sufficient inhabitants. From this the justices appointed the surveyor. The surveyors were, after the constable, probably the officers in the parochial hierarchy most dependent upon the magistrates, and least responsible to their fellow-parishioners in vestry.

The surveyor was appointed by warrant, sent to him by the hands of the constable. His first duty was that of interviewing his predecessor in office, taking over any cash balances and learning something of the manner in which the accounts were kept, with their complicated fines, compositions and commutations. Thrice a year he had to view the roads and present their condition to the nearest justice. His duties included looking out for vehicles with more than the statutory number of horses, attending at the high-ways sessions in the neighbouring town with due attention to the 'charge' delivered thereat, the fixing of days whereon the statute labour was to be performed and the supervising of his fellow-parishioners in their unpleasant task. He had to report to the nearest justice all defaulters, and to collect all commutations and compositions. He was supposed to receive no pay whatsoever for his year's work, and consequently it is not surprising that the office was not sought after. Its acceptance was compulsory upon the person chosen, under a monetary penalty (£1 from 1555 onwards, raised to £5 in 1691). It seems that the position, probably again after the constable's the most unpopular in the whole parish hierarchy, was often passed round in rotation or by house row, so that its bearer had at any rate the consolation of thinking that when his term was expired it would be several years before his turn came round again. (Incidentally this would mean that any little practical knowledge he had acquired of the duties belonging to the position would be quite wasted when another inexperienced officer took his place at the year end.)

The justices who were supposed to supervise the whole system acted generally upon the sound old English principle of leaving well alone. Even the theorists often considered that, given occasional lopping of hedges and scouring of ditches, the roads would 'grow better of themselves'. Naturally enough their condition became more abominable every year. Here and there, however, defaulting parishes were indicted or presented and ordered in a dual sense to ' mend their ways ', and the justices compelled obedience to their orders. Such a justice's order of 1629 was transcribed into the parish register of Brotherton, Yorks.:

Brotherton Causeway. } Forasmuch as it is presented at this session that Brotherton Causeway within this west ridding is in greate ruyne and decaye for want of repayre and that it ought to be repaired in part by the inhabitants of Brotherton, it is therefore ordered that a payne of 8^1 shall be ymposed upon the inhabitants of Brotherton for the present repairs of all but an hundred yards next unto the Bridge called Ferrybridge at or before Andersmas next....

But despite spasmodic efforts of this kind no serious progress was made. Before the end of the seventeenth century the statute labourers had become a by-word for inefficiency and neglect. The cottagers did almost everything on earth except the unpaid work in which they were supposed to be engaged, and in particular used the occasion for gathering alms from the passers-by; the surveyor, if he appeared at all, often spent the time in setting the teams upon carting work in connection with his own land. Nevertheless the system lasted until the General Highway Act of 1835.[15] The farmers' supplying of teams in lieu of paying rates remained even longer and, say the Webbs,[16] is still law. At the farmers' instance a proviso was inserted in the 1835 act permitting them to continue the old system, but fortunately the clause enacted that the rate at which the piecework was to be assessed should be fixed by the justices, so that this part of the act has remained a dead letter.

Even in the seventeenth century the provisions of the law had proved quite insufficient to carry out the work. Consequently in 1654 an ordinance was passed allowing, *inter alia*, the parishioners to make a highway rate not exceeding one shilling in the pound. This of course lapsed at the Restoration, to be replaced in 1662 by a statute drawn up on similar lines, but imposing a sixpenny limit. This, however, was but a temporary measure, and it was not until 1691 that highway rates were set upon a permanent basis.

Even after this, rates were not systematically levied in a great number of parishes, but advantage was taken of a clause in the 1691 act providing that any person fined—as representing a parish—by the justices for neglect to repair the roads might be reimbursed by a levy, made upon all the inhabitants and applied by the surveyor for highway repair. By the use of this curious device the old shilling and sixpenny limits were avoided, and what was virtually a highway rate of unlimited amount could be raised in any parish.[17] In many parishes it was not worth while to levy a highway rate and the items are included in the poor rate: in 1701 at Gnosall, Staffs.:

pd Jo Aldwin being on of ye surveyors of the highways for ye
   year last 1701 for picking of stones and drinck for the
   labourers but for the time to come no drinck allowed   1. 1. 6

In most parishes the standard of highway maintenance throughout the eighteenth century fell steadily further below the modest requirements of the age. So far as the main roads were concerned, the problem was met by the introduction of the turnpike trust, with its devices for compelling those who used the road to maintain it.[18] As Mr Cossons points out, 'The statute labour system was fairly satisfactory as regards parishes where all or most of the traffic was local. The farmers and other villagers under their surveyor naturally repaired those roads useful to themselves, and in a parish with little outside traffic the standard of maintenance of each would be in approximate ratio to the amount of wear and tear to which it was subjected.'

But it was an age of rapid transition in villages and towns. Of course statute labour was still supposed to be carried out to the trustees' directions, supplementing that which they paid for from the produce of their toll bars. But statute labour was becoming more inadequate than ever. The justices had the right to apportion the statute labour between the turnpike trust and the parish. Transport was developing at an enormous rate along the great trunk roads, and unless and until such roads were turnpiked[19] their maintenance was entirely the responsibility of the parishioners, who might seldom use them. In 1655 the inhabitants of Battlesden, Beds., were indicted for failing to repair their highways and to appoint surveyors. There were some twenty householders who were legally responsible for the repair, *inter alia*, of a mile of the London-Northampton road, and a mile of Watling Street. Of course the only thing the justices could do was find them 'not guilty through insufficiency'. We reproduce (*see* Fig. 4) Mr Cossons's sketch map of the parish roads of East Markham,[20] Notts., a parish lying athwart the Great North Road.

It will be seen that of the considerable length of the Great North Road in this parish, all repairable by the inhabitants until turn-piking took place,[21] the farmers of East Markham on their journeys to market at Tuxford or East Retford used very little. One may well share Mr Cossons's sympathy with the inhabitants who tended to spend their labour and their rates upon the network of roads in the middle of the parish, and remained profoundly indifferent when 'Angus MacTavish was bogged on his way to Aberdeen, or the Member for Newcastle lost his carriage wheels in the mud of the Moor when driving down to his constituency'.

For some reason which does not seem apparent, in many parishes the care of the parish bull,[22] formerly one of the duties of the constable, became attached to the position of waywarden. A typical extract from highway accounts, illustrating this point, is given below, from the records of Sutton Bonington, Notts.:

1752 Dec. 12th. Ann Winfield gave her accompts as Surveyor of the high Ways.

Rec. by Levy.	£5.	6.	11
made of the Bull	1.	14.	3½
Laid out	6.	8.	0
Remains due to yᵉ Town	0.	13.	2½ ...

Such was the system or lack of system under which all the minor roads of the country were maintained until at any rate 1835. References to it are to be found in parish chests in such documents as waywardens' appointments, their accounts and rate books, and justices' orders to defaulting parishes. Statute labour lists are also found.

It is perhaps an indication of how unsatisfactory the system must have been, that highway accounts are much rarer than are such documents as the accounts of constables and overseers.

Probably this is not so much because they have perished as because they have never existed. In some parishes, however, the accounts were carefully preserved in order to give details of composition and statute labour for the guidance of future surveyors. Presumably most parishes had waywardens—the justices took care of that—but in a great many of them the waywardens did nothing whatever save when, by the action of the justices, they were stimulated into spasmodic bursts of activity.

A few counties seem to be fairly rich in highway accounts, perhaps because the magistrates took seriously their supervisory duties. Nottinghamshire and Surrey have a few and Kent is really rich in them, e.g. Birchington has some of 1605, Woodchurch many from 1630, Tenterden a great many from 1671, Kenardington several series from 1693, Kingsnorth a set, 1695–1704, Stelling two volumes, 1703–1829, while Wingham is fortunate in the possession of almost a complete series, 1705–1875. Blackford, Castle Cary, Som., has a set, 1728–1815, and Bicknoller in the same county has a

Composition for the teams, draught or plough, for the Estates, Labourers and other inhabitants of the Parish of Bicknoller, liable to Statute work and duty for the repair of the highways in the said Parish, 1768–1832.

In 1932 the authorities of Bedfordshire arranged an exhibition of highway records (both those properly belonging to the county and those collected for safe custody from various parish chests). The earliest volume of surveyors' accounts on view was one relating to Houghton Conquest:

The Accompts of Jno Clarke & Tho: Impey, Surveires of the Highways for the year of Our Lord 1720.

	li. s. d.
Pd for 20 poles of Bushes at 9d per pole	15. 0
Pd to Ed Childs & Richard Piercon for makeing a way in Short Lane	1. 0. 0
Pd to Tho: Beale for worke in ye Highways	0. 2. 6
Pd to Abraham Pusser for Beare for ye Labours & Teames etc.	0. 17. 0

There are five such entries of payments for beer, suggesting that each innkeeper in turn was given his share of parochial custom.

On the opposite page of the accounts is an early agreement for the commutation of statute labour. It is dated the next year, 1721, and is made between the parishioners and Henry Peace. Thereby he is allowed a twopenny rate for six years,

> conditionally that he keeps all the ways and roads within our parrish in good repair and that he shall be att the expense of all presentments or indictments whatsoever, and excuse us the subscribers to this agreement from all manner of duty, work, or service to the heighways.

The careful reader will notice an analogy between this contract and those dealing with lump sum payments by the parishioners in discharge of other parochial duties and obligations referred to above.[23]

THE HIGHWAYS IN LATER TIMES. In the early part of the nineteenth century two of the heaviest burdens the parish officials had to bear were caused by the condition of the roads and a superabundance of unemployed and largely unemployable poor. It was natural that amateur administrators should endeavour to make the two problems solve one another. Here and there where proper supervision was available the plan seems to have worked tolerably well, and pauper labour on the roads took its place with the Roundsman System and the Labour Rate[24] as a recognised method of dealing with poverty. Generally, however, one is not surprised to find that it failed alike to employ the poor and to maintain the roads. The only satisfactory feature of its operation was that it provided in some circumstances a test of destitution.

To avoid friction between overseer and surveyor the offices, each of which would have taxed the ability of a genius, were combined in one person who was rarely, of course, anything of the kind. When the Poor Law Commissioners[25] reported in 1834 they came to conclusions thus summarised by the Webbs:[26]

> ...of continuous employment at wages of paupers who were not chosen for efficiency and could not be dismissed for idleness the results were unmistakable. The dissolute idleness of the little groups of able bodied paupers on the roads became notorious. 'Whenever the Surveyor is present the men bestir themselves a little, but the moment his back is turned a man who gives himself any trouble in working more than he can help is laughed at by his companions.... Of course, under these circumstances they do anything but work.'

In the general reform of local government after 1832 parochial autonomy in the management of roads was not done away with at once, and the vestry took control of roads and surveyors. Because of natural antipathy between a Whig Parliament and a Tory magistracy, the parish even succeeded in adding to its powers in road management at precisely the same time as it was losing the last vestiges of its autonomy in other matters. Fifteen thousand 'Highway Parishes' were freed almost entirely from such control as had formerly been maintained by the justices.

Some breaches were made in the system by the Public Health Act of 1848, the Local Government Acts of 1858 and 1863, and the Highways Act of 1862. Highway Boards under the 1862 act began to spread throughout the country, but after 1880 there still remained over six thousand independent parishes. The Public Health Acts of 1872 and 1875 and the Highways Act of 1878 made it clear that in the minds of administrators the new local government area was to be neither the county nor the parish, and in 1894, when there remained still five thousand 'Highway Parishes', the Local Government Act[27] abolished both 'Highway Districts' and 'Highway Parishes'. Gradually between 1894 and 1899 the last highway parishes became merged in 'Rural Sanitary Authorities', and almost the last vestige of English parochial autonomy had been destroyed.

Even now, however, the proper method of securing the repair of a road is the indictment in a criminal court of the inhabitants of the parish in which it lies. So cumbersome is this process that its use is rare; there was however instance of it in 1921, when there was such an indictment of Ewell, Surrey. As lately as Friday, 7 January 1938, the inhabitants of Poole,[28] Dorset, went (theoretically) into the dock at Poole quarter sessions, charged with neglecting to repair a highway in their parish. They were bound over!

X. RECORDS OF OPEN-FIELD AGRICULTURE. ENCLOSURE

ENCLOSURE ACTS AND AWARDS

THE OPEN-FIELD VILLAGE. Mediaeval open fields. Subsistence agriculture. Two- and three-course rotation of crops. The common meadow and pasture. THE OPEN ARABLE FIELDS. The operation of the three-field system. The management of open-field agriculture. Shifting severalties. The origin of open-field agriculture. The development of the one-field system through the two-field system into the three-field system. THE REGULATION OF OPEN-FIELD AGRICULTURE. THE COURT BARON'S PART IN SUPERVISING AGRICULTURE. A typical series of manorial by-laws from Oxfordshire. A comparable series from Nottinghamshire. A Yorkshire set of manorial rules for the re-allotment of meadows. THE TRANSFER OF POWERS FROM THE COURT BARON TO THE VESTRY. A CAMBRIDGESHIRE EXAMPLE OF INHERITANCE OF FUNCTIONS BY THE VESTRY FROM THE COURT BARON. VESTRY REGULATION OF OPEN-FIELD AGRICULTURE. Some Hertfordshire vestry by-laws. An Oxfordshire series of vestry by-laws. The Laxton (Nottinghamshire) instance of the re-transfer of powers from the vestry back to the manorial authorities. THE VESTRY AND THE MODERNISATION OF OPEN-FIELD STRUCTURE AND TECHNIQUE. A Nottinghamshire example of the complete re-casting of open-field structure by vestry agreement. The adaptability of the open-field organisation. THE DISADVANTAGES OF THE OPEN-FIELD SYSTEM. ENCLOSURE. Early references to enclosure. Governmental attempts to check enclosure. Early controversy as to the causes and effects of enclosures. Agricultural progress. ENCLOSURE BY THE COURT BARON. ENCLOSURE BY AUTHORITY OF THE VESTRY. PARLIAMENTARY ENCLOSURES. The development of the Enclosure Act. Enclosure Acts. The General Enclosure Acts. Controversies concerning the Enclosure Movement. Enclosure Commissioners. Enclosure and depopulation. THE ENCLOSURE RECORDS OF THE PARISH CHEST AS SOURCES OF EVIDENCE UPON DISPUTED TOPICS. ENCLOSURE AWARDS. The primary purpose of enclosure awards. Other data given. The evidential value of enclosure awards. Sources of information supplementing that given in enclosure awards.

THE OPEN-FIELD VILLAGE. No English village community has survived in entirety into modern times, but there are several in which there have persisted different features of the open-field system of land use which formed the economic basis of the village of former times. It will not be difficult to abstract from three or four villages their characteristic survivals, and then to form these into a sort of composite picture of an imaginary 'typical' village of centuries ago.

It is difficult for a modern, even if he is a countryman, accustomed as he must be to an agriculture carried on by farmers whose main concern is 'what crop will sell', to carry himself in imagination into an organisation of agriculture in which the individual's primary concern was 'what crop must I (and my stock) have to eat'. Yet only three or four or more centuries ago this, or something very like it, was the farmer's first consideration. It needs no profound knowledge of agricultural technique for one to grasp the elements of the old tripartite division of ground used in agriculture into arable, meadow and pasture. The farmer needed arable land to produce wheat and rye for his bread, and barley for his livestock, his bread and his beer; he must have pasture for his stock in the summer months. He must have meadow so that in summer he could lay on one side a stock of hay for the keep of his cattle during the winter, in an age long before the introduction of roots, and still longer before the use of cake and similar winter feeds. Otherwise the whole of his stock, instead of merely the major part, must be butchered at Martinmas.

Yet the part played by each of these three classes of ground in the agrarian economy of the Middle Ages was very different from the role of its modern counterpart. Instead of the host of crops grown by a modern arable farmer there was little cultivation save that of wheat and rye as bread corn, with barley (beer corn) and the pulses. Instead of modern artificial manuring, the usual manner of allowing the soil to recover its fertility was the ancient method of fallowing. In some areas the 'rotation of crops' was simply wheat or barley, fallow: wheat or barley, fallow (the two-course rotation, and the two-field system); in others, wheat, barley, fallow: wheat, barley, fallow (the three-course rotation, and the three-field system).

No artificial meadow was available before the introduction of phosphatic manures, so that the only mowing at the farmer's disposal was the natural water meadow by the river side.[1] The pasture consisted of the arable fields in their fallow year, of the meadow land after haysel, of a great many odd scraps here and there, which were of little use for anything else, of one or two pasture closes set on one side for rearing stock, and of the unredeemed waste not yet taken into cultivation. This might be open to all the occupiers of houses or land in the village, for as much stock as they pleased (unstinted pasture), or its use might be regulated according to the number of acres, yardlands, or oxgangs in each proprietor's hands, or the number of common rights attached to his cottage or messuage (stinted pasture).

THE OPEN ARABLE FIELDS. There were other complications too. In a village where the open-field system was in operation, virtually the whole of the arable land of the place was in two or three enormous 'open' fields, properly so called (modern 'fields' are in reality not *fields* at all, but 'closes'). These again were made up of roughly rectangular blocks (furlongs, shots, flats, wongs, 'quarentenae'), and these composed of long, narrow strips (acres, selions or lands). Perhaps originally these had been something approaching a furlong (furrow-long) in length, by four poles in width, and hence contained something in the region of an acre (a day's work) of land. In between the selions there might be rather more marked furrows, serving as boundaries, or sometimes narrow boundary balks of rough grassland, and in between one furlong or field and its neighbour often there were larger strips styled meers. These formed no inconsiderable proportion of the rough pasture referred to above. And for some reason, which is difficult now to ascertain definitely, every proprietor's land was mixed up with that of every other proprietor. Every farmer had land in every field (probably at one time roughly equal amounts in each one), and at first probably the average holder had strips in every furlong. In short, the plan of the arable fields was very much after the pattern of an enormous patchwork quilt, in two or three main divisions, each roughly equal to the other(s), and each made up of smaller, roughly rectangular subdivisions. Each of these subdivisions in turn was made up of long, narrow strips, roughly ten times (say from five to twenty times) as long as they were broad.

It may be that the origin of the system was, as often alleged, a desire to give each proprietor a fair share of both good and bad land, over-wet land and over-dry, so that whatever the season might be, each cultivator could at any rate count upon a subsistence. It seems likelier that the division originated as the land was gradually taken into cultivation, the strips being shared among those undertaking the enterprise in much the same fashion as children will share a parcel of sweets or a bag of nuts: 'one for me, one for you, one for Johnny, one for me, one for you, one for Johnny' and so on. At first apparently the incumbent's glebe and the lord of the manor's demesne were composed of scattered strips interspersed among those of the other cultivators. Although the proprietors of these, as a relatively small, enlightened and influential class, early endeavoured to withdraw their strips from the general arrangement, and to secure compact blocks of land 'in severalty' in lieu thereof, there are villages where this interspersal continued until within the time of living memory.

Since, after the crop had been lifted, the land was a common pasture, either for a month or two (when winter wheat was followed by spring barley), or more than a year (when spring barley was followed by a year's fallow, and then winter wheat), common regulation and government were necessary. Every proprietor must grow the same crop as his neighbours: he could not sow before his fellows (for the stock remained on the land until the generally accepted sowing time): he must harvest his crop at the same time as they removed theirs (since after the generally agreed on harvest time, the stock were turned on to the stubble). In short the system was admirably designed to maintain a stable agriculture, but it discouraged experiment, and persons having a taste for pioneering would quickly abandon agriculture in despair, since the only way in which they could secure liberty to try out new crops and new methods was to convince a hundred per cent of their more conservatively minded neighbours that such experiments were worth trial by the community *en bloc*.

In some ways the management of the meadow was even more primitive than that of the arable land. It seems likely that originally the ownership of the scattered plots of arable changed from year to year, so that no proprietor had the same plot from one year to another. The obvious inconvenience of such an arrangement, and the impassable obstacle which it presented to any sort of permanent improvement, early caused the abandonment of the shifting of severalties so far as arable land was concerned. But for some reason which is not apparent, shifting severalties often still persisted in the management of the meadows. A great part of the meadows over whole counties seem to have been allocated each year afresh amongst the proprietors of arable land in proportion to their arable holdings, the allocation being carried out by the most complicated methods in order to secure absolute fairness in distribution.

The common pastures which form the most primitive and archaic of the three types are those which have persisted most, so that many corporate towns and not a few villages still possess their greens, town moors and commons; the lot or rotation meadows which seem to represent the next stage of evolution are much rarer, but are still to be found; while the open arable fields, with interspersed lands but ownership in severalty, which mark the stage next before the modern state have almost entirely disappeared.

Scotland, Ireland and Wales had open-field systems of their own, but there are the most marked and essential divergencies between these systems and that formerly prevalent in the great central plain of England. In the west country and in such border regions as that along the boundaries of Wales and Scotland it is not difficult to find traces of transitional types of cultivation. The true open-field system spoken of here is that characteristic of the fertile plains of the English midlands.

Historically no doubt a one-field system came first. This was cultivated by an early 'field-grass husbandry', naturally evolving in a community where there was still a fairly considerable reserve of unoccupied land. When the fertility of the ground was exhausted, the community at large moved elsewhere, leaving the soil to recover by a natural fallowing until it was again taken into use by a fresh body of occupiers.

With the growth of population and the absorption of a great part of this reserve, it seems natural that a community having determined its boundaries should divide its available land roughly out into halves, and should cultivate the two halves in alternate years. Then, when further pressure of population developed, there would be a tendency to cultivate two-thirds or three-quarters of the land each year, leaving the remaining third or quarter to its fallow. Partly perhaps because the land was so exhausted that a rest of one year in three was almost the minimum required to maintain anything of its fertility, partly because the triparitite division marched closely with a tripartite division of the three main necessaries of life, bread, beer and plough-oxen-and-beef, the two-field system early evolved into a three-field system over the greater part of England. This was only exceptionally ready for the next stage of evolution into a four-field system before the time of the Norfolk four-course rotation, which was not generally adopted until well into the eighteenth century. And then the thoughts of reformers were concerned with abolishing open-field agriculture rather than with modernising it.

Before dealing with the disappearance of the open-field system, and the records of this disappearance which may be found in parish chests in the form of enclosure agreements, acts and awards, it may be well to refer briefly to the records which survive dealing with the administration of open-field agriculture and the manner in which the village community organised its rules for open-field cultivation in administering the territory of its petty republic.

THE REGULATION OF OPEN-FIELD AGRICULTURE. Above[2] we have referred to glebe terriers as sources of information as to open-field management, and below[3] we refer to enclosure acts surviving in parish chests. Such rights as the vestry had in directing the use of the open fields and the management of the common, it inherited, like many more of its functions, from the court baron.

THE COURT BARON'S PART IN SUPERVISING AGRICULTURE. Many

entries in the court rolls of the manor of Digby,[4] Lincs., 8 May 1707, relate solely to agricultural matters of the type:

	l	s	d
We pt Antho Wilkinson for his geese trespassing in the corne feild	0.	0.	6

and a great many more entries for:

'neglecting to do Common work ith fenn and for diging up the ground about his turfs at the hed of his dale whe the folks should cart to and fro' (£0. 1s. 0d.) 'making a highway up and down our fenn & Cowpaster' (£0. 1s. 0d.) 'neglecting to dress his cow dike' (£0. 0s. 4d.) 'making a highway over the leays' (£0. 0s. 6d.) and 'breaking the Westfield with his horses before the town consented'.

The classical instance of manorial regulation of agriculture is to be found in the by-laws of the manor of Great Tew, Oxon, a study of which was printed by the late Professor Vinogradoff,[5] while the laws themselves were printed by the Webbs.[6]

A similar document for the manor of Chipping Norton,[7] Oxon, in 1764 deals largely with the use of the common:

Orders made in the Court Baron as follows:

1. That the Great Common below the Town be heyned from all manner of Cattle on the 13th day of February next, every offender for every offence contrary to this order to incur a penalty of Ten shillings to the Lords of this Manor and one shilling to the Drivers or Person that shall impound the cattle or present the offender.

2. That the said Common shall be broke on the 2nd day of May next and not before, and then not till after sunrising (Penalty 2s. 6d. to Lords and 1s. to Drivers etc.)

3. That every person who shall put any mare gelding or cow kine on the said common or on any commonable place within this manor shall first bring it to the Drivers and declare whose beast it is and on whose common it is to be pastured and have it branded before it is turned on any commonable place within this manor for which branding shall be paid ½d. per head to the Drivers and 3d. to the Inspectors towards moulding Southcombe. (Penalty 3s. per head to Lords, and 2s. per head to Drivers etc.)

[and twenty-three more articles down to]:

27. That the owners or occupiers of the land lying next to the Churchill Field side from the Meads to Burford Road, do make their respective mounds good by opentide and continue them in sufficient repair until Stow Fair or they shall be prosecuted as the law directs.

And that the Mounds from the bottom of Haywards Plot to the lower end of the Meads be made a sufficient mound before the Meads are rid by the respective owners or occupiers of the Meads or Grass ground abutting upon the Corn Fields or they shall be prosecuted in like manner.

The reader may be interested to compare this set of by-laws drawn up for a semi-urban body by the corporation of the borough, who were lords of the manor, with the following series, drafted for a purely rural community where the lordship of the manor was in the hands of the local squire. They relate to East Leake,[3] Notts.:

Pains, Amercements, and by Laws made at the Court Leet and Court Baron of Sir Thomas Parkyns, Bart., for his Mannors of Great Leake, *alias* East Leake, there held the 21st day of Aprill 1730 [omitting 'Item' and 'We make a Pain that' which occur before each decree].

If anyone Teather in the Barley Field any Mare that has a Fole above a month old, whereby any Man's Corne or Meadow may be damaged, Or, in the Peas field after midsummer, to destroy the corne or pease, except the Fole be under a month old, they shall pay for every such defalt £0. 5. 0.

If anyone shall put a horse, mare, or cow, to pasture or comone without pasture or Comon they shall pay for that offence £0. 10. 0.

If anyone keep any close Tupps or Riggles, in the Fields betwixt Goose Fair and Martlemas they shall pay for that offence £0. 2. 6.

[and nineteen more articles down to]:

That Lambs take sheep places at Lady Day. If any persons take them not of then they shall pay for such Defalt five shillings for a score for one month (or till the first of May) and if they take them not of by the First of May for every such Defalt every sheep to pay £0. 1. 0.

Concerning the communal regulation of the meadows, and the arrangements for their annual re-allotment, one of the most interesting records is a series of rules found by Dr J. A. Venn in the chest of Brotherton, Yorks., and reprinted here by his permission. It runs:

A True and perfect copy of the Terrier of the meadow land within the Townships of Brotherton (Yorks) called Brotherton Ings, divided by lots and possessed in the year of our Lord 1773 [from an original drawn up in 1701].

BROTHERTON INGS

I.   The By Law men and others are to meet on Vicar's Hill to draw lots after this manner. Three small sticks marked with one, two, and three nicks are put into a Bunn. The stick marked with one nick is for the Lord; with two nicks for the Bishop; and with three for Peter Liberty. The Bunns are laid upon a long stick, and the first stranger that passeth by may be stopt to take them up. According to the order they are taken up, so they begin to measure that year, viz if the stick with three nicks be taken the first, then Peter Liberty begins at the Tythe Piece, and so the rest go on as they be taken up.

II.   The shorter rod is just sixteen feet long, and the long rod is two inches more.

III.   The placing of the rods in measuring from the Tythe piece is as followeth.

(1)   The short rod at the upper end, or river side, from the Tythe Piece to Curty's Acre.

(2)   The long rod at the upper end in measuring long of the upper Lowance, and short of the upper Lowance.

(3)   The short rod at the upper end in Bradmire's, short and long of the Ings' end.

(4)   The long rod is next the hedge in the short Lowance, and they begin from Bradmire's backwards.

IV.   At the far and long Doles allow on measuring each rod only half a foot breadth.   At the long of the upper Lowance to the end of the Ings allow a foot breadth every rod.   At the short Lowance, at the end of each rod allow a whole foot length.

V.   In the end of each Doal allow as followeth.   Three foot at the end of Peter Dole, one foot and a half at the end of Bishop Hold, and only the common allowance at the end of the Lord's Dole.

Note.   That lest the lower end of the Ings should be overrun by those who might get their hay very forward at the upper end and Tythe Piece, they begin at first to measure from the Long acres to the Ings' end, and sometime after they measure out the far Doals, and long Doals....

Besides these acres there is also the Bull piece and St. Maries pieces, one of which lies at the end of the Ings and the other at the end of the Nether or Short Lowance belonging to the By law men for their care and trouble.

*Each person's quantity of land in the Ings and
number of their pasture gates.*

....

	a. r. p.	Pasture gates
M. Hallilay T. Wilkes and T. Gilson have among them	o 1 o	6 Overgates to repair the pasture dykes

....

A contemporaneous note adds the information that ' $5\frac{1}{2}$ rods of meadow go to an oxgang in the Ings, and also $5\frac{1}{2}$ yards of fencing to an oxgang'.

THE TRANSFER OF POWERS FROM THE COURT BARON TO THE VESTRY. It appears that the control of open fields and commons was never formally transferred from the court leet to the vestry. The only act having the slightest reference to the matter is that of 1773,[9] noted below, and this entrusts the management of common fields not to a true vestry but to a meeting of proprietors, in which a three-fourths' majority in number and value should have the final determination. The history of the position seems to be that as, at various times during different centuries, throughout England the court baron gradually lapsed, without any formality the vestry, in this as in some other matters, stepped into its place.

A CAMBRIDGESHIRE EXAMPLE OF INHERITANCE OF FUNCTIONS BY THE VESTRY FROM THE COURT BARON. At Stretham, Cambs., the documents are interesting in that a series of

Orders and Bylawes and Paynes made and agreed upon by the Court Leet and alsoe the Court Baron holden at Stretham within the Ile of Elie the 29th of April in the 12th yeer of the Reigne of our Soueraygne Lord James by the Grace of God King of England &c and of Scotland the 47th A° Doj 1614:

is followed only eight years later by:

Certayne Orders and Bylawes made by the consent of the Most Part and the Greatest Number of the Inhabytants of Stretham both Coppie-howllders and Freehoullders and other Communers there according to the Decree and Order unto them prescribed and sett downe out of the Honourable Cort of His Majesty's Excheckure as followeth the fowre and twenty Daye of February 1622.

VESTRY REGULATION OF OPEN-FIELD AGRICULTURE. The parish register of SS. Peter and Paul, Mitcham, Surrey, has on its fly-leaf this entry under 1637:

It is this day agreed upon by the Inhabitants above named in the behalfe of the rest of the Inhabitants that the common fields shall be layd open so soone as all the corne of the said fields shall be carried out. And then and not before it shall be lawfull for the said Inhabitants that have been accustomed and to have benefitt of the common of the said field to put in their cattle untill St. Luke Day following, and not after any sheepe or other cattle to be suffered there, but if any be taken they are to be put in the pound or to be trespassers upon paine for every horse sixpence etc....

At Clayworth, Notts., such agreements were entered in the rector's commonplace book, e.g.

ye 28th of May this p^{e}sent year 1700.
Law. That none let any Gates save to those y^t are Inhabitants. If no Inhabitants take those Gates y^t others w^d let, y^n ye By-law Men (after 40 days notice) to pay to ye owners 2^s ⅌ Gate ⅌ An & so be reim-burs^d by an assessm^t at one Peny ⅌ Gate on ye said Comons. All Cattle to be taken off ye Comons ye 25th of March & not to be put on ye Carr again till ye 1st of May nor upon ye Cow-Pasture until ye 16th of May & ye By-Lawmen to impound all Cattle as shall be put on otherwise or y^t more in number than is here stinted & limited & ye same to detain till reasonable satisfaction be made to ye s^d By-Law men to ye use of ye Town.[10]

Among the most interesting vestry orders are these concerned with the management of open fields and commons. At Cobham, Surrey, e.g. in 1739 the vestry made an order as to the cutting of peat in the common turbary. A happy mixture of sporting and

business instincts is revealed in the register of St Nicholas, Durham,
April 1683, when Simon Lackenby was ordered by the vestry to

keep in lieu of his Intercommon ground one sufficient Bull for the
use of the City and Borough Kyne, for three years next ensuing; and
to give ten shillings towards a Silver plate for a Course.

Agreements and contracts for catching moles are often found.
Bedfordshire has several, now removed from the parish chests to
the County Record Office, including early ones at Maulden, 1710
and Oakley, 1720. At Sutton Bonington, Notts., referred to above
as the place where in 1757 the parishioners agreed to stint their
common, it seems that in this year there was a wave of agricultural
fervour, for they also at the same time entered into an agreement
with George Carver for catching moles throughout the parish at
a salary of 30s. the first year (when he had the arrears of neglect
to make up!) and 25s. each year thereafter for the rest of his life.
Thirty years before they had entered into an agreement concerning
vermin even more noxious than moles, in a resolution of 1728 which
still stands in the parish book:

to pay for everre Fox that is caht in sutton parish for Ever
a Greed on at a meeting   2s. 6d.

At Barton-in-Fabis, Notts., are articles of agreement of 1718,
1729 and 1766 for the improvement of the (common) sheep
pasture. A similar agreement for stinting the common, levying a
fine on commoners who exceeded their stint, and using the proceeds to compensate those who turned on fewer cattle than they
were entitled to, was drawn up in the neighbouring parish of
Sutton Bonington in 1757.

At Cottenham, Cambs., where there were disputes as to the
extent of the manorial pasture rights, an agreement, apparently
a very one-sided affair, was made in 1580 by the lord and the

greatest number of welthiest and substancyalist inhabitants and tenants
of Cottenham in the behalfe of themselves and of all the rest of the
inhabitants of the said town.

This was set aside and a new agreement was drawn up in 1596, and
confirmed by a Chancery decree. This seems to have been a
genuine agreement with the inhabitants at large, and it gave a
written democratic constitution to the village community—a constitution which lasted until the general enclosure of the place in
1842.[11]

A century or a century and a half later in many parishes the making of such rules was an undoubted function of the vestry. At Ardeley,[12] Herts., e.g.

2nd Aug. 1713.   Whereas there has been a Complaint made, by ye Inhabitants of this Parish, that ye said Parish does sustain great damage by those persons which come in by a certificate by over-burthening ye common, which they have no right to; and likewise hinder ye poor Inhabitants, by taking ye benefit of gleaning in the several and respective fields belonging to ye said Parish: therefore, it is now ordered at this Convention, held on Sunday ye 2nd day of August 1713, by ye major part of ye parishioners here present, that ye hayward doe give notice to them, and every of them, to take their Cattle off of ye Common, or else they will be impound.....

This order is to be set upon the Church door ye next Sunday.

At Steeple Aston,[13] Oxon, in 1762, the vestry drew up a whole series of by-laws very closely resembling those printed above, which were issued by manorial courts:

Articles agreed upon by the Inhabitants of
Steeple Aston Jany. 5th, 1762

1st   We agree to lay down Saintfoin in the Furlong called Slater-Lot to Pudding edge to be mounded by the Yard Land. No horse or sheep to be turn'd in under the Penalty of twenty shillings for every head of cattle for each offence. No person to turn his Plow to damage his Neighbour, if detected to pay five shillings.

2.   We agree to sow one hundred of Clover-seed in Barley Field, to be bought by the Constable, every Person to pay according to the Yard Land.

3.   No pigs to be turn'd into the Field without being ring'd, under the Penalty of five shillings for each offence.

[and eight more articles down to]:

12.   We agree that these Articles shall continue in force for the space of twenty years commencing from the fifth day of January 1762. We whose names are hereunto subscribed do promise and agree to conform to the above written Articles under the several Penalties annexed.

In witness whereof we have hereunto set our hands this fifth day of January 1762...

again:

Agreed by the Vestrey that Thos. Dean is Hired to look after the field; to look after the Crowes and Cach the moulds if he can: and to look after the mounds at Headon way, Dean headge and Slaterfoot that is now laid down Sandfine. And it [is] further agreed that the field men now apointed shall be all agreed to lett Thos. Dean the field keeper know when the field shall be stocked. Thos. Dean agrees to keep the field at the Yearly [sic] of foure pounds and ten shillings and ye s^d Thos. Dean is to find his own powder and shot all the time he keep the s^d field, and if the s^d Thos. Dean neglects or refuses to do His Duty he shall forfitt to the fieldmen now apointed the sume of twenty shillings to be reducted out of the sume above menchoned and if the said fieldsmen should neglect to pay the s^d Thos. Dean when he has proformed his above contract they agree to pay him the s^d Thos Dean the sume of Twenty shillings over & above the agreed wages as Wittness I have set our hand this 7 day of Novr 1763.

In later years such vestry resolutions as we have been discussing were sometimes ordered to be printed in the local newspapers. The notice below, relating to Beeston,[14] Notts., appears in the county paper:

BEESTON April 15, 1795

The Inhabitants and Occupiers of Beast-gates upon the Common Pasture, at a Vestry Meeting held at Beeston aforesaid, having agreed to HALF STINT in said Pasture, the Inhabitants at said Vestry Meeting will give this public Notice, that, in future, no Gates upon such Pasture as usual be let. ROBERT NUTT, Constable, ROBERT LACY, Churchwarden.

An interesting and probably almost unique example of the reversal of the process noted above, the transfer to the court baron of the rights formerly exercised by the vestry, occurs in the celebrated Nottinghamshire open-field parish of Laxton.[15] Here some sort of communal regulation survived side by side with the common fields to which it was applied, but as the late lord of the manor, Earl Manvers, had gradually been buying up toftsteads in order to secure more complete control of the place, so regulation of agriculture by a committee of proprietors came to be replaced by government according to a series of rules drawn up by the lord's agent.

The two last sets of rules, those drafted in 1871 and in 1908 respectively, are well worth comparison:

1871	1908
	Rules and Regulations for Grazing Laxton Open Fields.
Laxton Commons and Fields.	
At a Vestry Meeting held in the School Room at Laxton on Thursday 2nd day of March 1871, the following RULES for regulating the stocking of the OPEN COMMONS AND FIELDS were agreed to:—	

[after a long series of rules as to open fields and common]:

All persons breaking any of the above Rules will be presented at	(7) The Foreman of the Juries and the Parish Pinder are to see

1871	1908
the Court of the Lord of the Manor and dealt with as the Jury may decide.	that these Rules are carried out, and are to report any one breaking them to the Thoresby Estate office at once, and anyone so reported may, after one caution, be given notice to quit his farm.
The brander appointed by the Committee is MR JOSEPH MERRILLS	Lord Manvers appeals to his Tenants in their common in-terests to help him and the Fore-man of the Juries to carry out the above. He asks them specially to be careful to shut the Gates on the Commons when passing through them, and also the gates on the lands which he has lately enclosed
The following persons are to be a Committee for carrying these Rules into effect:	
Mr. John Keyworth. Mr. George Peck. Mr. William Pinder. Mr. Richard Harpham. Mr. Charles Wilcox. Mr. John Atkinson.	

R. W. Wordsworth.

Agent for Earl Manvers, Estate Office, Thoresby Park, April 1908.

THE VESTRY AND THE MODERNISATION OF OPEN-FIELD STRUCTURE AND TECHNIQUE. One of the strongest objections to the open-field system was the scattering of land in minute parcels throughout the area of the common fields. Before general enclosure, private agree-ments for the exchange of lands between neighbours were often the means of rearranging the open-field estates into more manage-able parcels. Such an agreement, this time for six years only, appears in the vestry book of Steeple Aston,[16] Oxon:

March 2 1765

It [is] agreed to change land in the Dean by Willm. Wing Richd. Prentice and Richd. Fox for Willm. Wing to have Richd. Fox peice above the stile for his peice below and for Richd. Prentice to have three lands of Richd. Fox next to his land under the Dean hedge shooting into Short Clay Furlong for his two lands in the Dean and for six years at Saint Micahill next. By we

W. Wing.
Richd. Fox.
Richd. Prentice.

A much more general and substantial reorganisation of the open-field structure of their village was undertaken by the parishioners of Sutton-cum-Lound, Notts., about the same time:

AGREEMENT OF THE INHABITANTS OF SUTTON AND LOUND FOR TAKING IN TURNIP FIELDS.

Dated the 28th February, 1766...

AND FIRST, each and every of the parties aforesaid for himself and herself severally, and for his and her respective Heirs, Executors and Administrators, DOTH Covenant, Promise, and Agree, with each and every other of the said parties jointly and severally, and with each and every of their joint and several Heirs, Executors, Administrators and Assigns, in manner and form as followeth (that is to say):

[in a different hand]

the Fields after Harvest shall be gotten shall be open for all Beasts.

[in the first hand]

THAT, from and after the twenty-fifth day of March next, for and during and unto the full end of Twenty Years, the Cõmon pasture called the West Cõmon, shall be used and kept for young Beast and Sheep, according to the former custom of the Parish aforesaid.

[in the second hand]

And that the Fields after Harvest shall be gotten in shall be Common for all Cattle as heretofore used and accustomed.

[and seven more articles, all in the first hand, down to]:

And likewise it is hereby AGREED. That there shall be separate Turnip Fields, taken in and formed in each of the Cõmon Fields at Sutton and Lound, in every Year during the said Term, at each Gate's expense, to be paid by the Owner of each Gate. And the Turnip seed shall be sown before the eighteenth day of July in every year during the said Term. And that every Cottager who hath a right of Cõmon and hath Cattle to shack (withall?) during the whole Summer, shall have a Gate on the said Turnip Fields (that is to say, a Cow or three Calves, or Six Sheep, or eight Hogsheep, or a Gelding, or Mare against a Cow).

[and eight more articles down to]:

AND for the due performance of all and every the Covenants and agreements, each and every of the parties hereunto signed and sealed do hereby bind himself or herself and their heirs, executors, and Admins., unto the other in the (full)? sum of twenty shilling sterling, well and duly to be recovered by virtue of these presents.

[82 names.]

There are several points of interest arising from the consideration of this document. Here we can but indicate one or two of them. Perhaps the most important is this, that during the eighteenth century, when, according to current views, the ancient agricultural village community was in the last stages of decay, crying out for its final extinction at the hands of the enclosure commissioners, this particular community was capable of very active and vigorous life. Through its vestry meeting it regulated the usage of its open fields, common meadows, and pastures, with the same vigilance and minuteness of detail which had formerly been applied through the manorial rule of the court baron. Another Nottinghamshire Sutton, Sutton (Bonington) St Anne's, undertook a similar modification of open-field structure, about the same date and probably for the same purpose.

THE DISADVANTAGES OF THE OPEN-FIELD SYSTEM. ENCLOSURE.
Despite some evident social advantages in cultivation by village
communities, clearly there were many inconveniences and extra-
vagances of time and labour involved in such a system of husbandry
as that outlined above. These early led to attempts to modify it.
In 1235 and 1285 the Statutes of Merton and Westminster II[17] gave
powers to the lords of manors to approve (enclose) portions of the
still unredeemed waste which were not needed by their tenants.
And a whole host of mediaeval records shows that this power was
very often exercised, though apparently rarely with respect to
any considerable acreage. As a rule, action under these statutes
seems to have been generally acquiesced in, and there are few
records of forcible protests against their operation.

Towards the end of the fifteenth century, however, enclosure
began to be alleged as a grievance. From the protest of John Rous,[18]
a chantry priest of Warwick c. 1480, until the end of the Tudor
period there is a long stream of propaganda, setting forth that enclosure for emparking involved the conversion of arable to pasture,
the rearing of sheep rather than man, the depopulation of the
countryside and the decay of the commonwealth.

In 1516 More's *Utopia* contained a celebrated passage in which
he brought to the eye of authority his complaints as to the neglect
of the interests of the small proprietors by lords, abbots and
bishops, and pressed for a remedy to be put in force against these
ills. Even before this time anti-depopulation measures had been
placed upon the statute book,[19] and now there followed a long
stream of statutes, proclamations, and commissions, all designed
to check the process which was felt to be utterly destructive of the
common weal. In 1517 a commission,[20] whose returns are still
extant, inquired into the whole problem; in 1518 Wolsey as
Chancellor ordered that those claiming the royal pardon for enclosure should destroy the hedges and ditches made since 1488.
A proclamation of 1526 made a similar order. In 1533–4[21] an act
forbade the engrossing of farms. Evidently the act was little
observed, and in 1548 the Protector Somerset issued yet another
proclamation.

Wholesale enclosure was one of the principal grievances alleged
by the rebels who revolted under Ket in 1549, as it was half
a century later when the midland counties of Northampton,
Warwick, Leicester and Bedford rose to redress agrarian grievances.
In Charles I's reign steps were taken to check the growth of
enclosure in 1630, 1632, 1635 and 1636, and Star Chamber dealt

very effectively with offenders. Cromwell and his major-generals had the same problem to deal with when Everard, Winstanley and the 'Diggers' kept the midlands in a ferment from 1649 to 1654 with their Christian-Socialist agrarian programme. But after this there were no attempts by the national government to stem the tide of enclosure and the weight of propaganda began gradually to turn the scale in favour of agricultural improvement at all costs. Even so, throughout the seventeenth century and for a great part of the eighteenth, a war of pamphleteers went merrily on, and as late as 1792 a propagandist alleged enclosure as among the principal causes of rural poverty and misery.

At the numerous inquiries resulting from all this controversy it was rarely alleged in later times, as it had been in earlier days, that men enclosed lands not properly belonging to them. The grievance was rather that land was put out of cultivation, involving lessened labour, and resulting in rural depopulation, and, therefore, that the movement was against public policy. After 1631, enclosure for such purposes may have slackened. Certainly recorded enclosures in the midlands between 1640 and 1740 were for the most part small in area and scattered in occurrence.

In the first half of the eighteenth century came great changes to agriculture, which, in the course of a couple of generations, altered the general public's whole attitude to land enclosure. Husbandry began to be studied scientifically and experimentally, and two new factors of undoubted advantage could not be made use of under the system of open-field arable agriculture. These were the introduction of roots as a field crop and the results attainable by subsoil drainage.

But how grow roots on open ground, when it was a crop that ripened only after the corn was all carried, and the neighbours turned their cattle loose over the wide stubbles? And how put in subsoil drains when one's land lay in narrow scattered strips and patches, cheek by jowl with the narrow selions of others, and with no control of the outfalls? Occasional attempts were made to graft a root-growing husbandry on to the open-field system, and a most interesting example of this occurred at Sutton-cum-Lound, Notts., an agreement for which is printed above. In 1772–3 provision was made by act for introducing improvements in open-field agriculture without enclosure. The act was rarely adopted, though hardly so rarely as some historians have asserted, and it seems to have had little effect upon agricultural technique.

ENCLOSURE BY THE COURT BARON. When the general current of

agricultural progress made enclosure of commons and open fields almost a national necessity, it is not surprising to find that often the local vestry was closely concerned in the process. Probably in this, as in so many of the other functions discharged by the vestry, it was acting as the legitimate successor of the court baron, in the rolls of which many early enclosure agreements had been registered, e.g. at Edwinstowe,[22] Notts., the court rolls of 1640 have:

WHEREAS...
nowe at this tyme John Goslinge gent. hath inclosed in the East feild of his owne lands eight acres or thereabouts, whereof part of the same he is to have in exchange by surrender from John Snoden of the same towne for other land lyinge in the West feild, Wee the Inhabitants of the towne of Edwinstowe aforesayd have thereunto assented and are contented with the same inclosure that it may soe continue inclosed & stand, without Molesta̅con of any of us our heires or assignes...

ENCLOSURE BY AUTHORITY OF THE VESTRY. Mr Toulmin Smith, as one would expect, regarded enclosure of common by the vestry as the only proper mode of carrying out the process:

precisely analogous to the steps taken as to the Folkland by the General Assembly of the Nation.

An example of authorisation by the vestry to enclose part of the common occurs at Ham, Surrey, where the civil records of the parish include a copy of an instrument dated 16 December 1730, purporting to sanction the enclosure by the Duke of Argyle of waste near Sudbrook Park. A monetary acknowledgement was exacted and the same records include a declaration of trust of 1762 respecting the use of the money paid. The vestry of Keston, Kent, on 6 July 1790 authorised Pitt, who had purchased Holwood, the local great house, some half-dozen years previously, to enclose thirty acres of the common known as the Bulwarks, upon payment of a perpetual annuity of £10 to the poor of the parish.

The vestry minutes of Tooting and Mitcham, Surrey, contain several agreements for the enclosure of scraps of common, 1795 and 1797. Even where agreements for enclosure were drawn up by the proprietors as such, rather than by the parishioners *qua* parishioners, the records of such agreements, when they have survived at all, have generally been preserved in parish chests. Nottinghamshire has two sets of articles of agreement for enclosing Torworth, 1792 and 1797, in the parish chest of the mother church at Blyth. Shropshire has at least three sets, those for Lee Brockhurst, 1800, Fitz, 1822, and Pontesford, 1826.

PARLIAMENTARY ENCLOSURES. Enclosure by private agreement was, however, a long and painful process, far too slow for the enthusiastic agricultural pioneers of the eighteenth century, so, from about 1760, the normal method of carrying out enclosure was by private act of Parliament. Usually the act appointed a number of commissioners, who had the duty of visiting the parish, having it properly surveyed, hearing all the claims of those having either open land or common right, and allotting all proprietors an equivalent in land, or occasionally in cash, for the rights they had enjoyed. And such land was allotted in severalty, after the modern fashion, and in general was entirely discharged from ancient incidents of almost every kind. The commissioners' final determination was expressed in an award, which, after proclamation in the parish church, became final and legally binding upon all the parties concerned.

Not, of course, that the English enclosure act sprang suddenly into existence in 1760 or thereabouts. As we have already indicated, enclosure by agreement had been quite usual for centuries before. Then, in the seventeenth century, a custom developed of securing confirmation of such private agreements in the courts of Chancery or Exchequer. Often, it appears, a collusive suit was undertaken in order to obtain a decree which would bind a recalcitrant minority. Various bills dealing with the matter, some of them giving general powers to confirm such decrees, were introduced into Parliament in 1656, 1661, 1664, and 1666, but none of them passed. The same end was ultimately achieved by a whole series of private acts, most of which, at first, merely confirmed arrangements already come to by agreement. From this it was but a short step to acts of the more usual type appointing commissioners to make the enclosure, and confirming in advance the decision they should make.

Altogether after 1760 there were rather more than 5100 enclosure acts and enclosures under general acts, affecting, it is estimated, well over six and a half million acres of England land. Before 1760 there were but 255 in all, and more than half of these are accounted for by the three midland counties of Warwick, Northampton and Gloucester, and by the vast waste spaces of the North and West Ridings of Yorkshire. The enormous expense attaching to enclosure by parliamentary means early caused a demand for a general act to simplify procedure and to cheapen proceedings. After 140 years of more or less continuous agitation the first general enclosure act was passed in 1801. This, however, was a 'clauses act' only. The next important general act was one of 1836. This permitted enclosure by the consent of a majority of the proprietors (generally at least two-thirds), without the requirement of any special application to Parliament. The next major enactment as to enclosure was the General Act of 1845. This set up a body of standing Enclosure Commissioners who had authority to sanction the enclosure of land by provisional order and enclosure award.

There are, of course, a great many hotly controverted points in the history of these Parliamentary enclosures. For information upon these matters generally historians have had to rely upon contemporary pamphleteers, quite regardless of the fact that these were almost invariably bitter and unscrupulous partisans, anxious to prove either that the great wave of enclosure which swept over the country was the greatest social and moral improvement which had occurred for centuries, or that it was a colossal legalised robbery —an unscrupulous confiscation of the scanty effects of Lazarus in order to cram them into the overflowing coffers of Dives—a gigantic and heartless swindle, equally hateful to God and man.

It is even sometimes suggested e.g. that private land ownership in England is really a result of the enclosure movement. It will be clear from what has been said above that while the land of England was largely *cultivated* in common until comparatively recent years there is very little evidence of common land-*ownership* in historic times.

Since the actual operation of the enclosure act was left so largely in the hands of the commissioners it is clearly of some importance to determine who exactly these commissioners were, and with what zeal and efficiency they carried out the well-remunerated duties with which they were entrusted. Those writers who have approached the enclosure question rather from the standpoint of modern politics than from that of historical fact have alleged that these same commissioners were commonly members of the landed class, and that in the performance of their duties they were often deliberately furthering class interests. Upon all such points a good deal of information is to be obtained from the awards themselves by anyone who will take the trouble to consult them.

With regard to the effect of these enclosures, it has commonly been alleged that they caused depopulation of the rural parishes. That this was often the consequence of the Tudor and Stuart enclosures is certain; there is a general weight of evidence to the effect that the enclosures of the eighteenth and nineteenth centuries —that is, the period covered by the Parliamentary enclosure acts

—derived from quite different causes and were carried out for entirely different reasons.

THE ENCLOSURE RECORDS OF THE PARISH CHEST AS SOURCES OF EVIDENCE UPON DISPUTED TOPICS. For really reliable evidence upon such points of controversy the enclosure records of the parish chest are invaluable. Here and there such agreements as those instanced above have survived. Copies of local enclosure acts occasionally turn up. As to the relation between enclosure and depopulation the official census returns mentioned below are the best source of information after 1801, and various unofficial estimates of population are found in some chests, covering earlier periods. Old rate books and land-tax assessments enable one to judge as to the connection (if any) between enclosure and the growth of land monopoly. Any or all of these may be found in the parish chest, and apart from the land-tax records they rarely survive anywhere else. Even enclosure commissioners' minute books, which are among the rarest of records (neither the British Museum, the London School of Economics, the Public Record Office, nor the Bodleian has any), are to be found in parish chests. East Drayton, Notts., has a most interesting one, 1819–25, Pontesford, Salop, has one, 1826–8, and several county record offices have collected one or two from various chests within their counties.

ENCLOSURE AWARDS. Most important of all the enclosure records are, of course, the enclosure awards. These acts almost invariably provided that the original award after execution and proclamation should be deposited in the parish chest, a copy only, for record purposes, being deposited with the Clerk of the Peace for the county. When the General Enclosure Acts were passed, this provision was incorporated in them.

Enclosure awards to be found in parish chests fall into four main classes: (1) early agreements and awards (including a great many made in the famine years at the end of the eighteenth century and the beginning of the nineteenth) under private agreements of the parties affected, (2) awards made by enclosure commissioners acting under private acts, (3) awards made without any application to Parliament under the General Act of 1836, (4) awards made by 'assistant commissioners' to the national enclosure commissioners under the general acts of 1845 *et seq.* There are few records, if any, to rival in interest and importance the awards. These enclosure awards of Georgian times are in their evidential value infinitely more weighty than all other enclosure records taken together.

Their primary purpose was to achieve and to register the

change from open-field ownership and cultivation to the modern system of land ownership and cultivation in 'severalty', but the awards have much more than historical or agrotechnical importance. They form the best—in many cases the only—source of accurate information as to the distribution of land ownership in the villages of a century and a half ago; they are full of useful information as to the prevalent types of tenure; in half the villages of the midlands they serve as ultimate title-deeds to the greater part of the land; they record the lands forming the endowments of ancient village charities and schools; and they are the final authority for information as to the course and breadth of the highways, the existence of footpaths and rights of way, and the courses, breadths and liability for cleansing of most of the surface drains. The awards, and the plans which are appended to them, register the ownership of hedges and fences; they distinguish between titheable and non-titheable lands—in many instances *enclosure* awards are better sources of information about tithe than are the *tithe* awards; and they specify allotments of land for public purposes, which are the origins of the greater part of what land still remains vested in such minor local governing bodies as parish meetings and parish councils.

Accordingly, the enclosure awards are invaluable sources of information, not only to the historian or the antiquary—and to him whether his interest be mainly ecclesiastical or civil, economic or social—but also to the present-day administrator. For the 4747 acts passed since 1709 there must have been about 6000 awards, many of them existing in one copy only, and of these a very considerable proportion have entirely disappeared.

It is clear then that when the parish chest contains an enclosure award the local historian is fortunate, and that when there should be one, but it is now missing, time and trouble spent in securing its return will be by no means wasted.

For further details as to the history of enclosure in England the reader is referred to a detailed bibliography on enclosure appearing in our *English Village Community and the Enclosure Movements*. Perhaps the most detailed county study is *Parliamentary Enclosure in Nottinghamshire*,[23] containing a fuller account of the many controversial topics bound up with the enclosure question, and a guide to the *House of Commons Journals* showing how the information in the *Journals* may be used to supplement and elucidate that to be obtained from the printed acts and the manuscript awards.

T

XI. MISCELLANEOUS RECORDS—CIVIL AND ECCLESIASTICAL

Early inventories of parish chest contents. Government returns and deposited plans. Census returns. Minute books of extinct *ad hoc* bodies. Counsel's opinions and other legal records. Bills and Acts of Parliament. Royal charters, etc. Fiscal records. School records. Court rolls and other manorial records. VARIOUS MEDIAEVAL RECORDS. Early ecclesiastical records. Early records preserved as wrappers or bindings of later ones. Mediaeval service books, etc. Wills of parish benefactors, etc. Early contracts for work about the church. Incumbents' diaries. Parish chest oddments and oddities.

The miscellaneous objects likely to be found in any parish chest, and not dealt with under any of the preceding heads, are so varied as to defy classification. Odd non-documentary contents which have been noted in one chest or another range from a fine (hitherto unrecorded) Elizabethan chalice to several good specimens of the pewter chamberpots in vogue in the seventeenth and early eighteenth centuries. Here we can but indicate a few of the most interesting types of record commonly surviving.

Occasionally eighteenth-century vestries ordered the making of proper inventories of the contents of the parish chests, and a number of these have survived. Meare, Som., has two such inventories, one undated, and one made at a vestry in 1770. Rode, Nunney and Othery in the same county have respectively a similar list of 1737, 'a Count of what Writtings are in the Coffer in the Chancel May 1732' and 'a Book of List of Writings belonging Nunney, 1773.'

Duplicate copies of Government returns are to be found in plenty, especially the constables' accounts of the poll tax of 1678–9, those concerning the collection of the hearth tax, and those relating to the assessment of the window tax of 1695–1851. It is not unusual to find also ancient copies of *The London Gazette*, particularly those containing references to presentations to or augmentations of the benefice, or its discharge from first-fruits and tenths.

Railway and canal plans ought to be found in a great many parish chests, but they seem rarely to have been preserved. Walton-upon-Thames, Surrey, has however a series of railway plans, 1845, 1856 and 1864, and Brushford, Som., has a book of reference of the Devon and Somerset Railway, 1864.

The 1801 census was taken through the parish officers, and such earlier inquiries as had been made concerning population all made use of the parochial organisation for collecting their data.

The vicar of Stevington, Beds., entered in his register:

Parishioners of Steventon in the village of Pavenham. Renewed and amended as the people dy or remove from the houses following at Christmas 1699....

Ardleigh, Essex, has on a loose sheet the census return of 1801, and, entered in Register VI (1790–1812):

The Names Qualities Ages & Numbers of the Inhabitants of the Parish of Ardleigh, as found by actual visitation in the month of September 1793.

This occupies twelve pages in all and is followed by the

No. of males from the age of 15 to 60 and capable of bearing armes 1796 (352 of a total population of 1145),

apparently compiled personally and unofficially by the vicar 'in case of a French Invasion, 1796'. Much more usual, of course, are the ordinary census returns. Streatley, Beds., has census returns for 1801 and 1811. Finchingfield, Essex, has census returns of 1815, 1821, as well as a 'List of Families in the Parish', c. 1750, and Berkswich, Staffs., has in Register IV, 1795–1812, the returns of 1801, 1811 and 1821. Portishead, Som., has the returns of 1831 in its fourth register, and Radstock, in the same county, has copies of the population returns of 1795 and the censuses of 1801, 1811, 1821, 1831, 1838, 1841, 1851 and 1861.

Combe, Berks., has such lists of 1782 and 1788. In Hampshire alone there are in the registers census lists of Burghclere, 1788, 1801, 1811, Hamble, 1795, South Hayling, 1788, Sparsholt, 1801. Croxden, Staffs., has in Register II a census of 1783. There must have been a great many other census lists in those civil records which have now largely disappeared, e.g. the overseers' book of Walsoken, Norf., has a copy of the census list of 1801. High Ham, Somerset, has a detailed description of the parish written by its (German) minister in Queen Elizabeth I's time.

Minute books of such extinct *ad hoc* bodies as Local Boards, Burial Boards, and School Boards are to be found here and there. In Somerset a Burial Board minute book of 1879 is in the chest of Dunster, another from 1855 onwards at Shepton Mallet, and a School Board minute book from 1888 has recently been transferred from Meare chest to Taunton.

Counsel's opinions and other legal records, especially those relating to tithe and similar matters, are often found. West Pennard, Som., has a document of 1528—Archbishop Warham's determination in a tithe suit. Hatfield Broad Oak, Essex, has a case for counsel's opinion concerning charity estates, dated 1813, and reciting an inquisition of 32 Charles II.

Lawford in the same county has a case of 1760, with counsel's opinion. Ickham, Kent, has an opinion of 1752 as to the rector's right to all parochial emoluments from the chapelry of Well. Walesby, Notts., has several bearing upon the disputed and disputable question whether the chapelry of Haughton was truly titheable, or whether a modus paid in lieu of tithe could be proved to have existed from time immemorial and hence to be binding.

Bath St Michael's has four volumes of correspondence, 1773–1806, relating to a lawsuit between the parish and the corporation. Bicknoller, Som., has an appeal to a judge by this parish and Stogumber, to decide which was responsible for the maintenance of a pauper, 1631. Chew Magna, Som., has a case and opinion of Prideaux, concerning the church rate, 1865. Bramley, Surrey, has an eighteenth-century memorandum of proceedings before the Guildford magistrates concerning settlement, and Shalford in the same county has several legal opinions upon settlement cases in 1812 and 1815. At Gnosall, Staffs., the vestry minutes of 1751 have this entry:

1751. Aug. 25th. Being a publick meeting it was agreed to have an opinion about Joseph Parkses and Joseph Bates settlements at the Parish Expence.

Acts of Parliament are occasionally found. Usually they are enclosure acts relating to the parish itself or to some other parish in which the incumbent had interests. Other acts, especially those relating to registration and similar ecclesiastical business, are by no means uncommon. Horne, Surrey, has a copy of an act of 1662 as to the 'safety and preservation of His Majesty's person'. Silchester, Hants., has bound in Register II a black-letter copy of the 1678 act for burial in woollen. Another is to be found at Gosbeck, Suff.

Appleby, Lincs., has a copy of the act 'to prevent profane cursing and swearing', 1745. In Somerset, Batcombe has its enclosure bill, 1795 (?); Chedzoy, Edington, Locking and West Lydford have copies of the enclosure acts of 1798, 1814, 1800 and 1826 respectively. Bath St Michael's has a copy of the poor law of 1815, Carhampton and East Harptree have copies of the 1822 marriage act, while Meare has copies of the marriage and registration acts of 1822 and 1836, and Bathwick possesses a copy of a local act 'for building a church and workhouse'. Of very great value to the economic historian are the Elizabethan and Jacobean rules to be observed by weavers and the (magistrates') assize of wages, 1684, in the chest of Donington in Holland, Lincs.

Royal charters, letters patent or 'inspeximuses' occur occasionally. St Mary's, Sandwich, has an inspeximus of Edward III concerning letters patent of Edward I; Hawkhurst, Kent, has letters patent of Henry VI concerning persons taking part with 'John Mortimer' [Jack Cade]; Worfield, Salop, has a royal charter of 16 Edward IV (1476); Walton, Som., has an inspeximus of 34 Henry VIII (1543), and Romsey, Hants., has the deed of sale by which Henry VIII in 1540 transferred the abbey church to the churchwardens and parishioners for £100. In the chest of St John the Baptist, Margate, is a royal charter of Mary I, 1553, giving offertories to the vicar, and in that of Westerham, Kent, are letters patent of Queen Anne, 1702-3, granting market rights to Sir Edward Gresham. Quite unique, we suppose, is the copy of the 'sealed book' of 1661 found at Ampton, Suff., apparently having found its way thither from the muniment room of some cathedral. Only thirty-one copies of the book were made, and neither the British Museum nor the Bodleian has one.

One would hardly expect to find land-tax records in a parish chest, but they are to be seen in several parishes, e.g. in Somerset alone there are at Batheaston returns for the parish, 1700-96, and those for a great many other parishes in the archdeaconry, 1719-35 and 1740-8. Kewstoke has in the vestry a framed copy of the land-tax assessment of 1707, Martock has assessments 1811-34 and 1837, and at Midsomer Norton, at the back of Register IV, are sundry notes on land tax, window money and rates. At Keysoe, Beds., is a detailed window-tax assessment of 1731.

Several Somerset parishes have also records of the ancient taxes of 'tenths and fifteenths'; Langford Budville e.g. has an assessment of these for 1579-94 on a page in its earliest register. Christchurch, Hants., has a list of the occupiers of land in five local hundreds assessed for a royal purveyance in 1575.

At Chiddingstone St Mary's, Kent, is a list of the subsidies levied in 1640 'towards raysing of an 100,000 pounds for the Scots' and a list of goods plundered from the parishioners during the Civil War. Lists of contributors for the defence of the realm in such times as those of the Revolutionary and Napoleonic wars are to be found in plenty; Keysoe, Beds., has a Bank of England receipt for such a contribution of £23. 14s. 6d. in 1798. A very odd discovery among the records of the Bedfordshire parish of Henlow was that of three original crown warrants, each bearing the royal sign manual. The first is a commission to the Earl of Macclesfield to attack the French coast, 1694, the other two, of 1781–2, are warrants for the holding of courts martial.

Very interesting to those concerned with the history of education is this extract from the Meppershall, Beds., charity school accounts, with its curious mixture of cultural and technical education. In this parish at the time it seems that a similar report was drawn up every quarter:

An account of the Schollars & their Learning taken
March 25. 1699

Taught by Dame Seal

Ann Leonard reads pretty well in her Testament, & this last week spun a pound & an half of hemp tare.

Hannah Tomson does little at reading, but has spun 3 pound of hemp tare this week.

Ann Endersby does little at reading, but has spun 3 pound of hemp tare very well this week.

Thomas Cherry proceeds in spelling....

Even court rolls, those most precious of local records, are sometimes to be found. Sometimes they are the court rolls of rectorial manors. A fine series of court rolls, 1327–1773, is to be found in the chest of Worfield, Salop. East Meon, Hants., has the records of the court of Bishop's Manor from 1754. The earliest court rolls known to have survived in Staffordshire are in the chest of Alrewas, which contains the series almost complete from 1259, with some of the Prebendal manor rolls. Chalton, Hants., has the court baron book from 1670 onwards. Somerset seems to be very fortunate in these, as in some other records it has preserved. They include court rolls for the manors (mostly rectory manors) of Batcombe, 1716–1921, Charlton Mackrell, 1724–1854, Curland, 'ancient and modern', Huntspill, 1597–1617 and 1687, Lympsham, 1807–71 (in the chest of the adjoining parish of East Brent), Mells, 1663–1843, Portishead, James I–1860, Weston Zoyland, 1819–44, Wookey, 1768–1869 (in the chest of the distant parish of Norton Fitzwarren), Yeovilton, 1710–1874; presentments for Banwell, 1791–1810, Charlton Musgrove, 1639–47, and Cheddar, 1834, with two customaries, one undated for Donyatt, and one of 1683 for Aller, and two surveys, Kingston Seymour, 1745, and Wookey, 1769.

Less important, but still very valuable and interesting, are such documents as extracts from court rolls, admissions, etc. Extracts from the court rolls of four manors, 1441–1753, are to be found at Gedney Hill, Lincs. Elstead, Surrey, has similar extracts of 1615–16; Priddy, Som., has separate 'admissions' of 1816–60, and Dummer, Hants., has extracts from the court rolls of the manors of Dummer and Popham, 1655–99. Great Dunmow, Essex, had a bundle of twenty admissions and surrenders of the middle of the nineteenth century (now preserved in the County Record Office), and Little Bentley in the same county has a volume, apparently a copy made c. 1600 from a mediaeval original, entitled 'Tenants of a Manor' (no place mentioned).

MEDIAEVAL RECORDS. St Nicholas, Stevenage, Herts., a model parish which has issued three detailed calendars of its records, and which rejoices in the possession of a set of vestry minutes from 1575 to the present day, has also the will of Steven Hellard, rector in 1501, the foundation charter of the grammar school, 1562, two fifteenth-century deeds and many dozens of deeds of the sixteenth, seventeenth and eighteenth centuries. Hawkhurst, Kent, has a collection of forty-three ancient deeds, the earliest of which is a copy made *temp.* Edward I of a deed c. A.D. 1180 executed by the abbot and convent of Battle. Wem, Salop, has a parcel of deeds relating to land now incorporated in the churchyard, the earliest document in the collection being dated 1584.

Newport, Essex, had a parcel of fifty-three deeds, mostly mediaeval, from 1265 onwards, many with fine seals, now deposited in the County Record Office. Eynesford, Kent, has a grant of 1521–2, and a release of 1552–3. Wymeswold, Leics., had of late, but we fear no longer has, in its porch chamber an enormous collection of deeds, many of them mediaeval in date. St Chad's, Shrewsbury, has a parcel of twenty-eight monastic deeds, 1280–1428. Rolvenden, Kent, has a copy of a Chancery petition of 1716. Alveley, Salop, has a collection of deeds relating to the charity lands, 1411–1626. Sellinge, Kent, has an escheat of 16 Edward II (1322–3). Thaxted, Essex, had amongst the records of the Yardley Charity, now deposited with the County authorities, a great many mediaeval deeds, the earliest being of c. 1200, and Wookey, Som., has a bundle of leases from Richard II to Elizabeth I, and a parcel of other deeds from 1390 onwards. Bedfordshire County Record Office has collected from the parish chests numerous such deeds, the earliest found so far being of c. 1280.

Often, of course, such records relate primarily to ecclesiastical business. At Hawkhurst, Kent, there is an indenture of 18 Edward IV concerning a 'light' in the church, and one of 1482 relating to an obit. St Dunstan's, Canterbury, has a deposition of 1552 concerning an obit in the church. At St Mary's, Sandwich, there is an ancient bede roll, and at Hedenham, Norf., there is a papal bull of Innocent IV, in a copy made by the rector in 1735; St Mary's, Sandwich, whose churchwardens' accounts were carried away by the French in 1456, has a contemporary copy, also a parcel of deeds including an agreement between the prior and convent of Christ Church, Canterbury and the mayor and commonalty of the town, and a letter c. 1448 from Humphrey, Duke of Buckingham. It has also the foundation deed of a light, and a chantry certificate of 1547. Herne, Kent, has the foundation deeds of two lights, 1296 and 1297, and an inventory of the ornaments in the chapel, 1341. Crondall, Hants., has an inventory of church goods, 1556. Linton, Kent, has an 'Inventory of all jewells of the Church of Cranbrooke', 1509, and a list of contributors to the 'work of making ye middle Ile', 1521–2. Deeping St James', Lincs., has the Corpus Christi Gild accounts, 1540–9, and North Cray, Kent, has a deed of 1557, signed by Cardinal Pole, for deconsecrating Ruxley church, and uniting the parish with that of North Cray. Nottingham St Peter's has the accounts of the gilds of St George, 1459–1546, and St Mary, 1515–41, with lists of churchwardens and aldermen, and churchwardens' accounts 1521–1648. The manuscript is bound in the leaf of a mediaeval processional. Early records of tithe disputes are sometimes found. At St Mary's, Southampton, there is a commission of c. 1290 for an inquiry as to tithe; Selsey, Sussex, has a parcel of old deeds, including one of 1526 concerning a tithe dispute between the rector and the prebendary. Old Romney, Kent, has a deed of 1547 as to the tithe payable to the rector by the rector of Midley. Berrington, Salop, of late had, but, alas, no longer has, a most interesting episcopal mandate of 1639 concerning the local custom of the vicar giving an annual love feast to his parishioners.

Sometimes odd scraps of early records have been preserved through their use to form part of the bindings of much later and sometimes much less valuable works. The overseers' account book of Dunton, Beds., is bound in a commission by the lord lieutenant of the county to three deputy lieutenants, 1625. At Yeovilton, Som., a little book of 1706–13 is bound in part of a patent of 1691 for the

use of rollers under carriages; at Kingsworthy, Hants., the register
is bound in part of a fifteenth-century astronomical book; at
Higham, Kent, in an Elizabethan deed, and at Grove, Notts., in
what appears to be a mandate to the local landowner, Sir Hardolph
Wasteneys, to appear at the coronation of King James I. At Highclere, Hants., the register is bound in part of an early fourteenth-
century *compotus*; at Castle Cary, Som., the fly-leaf is part of a
black-letter book of prayers; and at Compton, Surrey, the churchwardens' accounts, 1570–1638, are bound in a document of 1483,
signed by John Colingbourne, abbot of St Peter de Hida (the 'New
Minster' at Winchester), 1480–5. A manorial record of Little
Bentley, Essex, is bound in an Elizabethan deed concerning two
tenements in Southwark, and at Great Dunmow in the same county
the cover of the earliest churchwardens' account book, 1526–1621,
is part of a pre-Reformation work of some sort, with the words still
decipherable: JHESVS and MARIA.

Mediaeval parchments of one sort or another form the covers
of the registers of Boston, Lincs., Micheldever, Hants., and
St Bartholomew's, Winchester. At Brockenhurst, Hants., the
registers are bound in fragments of a mediaeval theological work,
and those of Thorncombe and Winsham, Som., are bound in
fragments of a Latin manuscript of the *Aurea Legenda*. The
churchwardens' accounts of Fordwich, Kent, 1509–38, are bound
in parchment leaves from a mediaeval service book, and fragments
of similar books are used for similar purposes at St Andrew's,
Canterbury, and Colmer, Hants. A calendar from such a book has
been used as a cover for the first part of the register of Luddenham,
Kent, 1554–1772, and two odd leaves of a similar book are pasted
in a scrap-book belonging to St Dunstan's, Canterbury. Several
pages of a black-letter psalter, apparently used in the first place as
packing for the binding, are now inserted at the end of the first
register, 1558–1634, of Farnham, Essex. A leaf of a thirteenth-
century manuscript psalter forms the original cover of the first
register of Brenzett, Kent. Two leaves from a fourteenth-century
benedictional make up the binding of the first register of Edenbridge, Kent. The earliest register of Treswell, Notts., is bound in
a fragment of a fifteenth-century Vulgate. The register of Oakley,
Beds., has as loose cover a leaf from a fifteenth-century gradual.
The vestry book of Donington in Holland, Lincs., 1586–1768, has
bound up with it two leaves of a mediaeval antiphonary. Fragments of mediaeval missals are not uncommon. Four pages of one

formerly covered the earliest register of Linton, Kent, 1558–1681 (they are now bound up in the volume), and pages from fifteenth-century missals cover the earliest registers of Southampton St Michael's and Southwick, Hants. The churchwardens' accounts of Cheswardine, Salop, were bound in several pages of a most interesting breviary following a use not yet identified, and the register of Greatham, Hants., is bound in part of a fifteenth-century gradual.

Wills of parish benefactors are sometimes found among parish records. Keston, Kent, has one of 1602 in a copy of 1637, the register of Heptonstall, Yorks., has one of 1638, with extracts from others of 1645, 1687 and 1721, and an old terrier of the same parish has copies of or extracts from four more wills of benefactors, 1609–42. Somerton, Som., has a will of 1638, and Ashill in the same county had until recently a bundle of wills proved in the peculiar court, 1663–1801. At Stevenage, Herts., the will of Thomas Alleyne is entered in abstract in the earliest register, in a beautiful hand showing the pious fervour of the scribe who commemorated his virtues. Costock, Notts., has a valuable collection of wills and marriage settlements of the lords of the manor.

Contracts for work to be done about the church may be met with occasionally. The register of Cowden, Kent, has e.g. a Latin contract with a bell-founder in 1635, and that of Brotherton, Yorks. (which also contains the churchwardens' accounts for 1661, 1663, 1664, 1665, 1666), has a contract for whitewashing the church in 1664.

Costock, Notts., has a melancholy object lesson as to the ultimate fate of the wordy testimonials with which parishioners even nowadays delight to honour a parting incumbent. Such a testimonial, of the early eighteenth century, forms the wrapper of a parcel of wills. It contains the signatures of twenty-five clergy and one schoolmaster in north-west Norfolk.

Such well-known diaries as those of Parson Woodforde are members of a very large class, and a great many of them are to be found in parish chests. The rector of Hedenham, Norf., e.g. kept such a diary from 1812 onwards. A typical entry is:

1830 Dec. 4. Mary Shorten, village schoolmistress in consequence of not being allowed to add a double cottage to the School (and other buildings wch she had been in the habit of erecting at various times without permission) thought proper having been ordered by Mr. Kent to pull down the new building, to pull down also the School room, and not leave one stone upon another (such are the blessed effects of Radical Reform).

In Nottinghamshire there are very interesting diaries at Clayworth and Sutton (Bonington) St Annes, the former, 'The Rectors' Book of Clayworth, 1676–1701', being a journal kept by the Rev. William Sampson, and the latter, one of 1740–70, by the Rev. Chas. Allen. Bainton, Yorks., has the parish visiting book of the Rev. Joseph Carter, 1830–40, and Walkeringham, Notts., has a similar book of about the same period, in which the vicar has entered some frank, and occasionally very uncomplimentary, references to his parishioners. Kent has at least six such books, at Acrise, 1819–44, Brabourne, 1786 to the present day, Crundale, 1698 onwards, Ospringe, 1848 onwards, and Rolvenden, 1884 to the present day. Brotherton, Yorks., has one from 1779 onwards, and Stevenage, Herts., one of 1764. Batheaston, Som., has a register of household accounts kept by two vicars and their sisters, 1711–86.

Plans of the church with reference to appropriated pews may be found. Trull, Som., has a fine series of such plans, 1569, 1635 and 1731. The chapel of Newchurch, Culcheth, Lancs., had one of the mid-eighteenth-century which is at present in our possession, but which will ultimately be restored to the parish chest whence it was abstracted many years ago.

Among the oddest contents of parish chests must be the eighteenth-century cobbler's account book preserved at Kingston-on-Soar, Notts.; the 'catalogue of Mr. Miller's books', dated 1750 (Mr Miller being a vicar who died in 1724), at Effingham, Surrey; the schoolboy's exercise book, c. 1650, with examples of the methods of solving three arithmetical problems, found at Luccombe, Som.; the

true and most dreadful discourse of a woman possessed with the devill, 1584

in the chest of Ditcheat in the same county; the estate account book, 1749–63, in no way concerning church or parish, found at Kingston-on-Thames, Surrey; the cast of the local Plough Monday play, 1563, in the chest of Donington in Holland, Lincs.; the Corporation records from 1600 and assizes of wages from 1620 in the chest of St Mildred's, Tenterden, Kent; and our own favourite, a medical secret discovered by the vicar of East Retford, Notts., and entered in the register for the benefit of posterity, by Thomas Gylby, vicar 1701–51:

In ye time of a Plague let ye person either infected or fearfull of ye infection take a penny worth of Dragon Water, a penworth of oyle Olive, methredate 1d. & treacle 1d., then take an unyon & fill it full of pepper w^n you scouped it, y^n roast it; and after y^t put it to ye liquor & strain & drink it in ye morning, & if you take ye same at night lay soap and bay salt to your feet & sweat upon it & with God's blessing you shall recover.

We suppose that *cacoethes scribendi* may fairly be described as a plague, but so far we have not ventured to try the prescription!

Notes

INTRODUCTION: pages 1–42

THE ENGLISH PARISH   **page 1**

1. *Argument against the Abolishing of Christianity*, 1708.

2. Under the Local Government Act of 1893–4, 56 & 57 Vict. c. 73, s. 17 (8). This was re-enacted in the Local Government (Consolidation) Act, 23 & 24 Geo. V, c. 51 (1932–3), s. 281, and developed in 10 & 11 Eliz. II, c. 56 (1962). Any list of briefs (for which see below, pp. 120–25) shows what an enormous number of churches were damaged or destroyed by fire in the seventeenth and eighteenth centuries. It must often have happened in such cases that the old parish records were destroyed too, or that even if they were saved from the fire, nearly all save the registers were cleared out in the reorganisation of church affairs while arrangements were being made for rebuilding the fabric. At Beaulieu, Hants. (Fearon, *op. cit.* p. 96), the parish civil records were 'destroyed when the Local Government Act came into force'. At Warlingham, Surrey, the (civil) parish council took steps soon after its formation to ascertain what documents were in the church. Inquiry elicited that about 1835–40 a certain Simon Baker was overseer, and that he had the chest in his private possession. He emigrated to America, and neither the chest nor its contents was ever heard of again. To make matters worse the vicar informed the council that the previous day he had turned out another old chest in the church, and destroyed its contents of 'worthless papers'. One is not surprised to find that in this parish the surviving records consist solely of the registers, the enclosure and tithe awards, and a few late account books of no particular interest or value.

3. It is sad to note such parishes as Church Stretton, Salop, where the documents referred to are not now to be found, though only a few years ago 'a very considerable mass of records remains in the belfry, from which apparently nothing has been removed, and to which nothing seems to have been added since the beginning of the nineteenth century'. Register III of St Peter's in Thanet, Kent, has:

'17th March 1759. At a meeting of the Ministers Churchwardens and other principal inhabitants of this Parish, all the writings in the Church Chest were carefully examined. Such of them only as by the length of time and their nature were become *absolutely useless* were destroyed, and every paper which *was* or hereafter possibly might be, of the least use or service was preserved. This Memorial is inserted to the intent that no false or malicious reports may ever be able to impose upon Posterity in this matter.

Cornelius Wilks, Vicar,   Elijah Mocket   } Churchwardens.
Vincent Underdoun }

4. Public Records Commission, 1912–19, *Report* III, p. 10.

5. In 1535–6, 27 Hen. VIII, c. 25 orders the accounts of the voluntary collectors of alms to be kept by 'the parson or some other honest man', though the book was to remain in the custody not of the parson but of two or three of the constables and churchwardens.

6. Public Records Commission, *Report* above cited, Pt. 1, p. 13.

7. *Ib.* Often the records consist of a series of books dating from c. 1691 when, by 3 Wm. & M. c. 11, s. 11 it was enacted that 'there shall be provided and kept in every parish at the charge of the said Parish a book or books wherein the names ... of such persons ... as may receive collection ... shall be registered' and that 'yearly in Easter week or as often as it shall be thought convenient the parishioners of every Parish shall meet in their Vestry ... before whom the said book shall be produced'.

8. Essex and Bedfordshire, e.g., have collected in their record offices almost the whole of the parish records of their areas (apart from registers, church-wardens' accounts, and vestry minutes). Some county archive authorities feeling, however, that wherever possible parish records should remain in their parishes, make no general appeal for the deposit of such records with the county archivisty, though they will, of course, accept deposit if this seems to be the only means of providing for the future safe custody of the documents. On this point see below *App. II.*

9. 58 Geo. III, c. 69 (1818).

10. 56 & 57 Vic. c. 73 (1893–4). See also *App. I sub anno* 1962.

page 9 THE ENGLISH PARISH AND ITS OFFICERS

1. Bryant, *Humanity in Politics*, 1937, pp. 86–8.

2. Cripps, *On the Law of Church and Clergy*, 1921 edn., p. 344; Blackstone, *Commentaries*, 1778 edn., Vol. I, p. iii.

3. 29 & 30 Vic. c. 113 (1866), s. 18; 52 & 53 Vic. c. 63 (1889), s. 5.

4. *Commentaries*, edn. above cited, Vol. I, p. 114.

5. By an act of 1662, 14 Car. II, c. 12, dealt with later (p. 192), parishes might be divided. During the eighteenth century there was some alteration of parish boundaries, and in the nineteenth and twentieth there has been a constant succession of changes in the boundaries of ecclesiastical parishes under local acts, under the Church Building Acts, the Divided Parishes Acts, and the New Parishes Acts, all now administered by the Church Commissioners. Civil parish boundaries have been altered under local acts, by the discretionary powers of the justices, and by the boundaries committees of modern County Councils. Alterations suggested by the last-named were effected by provisional order of the Ministry of Health as successor to the Local Government Board. There was a Ministry of Health Boundary Commission of 1945, but this was replaced in 1958 by the Local Government Commission, now responsible to the Ministry of Housing and Local Government.

It has been stated that there are no less than four kinds of parish: the ecclesiastical parish, the civil parish, the highways parish, and the land-tax parish. Here the third and fourth are regarded as special varieties of the second, so that we are left with the convenient, though not wholly accurate, division of parishes into two classes, civil and ecclesiastical.

6. Archbishop 668–90. Camden went further still and suggested that probably the division was made by Honorius, c. 630 (Blackstone, *op. cit.* p. 111).

7. See below, pp. 134–43.

8. Blackstone, *op. cit.* p. 112.

9. This contains a valuation of the whole country in parishes, made upon Pope Nicholas IV's grant of tenths to King Edward I in 1288, for six years, towards the expense of a crusade. This valuation held good until the valor of 1534–5 mentioned below. *Taxatio Ecclesiastica . . .* , c. 1291, edited by the Rev. S. Ayscough and J. Caley, and published by the Record Commission in 1802.

10. Ordered by King Henry VIII, upon the decision to transfer the receipt of first-fruits and tenths from the Papacy to the Crown: *Valor Ecclesiasticus . . .* (1534–5), Vols. I–VI, and Introduction, edited by J. Caley and the Rev. J. Hunter, and published by the Record Commission, 1825–34.

11. 14 Car. II, c. 12 (1662). The act relates to Lancashire, Cheshire, Derbyshire, Yorkshire, Northumberland, Durham, Cumberland and Westmorland, but was held judicially to extend to the country at large because of a reference to 'other counties'. See Nolan, *Poor Laws*, edn. 1808, Vol. I, pp. 737, and Burn, *Justice of the Peace*, edn. 1758, Vol. III, pp. 4–5. Although the act had fallen into abeyance the clauses referred to were not repealed until 1844.

12. The first Sturges Bourne Act, q.v.

THE MINISTER OF THE PARISH AND HIS CIVIL AND
page 12   ECCLESIASTICAL DUTIES

1. An incumbent might be rector, vicar, or perpetual curate. Only a rector was properly styled parson, but rector and vicar both held freehold benefices.

A curate was not normally 'beneficed' at all. For the technical distinctions among these three classes of clergy see Glossary, *sub Tit.* Curate, Incumbent Minister, Parson, Vicar.

2.   The Webbs, *The Parish and the County*, p. 36.

3.   15 Ric. II, c. 6 (1391), reinforced by 4 Hen. IV, c. 12 (1402).

4.   Burn, *History of the Poor Laws*, p. 105, quoted by Nolan, *op. cit.* Vol. 1, p. 5, fn.

5.   Though church rates had been levied as early as 1370: Cripps, *op. cit.* p. 436, canon 89.

6.   7 Jac. I, c. 4 (1609–10).

7.   The Webbs, *op. cit.* p. 37 and, I suppose, 5 Eliz. c. 4 (1562–3), s. 10.

8.   5 Eliz. c. 4 (1562–3), s. 10, and 13 Geo. II, c. 24 (1739–40). The wording of the testimonial is given by Burn as: 'Memorandum that A.B., late servant to C.D. of E., husbandman, or taylor etc., in the said county, is licensed to depart from his said master, and is at his liberty to serve elsewhere, according to the statute in that case made and provided. In witness whereof etc., Dated the day, month, year, and place etc., of the making thereof.' The acts provide that the testimonial is to be given by the constable and two other honest householders, and registered by the minister at a fee of twopence. Persons departing from service without such a testimonial are to be whipped as vagabonds, and their employers are to forfeit £5, half of which is to go to the informer.

9.   26 Geo. II, c. 31 (1753), and 26 Geo. III, c. 71 (1786).

10.   Blackstone, *op. cit.* Vol. 1, p. 377.

11.   Cripps, *op. cit.* pp. 33–48, 89–94, 145–50.

12.   Supposedly the incumbent and the parishioners jointly choose the two, but, as pointed out below, p. 85, in case of disagreement each chooses one.

13.   In an ordinary diocese this would be the Bishop's Consistory Court.

THE VESTRY MEETING   **page 13**

1.   *Op. cit.* p. 45 *et passim.*

2.   *Op. cit.* pp. 37–8, fn. 6.

3.   See below, pp. 92–4.

4.   Toulmin Smith, *op. cit.* p. 47 *et passim.*

5.   Peyton, *op. cit.* pp. 111, 330.

6.   5 & 6 W. IV, c. 50 (1835).

7.   5 & 6 Vic. c. 109 (1842).

8.   See the instances given below, pp. 197, 229.

9.   Various acts have such phrases as 'the Mayor and two or three of the chief parishioners', 'two or three of the most wealthy inhabitants', 'two or three of the most substantial householders'.

10.   Cripps, *op. cit.* p. 44.

11.   There were popular incursions into close vestries during the Commonwealth, but after the Restoration the old tendency continued with renewed vigour.

12.   The Webbs, *op. cit.* pp. 175–97.

13.   Toulmin Smith, *op. cit.* p. 238, and Lord Tenterden's judgment in Golding *v.* Fenn, 1827.

14.   But the vestries set up under the later acts, 10 Anne, c. 20 (1711), 58 Geo. III, c. 45 (1818) *et seq.* (the Webbs, *op. cit.* p. 204), were expressly confined to ecclesiastical business only.

15.   These parishes had, however, no power over the levying or expenditure of church rate, highway rate, or poor rate.

16.   See below, pp. 235–7.

17.   58 Geo. III, c. 69 (1818), and 59 Geo. III, c. 12 (1819).

18.   Persons rated at less than £50 were to have one vote, others one more for each £25 of rateable value in excess of £50 up to a maximum of six votes.

19.   The Webbs, *op. cit.* pp. 162–3.

20.   1 & 2 W. IV, c. 60 (1831), 'For the better regulation of Vestries', the Webbs, *op. cit.* p. 274.

page 25 RATES AND RATING

1. Cannan, *op. cit.* pp. 4, 327.
2. E.g. the land tax.
3. E.g. the provision of schools, roads, hospitals, etc. See below, p. 118.
4. E.g. labour on the roads, regularised, not introduced, by the act of 1555 (below, pp. 242–4).
5. Bridges especially were often reparable in this way.
6. See below, pp. 93–4.
7. Cannan, *op. cit.* pp. 18–21.
8. *Ib. passim.*
9. *The Ingatherer*, No. 66, 1938.
10. 6 Hen. VI, c. 5 (1427).
11. 22 Hen. VIII, c. 5 (1530–1).
12. 23 Hen. VIII, c. 2 (1531–2).
13. See below, p. 106.
14. 24 Hen. VIII, c. 10 (1532–3).
15. 2 & 3 P. & M. c. 5 (1555).
16. 2 & 3 P. &. M. c. 8 (1555). See below, p. 243.
17. 27 Eliz. c. 13 (1584–5).
18. 35 Eliz. c. 4 (1592–3).
19. 39 Eliz. c. 3 (1597–8).
20. See below, p. 191.
21. 43 Eliz. c. 2 (1601). See below, p. 191.

22. 3 Jac. I, c. 10 (1605–6), and 7 Jac. I, c. 4 (1609–10).
23. See above, p. 14, also below, pp. 93–5.
24. 14 Car. II, c. 6 (1662).
25. 22 Car. II, c. 12 (1670).
26. 3 W. & M. c. 12 (1691).
27. 14 Car. II, c. 12 (1662).
28. 18 & 19 Car. II, c. 9 (1666).
29. 11 W. III, c. 19 (1698–9).
30. 13 Anne c. 26 (1714).
31. 12 Geo. II, c. 29 (1738–9).
32. 17 Geo. II, c. 38 (1743–4).
33. 55 Geo. III, c. 51 (1814–15).
34. 3 & 4 W. IV, c. 90 (1833).
35. 31 & 32 Vic. c. 109 (1867–8).
36. 37 & 38 Vic. c. 54 (1874).
37. 15 & 16 Geo. V, c. 90 (1924–5).
38. 19 & 20 Geo. V, c. 25 (1928–9).
39. 41 Geo. III, c. 23 (1801).

page 29 THE OFFICERS OF THE PARISH

1. See below, pp. 84–108.
2. See below, p. 44.
3. See above, pp. 13–15.
4. See below, pp. 189–91, 226.
5. See below, pp. 176–87.
6. See below, pp. 242–50.
7. See below, pp. 255–64.
8. Published by the late Index Society, now absorbed in the British Record Society, as its third volume, 1879.
9. Blackstone, *op. cit.* Vol. I, quoting Gibson's *Codex*. There were perhaps 9000 parishes in 1688, and there are said to have been 10,693 in 1821, The Webbs, *The Parish and the County*, p. 13.
10. 59 Geo. III, c. 12 (1819), s. 6.
11. 13 Geo. III, c. 78 (1772–3).
12. ʻ5 & 6 W. IV, c. 50 (1835).
13. 3 W. & M. c. 11 (1691); cf. 59 Geo. III, c. 12 (1819).
14. See also 5 & 6 Vic. c. 109 (1842).
15. *Op. cit.* p. 86.
16. 59 Geo. III, c. 85 (1819).
17. In 1927 under 15 & 16 Geo. V, c. 90 (1924–5).
18. 7 & 8 Geo. V, c. 64 (1917–18).

page 35 THE CHEST ITSELF

1. *English Church Woodwork*, p. 342
2. A.D. 1166.
3. Roe, *op. cit.* p. 108.
4. 5 & 6 Ed. VI, c. 2 (1551–2).
5. Canon 84.
6. Below, p. 44.
7. Cox and Harvey, *English Church Furniture*, p. 300.
8. *Op. cit.* p. 79.
9. *Ib.* p. 70.
10. 52 Geo. III, c. 146 (1812), dealt with below, pp. 50–1.

PART I: pages 43–161

RECORDS MAINLY ECCLESIASTICAL

I. PARISH REGISTERS page 43

1. Hume, *History of England*, 1754–61, quoted by Sir Francis Palgrave, *Quarterly Review*, Vol. LXXIII, p. 561; Burn, *op. cit.* p. 4.
2. See Cox, *Parish Registers of England*, pp. 2–3, and Chester Waters, *op. cit.* pp. 7–8. The allegation was made by the deprived Romanists that the king intended to levy a tax of half a crown upon each baptism, marriage, or burial.
3. *State Papers Domestic*, Vol. XIII, Pt. II, No. 281.
4. See e.g. Froude, *Henry VIII*, Everyman edn. Vol. II, pp. 240–1.
5. See Cox, *op. cit.* p. 2, and Burn, *History of Parish Registers*, p. 17, for the text.
6. Cox, *ibid.* See below, p. 52. The present ruling on the matter is in canon 70.
7. Firth and Rait, Vol. I, pp. 582, 601.
8. *Ib.* Vol. II, pp. 715–18.
9. These two points are illustrated by the history of the registers of Sutton Bonington, Notts. For centuries the amalgamation of the two parishes of St Anne and St Michael was needed, but every time it was suggested it was blocked by vested interests of one sort or another, until it took place at last in the 1950's. During the Interregnum, union for registration purposes actually existed. John Savage, the 'Register' elected in 1653, stitched together the registers of the two parishes, and they remained so united (though, of course, the parishes had been severed again at the Restoration) until they were separated, in accordance with the archdeacon's instructions, in 1921.
10. *Op. cit.* p. 70.
11. Firth and Rait, Vol. II, p. 1139, 12 Car. II, c. 33 (1660).
12. Chester Waters, *op. cit.* p. 16.
13. See below, pp. 66–9.
14. 5 & 6 W. & M. c. 21 (1693–4), taxed marriages, 6 & 7 W. & M. c. 6 (1694), taxed marriages, births, deaths and burials, also bachelors and widowers; penalty clauses added the next year by 7 & 8 W. & M. c. 35 (1695).
15. 4 & 5 Anne, c. 23 (1705). **16.** Chester Waters, *op. cit.* p. 83.
17. 10 Anne, c. 10 (1711). **18.** 26 Geo. II, c. 33 (1753).
19. Wilkie Collins, *The Woman in White*, The Story continued by Walter Hartright, chap. 9.
20. *Op. cit.* p. 9. **21.** 23 Geo. III, c. 67 (1782–3).
22. 25 Geo. III, c. 75 (1785). **23.** By 34 Geo. III, c. 11 (1794).
24. Malthus' great *Essay* appeared in 1798. See also below p. 82.
25. See above, p. 45 and below, p. 55.
26. 52 Geo. III, c. 146 (1812), coming into force on New Year's day, 1813.
27. No. 298 of 1831. **28.** No. 669 of 1833.
29. The Births and Deaths Registration Act, 6 & 7 W. IV, c. 86 (1836), and the Marriage Act, 6 & 7 W. IV, c. 85 (1836), coming into force on 1 July 1837.
30. *The Story of the General Register Office.* See above, p. 45.
31. By Mr Chester Waters.
32. See below, note 44.
33. Public Records Commission, 1912–19, *Report* III, Pt. III, p. 58. According to Cox, *Parish Registers of England* there are also 205, beginning in 1539, and 16 prior to 1539, a total of 877 continuous from the early period. This total ought, of course, to be in the neighbourhood of 11,000. (Dr Cox's book gives: on pp. 234–9 particulars of all registers before 1538; on pp. 264–9 lists of registers beginning in 1538; on pp. 270–1 a list of registers beginning in 1539.) Mr F. G. Emmison, Essex County Archivist, is in a better position

U

than are most of us to give a reasoned estimate. He suggests, *Archives and Local History*, p. 52, that [I reckon ten thousand or so old parishes] the paper registers survive for perhaps a hundred or two hundred, the parchment ones from 1538 for about 1250, those from 1558 for perhaps 2500. These estimates will, of course, be subject to some revision on the appearance of Mr Steel's survey, elsewhere noted.

34. *Ib.* Vol. I, p. 16.

35. Instances of registers lost in this fashion appear in Buckland, *op. cit.* pp. 36–7, Thiselton Dyer, *op. cit.* pp. 214, and in the Report of the Commission of 1912–19. According to these, many of the missing registers have suffered such fates as burning, loss, lending without return, destruction by fire, water, damp, lightning, 'silverfish', rats, mice, or parish clerks. Other typical notes are 'removed with the vicar's books', used by the village grocer for wrapping his wares, abstracted by the churchwardens, purloined by the lord of the manor, 'thrown on a dung heap', 'made into tea kettle holders by the curate's wife', thrown on the fire by the parson's wife, in a rage with her husband, and cut into labels by a sporting parson for addressing presents of game to his friends. Leaves have been cut out for a variety of purposes, some to tack together as a covering for a bed tester, some removed bodily to save the clerk the trouble of finding paper and ink when persons applied to him for certified copies of entries. In one place the registers were given away in odd leaves as souvenirs to visitors to the church, in another they were 'burnt by the parish clerk in singeing a goose', in still another they were cut up to make tailor's patterns. One set were given to the old women in the village 'to wrap their knitting pins', another were used by the village schoolmaster for covering his children's primers. Perhaps the most grotesque of all fates that overtook any series of registers was that of a set which were buried in the churchyard, the leaves being cut out to swathe round the corpse of the parish clerk's grandmother. Another set suffering a curious fate had their entries obliterated during the accouchement of the parson's pet greyhound bitch, who had chosen the parish chest for her whelping, and whom the parson declined to disturb, since evidently he valued his bitch more than his registers.

Again, as late as 1824 a register was taken away and never returned, the culprit being, of all people, the archdeacon! Generally, though by no means invariably, such losses as those indicated have taken place many years ago. At Kingsdown, Kent, the incumbent entered in his register in 1814, the record of the burial of one Phillips, 'Clerk of the Parish 19 years. A respectable man & an excellent reader. The man who burnt the old Parish Registers.'

Since I have had a good deal to say above concerning the delinquencies of parish clerks, it seems only fair to note one record of an exceptionally virtuous one. According to the registers of Sutton, Surrey, after the death in 1678 of the Rev. H. Wycke, who had been incumbent since 1636, his widow carried away the volume with her into Lincolnshire, whence it was restored by one of her sons in 1703. 'But in yᵉ meane time Wᵐ. Stewart an honest man who was clark of this parish from Mʳ Wych's time til now kept an account of yᵉ Baptisms, Marriages and Burialls wh. I am now goeing to transcribe over yᵉ leafe. Wᵐ. Stephens.'

36. In Canterbury diocese it was usual for the transcripts to be made in duplicate, one for the consistory court, handed in at Michaelmas, one for the court of the archdeaconry, given in at Easter. The Canterbury series of transcripts is probably the most complete in the country. The earliest transcripts are at Lincoln and at Leicester. They date from 1561 and relate to the archdeaconries of Lincoln, Stow and Leicester, the first two still, and the last-named originally, in the diocese of Lincoln. They were made, some forty years before the 1597/8 Constitution, in obedience to an order of the Court of High Commission.

37. E.g. the transcripts of the registers of the fifty-five Lichfield Dean and Chapter peculiars (in Derbyshire and Staffordshire), at Lichfield, and those of the collegiate church (now the cathedral) of Southwell. In Nottinghamshire there were the Southwell peculiars and several peculiars of the Archbishop, of the Dean and Chapter, and of two prebendaries of York, Apesthorpe (Habbles-thorpe) and Bole. All the register transcripts of the parishes last named, plus the ordinary diocesan transcripts (Nottinghamshire was formerly in York diocese) have recently been discovered at York, and have been transferred to their proper place, the diocesan muniment room at Southwell.

38. See upon this point G. Hill, *English Dioceses, a history of their limits from the earliest times to the present day*, 1900, and below *App. II*.

39/40. All published references to guides to parish registers, register transcripts etc. will shortly become obsolete, on the appearance of Mr D. J. Steel's monumental *National Index of Parish Registers, Bishop's Transcripts and Marriage Licences, and of Printed, MS., TS., and Microfilm Copies*. This is to be a twelve-volume work, the first nine volumes covering England, but Monmouthshire 'in South Wales' in Vol. II. Inquiries as to the state of completion of the work at any time in the future, orders for copies, notes of *addenda* and *corrigenda* etc. may be sent to Mr Steel at the address given above, p. 54.

41. Based upon my own inquiries, Dr Cox's book, and information furnished by the late T. M. Blagg, Esq., F.S.A.

42. The Devon and Cornwall Record Society prints mainly registers.

43. Various publications of the Institute of Historical Research supplement its *Guide to the Historical Societies of England and Wales* (not published, but available in typescript in the Institute).

44. The fees laid down in the 1836 by the Births and Deaths Registration Act applied to the Marriage Registers until a few years ago, for the scale was incorporated in the Marriage Act of 1949, 12 & 13 Geo. VI, c. 76, and it held good till the amounts were increased to one shilling and sixpence for the first year, and ninepence for each subsequent year, by a 'Statutory Instrument' in 1952 (No. 991 of 1952). For Baptismal and Burial Registers they have, in general, been doubled, instead of merely increased by 50%, and this by various 'Instruments' of the Ecclesiastical Commissioners/Church Commissioners, issued by them at different dates, but all under the powers given by the *Ecclesiastical Commissioners (Powers) Measure*, 1-2 Geo. VI, no. 4 (1938).

45. Chester Waters, *op. cit.* p. 70.

46. See above, note 35, for lists of registers regarded as 'early'.

47. Clay, *History of Landbeach* (Cambs.), C.A.S. 1861, p. 81.

48. See above, pp. 47-8.

49. See Archdeacon W. M. Sinclair, *The Chapels Royal*, 1912.

50. E.g. this entry from the Register of the Chapels Royal of St James's, Whitehall, and Windsor, reproduced in the Registrar-General's pamphlet above cited (facing p. 7): '1685 James Scot late Duke of Monmouth Landed at Lyme Rs. in Dorsetshire wth about 150 men on the 11th day of June 1685. Hee was Routed at Weston-moore near Bridgwater on monday July ye 6th following. He was taken July 8th in Dorsetshire near Ringwood on the borders of Hampshire; He was brought to Whitehall July 13th and fro' thence carryed to the Tower, and Executed on Tower-Hill July 15th. Hee dyed a Refractory Fanatick owning, (at the last), he had lived happily for 2 years past wth ye Lady Harriot Wentworth as his wife; His Dutchess when hee saw her in the Tower he used but coldly.'

REGISTER ENTRIES   **page 58**

1. E.g. at Chelsfield, Kent, they are entered 1575-1602; at Edenbridge in the same county 1575-86.   **2.** The date of the 'Directory.'

3. The *Office for the Baptism of such as are of Riper Years* was approved by Convocation in 1661, and in February 1663 the Prayer Book in its present form was re-introduced.

4. See above, p. 48. **5.** See above, pp. 46-47. **6.** See above, pp. 49-50.

7. Canons 68 and 69, Lyndwood, Bk. I, Tit. VII, Chap. 3 (*Quod in Constitutione*), Tit. X, Chap. 1 (*Ut Archidiaconi*), Tit. XI, Chap. 2 (*Item commoneant*), Bk. III, Tit. XXIV, Chap. 2 (*Circa sacramentum*). On occasion baptism could take place even before birth, since, in a dangerous delivery, the appearance of the head or of any limb gave proof of the separate existence of the child, and hence formed justification for the christening. It was because of the midwife's duty to christen in emergency that the licensing of midwives was entrusted to the bishops. For the midwife's oath see Strype, *Annals*, I, p. 537, and Chester Waters, *op. cit.* p. 36.

8. Lyndwood, Bk. I, Tit. VI, Chap. I (*Panni chrysmales*).

9. Act II, Sc. 3.

10. Chap. I, Sec. (II), (2).   **11.** Everyman reprint, pp. 240–1.

12. See below, pp. 214–21.   **13.** See below, pp. 309–22.

14. Crabbe, *The Parish Register*, 1807, *Works*, 1834, Vol. II, p. 168.

15. *Oliver Twist*, chap. I.

16. The last-named being omitted and the other two shortened. In 1918 the Roman Catholic authorities reduced the period still further. It is to be noted that here the prohibition is not of marriage, but of the 'solemnities' of marriage. There is no nuptial mass, and the parties are warned to avoid unnecessary display (*ut a nimia pompa abstineant*).

17. Canon 62. The phrase under discussion was repealed in 1888.

18. Quoted by Dr Cox, *op. cit.* p. 79, from the register of Cottenham, Cambs., beginning 1572.

19. Everton, Notts., Register I, beginning 1567. See Cox, *op. cit.* p. 82, and Lyndwood, Bk. IV, Tit. I (*Matrimonium*) and Tit. III (*Quia ex contractibus*), for constitutions as early as A.D. 1200 ordering the calling of banns, and for references in 1328 to the archbishop's dispensing power.

20. He took over at the Reformation the powers formerly exercised in this matter by the pope (25 Hen. VIII, c. 21 (1533–4), which powers are still reserved to him by the Marriage Act of 1823, 4 Geo. IV, c. 76.

21. The Fleet, the King's Bench Prison, and the Mint.

22. E.g. in London, St James's, Duke Place, and the Mayfair Chapel, in Derbyshire, the Peak Forest Chapel and the Dale Abbey Chapel. There were also such parishes as Fledborough, Notts., not technically peculiars, but having accommodating incumbents who were ready to marry couples on demand.

23. A particularly glaring scandal occurred in William III's reign when Captain Campbell abducted Miss Wharton. The marriage was annulled by act of Parliament in 1690, and Campbell's accessory, Sir John Johnstone, was hanged. Another, much later, was occasioned when Edward Gibbon Wakefield abducted a Miss Turner. He was tried for this in 1827, the marriage was annulled by special act, and he was transported (to become a pioneer of empire. He later played a most distinguished part in the history of reform in Australia and New Zealand).

24. *Op. cit.* p. 100. See also pp. 81–2.

25. Chester Waters, *op. cit.* p. 68.

26. *Ex inf.* E. Freckingham Esq., of Fiskerton, Notts.

27. 18 & 19 Car. II, c. 4 (1666), 30 Car. II, c. 3 (1678), amended by 32 Car. II, c. 1 (1680).

28. E.g. at Holy Cross, Shrewsbury, Vol. 1678–1737.

29. The act assumes as necessary a shroud, but not a coffin. It was not until the eighteenth and nineteenth centuries that coffin burial became universal. See e.g. the rubric in the Burial Service, 'the earth shall be cast upon the *body*', and the references given by Dr Cox, *op. cit.* pp. 120–1. Easingwold and Howden parishes, Yorks., are said still to have the parish coffins provided for general use many years ago.

30. 54 Geo. III, c. 108 (1813–14).

31. *Moral Essays*, Ep. I, ll. 246–51.

32. Lyndwood, Bk. I, Tit. III, Chap. I (*Statutum et infra*), Bk. III, Tit. XIV, Chap. 2 (*Quia inter Rectores*). See also my suggestion, p. 305 (Pt. IV), note 22.

33. 21 Hen. VIII, c. 6 (1529). See below, p. 131, for a terrier incorporating the scale of dues.

34. 7 Geo. III, c. 14 Pr. (1766–7).

35. 2 & 3 Vic. c. 62 (1839), s. 6.

36. See above, p. 49.

37. On these associations see Gandy, *Guide to . . . the Association Oath Rolls*, 1921.

38. Lyndwood, Bk. V, Tit. xv, Chap. 1 (*Eternae sanctio voluntatis et infra*).
39. *A Priest to the Temple*, Chap. xxv. See also Herrick, *Hesperides*, 'To Anthea'.
40. *Hadden's Overseer's Handbook*, edn. 1920, pp. 314–15. The Poor Law Amendment Act, 7 & 8 Vic. c. 101 (1844), s. 60.
41. The MS. text has been checked. It certainly has, what appears in earlier printings of the present work, *est* for *erat*, *quia* for *qui* (which together spoil the third line of the hexameters), etc. A friend suggests the version given as containing some possible emendations.
42. *The Story of the General Register Office*, p. 5.

A NOTE UPON REGISTERS AND POPULATION STATISTICS

page 80
1. *Introduction to English Historical Demography*, 1966.
2. See above, pp. 47, 48, 63, 65.
3. See above, pp. 52–3, 64.
4. *Ed.* E. A. Wrigley; D. C. Eversley *et al.*, *Introduction to English Historical Demography*, 1966.

page 84 II. CHURCHWARDENS' ACCOUNTS

1. Cox, *op. cit.* pp. 15–32, describes three fourteenth-century and fifty-three fifteenth-century sets of accounts, and lists 323 series older than A.D. 1700.
2. In 1915 that great antiquary, the late Canon Foster, said that of early accounts there were in the huge diocese of Lincoln 'a few, about eight, I think', but in 1912 Dr Cox knew of more than four hundred in the whole country, and new sets were being discovered almost every week because of the new interest in local records which was aroused by the labours of the Commission of 1912–19. *Report* III, Pt. III, pp. 19 and 55.
3. Cripps, *The Law relating to the Church and Clergy*, p. 175.
4. See e.g. *The Freres Tale*, c. 1386, l. 7, below, p. 145.
5. Cripps, *op. cit.* p. 174.
6. Numerous other dates have been suggested. Toulmin Smith thought they could be traced as synodsmen (*decani*) as far back as the Council of Rouen, A.D. 550, at the Council of Narbonne in A.D. 1227 (as *testes synodales*), and in 1236 when Archbishop Edmund (Rich) of Canterbury directed the appointment of two or three questmen in each rural deanery, Lyndwood, Bk. V, Tit. I (*Sint in quolibet decanatu*). Pollock and Maitland's *History of English Law*, Bk. II, Chap. III, p. 602, says 'it is a moot point whether or not already in the 13th century the parishioners elected the churchwardens'. They are first mentioned as such in Archbishop Walter Reynolds' Constitutions of 1322, but the first quite indisputable reference to them in the legislation of the church is in the constitutions of Archbishop Henry Chichele in 1416.
7. 21 Jac. I, c. 12 (1623–4), s. 3, 'Churchwardens and other persons called sworn men'.
8. Based upon a canon of 1571 (Cox, *op. cit.* p. 5), ordering their election by the parishioners and minister according to the custom of the parish.
9. In later years by either 'open' or 'select' vestries (for which see pp. 13–22). For details of pre-Reformation usages see Cox, *op. cit.* pp. 3–6; The Webbs, *The Parish and the County*, pp. 21–2; or Cripps, *op. cit.* pp. 177–9.
10. With a few minor exceptions such as members of Parliament, sheriffs, ministers of all denominations, members of certain professions, and certain classes of Government officials. Dissenters and Papists were, and still are, eligible, though by the Toleration Act of 1689 they might serve the office by deputy. Quakers, however, were exempt from the obligation. Resignation of the office, with the consent of the electing body, has been possible since 1921; resignation without this was authorised only in 1964.
11. At Pittington, Durham, according to Miss Trotter, *op. cit.* p. 27, the parishioners grazed one sheep for the church flock for each £4 of their annual rent. For forty years the profit upon this covered all parish expenditure.

12. Clay, *op. cit.* pp. 45–6.

13. *A Priest to the Temple*, Chap. XIII.

14. 56 & 57 Vic. c. 73 (1894).

15. Dr Cox, *op. cit.* pp. 67 and 188, quotes examples of pew rents as early as 1454–5 and 1477–8, and follows in detail the history of pew renting and pew allocation from the fifteenth century to the middle of the seventeenth. Evidence is not lacking of pew appropriation before the Reformation. See Cox, *English Church Fittings*, p. 110, for an account of fifteenth-century appropriated pews in Cornwall. On this same matter of pews the work mentioned contains the interesting suggestion that the right of the 'squire to a pew or other seat in the chancel often attaches to him not as rector, but as patron, and that this was recognised in the diocese of Exeter in the thirteenth century'. Another interesting suggestion is that manor pews had their origin in the parcloses surrounding the chantries of manorial lords.

16. *Natural History and Antiquities of Selborne*, Letter III.

17. *The Romany Rye*, Chap. VIII.

18. *Pepys Diary*, 25 December 1661.

19. *Baucis and Philemon*, ll. 101–7.

20. Toulmin Smith, *op. cit.* pp. 582–3.

21. Cox, *op. cit.* p. 11.

22. Lyndwood, *Constitutiones . . . Othonis et Othoboni*, edn. 1679, p. 113.

23. Lyndwood, *Provinciale*, Bk. III, Tit. XXVII, Chap. 4 (*Licet parochiani et infra*).

24. Cripps, *op. cit.* p. 437.

25. Cox, *op. cit.* p. 11.

26. 9 February 1647, Scobell, *Acts and Ordinances*, 1658, Pt. I, p. 139.

27. 18 May 1661, The Webbs, *op. cit.* p. 14 fn.

28. *House of Lords MSS.*, Vol. I, N.S. 1900. The Bill became law as 7 & 8 W. III, c. 6 (1695–6).

29. 31 & 32 Vic. c. 109 (1867–8).

30. It is noteworthy that the archdeacon's function is purely ministerial. He has no power to exercise discretion as to the fitness of the persons appointed, and unless he is aware of some statutory disqualification he must admit them, whether or not he approves of the choice.

31. Canons 90 and 109–110.

32. Canon 19.	**38.** Canon 85.
33. Canon 27.	**39.** Canon 88.
34. Canon 28.	**40.** Canon 90.
35. Canon 52.	**41.** Canon 91.
36. Canon 53.	**42.** Canon 26.
37. Canon 57.	**43.** *Op cit.* p. 185.

44. 37 & 38 Vic. c. 85 (1874), The Public Worship Regulation Act.

45. First rubric prefacing the Prayer for the Church Militant.

46. Ninth rubric following the Communion Service.

47. Canon 20, and seventh rubric following the Communion Service.

48. 1 Eliz. c. 2 (1558–9), and Preface before the *Order for Morning Prayer*. For an interesting pre-Reformation list, incorporated in a canon of Archbishop Winchelsea, see Lyndwood, Bk. III, Tit. XXVII, Chap. 2 (*Ut parochiani*).

49. Canon 82, incorporating the injunction of 1550.

50. See below, pp. 104–5.

51. Canon 88.

52. *A Priest to the Temple*, Chap. XXIX.

53. See below, pp. 105–7.

54. Cox, *op. cit.* pp. 89–90. See above, p. 89.

55. After his visitation of 1633.

56. In 1641 Parliament forbade the use of altar rails.

57. According to Miss Trotter, *op. cit.* p. 24, at Houghton le Spring, Durham, for Easter 1662 there was bought 17 gallons and one pint of wine, at a cost of £1. 17s. 6d., with bread to a value of 2s. 2d.

58. *Shropshire Parish Documents*, p. 138.

59. Rubric 7.

60. Dr G. R. Owst, *Preaching in Medieval England*, 1926; *Literature and Pulpit in Medieval England*, 1933. The supposed antithesis between preaching and sacerdotal tendencies is, of course, a false one, as the history of the church from the time of St John Chryostom onwards most plainly shows.

61. See Cox, *English Church Fittings*, p. 127.

62. See e.g. canons 46, 47, 49, 50, 52.

63. 15 August 1781. A similar pulpit still remains in the Chapel of King's College, Cambridge.

64. Lyndwood, Bk. III, Tit. xxv, Chap. 1 (*Fontes baptismales*).

65. See e.g. Cox, *op. cit.*, p. 149, *sub* East Dereham, Norf. 1466.

66. See above, p. 58.

67. Lord Macaulay, *History of England from the Accession of King James II*, Vol. 1, Chap. 8.

68. In 1536 the English Bible (Coverdale's) and a Latin one were ordered to be placed in every church, and the injunction was repeated in 1537 for Matthew's translation, which was to be available by 1 August 1537. In 1547 the *First Book of Homilies* was issued by Edward VI's Council, and the same year, and again in 1559, it was ordered that the Bible (Cranmer's or the Great Bible) and the *Paraphrases* of Erasmus should be deposited in every church. The Order of Communion was approved by Convocation on 30 November 1547, and issued under a royal proclamation on 8 March 1548; Edward VI's First Prayer Book was issued in 1549, the second one in 1552, and the Prayer Book of Elizabeth in 1559. In 1563 the *Second Book of Homilies* was issued first by Convocation, and in 1563 also the Government required a translation of Foxe's *Book of Martyrs* to be obtained for each church. Archbishop Parker in 1564 added Jewel's *Defence of the Apology* to the other books, and Bancroft added Jewel's *Collected Works*, and again ordered the inclusion of Erasmus. The Presbyterian Directory was issued in 1645, when every parish was ordered to buy a copy.

69. Canon 82.

70. See above, pp. 43–4 and below, pp. 145–6 and f.n.

71. See Cox, *English Church Fittings*, pp. 169–70.

72. Until the Local Government Act of 1894, 56 & 57 Vic. c. 73; Prideaux, *op. cit.* p. 3.

73. See below, p. 192.

74. 13 Eliz. c. 19 (1571). The act was repealed in 1597–8.

75. 24 Hen. VIII, c. 10 (1532–3).

76. 8 Eliz. c. 15 (1566).

77. 14 Eliz. c. 11 (1572).

78. 39 Eliz. c. 18 (1597–8).

79. An *Observer* correspondent, 20 October 1937.

80. Pope, *Works*, edn. 1757, Vol. 6, p. 244.

81. Ezek. i. 15–28: ' Now as I beheld the living creatures, behold one wheel upon the earth by the living creatures, with his four faces. The appearance of the wheels and their work was like unto the colour of a beryl: and they four had one likeness: and their appearance and their work was as it were a wheel in the middle of a wheel . . . etc.'

82. The Webbs, *op. cit.* p. 35.

83. See Cox, *English Church Fittings*, pp. 294–5 and 301.

84. For references to a fuller list see above, pp. 30–1.

III. CHARITY ACCOUNTS AND OTHER **page 109**
CHARITY RECORDS. BRIEFS

1. See e.g. the Nottinghamshire rolls printed in the *Transactions* of the Thoroton Society, 1912–14, the Yorkshire surveys published by the Surtees Society as Vols. 91 and 92 in its publications, and a few similar county volumes, listed in R. Hist. S. *Texts and Calendars*, 'Indexes and Handbooks Series', no. 7, 1958, p. 651.

2. 37 Hen. VIII, c. 4 (1545).

3. 1 Ed. VI, c. 14 (1547).

4. But there is contemporary evidence to the contrary from those who had no undue affection for Romanism. Thomas Lever in his *Sermon preached the Fourth Sonday in Lent*, 1550, says, 'Alas, what a iudgement is this, a supersticious papiste, whiche hathe made the faulte, shall haue a pension out of a Chauntrie, so long as he lyueth, and a poore paryshe whiche hathe great neede and doone no faulte, shall lose and forfayte many Chauntries vtterly for euer' (*Sermons*, Arber's Reprint of 1901, p. 69).

5. 43 Eliz. c. 4 (1601).

6. 32 Geo. II, c. 28 (1758–9), and see 7 below.

7. Since the earlier editions of this present work appeared, the whole situation as to (educational and other) charities has been clarified by the Charities Act of 1960 (8 & 9 Eliz. II, c. 55, 1960). This authorises the establishment of a central register of charities, to be kept jointly by the Charity Commissioners, 14 Ryder Square, St. James's, London W.C.1, and by the Secretary of State for Education and Science. Registration is compulsory; review (of the working of groups of local charities often by or with the blessing of the local authority for the area concerned) is not. A good deal of this, however, is taking place by agreement.

Since the register began in 1961, over 50,000 social welfare charities have been entered in it, and the Official Custodian (an officer of the Charity Commissioners) now holds securities and other assets to a nominal value of more than £150 million. The Commission issues (circular letters July 1965 and Feb. 1966) some very sensible suggestions for modernising the administration of many charities, and getting them to co-operate with one another and with the statutory welfare services in meeting such exceptional needs as, in the nature of things, cannot always be dealt with by publicly provided facilities. It is to be noted in this connection that after the introduction of free, virtually nation-wide education, the distinction between educational and other charities has still been maintained. It is possible for the Department of Education and Science to sanction the re-allocation to 'welfare' a branch of a foundation which originally was both 'for the poor' and 'for education'. It has, however, no power to apply to welfare a charity originally established solely for educational purposes. The educational purpose may, however, now be served in a fashion differing very considerably from that prescribed by the original benefactor.

8. A very few may have been, but Dr Gilbert Slater in *The English Peasantry and the Enclosure of Common Fields*, 1907, p. 128, thinks that 'not one enclosure act in a hundred showed any care whatever for the interests of the poor'. Probably fewer still ordered the allotment to them of any land. From the legalist point of view there was indeed not the least reason why any such allotment should be made, since land given to them could only be at the expense of the other proprietors, its legal owners. When the open-field village was liquidated, its assets were divided, like those of any other business concern, after satisfying the creditors among the shareholders.

9. List X (P.R.O. 'Lists and Indexes Series', no. X, H.M.S.O., 1899, purports to give 'a list of proceedings pursuant to the statutes of 1598 and 1601'. It has long been out of print, but it was reprinted at what seems to us an extortionately high price in 1963 by an American reprint corporation. Although it includes, as it claims, some 'calligraphic amendments' from the master copy in the P.R.O., it is still very imperfect, and it should be supplemented by reference to the MS. indexes in the P.R.O. The original documents are thus classified: C 93 (Commissions, Inquisitions and Decrees*) 61 bundles, C 92 (Exceptions, Answers, Replications and Rejoinders*) 22 bundles, C 91 (Writs, Interrogatories and Depositions*) 23 bundles and C 90 (Confirmations and Exonerations*) 37 rolls. All of these except C 92 are said to be indexed

---

* Even if I were competent to give it, this is not the place for an exposition of the technicalities of Chancery procedure, or for definitions of the terms used. Some account of the procedural oddities of Chancery will be found in archaic legal works of reference. On the special matter under consideration there is a good deal of useful and understandable matter in such specialised volumes as G. Duke, *Law of Charitable Uses* . . . etc., 1676.

in List X—it is indexed in MS. in Index 16817, in a highly contracted and somewhat exasperating dog-Latin. The documentary series are, however, very incomplete, and the correlation of the separate ones is imperfect. It is not unusual, for example, to find documents relating to the same place, but to two or three different inquiries of widely differing dates, wrongly ascribed to the same series of proceedings. The parish historian cannot afford to disregard the existence of this series of records, which very often supplies the want of records which should be in the parish chest, but in fact are not. He should, however, use rather cautiously both the documents themselves and the printed and MS. indexes to them.

BRIEFS **page 120**

1. By John Hough, Bishop of Worcester, 1717–43.
2. 25 Hen. VIII, c. 21 (1533–4), and 28 Hen. VIII, c. 16 (1536).
3. 22 Hen. VIII, c. 12 (1530–1), etc. See below, p. 190.
4. Ely Visitation Book F i, p. 21, quoted in Palmer, *History of Borough Green* (Cambs.), C.A.S. 1939, p. 133.
5. 24 April, 13 May, 15 May, 25 May, 1624, 26 April, 23 May, 25 May, 1625, and 24 May, 1626. See also Overbury, p. 55 of work cited below (p. 297).
6. 4 & 5 Anne, c. 25 (1705).
7. Walford, *op. cit.* pp. 46–8.
8 1 August.
9. 1 March.
10. 9 Geo. IV, c. 42 (1828), An Act to abolish Church Briefs.
11. *A Priest to the Temple*, Chap. XIX. See also, Herrick, *Hesperides*, 'Upon Cuffe'.
12. 3 December 1667. See also Evelyn, *Diary*, 23 September 1683.
13. Book II, ll. 24–34.
14. *Table Talk* and Other Poems, edn. 1825, p. 139, ll. 461–78.
15. *Works*, edn. 1757, Vol. VI, p. 247.

IV. GLEBE TERRIERS AND TITHE RECORDS

GLEBE TERRIERS **page 126**

1. The homonym *terrier-terrier* sometimes amuses, (?) often puzzles, beginners in record work. It is easily explained; the dog, *terrarius* 'has a digging propensity', the document, *terrarium* is essentially a list of landed property.
2. Lyndwood, *Provinciale*, Bk. I, Tit. x, Chap. 1 (*Ut Archidiaconi*); Cripps, *On Church and Clergy*, p. 139.
3. For an explanation of this term see below, pp. 252–54.
4. Cox, *English Church Fittings . . .* , pp. 38–41. See below, pp. 133–4.
5. Dr J. A. Venn, *Foundations of Agricultural Economics*, edn. 1923, pp. 17–21.
6. See below, pp. 134–43, on Tithe.
7. So dated, but in the same hand as the 1726 terrier, and apparently a copy of an original now lost. The Duchess of Newcastle may be Henrietta [Godolphin] or Margaret [Holles].
8. See above, p. 69, for reference to the provisions of 21 Hen. VIII, c. 6 (1529).
9. Pope, *Works*, edn. 1757, Vol. VI, p. 248.
10. Crabbe, *Works*, edn. 1834, Vol. III, pp. 301–11.
11. Prynne, *Canterburies Doome*, 1646, p. 143.
12. Clay, *History of Landbeach*, C.A.S., 1861, p. 79.

TITHE RECORDS **page 134**

1. See e.g. Gen. xxviii. 22; Lev. xxvii. 30–33; Num. xviii. 21–32.
2. *History of Tithes*, p. 35.
3. Floyer, *op. cit.* p. 96. This followed an order by Charlemagne to the

Frankish Church in A.D. 779. It was duly confirmed by the kings and witans of Mercia and Northumbria, and by the king of Wessex.

4. Strictly speaking, in the laws drawn up in pursuance of treaties made between Guthrum and Alfred and Edward the Elder.

5. On the quadripartite division of tithes, a quarter each to the bishop, the church fabric, the poor, and the incumbent, and the theory that the bishops relinquished their share upon receiving other endowments in lieu, see Blackstone, *Commentaries*, Bk. I, Chap. 2.

6. 15 Ric. II, c. 6 (1391).

7. 37 Hen. VIII, c. 12 (1545).

8. 2 Hen. IV, c. 4 (1400–1).

9. 4 Hen. IV, c. 12 (1402).

10. 32 Hen. VIII, c. 7 (1540); 2 & 3 Ed. VI, c. 13 (1548).

11. Lyndwood, Bk. III, Tit. xvi, Chap. 1 (*Quia quidam maledictionis*), Chap. 2 (*Erroris damnabilis*), Chap. 3 (*Quanquam exsolvendibus*), Chap. 4 (*Immoderatae temeritatis*), Chap. 5 (*Quoniam propter diversas*), Chap. 6 (*Quoniam ut audivimus*), Chap. 7 (*Sancta ecclesia et infra*).

12. *Foundations of Agricultural Economics*, edn. 1923, pp. 100–9.

13. *A Paper sent forth by the . . . Quakers*, 1654 (Reprint in A. C. Ward's *Miscellany of Tracts and Pamphlets*, 1927, pp. 249 and 259).

14. Pope, *Works*, edn. 1757, Vol. vi, p. 247.

15. See below, pp. 251–5, 264–5.

16. See below, and W. Cobbett, *Political Register*, Vol. v, No. 7, p. 246, 18 August 1804.

17. *An Act for Dividing and Inclosing certain Open Arable Fields Meadows and Stinted Common Pastures in the Parish of West Retford in the County of Nottingham*, 14 Geo. III, c. 9 (Pr.) (1774). According to a return of 1831 (Cripps, *op. cit.* p. 295), there were more than 2000 private acts between 1757 and 1830 which contained clauses as to tithe commutation. Not all these were enclosure acts, and the number of enclosure acts alone from 1719 to 1845 was, according to my reckoning 4185. So clearly rather less than half the enclosure acts authorized the commutation of tithe.

18. 1 Ric. I, A.D. 1189.   **19.** 2 & 3 W. IV, c. 100 (1831–2).

20. 6 & 7 W. IV, c. 71 (1836).

21. 26 Geo. V and 1 Ed. VIII, c. 43 (1935–6).

22. See e.g. the cases cited below, pp. 130–1, 273–4.

23. See below and a most interesting study of 'Tithe Commutation as a Factor in the gradual Decrease of Land ownership by the English Peasantry', by Professor Vladimir Lavrovsky, in *Econ. Hist. Rev.* Vol. iv, No. 3, October 1933, p. 273.

24. According to Cripps, *op. cit.* p. 5, a shilling, but 2s. 6d. according to the Ministry of Agriculture circular letter Form A. 16/LT. The address of the Tithe Redemption Commission is Finsbury Square, London, E.C.4. Its copies have lately been deposited in the Public Record Office.

25. 6 & 7 W. IV, c. 71 (1836); 5 & 6 Vic. c. 54 (1842).

26. 9 & 10 Vic. c. 73 (1846).   **27.** 23 & 24 Vic. c. 93 (1860).

28. 56 & 57 Vic. c. 73 (1893–4), s. 18 (8).

29. The statutory prices were: wheat 7s. 0d., barley 3s. 11½d., oats 2s. 9d. The rent charge was to consist of such a sum as would, if divided into three equal parts, purchase the same quantity of these three grains as the tithe produced in 1836. The idea was, of course, to guard against unfairness to either tithe owner or tithe payer arising from unforeseen variations in the value of money and in the price of corn. Averages were to be worked out over ten-year periods. The Tithe Act of 1918, 8 & 9 Geo. V, c. 54, substituted fifteen-year periods for the previous ten-year ones. The latest major Tithe Act (26 Geo. V and 1 Ed. VIII, c. 43, 1935–6) makes provision for the final extinction of tithe rent charge at a valuation of 80–90 per cent. The tithe is now being bought out by means of a sinking fund, largely extracted from the tithe owners, a most ingenious example of the feeding of the ecclesiastical cat upon small sections of her own tail. There are, however, 'compassionate' allowances for the poorer clergy.

V. OTHER ECCLESIASTICAL RECORDS

RECORDS OF CHURCH COURTS **page 144**

1. Mr Hill's work above cited, note 38 on p. 289, is a mine of information upon this subject.

2. Blackstone, *Commentaries*, edn. 1778, Vol. 1, p. 111.

3. Cripps, *op. cit. passim*.

4. The Judicial Committee's proceedings are now governed by rules drawn up under the Appellate Jurisdiction Act, 39 & 40 Vic. c. 59 (1876).

5. Established by 25 Hen. VIII, c. 21 (1533–4), and abolished by the Privy Council Appeals Act, 2 & 3 W. IV, c. 92 (1831–2).

6. The Ecclesiastical Courts Jurisdiction Act, 23 & 24 Vic. c. 32 (1860).

7. See above, pp. 95–6.   8. See above, pp. 134–43.

9. See above, p. 127, and eighth rubric at the end of the Communion Service.

10. Dr J. C. Cox, *Parish Registers of England*, p. 110.

11. *The Freres Tale*, ll. 1–22.

12. The apparitor was equally unpopular, both then and in later times. Sir Thomas Overbury in 1614 (*Characters*, Henry Morley's reprint of 1891, pp. 54–5) tells us of him that he is 'a chick of the egg abuse, hatched by the warmth of authority; he is a bird of rapine, and begins to prey and feather together . . . his happiness is in the multitude of children, for their increase is his wealth, and to that end he himself yearly adds one. He is a cunning hunter, uncoupling his intelligencing hounds under hedges, in thickets and cornfields, who follow the chase to city suburbs, where often his game is at covert . . . he and the pursuivant of hell both delight in sin, grow richer by it, and are by justice appointed to punish it; only the devil is more cunning, for he picks a living out of others' gains. His living lieth in his eye, which (like spirits) he sends through chinks and keyholes to survey the places of darkness; . . . Thus lives he in a golden age till death by a process summons him to appear.'

13. *Passus* II, ll. 172–6.

14. Canons 2–12, 26, 27, 38, 59, 65, 76, 85, 119.

15. Canons 92–108, Courts belonging to the Archbishop's Jurisdiction; 109–126, Courts belonging to the Jurisdiction of Bishops and Archdeacons; 127–128, Judges Ecclesiastical and their Surrogates; 129–133, Proctors; 134–137, Registrars; 138, Apparitors.

16. Canons 105–7.

17. Lev. xviii. 6.

18. At any rate since 1215 when the Lateran Council IV so decided. Previously the prohibition had extended to the seventh degree. See on this point Dr Coulton's *Mediaeval Village*, p. 80 and App. 16, pp. 471–7.

19. For an illustrative diagram see Phillimore, *How to write the History of a Family*, p. 32.

20. Whence, I suppose, the curious, still-surviving folk-lore tradition: 'In England you may marry your "own" cousin (cousin-german), but not your second cousin.'

21. Ollard and Cross, p. 355, s.v. *Marriage*, give a most interesting, but what seems to me a somewhat 'slanted' account of what they say is the present position of the Church of England on this.

22. *Commentaries*, edn. 1778, Vol. 1, p. 435; 32 Hen. VIII, c. 38 (1540).

23. Canon 99. Punishments for infraction of the Roman canon occur in the reign of Mary I, but not, of course, later. The present canon received the royal assent and was promulgated in May 1946.

24. Chester Waters, *op. cit.*   25. See above, p. 95.

26. Canons, *passim*; Lyndwood, Bk. V, Tit. xvii, Chaps. 1–8.

28. Cox, *Parish Registers of England*, p. 110.

LISTS OF STRANGE PREACHERS **page 150**

1. Canon 52, based upon a canon of Archbishop Arundel, for which see Lyndwood, Bk. V, Tit. v, Chap. 1 (*Reverendissimae synodo et infra*). See above, p. 96.

page 150 SPECIAL FORMS OF SERVICE

1. Cripps, *op. cit.* p. 545; 2 & 3 Ed. VI, c. 1 (1548); 5 & 6 Ed. VI, c. 1 (1551–2); 1 Eliz. c. 2 (1558–9); 14 Car. II, c. 4 (1662); and, of course, such recent legislation as the Prayer Book (Tables of Lessons) Act, 34 & 35 Vic. c. 37 (1871); the Act of Uniformity Amendment Act, 35 & 36 Vic. c. 35 (1872), and Church Assembly Measure, 12 & 13 Geo. V, No. 3 (1922). Canon 36 was amended in 1865, but the emendation does not affect the clause mentioned.

2. See Bishop Ryle, *Lawful Authority*. A Commission on this subject, set up by the Archbishop of Canterbury, sat quite lately, but its findings have been controverted.

page 151 NOTICES AND PROCLAMATIONS

1. 10 Geo. III, c. 73 (Pr.) (1770).
2. The Parish Notices Act, 7 W. IV and 1 Vic. c. 45 (1837).
3. Rubric after the Nicene Creed in the Communion Service.
4. For a brief account of the movement 'for the reformation of manners', see the Webbs' *History of Liquor Licensing in England*, 1903, App. pp. 137–51.

page 154 FACULTIES AND LICENCES

1. See above, p. 139.
2. See above, p. 92.
3. See above, pp. 19–20.
4. Preface to the Ordinal, par. 2.
5. Prideaux, *op. cit.* p. 226.
6. Canons 48 and 50. See above, p. 97 and fn. 49.
7. Cripps, *op. cit.* p. 139, quoting Lyndwood and I suppose Johnson, *Collection of Ecclesiastical Laws . . . and Canons . . .* , 1720, Vol. II, 1222–25.
8. Printed in *Lincolnshire Notes and Queries*, Vol. XXIV, No. 190, April 1936 and reproduced here by courtesy of the editor.
9. Canons 77–9. For further information on this see my article in the *Church Quarterly Review*, CLVII, 325, pp. 426–32, with one or two further notes by other writers in following issues.
10. Canons 48–9.
11. Canons 45 and 47.
12. 1 W. & M. c. 26 (1688), Canon 41.
13. Under statutes made at the Reformation and in George III's reign. The law on the subject is now expressed in the Pluralities Act of 1838, 1 & 2 Vic. c. 106 (1837–8), and Church Assembly Measure, 20–21 Geo. V, No. 7 (1930), s. 2.
14. Canon 72.
15. See Cox, *Parish Registers*, pp. 221–5, *id. Churchwardens' Accounts*, pp. 251–2, and references there cited, also Herrick, *Hesperides*, 'Upon Bungie'
16. See above, pp. 62–3.
17. The Marriage Act, 6 & 7 W. IV, c. 85 (1836).
18. 20 & 21 Vic. c. 77 (1857). For registered wills see ed. A. J. Camp, *Wills and their Whereabouts*, edn. 1963, which will shortly be superseded, in some respects at any rate, by Mr D. J. Steel's survey referred to above p. 53 and fns. 39–40.
19. 5 Eliz. c. 5 (1562–3).   **20.** 16 Car. I, c. 1 (1640).
21. 26 & 27 Vic. c. 125 (1863).

page 157 RECORDS OF TOUCHING FOR THE KING'S EVIL

1. Chester Waters, *op. cit.* pp. 81–2.
2. Printed in Crawfurd, *The King's Evil*, pp. 164–85.
3. Proclamation of 9 January 1683.
4. Thiselton Dyer, *op. cit.* p. 80.
5. Reprint (n.d.) edited by Henry Morley, p. 65.
6. Act IV, Sc. iii. See also Herrick, *Hesperides*, 'To the King to Cure the Evil', Sir Thomas Browne, 'Letter to a Friend', and a variety of other writers

from William of Malmesbury and Polydore Vergil to William Tooker *alias* Tucker.

7. Pepys, *Diary*, 23 June 1660, and 13 April 1661.
8. Evelyn, *Diary*, 6 July 1660, 28 March 1684, and 5 November 1688.
9. Letter 22, 28 April 1711.
10. *Life of Johnson*, Everyman edn., Vol. I, pp. 16–17.
11. *History of England from the Accession of James II*, Chap. XIII.
12. Cited below, p. 352.
13. Reproduced as the frontispiece to Dr Crawfurd's book.

PART II: pages 162–282

RECORDS MAINLY CIVIL

VI. VESTRY MINUTES AND AGREEMENTS
page 162

1. See above, p. 91.
2. See above, pp. 120–5.
3. See other agreements of a similar type, above, pp. 15, 23–24.
4. G. Ewing, *History of Cowden*, Kent, n.d.
5. See below, pp. 221–6.
6. See below, pp. 214–21.
7. Clay, *op. cit.* p. 66.

VII. PETTY CONSTABLES' ACCOUNTS **page 176**

1. The law writers treat these terms as synonymous with that of constable, but in many places, during the seventeenth and eighteenth centuries, they were applied to deputy or assistant constables.
2. *Commentaries*, edn. 1778, Vol. I, p. 356.
3. *Ib.* quoting Spelman's *Glossary*, p. 148.
4. *Op. cit.* p. 45.   5. *Op. cit.* p. 27, fn. 1.
6. 13 Ed. I, St. II, c. 6 (1285), The Statute of Winchester. 2 Ed. III, c. 3 (1328) seems much more clearly a reference to the *petty* constable.
7. Professor Helen Cam, *The Hundred and the Hundred Rolls*, 1930, pp. 188–94, regards him as originating in 1242, when Walter de Gray, Archbishop of York and Justiciar, during his government of the realm while the King was in France, improved the national defence organisation, as outlined by Henry II, and developed by John and Henry III.
8. E.g. Hone, *op. cit. passim*, and *Modus Tenendi Curiae Baronis*, 1510, reprinted by the Manorial Society in 1915, as Publication No. 9.
9. These constable's staves, usually locally made, and bearing the royal arms and cipher, and the initials of the parish, are very attractive little curios. Specimens may often be picked up for a trifle in 'antique' shops. Many museums have collections of them. We have noted such at the Curtis Museum, Alton, Hants., the Devizes Museum, the Ashmolean, Oxford, and the York Castle Museum.
   When, as sometimes happens, one finds in a parish church the effigy of a mediaeval knight with, hanging over it, a wildly anachronistic, perhaps seventeenth century, sword, or headpiece or scrap of armour, it is doubtless because some romantically-minded Victorian incumbent, finding, possibly, in the belfry, the remains of the parish armour, has jumped to an incorrect inference about it.
10. 2 & 3 Vic. c. 93 (1839).
11. 3 & 4 W. IV, c. 90 (1833).
12. 5 & 6 Vic. c. 109 (1842); 35 & 36 Vic. c. 92 (1872).
13. With the assistants specified in the Statute of Winchester II (reinforcing the old common law obligation).
14. 2nd Inst. p. 73.

15. 17 Ed. IV, c. 3 (1477–8), ordered every man to shoot each Sunday and holy day, under a penalty of a halfpenny. Other acts were passed 3 Hen. VIII, c. 3 (1511–12), 33 Hen. VIII, c. 6 (1541–2), 8 Eliz. c. 10 (1566), etc.

16. The Statute of Winchester, elaborated by 4 & 5 P. & M. c. 2 (1557–8), commanded the constables to make view of armour in each hundred and franchise twice a year.

17. Cox, *English Church Fittings*, p. 165.

18. Cf. Evelyn, *Diary*, 18 June 1685, 18 July 1686.

19. Reprinted by permission of the editor of *Lincolnshire Notes and Queries*, in which it was published, Vol. XXIV, No. 190, April 1936, pp. 27–8.

20. Exempted from the monopolies legislation of 1623–4 (21 Jac. I, c. 3, s. 10), checked by proclamation in 1627, but recognised in other proclamations in 1625 and 1634, when it was forbidden to pave stables and dovehouses because of the ill-effect such paving would have upon saltpetre formation: mentioned in the *Remonstrance of the State of the Kingdom* in 1641, but not finally checked until 1656 (Scobell, *Acts and Ordinances*, p. 377).

21. *Passus* IV, ll. 47–59.

22. Printed in *The Local Historian*, March 1936, and here reprinted by permission of the editor.

23. Toulmin Smith, *op. cit.* pp. 191, 373.

24. See below, Settlement and Removal, pp. 197–204.

25. The Webbs, *History of Liquor Licensing in England*, p. 10, and Massinger, *A New Way to Pay Old Debts*, Act IV, Sc. 2, ll. 90–5:

'For which gross fault I here do damn thy license,
Forbidding thee ever to tap or draw;
For, instantly, I will, in mine own person,
Command the constable to pull down thy sign,' . . .

26. See above, p. 152.

27. *Much Ado About Nothing*, Act III, Sc. 3, etc.

VIII. RECORDS OF POOR-LAW ADMINISTRATION

page 188 THE POOR LAW

1. Instances of the observance by manorial lords of ancient customs that each lord should maintain the poor of his own manor occur as late as the middle of the seventeenth century.

2. See above, p. 135 and below, Glossary *passim*.

3. *Church History*, edn. 1656, p. 298. The George Herbert reference is *A Priest to the Temple*, Chap. XII.

4. 12 Ric. II, c. 7 (1388).

5. Note in this the germ of the later law of settlement (below, pp. 192–3, 198–205).

6. R. Garnier, *Annals of the British Peasantry*, p. 91, and references there cited.

7. 22 Hen. VIII, c. 12 (1530–1). **8.** 27 Hen. VIII, c. 25 (1535–6).

9. 1 Ed. VI, c. 3 (1547). **10.** 3 & 4 Ed. VI, c. 16 (1549–50).

11. 5 & 6 Ed. VI, c. 2 (1551–2). **12.** 2 & 3 P. & M. c. 5 (1555).

13. 5 Eliz. c. 3 (1562–3). **14.** 14 Eliz. c. 5 (1572).

15. 39 Eliz. c. 3 (1597–8). **16.** 43 Eliz. c. 2 (1601).

17. 1 Jac. I, c. 25 (1603–4); 3 Car. I, c. 5 (1627); 16 Car. I, c. 4 (1640).

18. 7 Jac. I, cc. 3 and 4 (1609–10).

19. 14 Car. II, c. 12 (1662). **20.** 1 Jac. II, c. 17 (1685).

21. 3 W. & M. c. 11 (1691). **22.** 8 & 9 W. & M. c. 30 (1696–7).

23. 9 W. III, c. 11 (1697–8); 2 & 3 Anne c. 6 (1703); 8 Anne c. 5 (1709); 12 Anne c. 18 (1712), and 5 Geo. I, c. 8 (1718–19).

24. 9 Geo. I, c. 7 (1722–3).

25. 3 Geo. II, c. 29 (1729–30), and 6 Geo. II, c. 31 (1732–3).

26. See below, pp. 211–12.

27. 22 Geo. III, c. 83 (1781–2). **28.** 32 Geo. III, c. 45 (1792).

29. 35 Geo. III, c. 101 (1794–5). **30.** 36 Geo. III, c. 23 (1795–6).

31. 55 Geo. III, c. 137 (1814–15). **32.** 17 Geo. II, c. 38 (1743–4).

33. 26 Geo. III, c. 56 (1786), and 30 Geo. III, c. 49 (1790).
34. 33 Geo. III, c. 55 (1792–3).   **35.** 20 Geo. II, c. 19 (1746–7).
36. 7 Geo. III, c. 39 (1766–7), and 18 Geo. III, c. 47 (1777–8).
37. 32 Geo. III, c. 57 (1792).   **38.** 33 Geo. III, c. 55 (1792–3).
39. 42 Geo. III, c. 46 (1801–2).   **40.** 43 Geo. III, cc. 47 and 61
41. 5 Geo. IV, c. 83 (1824).   (1802–3).
42. The main later acts are 4 & 5 W. IV, c. 76 (1834), 19 & 20 Geo. V,
c. 17 (1929), 11 & 12 Geo. VI, c. 29 (1948), and the Ministry of Social Security
Act, 1966.
43. See C. D. Stooks, *Account of Crondall Records*, n.d.
44. 6 Geo. II, c. 31 (1732–3).
45. P. 121, quoted by Aschrott, *op. cit.* p. 12, fn.

(*a*) Settlement and Removal   **page 198**

1. R. Garnier, *Annals of the British Peasantry*, p. 249.
2. Sir F. M. Eden, *State of the Poor*, edn. cited, pp. 27–8.
3. 39 & 40 Vic. c. 61 (1876).   **4.** *Commentaries*, Vol. I,
5. See above, pp. 15, 163–4.   pp. 361–2.
6. Aschrott, *op. cit.* pp. 111–12.   **7.** Nolan, *op. cit.* Vol. I, p. 223.
8. *New Discourse of Trade*, 1668, quoted by Garnier, *British Peasantry*,
p. 251.
9. *Wealth of Nations*, 1776, Bk. I, Chap. XI.
10. The Mendicity Report of 1815, dealing with the work of a Mr Davies,
vagrant contractor for Middlesex (at a salary of £300 per annum), whose work
was concerned only with the vagrant poor and with these only when they had
been commited to Bridewell and released therefrom, says he 'passed' as many
as 12,000 or 13,000 a year, often 'passing' the same person several times in a
year. Miss Marshall, *op. cit.* 243.
11. On the genealogical interest of these and similar poor-law records see
Bernau, 'The Genealogy of the Submerged', in *Some Special Studies in
Genealogy*, 1908.
12. *Justice of the Peace*, edn. 1758, Vol. III, pp. 83 and 101, 9 Geo. I, c. 7
(1722–3, s. 8).

(*b*) Parochial Generosity, Parochial Deterrent
Measures and Parochial Experiments
page 205

1. From *The Local Historian*, January 1936.
2. *Op. cit.* p. 34.
3. *Some Proposals for the Employment of the Poor and the Prevention of
Idleness*, 1681, pp. 18, 38.
4. Dr Marshall, *op. cit.* p. 102.
5. 8–9 W. III, c. 30 (1696–7).
6. Dr Marshall, *op. cit.* pp. 3–4, quoting *Hertfordshire County Records*,
Vol. II, p. 70.
7. See above, p. 108.
8. Dr Marshall, p. 104, refers to the act as 'in force until nearly the close of
the 18th century', and Sir F. Eden (*op. cit.* pp. 274, 314 and 343) notes three
parishes where the system was in vogue in 1797. The official *Index to the
Statutes* gives this section (s. 11) of the act as repealed in 1810 by 50 Geo. III,
c. 52, though other parts remained in force until 1867.
9. *Op. cit.* pp. 8–12.

(*c*) Overseers' Accounts and the Information to
be obtained from them
page 210

1. (Nottinghamshire) *Thoroton Society Transactions*, Vol. 34, 1930,
pp. 53–59.

(*d*) Vagrants and Vagrancy   **page 211**

1. 17 Geo. II, c. 5 (1743–4). See above, p. 193.
2. This was a quite different reward from the 10*s.* payable for the appre-

hension of a rogue and vagabond. It was payable not by the county but by the parish of settlement (in order to punish it for suffering one of its parishioners to beg within its bounds). If the offender begged *outside* the limits of his own parish he incurred a further degree of guilt, since he became thereby a rogue and vagabond. Burn, *op. cit.* edn. 1758, Vol. III, p. 398.

3. See above, pp. 120–25, Briefs.

4. As distinct from those merely threatening to do so.

5. This did not apply to genuine soldiers or sailors with their officer's pass.

6. 13 Geo. I, c. 23 (1726–7). This is an act for protecting the wool trade 'by preventing abuses in woollen manufacture'. Apparently 'end gatherers' were rag men.

7. *Op. cit.* pp. 416–25.

page 213 (e) BASTARDS AND BASTARDY

1. See above, pp. 60–2.

2. For a variety of such descriptive phrases see the glossary, pp. 309–22.

3. Dr Bradbrook, *The Parish Register*, pp. 3–4, states, quite erroneously we believe, that 'the evidence of the registers shows that sexual morality has not varied very much in quality since registers were instituted'.

4. This table was worked out by the late Dr J. C. Cox from the registers of Letheringham, Suff.:

Letheringham	Incidence of Illegitimacy		
Period	Baptisms of bastards	Total baptisms	Proportion
1588–1600	None	—	—
1601–1650	1	144	1 in 144
1651–1700	1	74	1 in 74
1701–1750	3	99	1 in 33
1751–1800	7	147	1 in 21
1801–1812	3	30	1 in 10

This one I owe to the kindness of Mr J. Meeds of Kirklington, Notts., who has examined the registers of many Nottinghamshire parishes:

Halam			
1774–1808	28	204	1 in 7
Woodborough			
1690–1749	8	463	1 in 58
1750–1835	8	148	1 in 18

5. For further references to enclosure see below, pp. 265–71.

6. The Webbs suggest that perhaps there may have been a connection between this tendency and the rapid growth of alehouses between the thirties and the eighties of the eighteenth century (*History of Liquor Licensing in England*, 1700–1830, 1903). There is a most interesting discussion of this point, the first-fruits of what will be a more detailed study of it when the Cambridge Group has proceeded further with its programme, in P. Laslett, *The World We Have Lost*, 1965, pp. 128–36. Laslett's provisional conclusion is that, at any rate until a couple of centuries ago, our ancestors, by this test of bastards born and registered as such, were rather more moral sexually than are we ourselves. In this matter so far little difference has been noted between the standards inferred in the countryside and those in the towns (even worldly London and seafaring Bristol!).

7. *Discourse of the Poor*, not published until 1753, p. 51.

8. *Political Arithmetic*, 1774, pp. 93–4.

9. *Eight letters on the Management of our Poor*, by an Overseer, Newark, 1822, p. 47.

10. Statute of Merton, 20 Hen. III, c. 9 (1235), and 9 Hen. VI, c. 11 (1430–1).

11. 18 Eliz. c. 3 (1575–6).
12. 7 Jac. I, c. 4 (1609–10).
13. 21 Jac. I, c. 27 (1623–4).
14. 3 Car. I, c. 5 (1627).
15. 14 Car. II, c. 12 (1662), s. 19.
16. 6 Geo. II, c. 31 (1732–3).
17. 17 Geo. II, c. 5 (1743–4), s. 25.
18. One cannot, of course, discover how many cases were dealt with by two justices.
19. *The Gentleman's Magazine*, Vol. LXXI, 1811, April, p. 336, July, p. 2.
20. The parish officers had, of course, no legal powers to do this, but it was certainly done, often, I think, by a judicious mixture of bullying with bribery.
21. This latter course seems seldom to have been adopted, probably because the security offered was often non-existent, as when e.g. a farm labourer stood surety for £100.
22. For instances see Miss E. M. Hampson's study, *The Treatment of Poverty in Cambridgeshire*. I have found none in Nottinghamshire.
23. *The Parish Register*, 1807, Marriages, *Works*, edn. 1834, Vol. 2, p. 179.
24. Possibly under the act of 1732–3.
25. This naturally leads one to suspect abortion, which seems, however, to have been comparatively rare. See, however, such references as that in *The Gentleman's Magazine*, July 1811, Vol. LXXI, p. 86.
26. Under the act of 1609–10.
27. E.g. at Halam, Notts., of the 28 bastards born 1774–1808, less than half belonged to mothers who had only the one illegitimate child. The numbers are:

Bastard children born to mothers with	1	2	3	4	children
Children born	12	3	2	1	
Total bastards	12	6	6	4	28

Lord Ernle, in *English Farming Past and Present*, p. 329, quotes the instance of a woman at Swaffham, Norf., who had five bastard children, and who, in consequence, received from the parish a weekly allowance of 18s. (considerably more than the wage upon which a respectable married labourer was expected to keep his wife and family in the same district in my own early days).
28. Since Parliament thought it worth while to make the practice illegal, probably it may be taken that it must have been fairly general in some districts.
29. See below, pp. 231–7.
30. Quoted by Aschrott, *op. cit.* p. 30, fn.
31. Legally not until 1819, but in many parishes assumed by the Vestry long before this, in one (Welsh) instance as early as 1693, Webb, *The Parish and the County*, pp. 128, 166.
32. Inventories of goods might be either for reimbursing the parish upon the death of a pauper for as much as possible of the relief he had received, for the relief of a deserted wife, or for that of an unmarried mother, and it is rarely stated for which of these reasons any particular inventory has been taken. As to apprenticeship indentures see below, pp. 221–6. For some reason not very clear to us nowadays, these bonds seem especially full of detail in the period c. 1690–1720.
33. Recognised by the law, but very rarely found.

(f) APPRENTICES AND APPRENTICESHIP INDENTURES
page 221

1. Under 5 Eliz. c. 4 (1562–3).
2. By 43 Eliz. c. 2 (1601).
3. 3 W. & M. c. 11 (1691); 31 Geo. II, c. 11 (1757–8).
4. *Op. cit.* pp. 53–62.
5. 8 & 9 W. III, c. 30 (1696–7), s. 5, making explicit the powers implied in the 1601 act, gave the right of compulsion on condition that the churchwardens' and overseers' request was confirmed by two justices.

6. *Op. cit.* p. 199.

7. *Das Kapital*, Eng. trans. by E. and C. Paul, Everyman Series, Vol. II, p. 838.

8. See above, p. 167.   **9.** *Op. cit.* pp. 94–5, App. I.

10. 6 Geo. III, c. 25 (1765–6).   **11.** 7 Geo. III, c. 39 (1766–7).

12. Sched. E.

13. 18 Geo. III, c. 47 (1777–8); 20 Geo. III, c. 36 (1779–80); 42 Geo. III, c. 46 (1801–2).

14. 20 Geo. II, c. 19 (1746–7); 32 Geo. III, c. 57 (1792); 33 Geo. III, c. 55 (1792–3).

page 226   (*g*) In-relief and out-relief—Workhouses

1. *Commentaries*, edn. 1778, Vol. I, p. 360.

2. Stanley's *Remedy*, quoted by Eden, *op. cit.* pp. 25–6, and Aschrott, *op. cit.* p. 15.

3. Which, *inter alia*, set up a 'corporation or corporations, work house or work houses for the cities of London and Westminster, and those parts of Middlesex and Surrey lying within the Bills of Mortality'.

4. By Messrs Peter Davies, ed. Charles Whibley, Preface, p. iii, and pp. 27–36.

5. 7 & 8 W. III, c. 32 Pr. (1695–6) and amending Acts noted in App. I; 2 & 3 Anne, c. 8 (1703); 6 Anne, c. 46 (1706–7); 10 Anne, c. 15 (1711), etc.

6. 9 Geo. I, c. 7 (1722–3).

7. From £819,000 in 1698 to £619,000 in 1750. Aschrott, *op. cit.* p. 16.

8. *Works*, edn. 1834, Vol. II, pp. 83–4. A less harrowing but nevertheless very unfavourable picture of the hundred house appears in *The Borough*, first published in 1810, *Works*, edn. cited, Vol. III, pp. 287–9.

9. 22 Geo. III, c. 83 (1781–2).

10. It therefore had a bad effect upon many more parishes than actually adopted it. There were in 1834 but sixty-seven Gilbert Unions, covering 924 parishes.

page 231   (*h*) The Last Days of the Old System

1. Aschrott, *op. cit.* p. 21, quoting von Gneist. Cobbett was very fond of arguing to this effect.

2. 35 Geo. III, c. 101 (1794–5).

3. Hasbach, *The English Agricultural Labourer*, p. 182.

4. Dr and Mrs J. L. Hammond, *The Village Labourer*, pp. 161–2.

5. 36 Geo. III, c. 23 (1795–6).

6. E.g. in his *Short History of English Agriculture*, p. 239. probably on the strength of the fact that provisions for paying roundsmen, two-thirds from the rates and one-third by the employer, were included in his abortive poor law reform bill of 1788.

7. Emmison, *op. cit.* pp. 50–1.

8. *Ib.* p. 53.

9. *Kettering Vestry Minutes*, pp. xviii and 69.

10. Hammond, *op. cit.* p. 230.

11. *The Village, Works*, edn. cited, Vol. II, p. 82.

12. As e.g. at Eastbourne, where the paupers' standard allowance was 16s. a week, while independent labourers received only 12s. Aschrott, *op. cit.* p. 3.

13. 'The rental of a pauperised parish was like the revenue of the Sultan of Turkey, a prey of which every administrator hoped to get a share. The owners of cottage property found in the parish a liberal and a solvent tenant, and the petty shopkeeper and publican attended the vestry to vote allowances to his customers and debtors.' Art. *Edinburgh Review* (?) by Nassau Senior, Vol. VI, p. 149, quoted by Aschrott, p. 31.

14. Lord Ernle, *English Farming Past and Present*, p. 330.

15. *Eight Letters on the Management of our Poor, by an Overseer*, Newark, 1822, p. 4.

16. Lord Ernle, *loc. cit.*

17. Except for the law of settlement, which remained almost unchanged until very much later.
18. 4 & 5 W. IV, c. 76 (1834).
19. Cutlack, *op. cit.* p. 17.

(*i*) THE POOR AND THE POOR LAWS   page 237

1. Peyton, *op. cit.* p. 330, App. III, pp. 207–8.
2. Miss E. M. Hampson, *op. cit.* pp. 278–9; now C.R.O. P25/13/6: P25/18/13.
3. Unhappily this seems to have disappeared since the inventorying of the parish records in 1933, and its wording is not now recoverable.

IX. RECORDS OF HIGHWAY MAINTENANCE
    page 242

1. 'Court Rolls of the Manor of Tunstall', *Trans. N. Staffs. Field Club*, Vol. LXV, 1930–1, p. 69.
2. St. II, c. 5, 13 Ed. I, Statute of Winchester (1285).
3. *The King's Highway*, p. 8.
4. J. J. Jusserand, *English Wayfaring Life in the Middle Ages*, ed. Miss Lucy Toulmin Smith, 4th edn. 1892.
5. The Webbs, *op. cit.* pp. 7–8.
6. *Ib.* p. 13; 14 & 15 Hen. VIII, c. 6 (1523); 26 Hen. VIII, c. 7 (1534), etc.
7. 2 & 3 P. & M. c. 8 (1555).
8. Compare pp. 14, 189–91.
9. Later by 5 Eliz. c. 13 (1562–3), for six days.
10. 5 & 6 W. IV, c. 50 (1835); Blackstone, *op. cit.* Vol. I, pp. 357–9, quoting Cicero, *Ad Att.* l. I, ep. I.
11. The Webbs, *op. cit.* p. 214.   **12.** 14 Car. II, c. 6 (1662).
13. 22 Car. II, c. 12 (1670).   **14.** 3 W. & M. c. 12 (1691).
15. 5 & 6 W. IV, c. 50 (1835).   **16.** *Op. cit.* p. 201.
17. *Ib.* p. 46.
18. Although, of course, statute labour was still supposed to be carried out to the trustees' directions, supplementing the work paid for from the product of their toll bars. It was abolished in 1835, but the office of waywarden still remained until the 1862 Highways Act was put into operation. On the whole question of turnpikes see the Webbs' work already cited, and a most interesting and valuable pamphlet, A. Cossons, *Turnpike Roads of Nottinghamshire*, published by the Historical Association in 1934.
19. Some sections of such main roads, especially those passing over sound dry limestone or sandstone, were turnpiked very late, e.g. The Great North Road from Bawtry to Doncaster, 1776. The Fosseway, even in some sections which have always been parts of main routes, was never completely turnpiked.
20. *Op. cit.* p. 5.   **21.** Actually here in 1725–6.
22. References to a parish boar are less common than those to the parish bull. Where there was one, e.g. at Eckington, Derbys., and Keyworth, Notts., his maintenance was often charged upon the rector. Presumably the reason behind the arrangement was that the lord of the manor shouldered the heavier obligation (since he would receive each tenant's heriot—his best beast), the rector the lighter one (since he would benefit by the mortuaries—the second best beasts of his parishioners). See above, p. 69, and Burn, *Ecclesiastical Law*, etc., 1788, Vol. III, p. 467, for cases where the rector provided both bull and boar, and for a justification of the custom.
23. See above, p. 209, below, pp. 261–2.
24. See above, pp. 234–5.   **25.** See above, pp. 195, 235–6.
26. *Op. cit.* p. 199.   **27.** 56 & 57 Vic. c. 73 (1893–4).
28. The *Sunday Times*, 9 January 1938.

X. RECORDS OF OPEN-FIELD AGRICULTURE.
ENCLOSURE, ENCLOSURE ACTS AND AWARDS
page 251

1. Several historians have pointed out how in such records as Domesday the valuation set upon meadow land is proportionally much higher than that of land in the other two categories. And in Domesday Book, when arable land is measured by the carucate or the hide, waste, if at all, by the league, meadow is stated precisely by the acre. See upon this point, Simkhovitch, *Hay and History*, Reprint of 1938 *passim*.

2. See above, pp. 126–31.

3. See below, pp. 270, 274.

4. Printed in *The Local Historian*, March 1936.

5. *Quarterly Journal of Economics*, 1907, Pt. 4.

6. *English Local Government, The Manor and the Borough*, Vol. II, p. 80.

7. A. Ballard, 'Notes on the Open Fields of Oxfordshire', in *Oxfordshire Archaeological Society Report*, 1913, pp. 134–9.

8. The late Rev. S. P. Potter in *Local Notes and Queries* in *The Nottinghamshire Guardian*, 1 April 1933.

9. 13 Geo. III, c. 81 (1772–3).

10. Thiselton Dyer, *op. cit.* p. 31; *The Rectors' Book of Clayworth*, 1676–1701, of which there are four copies in the church chest.

11. *Common Rights at Cottenham and Stretham, Cambridgeshire*, ed. Archdeacon Cunningham, Camden Series, 1910, p. 193.

12. J. Toulmin Smith, *The Parish*, p. 258.

13. A. Ballard, *op. cit.* pp. 140–4.

14. *The Nottingham Journal*, 18 April 1795.

15. Dr J. D. Chambers, 'The Open Fields of Laxton', in *Thoroton Society Transactions*, Vol. XXXII, 1928, pp. 102–25.

16. A. Ballard, *op. cit.* p. 144.

17. 20 Hen. III, c. 4 (1235); 13 Ed. I, c. 46 (1285).

18. *Joannis Rossi Antiquarii Warwicensis Historia Regum Angliae* (ed. Thos. Hearne), editio secunda, Oxon, 1745.

19. 4 Hen. VII, c. 16 (concerning the Isle of Wight only), and c. 19 (1488–9); 6 Hen. VIII, c. 5 (1514–15); 7 Hen. VIII, c. 1 (1515).

20. *The Domesday of Inclosures of* 1517, ed. I. S. Leadam, Royal Historical Society, 1897.

21. 25 Hen. VIII, c. 13 (1533–4). See p. 4 above, and the summary of the act's provisions in Slater, *op. cit.* pp. 87–90.

22. MS. court rolls of Edwinstowe, Notts., lib. 11, p. 90, for reference to which I am indebted to T. M. Blagg, Esq., F.S.A.

23. 1967 and 1935 respectively.

A NOTE UPON HANDWRITING[1]

Since, in an average parish, the registers should date back well into the seventeenth century, and with any luck may go beyond the middle of the sixteenth, the student must expect a little difficulty in deciphering the handwriting in their earliest pages. In fact, at first the hand may seem quite incomprehensible, especially in the seventeenth century. Curiously enough, as a general rule Tudor hands do not present so much difficulty as those of a rather later period.

The form of court hand which for centuries had been evolving from the Caroline Minuscule began to fall into disfavour in the fifteenth century. A new form (secretary) developed rapidly, and is the normal hand of the trained scribe in the sixteenth and seventeenth centuries (see the alphabet, Pl. VII). The hand of the writer without special training is based on secretary, but employs freely letter forms of the older court hand and increasingly those of the Italian hand, until in the course of the seventeenth century it becomes entirely of the modern type. The letters and the combinations and distortions of letters used in this current writing, and to a less extent in the set secretary, are a source of difficulty to the beginner, but it is remarkable how understandable they become after a few days' practice.

The principal sources of difficulty are certain pairs of letters, the minor distinguishing features in which may be missed by a hurried writer, e.g., in the alphabet reproduced in pl. VII,

k and R	O and G	o and e	h and z
W and M	T and C	t and c	x and p
S and G	G and C	u, n, m, and i	y and g

k and R, G, C and T are probably the most difficult of all. The former pair may however be differentiated by the formation of the top loop, in which k reverses R. In other respects these in many hands are almost identical. ff (F) is often rather like a *modern* H. In the seventeenth century u and v are used almost indiscriminately. If one remembers these points, and bears in mind that English secretary hand of the seventeenth century bears a close resemblance to German Gothic script of the twentieth (e.g. in r, one form of which is 𝔯), much of the initial difficulty soon disappears.

1. Based upon W. P. W. Phillimore, *Pedigree Work*, 1914, p. 86. I am obliged to Messrs. Phillimore for permission to use this, and to Mr. N. Ker for help in revising it.
2. This is the work of Billingsley—a writing master, 1637. The hand of the average scribe was at once less elaborate (especially in the capitals), and more mixed.
3. There are three admirable modern guides to the amateur palaeographer: *ed.* Miss H. Grieve, *Examples of English Handwriting* . . . (Essex C.R.O., 1954 and edns.), N. Denholm-Young, *Handwriting in England and Wales* (Cardiff) 1954 and L. C. Hector, *Handwriting of English Documents*, 1955.

A NOTE UPON CHRONOLOGY

There are available a number of excellent books upon chronology which will help the amateur historian in such puzzling matters as the difference between Old Style and New Style, the beginning of the year of grace, and those of the regnal years of successive rulers, and so on. Most of these also contain a table for finding Easter, and a list of the saints' days commonly used in dating documents. Sir Maurice Powicke *et al.*; *A Handbook of Chronology*, R. Hist. Soc., 1939, 'Guides and Handbooks' Series no. 2, 2nd edn. 1961, is at once a very compendious and quite the clearest and most intelligible book I know of on the subject. A shorter work covering some of the same ground is C. R. Cheney, *Handbook of Dates*, 1945 and reprints, a companion volume to Sir Maurice's, and no. 4 in the same series.

A NOTE UPON MARRIAGE AND THE
PROHIBITED DEGREES[1]

The present statute law is laid down in Cripps, *op. cit.* p. 586 the Marriage Act of 1931, and the Marriage Enabling Act of 1960, which removes some of the last mediaeval restrictions which had survived until Archbishop Parker's time, and from thence to our own days. The canon law, which differs in that it still forbids marriage to one's deceased wife's sister, is in Burn, *Ecclesiastical Law*, Vol. III, pp. 405–15. It is not correct to say as Cripps does (p. 586)[2] that Pope Alexander II introduced a new system. His long letter on the computation of consanguinity is reproduced by Gratian (c. 2, C. 35, q. 5). But that very letter shows that he was not introducing 'a new system' at all, since he quotes Gregory the Great (590–604) as using the same system himself (cf. also, for Gregory, c. 20, C. 35, q. 2, where he explains that he only made a temporary relaxation of the restrictions for the English, who as recent converts must needs be given milk rather than solid food!).—Doubt seems to be rightly thrown on the quotations from Gregory as not being authentic, since nothing supports the idea of prohibition of marriage between sixth cousins in his time [cf. *Cath. Encycl. Consanguinity*, IV, 264–5].—But it is clear that the *system* of computation was already in use long before Alexander II.

This same system has been in force ever since. The Fourth Lateran Council (1215) reduced the impediments from the seventh to the fourth degree, and this survived until the new Code of Canon Law, 1918, when it was further reduced to the third (i.e. second cousins) [who therefore need a dispensation to-day].

1. *Cf.* pp. 43–4, 105, 106, 213.
2. For most of which I am indebted to the Catholic scholar, the Rev. Fr. M. Bevenot, S.J.

Glossary. *See also* General Index

The orthography of seventeenth- and eighteenth-century parish officers is often eccentric in the extreme, and the inquirer must be prepared to translate, e.g.

and setterer	*into*	etc.
arter david		affidavit
badderacks		(bell) baldrics
baggars		badgers
bagging (ye poore)		badging them
born on the bear		borne on the bier
cececary		certiorari
carvaers		surveyors
cilling a notter		killing an otter
cinges aremes		king's arms
disses		decease
double cats		(land tax, etc.) duplicates
fedomes (of bell rope)		fathoms
feyseytashyn		visitation
frant and sens		frankincense
(workhouse) inmetary		inventory
jelan orspitle (rate)		jail and hospital rate
melisha		militia
a mont of lenin		her month of lying in (the period for which a pauper woman was allowed relief)
a nabstrak		an abstract (of parish register entries)
a nomeley		a homily
pellitor, paritory, etc.		apparitor
(scavenger's) phes		fees
possessioning, pashon, etc.		processioning, i.e. perambulation
sillister		solicitor
sitacon		citation
stivacate and even cirstoviate		certificate
waichin ye sorples		washing the surplice
tarry		terrier
wart (for warrt)		warrant
yngeounseon		injunction

It is perhaps unnecessary to point out that an acquaintance with local dialect will often provide the clue to such puzzles, otherwise sometimes almost insoluble. Commonly used Latin phrases are printed below in italics. Much fuller Latin wordlists are to be found in Martin's *Record Interpreter, Latin for Lawyers*, Baxter and Johnson's *Mediaeval Latin Wordlist*, and the other works of reference cited elsewhere. Martin's book gives some lists of trades and vocations in English and Latin. A still better list appears as an appendix to the British Record Society's *Nottinghamshire Marriage Licences*, Vol. 1, 1930, pp. 589–94. Latin words appearing in the ordinary dictionaries, and used in the same sense as in classical times (*e.g. agricola* for farmer, husbandman, etc., *artifex* for craftsman), and such standard terms as *armiger* for esquire, *generosus* for gentleman, are not given hereunder, since they will be found in the ordinary works of reference.

ACTS OF PARLIAMENT. *See also* CHRONOLOGICAL TABLE
OF ACTS CITED.

Act of Submission, 25 Hen. VIII, c. 19, 1533–4.
Act of Supremacy, 1 Eliz. c. 1, 1558–9.
Acts of Uniformity, 2 & 3 Ed. VI, c. 1, 1448; 1 Eliz. c. 2, 1558; 14 Car. II, c. 4, 1662.

Lord Blandford's Act, The New Parishes Act, 6 & 7 Vic. c. 37, 1843.
Commons Registration Act, 14 & 15 Eliz. II c. 64 (1965).
East's Act, The Poor Law, 55 Geo. III, c. 137, 1814–15.
Gilbert's Act, 22 Geo. III, c. 83, 1781–2. The name is also sometimes given to the Clergy Residences Repair Act, 17 Geo. III, c. 53, 1776–7.
Lord Hardwicke's Act, 26 Geo. II, c. 33, 1753.
Hobhouse's Act, 1 & 2 W. IV, c. 60, 1831.
New Poor Law, 4 & 5 W. IV, c. 76, 1834. Old Poor Law, 43 Eliz. c. 2, 1601.
Pitt's Act, 35 Geo. III, c. 101, 1794–5.
Rose's Act, 52 Geo. III, c. 146, 1812.
Speenhamland Act. This term is applied both to Pitt's Act of 1794–5, and to Sturges Bourne's 1819 Act, *q.v.*
Statute of Merton, 20 Hen. III, cc. 4, 9, 1235.
Statute of Westminster II, 13 Ed. I, c. 46, 1285.
Sturges Bourne's Acts, 58 Geo. III, c. 69, 1818, and 59 Geo. III, c. 12, 1819.
Lord Tenterden's Act. The Tithe Act, 2 & 3 W. IV, c. 100, 1831–2.
Toleration Act, 1 W. & M. c. 18, 1688.
Lord Worsley's Act. The Enclosure Act, 6 & 7 W. IV, c. 115, 1836.

Advertisements, a series of injunctions issued to the clergy in 1566, pursuant to the Act of Uniformity.
Affeerers (afferatores), officers of the manorial court having the duty of assessing monetary penalties.
aftermath, herbage remaining after hay harvest.
albacio, whitewashing.
aleplays, mystery or miracle plays in aid of church funds; *see* church ales.
altarage, mortuaries, surplice fees, and other minor ecclesiastical offerings.
amercement or **amerciament,** monetary penalty levied in the court.
apparitor, the official messenger of the archdeaconry court.
(common) appendant, *see* common.
appropriate, an ecclesiastical benefice whose tithe is annexed in whole or in part to an ecclesiastical body or personage other than the incumbent.
approvement, enclosure of common, especially by the lord of the manor under the Statutes of Merton and Westminster II.
(common) appurtenant, *see* common.
Archbishop Parker's Table, the table of prohibited degrees, for which *see* pp. 43–4, 105, 146, 308.
archdeacon, an ecclesiastical dignitary ranking above the incumbent but below the bishop. In many matters the bishop's principal officer, *oculus episcopi.*
Arches, Court of, the Provincial court of the Archbishop of Canterbury.
ascertaciones sedilium, pew rents.
assart or **essart,** enclosure of forest or other waste land.
badgers, licensed beggars, later also pedlars or chapmen.
badging the poor, marking them in accordance with the act of 1697–8, for which see pp. 207–8.
baldric, the leather thong inside a bell, by which the clapper is hung.
balk, an untilled boundary strip either between adjacent selions in a common-field furlong, or, more often, between two adjacent furlongs in a common field. Hence a grass way over an open field. Sidebalks are those running parallel to the selions, waybalks those running at right angles to them, headlands. It has lately been shown that balks in the former sense were by no means so common as was formerly supposed; see Dr Orwin's address to the Historical Association Conference, January 1938.
basterino, bastard.
bastard, properly the base child of a father of gentle or noble birth, but more generally any illegitimate child.
beast gates, *see* gate.
bede roll, a list of benefactors to the church, for whose souls the faithful were asked to pray. The roll was usually read out from the pulpit each Sunday, and at Christmas and Michaelmas. It is now replaced by the Bidding Prayer.

Bills, Hay's of 1735, for centralising the administration of Poor Relief: **Pitt's** of 1795, for Poor Law amendment: **Whitbread's** of 1796, for fixing minimum wages.

bills, register, transcripts of parish registers, *q.v.*

Lord Blandford's Act, *see* Acts.

bond of indemnification, a device often adopted to secure the parish against pecuniary liabilities, and often demanded (*a*) from relatives or friends of potential paupers who might gain a settlement; (*b*) from masters engaging servants for twelve months, whose service would gain them a settlement; (*c*) from putative fathers of illegitimate children, in order to secure the observance of covenants for their maintenance.

boonmaster, *see* waywarden.

boots, *see* botes.

borsholder, *see* constable.

botes, haybote, housebote, firebote, ploughbote, etc. Common right of taking timber from the waste of the manor for the repair of hedges and fences, for house repair, for firewood, for the maintenance and repair of the tools of husbandry, etc.

bounties, (parochial) payments to militia volunteers. *See* pp. 180–1.

bovate, one-eighth of a ploughland. Oxgang.

brasses, the sockets in which the axles of a bell work.

brecks, breaks, (supposedly temporary) enclosures, especially from forest land.

bridewell, an early form of county gaol or house of correction.

brief, a letter from authorities civil or ecclesiastical commending a charitable appeal. *See* pp. 120–5.

broad oxgang, yardland.

brushing the road, *not* sweeping it, but repairing it by filling up the worst holes with bundles of brushwood.

buried, partly, having the heart buried separately from the rest of the body.

burleyman, officer appointed at the manor court for various local duties, also constable, or tithing man.

butts, lands in a common field abutting more or less at right angles upon another selion, or lands which because of the irregular shape of the field fall short of the full length.

byeblow, bastard.

bylawman, variant of burleyman, *q.v.*

canons, ecclesiastical laws relating to the church as a whole, cf. **constitutions.** Those now in force were issued by both Convocations in 1603.

cantle, small piece of anything, especially the holy loaf, *q.v.*

capellanus, chaplain.

capias, warrant for arrest.

cap money, a fine levied on the township and paid by the constable for breach of the 1571 act concerning the wearing of woollen caps on Sundays and Holy Days. *See* p. 106.

car(r), common, especially of a marshy sort.

cart, parish, a deterrent device consisting of a farm cart to which applicants for relief were harnessed in a few specially economical parishes in the early nineteenth century.

carucate (in the Danelaw), ploughland (assessed for taxation), varying in area, but on the average perhaps c. 160–80 acres, as much as an eight-ox team could plough in a year.

catchpole acre, an acre or strip on a parish boundary, the tithe of which belonged to the first incumbent who arrived at the spot to collect it.

certificate, (*a*) of settlement, *see* pp. 192–3, 198–205; (*b*) of good conduct, *see* p. 12.

cess, rate, tax, or assessment.

champion, open-field land as distinguished from land held in severalty.

chanceling, bastard.

chantry. The term is used loosely of almost any pre-Reformation religious foundation connected with a cathedral, parish church, or chapel—light, obit, stipendiary service, trental, etc. Properly a chantry is a service founded in a church for a special object either with a permanent endowment in land and rent, or celebrated for a terminable period for which funds have been bequeathed or otherwise allocated. Freehold chantries and most stipendiary services fall within the first division; the second includes obits and trentals.

chaplain, (in this sense) the priest of a chapel, i.e. a church not having full parochial rights of sepulture, etc. An unbeneficed priest existing on a stipend at the pleasure of his employer.

chosen sentences, the sentences, generally the Lord's Prayer, etc. etc. set up in church 'in convenient places', in accordance with Canon 82.

chrismatory, a silver or silver-gilt box used for holy oil in the mediaeval baptismal office and extreme unction.

chrism cloth, a silk cloth used for covering the chrismatory in transit from its aumbry to the font. Not to be confused with the Chrisom cloth, for which *see* pp. 59–60.

chrisom child, chrisomer, *see* pp. 59–60.

christened, technically not quite equivalent to baptised. *See* p. 59 for notes on the difference.

church ales, the mediaeval equivalents of the church bazaar or the vicarage garden party, their degenerate descendants. *See* pp. 87–8.

church hay, churchyard.

church house, the mediaeval prototype of the parish hall. *See* pp. 87–8.

churchmen, churchwardens, *q.v.*

church reeves, churchwardens.

churchwardens. *See* pp. 84–108.

churchwardens, tied, wardens compelled to serve the office in virtue of their occupation of certain houses or land whose turn on the rota had come round. *See* pp. 85–6.

churchyard rails, the churchyard fence, often repairable by the parishioners in specific shares, each apportioned to the owner or occupier of a particular house or farm. *See* pp. 133–4.

clericus pacis, clerk of the peace—the principal legal officer of the county authority.

clericus parochialis, parish clerk, for whom *see* pp. 131–3.

close, a hedged or fenced area of cultivable land such as is now generally (though incorrectly) known as a field.

close parishes, those taking stringent precautions against the gaining of settlements by strangers.

co-aration, communal cultivation of open fields.

collation, nomination of a clerk to a benefice by the bishop either as patron or because of the failure of the real patron to present within six months. Strictly speaking the benefice is collated to the man, not the man to the benefice.

collectioner, pauper receiving relief.

collector of the poor, the prototype under the 1572 act of the officer later known as the overseer of the poor. The term is also used in later years of a kind of assistant overseer.

common appendant, common right attached to land.

common appurtenant, common right attached to a house or the site of a house formerly existing.

common in gross, common right detached from both house and land.

common of shack, common right of grazing upon land after the crop has been lifted, e.g. in lammas lands, *q.v.*

common of turbary, common right of cutting turf or other fuel.

compatres, godparents.

conductio sedilium, pew rents,.

conjuncti fuere, (they) were married.

consistory court, the court of the bishop, presided over by his chancellor.

constablewick, the area of a constable's jurisdiction, generally more or less equivalent to township or tithing.

constant man, agricultural labourer working regularly for the same employer.

constitutions, ecclesiastical regulations adopted by a provincial synod, and valid throughout the whole province. Cf. **canons**.

correction, house of, a variety of county gaol. The term is applied correctly more especially to the gaols established in 1575–6 by 18 Eliz. c. 3.

cotarius, cottager.

cóttager, the occupier of a tenement having attached thereto a croft, a common right, and a little land, usually not more than eight or ten acres.

cotter, iron wedge put through a bell to secure it; lynch pin.

courage bater, gelder.

court baron, the assembly of the tenants of a manor under the presidency of the lord or his steward. (?) The link in development between the township moot of early English times and the vestry meeting of our own day.

court leet, a court of record held in some manors, though not in all, by the lord or his steward, and attended by freeholders and tenants. It could not be held unless at least two freehold tenants occupied lands in the manor. It had jurisdiction over various petty offences, and performed a variety of administrative duties.

cows, papers for the, schedules under 19 Geo. II, c. 5, 1745–6, an act relating to the distemper among horned cattle.

creature (*creatura Christi*), a baptismal name often applied in special circumstances. *See* p. 59.

cro(c)k, (processional) cross.

curate, properly *not* the assistant priest of a parish, but any minister having *cure* of souls, especially a deputy in full charge of a parish, but removable at pleasure by his employer.

custodes ecclesiae, custodes bonorum ecclesiae, etc., churchwardens.

dales, *see* doles. In some counties the word is used as equivalent to selions, *q.v.*

day labourer, labourer selling his work by the day in the open market, i.e. not attached to one employer, or hired yearly.

decimae, tithes.

decimer, *see* dozener.

dispensation, licence granted by the Archbishop of Canterbury, 'in any case not contrary to the Holy Scriptures and the law of God', or by diocesan bishops for non-observance of minor regulations, e.g. for non-residence, to eat flesh in Lent, etc.

distributer, assistant or deputy overseer of the poor, *q.v.*

dog-whipper, a minor official of the church. *See* pp. 107–8.

doles, (*a*) shares, especially of common meadow, distributed annually or periodically by lot or rotation; also (*b*) charitable donations of any kind.

dominus, 'sir', a courtesy title applied to a priest who was not *Artium Magister*, and therefore could not properly be styled *Magister*. Untranslatable into modern English, except perhaps as 'Sir' (in quotation marks).

donative (benefice), one wholly or partly withdrawn from the bishop's jurisdiction.

dozener, burghal official elected by the householders of each ward or street to make presentments at the court leet in towns. Probably originally having jurisdiction over twelve houses or families; cf. tithingman. In some places the word is used of jurymen, the jury being the 'douzaine'.

driving (the common), the lord of the manor's privilege of collecting and examining once a year all the beasts on the common in order to ascertain that only those persons having common right were turning on their stock.

duplicates, (*a*) of parish registers, the transcripts furnished annually or triennially to the bishop or archdeacon by the churchwardens; (*b*) of land-tax assessments, the copies furnished each year by the petty constable to the local commissioners and to the clerk of the peace.

East's Act, *see* Acts.

edge, balk or mear, *q.v.*

electioner, a person qualified for parochial office but not actually appointed to any.

enclosure, the conversion into severalty of open-field (champion) common meadow, or common pasture or waste.

engrossing, the gathering into single ownership or tenancy of lands and houses formerly supporting two or more families.

essart, variant of assart, *q.v.*

essoins, tenants making a monetary payment or other valid excuse for non-attendance at the court. Strictly speaking the essoin is the excuse itself and the tenant is the essoiner.

estovers, the Norman French equivalent of the Old English term botes, *q.v.*

examination (as to settlement), a sworn statement made before one or more magistrates, generally upon the demand of the parish officers with a view to removal. *See* pp. 202–3.

extra-parochial, outside the bounds of any (civil and/or ecclesiastical) parish, and therefore exempt from the payment of poor and/or church rates, and usually exempt from payment of tithes also, though strictly extra-parochial tithe was payable to the Crown. All extra-parochial places automatically became civil parishes in 1894.

farthinghold, half oxgang.

fidejussores, godparents.

field, a large area of open land, divided into furlongs, which again were sub-divided into selions, all of which were normally subject to the same crop rotation. Not the modern 'field', which is more properly styled a close.

field jury, a jury of the manorial court regulating the use of the common fields.

field master, field reeve, field(s)man, a communal officer regulating the use of the open fields, the appointment of whom was regularised by the act 13 Geo. III, c. 81, 1772–3. for which *see* p. 266.

fifteens, select vestry.

fire hooks, large iron hooks on long poles, used for removing the thatch from burning buildings; often stored in the church and occasionally still surviving there, e.g. at Iver, Bucks.

flat, furlong.

font tapers, a levy made by the churchwardens, originally for the taper used at baptism, but continued long after the Reformation as a customary fee at baptism.

foreman of the fields, fieldmaster, *q.v.*, or sometimes foreman of the field jury, *q.v.*

forthfare, passing bell.

fother, odd scrap of land in the open fields.

furlong, group of selions forming a subdivision of an open field.

gait, gate, *q.v.*

Gang Week, Rogation tide. *See* p. 74.

garbs, tithe of, that of sheaves, i.e. tithe of white corn, part of the great tithe.

garnishing the church, decorating it with appropriate flowers and branches, etc., upon the major festivals. *See* p. 101.

-gate (beast-, cow-, horse, ox-, sheep-), the right of pasture on the common for one animal.

gated pasture, stinted pasture, *q.v.*

Gateward's Case, a celebrated legal case of 1603 in which it was decided first as to Stixwould, Lincs., and then by extension generally, that common right could not attach to the inhabitants in a village or town unincorporate merely by reason of their inhabitancy.

Gilbert's Act, *see* Acts.

gore or **gored acre,** a scrap of land, generally more or less triangular in shape, in the open field.

gossips, gossibs, godparents.

(common) in gross, *see* common.

'hacking the ruts', a primitive method of road repair.

half-baptized, christened privately.

half-year's lands, lands commonable for about six months in twelve.

hamlet, a small settlement having neither a constable (so therefore not a township), nor an overseer, a parish church, and a separate rate (so therefore not a parish).

hapence, Easter dues.

Lord Hardwicke's Act, *see* Acts.

hayward, a manorial, burghal, or parochial officer having charge of the hedges, and by extension sometimes regulating open-field cultivation and the use of the common generally.

headborough, properly a deputy constable. In some districts the term was used as synonymous with that of constable.

headland, space left at the head of a selion for the plough to turn on. Often the headland was commonable or belonged to a different proprietor from the long lands. The word is now used for similar land in an arable close held in severalty.

he(a)rse, (*a*) a frame for holding candles; (*b*) a frame placed over a corpse to support the pall; (*c*) a similar frame attached to a tomb for the purpose of supporting hangings or lights.

hempland, small plot for the cultivation of hemp, in accordance with the statutes of 1533 and 1563; by extension any very small plot or pightle, especially one going with a dwelling.

hide, (in the part of England outside the Danelaw) a ploughland assessed for taxation.

highways, surveyor of, parish officer appointed in accordance with the 1555 highway Act to take charge of road repairs—waywarden.

hitched land, part of the common field withdrawn by common consent (especially in the fallow year) from the customary rotation, and used for some special crop, e.g. vetches or turnips.

Hobhouse's Act, *see* Acts.

Hocktide, the second Monday and Tuesday after Easter.

holy loaf, bread blessed but not consecrated, distributed to the congregation in the chancel after mass, and consumed in token of fellowship.

holy oil box, chrismatory, *q.v.*

homage, body of tenants attending a manorial court.

honour, aggregation of manors.

houseling bread, the small wafers used for the communion of the parishioners in general.

houseling cloth, a cloth used at the communion.

houseling people, parishioners of age to communicate.

house row, any parochial system of rotation among the inhabitants, especially with reference to the serving of parish offices or the taking of parish rounds-men or parish apprentices, etc.

hundred house, workhouse serving a district larger than a mere parish, especially in East Anglia, where workhouses to serve whole hundreds were very generally established as a measure of poor law reform from the middle of the eighteenth century onwards.

husbandland, ploughland.

husbandman, usually tenant farmer as distinct from yeoman, *q.v.*

iconomi, variant of *oeconomi,* *q.v.*

impropriate, ecclesiastical benefice whose tithe is held in whole or in part by a layman.

inclosure, the lawyers' spelling of enclosure.

increase, the profit on the church 'stock' lent by the wardens to parish gilds, etc.

increment, increase as above. The term is also used in some accounts for the balance of gild funds in hand at the end of the year, carried to general church funds.

incumbent, parson—rector or vicar,—but not of course unbeneficed clerk or curate, except perhaps a 'perpetual curate'.

induction, introduction of a clerk by the archdeacon or his deputy (except in peculiars or exempt benefices) into the temporal possession of his benefice.

information, affidavit as to burial in woollen, for which *see* pp. 66–9.

ingenuus, yeoman, freeholder.

ings, (common) meadows.

initiatus(a) fuit, he (she) was baptized.

injunctions, orders issued to the clergy in pre-Reformation times by the bishops, later especially by Cromwell as Vice-gerent in 1538, by Edward VI in 1547, and by Elizabeth in 1559.

innocent, chrisom child, *q.v.*

institution, installation of a clerk by the bishop or his deputy into the possession of the spiritualities of his benefice, i.e. to the cure of souls.

interred, often used of Quakers, Anabaptists, etc. to mean buried without Christian rites.

intruder, puritan minister installed in a benefice after the expulsion of the lawful incumbent during the Interregnum.

jack's land, scraps of land, largely unused and unusable, in a common field.

judas, dummy candle (from the sham disciple),

keeds, kids, bundles of brushwood used for road repair.

king ales, church ales, so called from the 'king' and 'queen' elected to preside over the revels.

kirkmasters, churchwardens. In some parishes the term is used of select vestrymen.

kirkwardens, churchwardens.

knobstick wedding, wedding of a pregnant woman, compelled by the churchwardens and attended by them in state. So called from the staves which were and are their badge of office. *See* pp. 215–16.

knocknobbler, dog-whipper, *q.v.*

labour rate, a device for employing the able-bodied poor. *See* pp. 234–5.

laine, (in the south of England) open field.

lairstall, a grave inside the church.

lairstone, a stone covering the above.

Lammas lands, meadows commonable after haysel (Lammas day is 1 August and Old Lammas 12 August).

lanatus, bewoolled, i.e. buried in woollen, for which *see* pp. 66–9.

lands, selions.

Land Tax, a tax levied rate fashion from 1692 upon the various counties, each of which had to apportion its share among its constituent parishes. It was made permanent but redeemable in 1797–8, upon a very inequitable basis, and is still payable upon lands which have not been compounded for. It was assessed by local commissioners and gathered by the petty constables.

lanebegot, bastard.

lawless parson, a cleric willing to marry couples at uncanonical times and places. *See* pp. 64, 81–2.

lawn, selion.

lay(e), variant of ley, *q.v.*

laystal, lestall, etc., variants of lairstall, *q.v.*

leawne, levy or rate, especially in Shropshire and the neighbouring counties.

leaze, (common) meadow.

lestall, variant of lairstall, *q.v.*

levant et couchant (common right for cattle), for as many in summer as the produce of the land in question will maintain during the winter.

lewne, *see* leawne *above*.

ley, (*a*) variant of levy or rate, *for which see* leawne *above*; (*b*) land ploughed for several years, and then put under grass for a period, then ploughed again, and so on.

liberty, group of manors, manor or subdivision thereof; strictly speaking a privileged area whence the sheriff was excluded, and where the lord had the return of writs.

light, stipendiary endowment in the pre-Reformation church.

litten, churchyard.

loon, selion.

lordship, liberty or manor.

lot meadow, (common) meadow the several occupation of which was determined every year or every two or three years by the casting of lots among a limited number of proprietors.

lune, rate, especially in Cheshire and the neighbouring counties.

mainport, a small tribute, usually of bread loaves, paid in some parishes to the rector in lieu of certain tithes.

maslin, mixed corn, especially rye and barley.

masters of the parish, selectmen, *q.v.*

mear, meer, boundary bank or hedge dividing furlong from furlong or field from field in open-field agriculture, as distinct from balk, which in some places, though not all, was used of a bank dividing selion from selion. In some districts balk and meer are used indiscriminately.

merry begot, bastard.

militia, the old constitutional force of the country, still surviving in a somewhat attenuated form, and corresponding more or less to the territorial army. Counties and parishes were informed how many men they must provide, and were fined if they did not produce their proper quota. Each parish raised its share by the method it preferred, generally by ballot, or by offering bounties for volunteers. Normally the militia arrangements in each parish were in the charge of the constable.

minister, a somewhat archaic word more or less equivalent to incumbent, *q.v.*

mislin, maslin, *q.v.*

mock of the church, banns called but not followed by a wedding. Often customarily fineable by the churchwardens.

modus, strictly *modus decimandi,* a customary fixed payment in lieu of tithing in kind. *See* pp. 139–40.

mortuary, customary payment to the incumbent upon the death of a parishioner. *See* pp. 69–70, 127, 131, and 299 (Pt. IX, note 22).

muslin, maslin, *q.v.*

naked (buried), buried unshrouded to escape the penalties of the burial in woollen Acts. *See* pp. 66–9.

New Poor Law, *see* Acts.

nomansland, variant of jack's land, *q.v.*

nothus, bastard. Strictly the base child of a gentleman by a plebeian mother, or, according to other authorities, the base child of a married woman. Actually in many parishes used indiscriminately of all illegitimate children.

odd man, labourer employed and paid by the day.

oeconomus(i) steward(s), churchwarden(s).

Old Poor Law, *see* Acts.

open parishes, (*a*) those in which open fields and/or commons still remained; (*b*) those in which, generally because of lax administration of the poor law, or wide distribution of land and cottage ownership, settlement could readily be gained.

open vestry, *see* vestry, open.

order, removal, *see* removal order.

ordinary, ecclesiastical superior of any kind, archbishop, bishop, or archdeacon.

overseer of the poor, the principal parish officer concerned with the administration of the poor law from 1601 until after 1834. *See* pp. 29–30, 34, 191–8, 209–11. Later a mere rate assessor and collector. Office abolished 1927 under Act of 1925.

overseer of the highways, waywarden, *q.v.*

oxgang or **narrow oxgang,** originally the area of land cultivable by one ox, half a yardland, or one-eighth of a ploughland. Later a conventional unit varying widely from parish to parish (and even within the same parish), from perhaps 10 to 25 acres.

oxgang, broad, yardland.

parish, civil, district for which a separate rate is or may be levied.

parish, ecclesiastical, the area of ground committed to the charge of one minister, and possessing a church with full rights of sepulture, etc.

parish, highway. *See* pp. 9, 249–50.

parish clerk, a temporal officer, not a spiritual one, discharging minor duties connected with the church, and often wrongly entrusted with the entering up of the registers.

parish priest, (properly) unbeneficed clerk to whom the cure of souls is deputed by the parson; curate.

Parker's (Archbishop) Table, *see* Archbishop Parker's Table.

parson, (properly) rector; a vicar is not strictly speaking a parson, nor, of course, is an unbeneficed curate.

paschal money, a levy originally for the cost of the paschal taper kept lighted from Easter to Holy Thursday, and lighted again at Whitsuntide. The levy was collected when the parishioners 'took their rights'; *see* rights.

paull, selion.

pauperum supervisor, overseer of the poor, *q.v.*

Peace, Clerk of the, *see clericus pacis.*

peace keeper, dog-whipper, *q.v.*

peculiar, an ecclesiastical district exempt from the jurisdiction of the ordinary.

pentecostals, a tax levied originally as Peter's pence, later paid by each parish church to the cathedral church of the diocese.

perambulation, beating the bounds of the parish at Rogation tide. *See* p. 74.

perpetual curate, clerk holding cure of souls, though formerly not strictly speaking beneficed, in a parish or chapelry where there was no regularly endowed vicarage, but nevertheless, unlike a mere stipendiary curate, not removable at the caprice of his employer—in this case the impropriator; incumbent of a parochial chapelry—*i.e.* one having some rights of burial, etc.

Peter's pence (farthings, etc.), *see* pentecostals *above.*

petty constable, parish constable as distinct from high constable.

petty sessions, *see* sessions, petty.

pightel, pightle (and even **pigtail**), scrap of land (in the open fields), in the eastern counties any small enclosure.

pinfold, (in the Midland counties) pound.

pingle, (especially in Nottinghamshire and neighbouring counties), a variant of pightle, *q.v.*

pit money, a customary fee for burial in church.

Pitt's Bill, *see under* Bills.

plough duty, (highway) statute duty assessed per ploughland.

Plough Monday, the first Monday after Epiphany, notable for rustic jollifications with monetary collections, often formerly for church funds.

ploughland, the area of land cultivable by one eight-ox plough, later a conventional amount containing anything from perhaps 80 to 200 statute acres, but always containing four yardlands or eight oxgangs.

Poor Law, New, and Poor Law, Old, *see* Acts.

possessioning, perambulation, *q.v.*

presentation, the nomination of a clerk by the patron to the ordinary.

presented, accepted in church after 'half baptism'. *See also* presentment *below.*

presentment, statement of fact made on oath by e.g. the churchwardens in the bishop's or archdeacon's correctional court, *see* pp. 84, 85, 99, the jurors in the manor court, *see* p. 256, or the petty constable at quarter sessions or assizes, *see* pp. 177–9, 185, 187.

processioning, perambulation, *q.v.*

procuratores ecclesiae, churchwardens.

provost, constable.

purveyance, the royal right of buying provisions, etc., for the household at prices below market rates, exemption from which was often bought by the villagers through the constable.

pyke, gore, *q.v.*; a leg of mutton shaped plot of land, as it were a spandril, in a corner of the ploughlands.

quadripartite division of tithe. *See under* tithe.

quarentena(e), furlong(s).

quarrells, panes of glass.

quarter, a division of a parish for poor law purposes, especially in large parishes. Often used as equivalent to township or constablewick.

quarterage, county rates paid quarterly through the parish officers.

quartering (a church bell), turning it through an angle of 90° so that the clapper may strike a fresh place.

questmen, sidesmen or assistants to the churchwardens. *See* pp. 84–6. The Canons seem to use the term as synonymous with that of churchwardens.

quietus, receipt.

quillets, surviving selions, still in separate ownership, but situated entirely within the boundaries of a close belonging to another owner.

R.R. (for *regni Regis*), in the — th year of King —.

rap, selion.

rean, meer.

rector (clerical), an incumbent having both great and small tithe, or lands or moduses in lieu thereof.

rector (lay), a layman owning the great tithe of a rectory impropriate. Until recent years the rector, whether clerical or lay, was liable to repair the chancel of the parish church.

recusants, nonconformists, especially of the Roman Catholic variety, declining to attend their parish church.

reeve, communal officer of almost any kind, especially one concerned with the management of open fields and commons.

register bills, *see* bills, register.

regulation (of commons), stinting, *q.v.* Under the General Enclosure Acts, regulation includes also such measures as fencing, draining, etc., thought necessary in order to maintain the utility of the common to the commoners and to the community at large.

removal, the transfer of a pauper or potential pauper to his place of legal settlement, *q.v. See* pp. 190–205.

removal order, justice's warrant for effecting the above.

ridges or rigs, selions.

rights, taking one's, communicating in one's parish church, the legal right of every parishioner 'devoutly and humbly desiring the same', unless there is lawful cause to the contrary. In pre-Reformation times this also included confession and the receiving of absolution. *See also* paschal money.

ring of the town, *see* vicar's ring.

rogue money, an annual payment by the constable of each parish to the high constable of the county for the maintenance of prisoners in the county gaol, by 39 Eliz. c. 3 (1597–8), 3 Jac. I, c. 10 (1605–6) and 7 Jac. I, c. 4 (1609–10).

Romescot, pentecostals, *q.v.*

rotation meadow, variant of lot meadow, *q.v. See also* shifting severalties.

roundel, iron ring for holding candles, trendal.

roundsman system, a device for employing the able-bodied poor: (*a*) the ordinary system, the parish paying the difference between the labourer's wages and an agreed scale; (*b*) the special system, the parish contracting with individuals to perform certain work, the work being done by pauper labour, and the parish paying the paupers; (*c*) pauper auction, each pauper labourer being auctioned off separately each week or month to the highest bidder. *See* pp. 232–4. *See also* labour rate *and* house row.

saunce bell, sanctus bell.

scapebegotten, bastard.

scot ale, church ale. *See* pp. 87–8.

season, two or more open fields or parts of such fields simultaneously under the same crop or fallow.

second poor, poor not in receipt of relief.

selectmen, vestrymen (of a select vestry, *q.v.*).

selions, (originally probably acre) strips of arable land in an open field, not of course uniform in size, and often very far removed in area from either statute or local acre.

seniors of the parish, select vestrymen.

serges, large corpse candles.

sess, variant of cess, *q.v.*

sessions money, county rate, paid quarterly by the constable at the quarter sessions.

sessions, petty, (until 1830) meetings of two or three local justices for minor local business.

sessions, quarter, the general sessions of the peace for the county, held quarterly for both criminal and administrative business.

sessions, special, monthly and somewhat informal meetings of the justices in each division of the county.

settlement. *See* pp. 31–2, 190–205.

settlement certificate, a written admission by a parish that a certain pauper

Y

or potential pauper was legally settled in it and undertaking to receive him back, or otherwise to indemnify any other parish to which he fell chargeable. *See* pp. 192–3, 198–205.

settlement examination, *see* examination.

several(ty), land held in individual ownership or tenancy as distinguished from that held in common.

shack, right of grazing upon open fields after the crop has been lifted, e.g. in lammas lands.

shifting severalties, land such as lot or rotation meadow, held in severalty for part of the year only, and the several ownership of which varies from year to year or through a prescribed period, being determined by lot, rotation, or some similar method.

shot, furlong, or sometimes selion.

sidebalk, *see* balk.

sidesmen, originally and still properly synodsmen or questmen, for whom *see* pp. 84–6. Actually deputy churchwardens. The derivation of the word from 'Synodsmen' is not accepted by all ecclesiastical historians.

singing bread, large wafers used for the communion of the priest.

sixteen, *see* vestry, select.

sluggard waker, dog-whipper, *q.v.*

smoke farthings, pentecostals.

Speenhamland Act, *see* Acts.

Speenhamland scale. *See* p. 231.

Speenhamland System, a device for proportioning rates of poor relief to family responsibilities and to the cost of living. *See* pp. 231–2.

squatters, persons enclosing scraps of common and building cottages thereon without the leave of quarter sessions and the lord of the manor.

statutes, *see* Acts.

sticking (the church), garnishing it, *q.v.*

stint, stinting, (*a*) the regulation of the number of cattle allowed to graze on a common. Hence commons were classified into stinted and unstinted; (*b*) the last two or three yards of a selion meeting another selion end to end, which the owner of the neighbouring selion had the right to use for access to his own land, and which therefore were not cultivable until after the sowing of the neighbouring selion had been completed.

stitch, selion.

stock, parish, (*a*) before the Reformation, the church capital in cash or cattle, lent out on bond by the wardens to suitable parishioners, in the former case for the whole profit, in the latter for an annual rent payable to church funds; (*b*) after the Reformation, the stock of 'wool, flax, hemp, wood, thread, iron, and other necessary ware and stuff to set the poor on work', provided by the overseers and churchwardens at the parish expense.

stoneman, waywarden.

striking (candles), casting them.

stropper, dry cow.

Sturges Bourne's Acts, *see* Acts.

substitute, person provided either by the parish or by an individual inhabitant to replace a parishioner drawn for service in the militia, *q.v.*

supervisores fabricae ecclesiae, churchwardens.

supervisores pauperum, overseers of the poor.

surcharging (the common), overstocking it.

sureties, (*a*) godparents, alternatively (*b*) those giving security for the performance of a bond of any sort, eg. marriage, indemnification for maintenance of bastards, etc.

surveyor of the highways, waywarden, *q.v.*

susceptors, *susceptores,* godparents.

taberna cerevisiae, church ales; the phrase is also used sometimes (and more properly) to mean simply alehouse.

Table, Archbishop Parker's, *see* Archbishop Parker's Table.

taking one's rights, *see* rights, taking one's.

Lord Tenterden's Act, *see* Acts.

terrier, inventory of possessions, especially of landed property. *See* above p. 126.

testes, witnesses, i.e. godparents.

testimonial, parish certificate of almost any kind, but more usually to labourers in husbandry wishing to leave the parish, under 5 Eliz. c. 4 (1562–3). *See* p. 12.

thirdborough, tithingman or deputy constable.

three-field system, the arrangement of open arable lands in three great open fields; corresponding to the three-course rotation: winter corn, spring corn, fallow. *See* pp. 251–5.

tied churchwardens, *see* churchwardens, tied.

tithe. *See* pp. 134–43.

tithe, great, that of corn, hay and wood.

tithe, mixed, that arising from beasts and fowls fed on the earth's produce.

tithe, predial, that arising from the produce of the earth.

tithe, quadripartite division of, a supposed former division into four parts, for the bishop, the church fabric, the poor and the maintenance of the priest respectively.

tithe, small, tithe, whether predial or mixed, upon everything save corn, hay and wood.

tithe, tripartite division of, an alleged former division of the total tithe received into three portions (after the diocesan bishops had been provided for in other ways), the equal shares being respectively for the church fabric, the maintenance of the priest, and the relief of the poor.

tithingman, (up to say the seventeenth century) an officer having no connection with tithe, and probably so called from his having been responsible, originally, for the supervision of *ten* families, just as the tithe was a *tenth* part of the produce. In some districts the constable, in others a sort of deputy constable, having charge of law and order in the tithing or township.

toftstead, a house or the site of a former house, especially one having common right, which attached to the site even if the house had disappeared.

token, communion. See Cox, *Churchwardens' Accounts*, pp. 100–1. A device for ensuring that the parishioners communicating had not omitted to make their offering towards the costs involved.

Toleration Act, *see* Acts.

townships, the ultimate units into which the country was divided for purposes of civil government before the development of the parish as a civil unit in Tudor times.

transcripts (of parish registers), the duplicate copies of entries transmitted annually or triennially to the archdeacon or bishop. *See* pp. 45, 51–3.

traverse, to, to appear in court to plead 'not guilty'.

trendal, a hanging circle of lights before the rood, also **trendal** or **trental,** thirty requiem masses or payment therefor.,

trinoda necessitas, the three fundamental obligations attached to landholding in the Dark and Middle Ages—military defence, the maintenance of roads and bridges and the upkeep of fortresses.

tripartite division of tithe, *see* tithe.

trophy money, militia rate. *See* pp. 180–1.

turbary, common of, *see* common of turbary.

twelve, also **twenty** and **twenty-four,** select vestry.

'Tyburn ticket', a certificate of exemption from parish office in reward for the capture and successful prosecution of a felon. *See* p. 32 and 10 W. III, c. 12 (1698).

uxoratus, married man.

uxoratus(-a, -i) fuit (fuerunt), he (she was (they were) married.

vestry, open, general meeting of all inhabitant ratepaying householders in a parish.

vestry, select, 'close' governing body of a parish, the members generally having a property qualification, and being recruited more or less by co-option.

viaticus, wayfarer, tramp.

vicar, originally the mere deputy of the parson (rector), later usually the incumbent of a benefice appropriate or impropriate, i.e. receiving small tithes or their equivalent, but generally not receiving great tithes. Exceptionally there were benefices neither appropriate nor impropriate, but having a clerical (sinecurist) rector as well as a resident vicar.

vicar's ring, the ancient enclosures of a township, often tithable to the vicar for both great and small tithe, although in the rest of the township the great tithe belonged to the rector.

viciatus, bastard.

vill, the Norman French equivalent of the Old English term township, *q.v.*

virgate, yardland.

visitation. *See* pp. 95–6, 144–5, 150.

visus franci plegii, view of frankpledge.

wall, balk or meer.

wax silver, Easter offering. *See* pp. 70, 127.

way balk, *see* balk.

wayman, waywarden, parochial officer in charge of the highways. *See* pp. 242–50.

wheel, spinning or jersey wheel, largely used in the employment of pauper women.

whirrer, spindle.

Whitsun farthings, pentecostals, *q.v.*

whole year lands, every year lands, lands in the open fields cropped every year, having no fallow in their rotation.

witnesses, godparents.

wong, (*a*) furlong in the open fields, especially in the counties of Danish and Scandinavian settlement, also (*b*) enclosed meadow.

workhouse test, refusal of outdoor relief, and the offer to applicants of the option of admission to the workhouse or nothing at all.

Lord Worsley's Act, *see* Acts.

yardland, virgate. A measure of land, originally, no doubt, as much as would serve to occupy a yoke of oxen. Later a conventional unit, varying very widely in area, from perhaps 20–50 statute acres, but always containing two oxgangs, and forming a quarter of a carucate, hide, or ploughland.

yconomi, See *oeconomi.*

yeoman, (properly) freeholder cultivating his own land—occupying owner—, but (because of the sentimental associations of the word), often used (not only by song writers) much more loosely to mean small or medium farmer generally.

Appendix I

TABLE OF THE PRINCIPAL STATUTES, ETC., CITED OR REFERRED TO

Acts of the Parliaments of England, Great Britain, and Great-Britain-and-Ireland, and Measures of the National Assembly of the Church of England. (Ecclesiastical legislation is entered in italics.) The capitulation is that adopted by the Statute Law Revision Committee in the official *Chronological Table and Index of the Statutes.* Only in special instances are acts indexed here and in the General Index.

---

* Commonwealth Ordinance.   † 'Act' of Barebones's 'Parliament'.
‡ Act of the Protectorate II Parliament.

1 W. & M. c. 18 (1688), **Toleration Act**, 65, 94, 310
1 W. & M. c. 26 (1688), pluralities, 155, 298
3 W. & M. c. 11 (1691), making permanent 1662 and 1685 poor laws, parish records, settlements, apprentices, 7, 31, 106, 192, 198, 221, 283, 286, 300, 303
3 W. & M. c. 12 (1691), highways, highway surveyors, 28, 106, 243, 244, 246, 286, 305
5 & 6 W. & M. c. 21 (1693–4), taxation on births, marriages, and burials, 48, 58, 287
6 & 7 W. & M. c. 6 (1694), taxation on births, marriages, and burials, 48, 58, 287
7 & 8 W. III, c. 6 (1695), church rates, 94, 292
7 & 8 W. III, c. 35 (1695), taxation on births, marriages, and burials, 48, 58, 287
7 & 8 W. III, c. 32 **Pr.** (1695–6), Bristol Workhouse, 227, 304
8 & 9 W. III, c. 30 (1696–7), poor, settlement certificates, badges, apprenticeship, 192–3, 199, 207–8, 222, 226, 300, 303
9 W. III, c. 11 (1697–8), poor, 193, 300, 310
10 W. III, c. 12 (1698), criminal procedure, 'Tyburn tickets', 32, 87
11 W. III, c. 19 (1698–9), county gaols, 28, 286
2 & 3 Anne c. 6 (1703), poor, 193, 300
2 & 3 Anne c. 8 (1703), Worcester Workhouse, 227, 304
4 & 5 Anne c. 23 (1705), indemnification of clergy, 48–9, 287
4 & 5 Anne c. 25 (1705), briefs, 123, 295
6 Anne c. 46 (1706–7), Plymouth Workhouse, 227, 304
8 Anne c. 5 (1709), poor, 193, 300
10 Anne c. 10 (1711), registration, 49, 287
10 Anne c. 15 (1711), Norwich Workhouse, 227, 304
10 Anne c. 20 (1711), church building, 20, 285
12 Anne c. 18 (1712), poor, 193, 300
12 Anne Sess. II, c. 15 **Pr.** (1712), amending Bristol Workhouse Act of 1695–6, 226, 304
13 Anne c. 26 (1713–14), vagrancy, gaols, 28, 286
4 Geo. I, c. 3 **Pr.** (1717–18), amending Bristol Workhouse Acts of 1695–6 and 1712, 226, 304
5 Geo. I, c. 8 (1718–19), poor, 193, 300
9 Geo. I, c. 7 (1722–3), justices, relief, workhouses, 193, 196, 198, 199, 205, 228, 230, 300, 304
13 Geo. I, c. 23 (1726–7), 'end gatherers', 211, 302
3 Geo. II, c. 29 (1729–30), poor, settlement, removal, 193, 300
6 Geo. II, c. 31 (1732–3), bastardy, 193, 196, 216, 217, 219, 300, 303
12 Geo. II, c. 29 (1738–9), rates, 28, 286
13 Geo. II, c. 24 (1739–40), servants leaving employment, 12, 13, 285
17 Geo. II, c. 5 (1743–4), vagrancy, bastardy, etc., 193, 196, 211–12, 216, 217, 301, 303
17 Geo. II, c. 38 (1743–4), **Poor Relief Act, 1743**, rating appeals, poor, accounts, 28, 194, 196–7, 286, 300
19 Geo. II, c. 5 (1745–6), disorder in horned cattle, 313
19 Geo. II, c. 21 (1745–6), profane swearing and cursing, 274
20 Geo. II, c. 19 (1746–7), apprentices, 194, 226, 300, 304
26 Geo. II, c. 31 (1753), alehouses, 12, 285
26 Geo. II, c. 33 (1753), **Lord Hardwicke's Act**, marriages, 49, 64, 287, 310
31 Geo. II, c. 11 (1757–8), apprenticeship, settlement, 221, 304
32 Geo. II, c. 28 (1758–9), charities, 113, 294
4 Geo. III, c. 56 (1763–4),
6 Geo. III, c. 25 (1765–6), runaway apprentices, etc., 225, 304
7 Geo. III, c. 39 (1766–7), apprentices in London, 194–5, 225, 304
7 Geo. III, c. 39 (1766–7), apprentices in London, 194–5, 225, 304
7 Geo. III, c. 14 **Pr.** (1766–7), **Private Act**, enclosure of Yaxley, Hunts., 70, 290
10 Geo. III, c. 73 **Pr.** (1770), **Private Act**, enclosure of Normanton on Soar, Notts., 152, 298

13 Geo. III, c. 78 (1772–3), highways, surveyors of highways, 31, 286
13 Geo. III, c. 81 (1772–3), improvement of open fields, 258, 266, 306, 314
14 Geo. III, c. 9 **Pr.** (1774), **Private Act,** enclosure of West Retford, Notts., 139, 296
17 Geo. III, c. 53 (1776–7), **Clergy Residences Repair Act, Gilbert's Act** (see also p. 310), repair of rectories and vicarages, 310
18 Geo. III, c. 47 (1777–8), apprentices, 194–5, 226, 304, 310
20 Geo. III, c. 36 (1779–80), apprentices, 226, 304
22 Geo. III, c. 83 (1781–2), **Gilbert's Act** (see also p. 310), poor, overseers, workhouses, badges, 193–4, 197, 228, 229, 230, 231, 233, 300, 304
23 Geo. III, c. 67 (1782–3), stamp duties, 49–50, 59, 287
25 Geo. III, c. 75 (1785), stamp duties, 50, 59, 287
26 Geo. III, c. 56 (1786), returns relative to the poor, 194, 301
26 Geo. III, c. 71 (1786), slaughterhouses, 12, 285
30 Geo. III, c. 49 (1790), workhouses, 194, 300
32 Geo. III, c. 45 (1792), removal of vagrants, 194, 300
32 Geo. III, c. 57 (1792), apprentices, 195, 226, 301
33 Geo. III, c. 55 (1792–3), **Parish Officers Act, 1793,** parish officers, apprentices, 194, 195, 226, 301
34 Geo. III, c. 11 (1794), repeal of stamp duties, 50, 287
35 Geo. III, c. 101 (1794–5), **Pitt's Act,** also **Speenhamland Act** (see also p. 310), removal, 194, 199, 231, 232, 304, 310
36 Geo. III, c. 23 (1795–6), out-relief, 194, 232, 300, 304
38 Geo. III, c. 60 (1797–8), **Land Tax Perpetuation Act,** land tax, 316
38 Geo. III, c. 1 **Pr.** (1798), enclosure of Chedzoy, Som., 274
39 & 40 Geo. III, c. 6 **Pr.** (1800), enclosure of Locking, Som., 274
41 Geo. III, c. 23 (1801), **Poor Rate Act, 1801,** rates, 28, 286
41 Geo. III, c. 109 (1801), **General Enclosure Act, 1801,** enclosure, 268
42 Geo. III, c. 46 (1801–2), apprentices, 195, 226, 301, 304
43 Geo. III, c. 47 (1802–3), relief of families of militiamen, 195, 301
43 Geo. III, c. 61 (1802–3), discharged soldiers and sailors, 195, 301
50 Geo. III, c. 52 (1810), repealing in part 8 & 9 Wm. III, c. 30, 208, 301
52 Geo. III, c. 146 (1812), **Parochial Registers Act, 1812, Rose's Act,** registration, 36, 50–1, 286, 287, 310
54 Geo. III, c. 108 (1813–14), repeal of burial in woollen acts, 68, 290
54 Geo. III, c. LXX **Pr.** (1814), enclosure of Edington, Som., 274
55 Geo. III, c. 51 (1814–15), county rates, 28, 286
55 Geo. III, c. 137 (1814–15), **Poor Relief Act, 1815, East's Act,** out-relief, 194, 274, 300
55 Geo. III, c. XVCI **Pr.** (1815), church and workhouse at Bathwick, Som., 274
58 Geo. III, c. 45 (1818), **Church Building Act, 1818,** church building, 20, 285
58 Geo. III, c. 69 (1818), **Vestries Act, 1818, First Sturges Bourne Act,** vestries, parish records, 8, 11, 21, 86–7, 195, 285, 310
59 Geo. III, c. 12 (1819), **Poor Relief Act, 1819, Second Sturges Bourne Act,** also **Speenhamland Act** (see also p. 310), vestries, 21, 23, 31, 195, 220, 285, 286
59 Geo. III, c. 85 (1819), **Vestries Act, 1819,** vestries, overseers, settlements, 34, 286
4 Geo. IV, c. 76 (1823), **Marriage Act, 1823,** marriages, 63, 273, 290
5 Geo. IV, c. 83 (1824), vagrancy, 195, 301
7 Geo. IV, c. 53 **Pr.** (1826), enclosure of West Lydford, Som., 274
9 Geo. IV, c. 42 (1828), abolition of briefs, 123, 295
1 & 2 W. IV, c. 60 (1831), **Vestries Act, 1831, Hobhouse's Act,** vestries, 22, 195, 285, 310
2 & 3 W. IV, c. 92 (1831–2), **Privy Council Appeals Act, 1832,** abolition of Court of Delegates, 144, 297
2 & 3 W. IV, c. 100 (1831–2), **Tithe Act, 1832, Lord Tenterden's Act,** tithes, 140, 297, 310
3 & 4 W. IV, c. 90 (1833), **Lighting and Watching Act, 1833,** lighting and watching, 23, 28, 177, 285, 299

Appendix II

COUNTY AND OTHER MAJOR LOCAL RECORD OFFICES IN ENGLAND*

Between 1946, when this book first appeared, and this present year 1968, there has been a very noteworthy growth in the establishment of county record offices (C.R.O.s). There has also been a marked extension of the services offered by these to historians, whether amateur or professional, interested in the archives, ecclesiastical or secular, of the areas dealt with. I have noted above in my *Preface* that anyone intending to do any serious study on any aspect of parish history should, at an early stage in his inquiries, make himself and his interests known to his local—almost always county—archivist (C.A.). Not only has the C.A. in his custody very considerable accumulations of MSS. coming to him officially from county sources, with a good deal more in the way of deposited MS. material; sometimes he has also been formally appointed by the bishop as archivist for the diocese, or certain archdeaconries or rural deaneries or other areas within it. Where he has not, it is usually much to be hoped that he soon will be. He is also much likelier than anyone else to know of the existence of other substantial deposits of archives locally, and to have some notion of their contents and of the possibilities of access to them.

I think it may be relevant to repeat here a note I published some years ago for the benefit of my fellow-amateurs of local history and my fellow-teachers. However patient—indeed, long-suffering!—and helpful a C.A. may be, his C.R.O. is most emphatically not the establishment to visit in order to brush up one's rusty or virtually non-existent Latin. Even less is it the place whither to send one's students needing to learn the elements of 'how to read courthand'. If the inquirer's Latin, or palaeography or diplomatic need attention, he may well find that classes in the appropriate subjects are being, or can be, offered by the local branch of the W.E.A., and/or by the local University Extra-mural Department. It is in response to the request of more than one C.A. that I add one or two further comments on this matter. 'It should be realised', says one C.A. plaintively, 'that it is not the C.A.'s place to act as supervisor of students' research projects. If original documents are to be used in his inquiries, they should be such as are within his capacity to deal with, and his theme should be chosen accordingly. Several C.A.s have drawn up guides and reports in order to help in this choice.' It seems unnecessary to suggest that 'these should be considered before, not after the subject is chosen'. Teachers, and for that matter other inquirers, will appreciate that 'it is in their own interest that before visiting the C.R.O. they should write to the C.A. outlining their needs and their special interests, so as to give him

* For help in checking the data for this I am obliged to the various C.A.s, every one of whom has seen the whole table in draft. For aid in giving it a final revision in proof I have to thank the Bristol City Archivist, Miss E. Ralph. I am responsible for all opinions expressed, and for any remaining errors.

ample time for considering how he can best help them'. I hope very
much that intending 'customers' of the various C.R.O.s will accept
these suggestions in the spirit in which they are tendered. Perhaps
it is permissible, here and in this connection, to pervert, deliberately,
pro hac vice, some of the technical terms of our subject, and of the
topics closely allied to it. If so, I leave the matter with the comforting
thought that the hints offered are but supplications, or at the most
admonitions, and have about them little of the injunction (and nothing
at all, of course, of the commination or the anathema)!

The table below sets forth, in as businesslike a fashion as I have been
able to hit on, the styles and addresses of the C.R.O.s covering the
(forty-two)[1] historic English counties, without too much regard to the
administrative changes which have lately taken place, and with none at
all to others which may well be impending. It indicates especially
(*a*) in which diocese(s) the county is wholly or mainly placed today;[2]
and (*b*) in which it has been situated during the last four centuries or
so, since the beginning of parish registers in Henry VIII's reign.[3]
(*a*) I hope may sometimes help the inquirer to locate a missing register,[4]
and (*b*) may aid him in obtaining access to diocesan transcripts of registers the originals of which are imperfect, or which have disappeared.
I hope that on occasion (*a*) may serve also to help him in obtaining
access to other documentary material useful for parish history. It is
to be noted that in some dioceses (especially, perhaps, the enormous
one of Lincoln as it existed for nearly five centuries, containing eight
and a half counties, and parishes which now make up six dioceses)
records of the archdeacons, and of the bishop acting through his
commissaries are often to be found at archidiaconal centres. It is worth
noting also that here and elsewhere there is often a correspondence in
boundaries between rural deaneries, and hundreds or wapentakes, and
between archdeaconries and counties. For various historical reasons

---

[1] (According to the general reckoning) there are 42 historic English counties. Quite certainly
there are today, in the provinces of Canterbury and York, 42 (ancient, elderly or modern)
dioceses. Moreover there is, as I have noted elsewhere, a relation between county (and Hundred)
boundaries and diocesan (and archidiaconal) ones. It would, however, be someone equally
ignorant of English topography and of the English attitude to administration generally who
assumed that therefore the 'normal' English diocese is, or ever has been, even approximately
co-extensive with a county.

[2] Though my book is concerned, in the main, with parish archives, and with these chiefly
since the beginning of parish registers in 1538, I have tried to indicate concisely (*c*) in which
diocese(s) the county lay throughout medieval times, say from the foundation of the last medieval
diocese (Carlisle 1133) to the first (lasting) Tudor one (Chester 1541). Similarly (*d*) I have of
purpose touched though but lightly upon various changes in diocesan boundaries between the
date of the first modern diocesan foundation or refoundation (Ripon 1836) and the present day
(1968). It may be worth noting in passing that while neither (*c*) nor (*d*) is likely to be of great
interest to the student of parish records as such, both may well give a clue to the whereabouts
of MS. material of great value to the parish historian, (*c*) in respect of medieval episcopal or
archidiaconal dealings with the parish and its parish priest, (*d*) chiefly perhaps with reference
to records of Visitation (above, p. 150) during the Victorian era.

In this connection it is to be noted also that a C.R.O. may well be recognised—in fact, normally
is recognised—as D.R.O. for the parish records of all the parishes in its area, but not so for
other types of record of ecclesiastical provenance. Thus it may well have deposited in it some,
or most, of the original parish registers, but not register transcripts (pp. 45, 52), or glebe terriers
(p. 125) or archdeacon's correctional court papers (pp. 144–50), or registered wills (p. 155). This
is a point on which the student will have to make his own inquiries in his own local C.R.O.

[3] The most convenient short guide to the past and present ecclesiastical topography of England
(and Wales), looked at from the point of view of the present-day county, is in Gardner, D. E.,
and Smith, F., *Genealogical Research in England and Wales* (Salt Lake City, Utah, U.S.A.),
Vol. II, 1959, 3rd printing 1966, pp. 211–30, 307.

[4] In order to avoid unnecessary detail, I have ignored references indicating only that parts of
one or two present-day civil parishes are ecclesiastically in different dioceses.

the patterns of mediaeval diocesan boundaries were not nearly so logical, and this is a matter which the inquirer must look into for himself, so far as 'his' chosen parish is concerned. I advise the beginner in parish history not only to check very carefully the present-day placing, ecclesiastically and civilly, of his chosen unit, but also to find out from such works as the earlier editions of Lewis[1] which diocese[2] (and which *county*) it was in from about the 1530's to the 1830's. Hence it is simple to ascertain whether it has changed in either respect, usually during the last century and a quarter or so. Despite all recent boundary rationalisations, a great many anomalies still remain, more of them (as one would expect) in ecclesiastical topography than in its civil counterpart.

Thus, to revert to Little Piddlington,[3] I fear that the illustration may appear, on a first glance, rather to obscure the general issue than to illumine it. I assure the reader, however, that it is, in view of the complexity of the matter dealt with, relatively both clear and concise, and that if he battles with it he will find that the struggle has not been in vain. It is true that the civil parish of Piddlington Parva is, and always has been, both topographically and administratively in Loamshire, which is more or less co-extensive with the diocese of Loamchester. This is why the Loamshire C.R.O. in the county town (and cathedral city) of Loamchester has custody of both copies of the Piddlington enclosure award,[4] of the Piddlington constable's and overseers' accounts,[5] and so on. However, by way of exception to its neighbouring parishes, for historical reasons of great interest to the Piddlingtonian historian, but not our business here, the ecclesiastical parish of Piddlington St Paul is not, and never has been, in Loamchester diocese. It has been placed for the last thousand years—and it may well remain for the next millennium—in the neighbouring diocese of Lynford, which we tend to regard nowadays as more or less Lynfordshire county, looked at from the ecclesiastical point of view. The Piddlington parish registers, if not still in the parish, may then perhaps have been collected, with the other parish records, by the Loamshire C.R.O. at Loamchester. Strictly speaking, if not in Little Piddlington they should have been deposited in the Lynford Diocesan Record Office (D.R.O.) (which is also the Lynfordshire C.R.O.), in the cathedral city (and county town) of Lynford. Such essentially ecclesiastical records as register transcripts and glebe terriers[6] are very

---

[1] [Ed. Haydn, J.], '*Lewis's Topographical Dictionary of England*, 1831, 1833 and edns. It is to be noted that since large-scale administrative reform in Church and State began in England in the years following 1832, the two earliest editions of 'Lewis' are, for our special purpose, much more useful than are the later ones. The *Third Report from H.M. Commissioners appointed to consider the Established Church with reference to Ecclesiastical Duties and Revenues*, 1836, has useful maps of the proposed boundary changes, and G. F. A. Best, *Temporal Pillars* (Cambridge), 1964, has two maps giving counties and dioceses before 1835 and c. 1850.

[2] It may be helpful to note the existence of some excellent large-scale diocesan maps of the post-Reformation dioceses in the Record Commission's (well-indexed six folio) volumes of the *Valor Ecclesiasticus* (the survey ordered by Henry VIII in 1535), published by the Commission 1810–34. It is not always realised that, although the survey was made in 1535, the arrangement of the printed text is due to the dioceses as they existed ten years later, after the last of Henry's major changes, the removal of Osney (1542) to Oxford, 1545.

[3] Above, p. xi.

[4] Above, pp. 270–1, etc.

[5] Above, pp. 176–87, 209–11, etc.

[6] Above, pp. 50–3, 126–34.

probably to be found there. For other documents of ecclesiastical origin, then, relating to our chosen parish, we may have to inquire in what appears at first sight to be the C.R.O. of the 'wrong' county. Local record offices (R.O.s) in England are in the main C.R.O.s. The reputable English local R.O.s are very largely the C.R.O.s.[1] Usually a C.R.O. is now approved as D.R.O. for the whole diocese, or certain archdeaconries or rural deaneries of it, or occasionally for those ecclesiastical parishes of the diocese which correspond to civil parishes within the county. There are a few civic and municipal R.O.s, usually attached to the MS. Departments of local public libraries, usually marked here B.L. for Borough Library, and which have in fact often developed from these. In quality they range from the admirable to the appalling. These last often mark nothing more than the vaulting ambition of some city or borough librarian, past or present, 'hatching vain empires', which has led him into meddling with matters he had far better have left alone. It is rather as though an over-enthusiastic vet. should decide to launch out in an allied branch of science. He has time on his hands, some expertise, a good stock of medicaments and instruments and he notices with regret that medical services in his area are inadequate. So he decides to establish a medical practice as a side-line. He certainly arouses some comment if he does! It is arguable that in the long run neither his original patients nor his newly acquired ones benefit by his ambitious indiscretion.

A city or borough is, of course, under a moral obligation to do what it can to ensure the safe custody and accessibility of its own archives. If it thinks them likely to be better cared for by its librarian than by its town clerk, it may well be right. And before the general establishment of C.R.O.s, if only from the 'salvage' point of view, there was a good deal to be said for the local library accepting temporary custody of private records, unless and until the county authority could be persuaded to do its duty. There still is an enormous and very wealthy county (which I am ashamed to name) where the major (county) authority never has been induced to act effectively in this. Here the city libraries of the two principal county boroughs in the area have very public-spiritedly supplied in part what was wanting. They have in effect partitioned between them the county area (except the other county boroughs) so far as the collection and caring for 'deposited' record are concerned, and have appointed qualified staff who have done most valuable work in collection, custody, conservation, indexing, calendaring and publication. The City R.O. at Bristol is as good as any in the country, and the City-and-County R.O. at Norwich, which is situated, as it happens, in the City Library, is a noteworthy example

---

[1] There is a more detailed survey of county and other R.O's in *Record Repositories in Great Britain*, H.M.S.O. (for the Historical MSS. Commission and the National Register of Archives) 1964, and a survey of D.R.O.s, corrected up to 1958, in an article by Mr C. E. Welch in *Archives*, IV, 22, Michaelmas 1959. Smith and Gardner (above p. 330, fn. 3) give also well-arranged 'potted histories' of the various dioceses. These usually indicate, if not always where are the records of the main types interesting the local historian, at any rate where they ought to be.

To 1541/2 ecclesiastically, wholly or almost wholly in the diocese of	*1541/2–1836*	*1831/3:* No. of ancient parishes returned county + major towns	*1836/40 onwards* ecclesiastically, wholly or almost wholly in the diocese of	*1968*
CORNWALL				
Exeter	**Exeter**	204	**Exeter**	*Truro*

Cornwall County Record Office,
County Hall, Truro.
This is recognised as 'diocesan repository', not technically D.R.O., for Truro diocese, virtually co-extensive with the county. As such it contains the glebe terriers and tithe maps for most Cornish parishes, the other archives of diocesan origin, before 1877, being still at Exeter. It also holds on deposit all or some of the records of some 60 Cornish parishes.

| **CUMBERLAND** | | | | |
| **Carlisle** **York*** | **Carlisle** **Chester*** | 138 + 5 | **Carlisle** | **Carlisle** |

Cumberland, Westmorland† and
Carlisle Record Office,
The Castle, Carlisle.

| **DERBYSHIRE** | | | | |
| **Lichfield** | **Lichfield** | 179 + 5 | Lichfield then *Southwell* | *Derby* |

Derbyshire Record Office,
County Offices, Matlock.
See also note under STAFFORDSHIRE.

| **DEVON** | | | | |
| **Exeter** | **Exeter** | 449 + 23 | **Exeter** | **Exeter** |

Devon Record Office,
County Hall, Topsham Road, Exeter.
(There is also a good deal of archival material for the County in the City Library, Exeter.)

| **DORSET** | | | | |
| **Salisbury** | Bristol | 252 + 8 | **Salisbury** | **Salisbury** |

Dorset Record Office,
County Hall, Dorchester.
(The diocesan register transcripts are at Salisbury.)
It is to be noted that 1542–1836, Dorset was ecclesiastically in the diocese of Bristol.

| **Co. DURHAM** | | | | |
| **Durham** | **Durham** | 86 + 7 | **Durham** | **Durham** |

Durham County Record Office,
County Hall, Durham.
The diocesan records, including the parish register transcripts, are in 'the Prior's Kitchen', Department of Palaeography, etc., Durham University.

ELY, ISLE of—see under (County of)
CAMBRIDGESHIRE-and-the-ISLE-OF-ELY

* I make an exception to my general rule of ignoring as far as possible the niceties of ecclesiastical topography in noting that the archdeaconry of Richmond (?unique in Christendom as a quasi-diocese) which extended into five counties, was until 1541 in **York,** thereafter in Chester, and that such of its later archives as have survived have been as far as possible apportioned among the C.R.O.s at Carlisle, Kendal, Preston and (for Yorks. W.) the Archives Department of the Public Library at Leeds *q.v.,* since *Ripon* diocese corresponds very roughly to part of the archdeaconry. On this see further notes under YORKSHIRE.
† For the associated Record Office at Kendal see under WESTMORLAND.

of city and county collaborating in discharging a public duty much better than either of them could have carried it out individually. Similarly, the C.R.O. at Hereford is in a sense an offshoot of the County Library, and, though it has now acquired a staff of its own, the County Librarian is the Hon. C.A.

In such exceptional instances as these, as well as in the more usual ones, the municipal authority may well claim to have established a *locus standi* in these matters. This has happened in several major provincial cities and county boroughs, where the local authority not only had inherited a mass of civic and other records, but also had the means and the intention to establish a properly organised and staffed local R.O., even as a sub-department of its central reference library. Clearly, in such cases vested interests will have to be considered whenever the Government sets itself to encouraging throughout England the provision of proper, systematic archive arrangements, based, of course, on the C.R.O.s.

Meanwhile there is little to be said in favour of the ill-considered and totally unco-ordinated proliferation of municipal and other alleged R.O.s, which has already done a disservice to local history and which is becoming a serious inconvenience to local historians. (*Soi-disant*) R.O.s and Archive Departments now exist not only in some major local libraries but in many minor ones; in a few local museums; lately they have been set up by the librarians of one or two of the civic universities, and unless the trend is checked, one may next expect to see them established by some of the more ambitious 'colleges of education'. It is a matter for regret that in a situation which was already chaotic enough, confusion is being worse confounded. The upshot of this note is a suggestion that if the reader becomes personally responsible for the disposal of any archival material, public or private, he should, at any rate in the first place, make contact with his C.R.O. The few civic or municipal R.O.s noted in the list below are not the target of the criticism advanced: there is, of course, no implication that any individual one omitted is necessarily in the category adversely commented upon.

Contractions used and conventions adopted:

The names of civil units I have had set in roman type, those of ecclesiastical units in *italic*. These—usually diocesan styles—I have further conventionalized. Since it is often very convenient to see at a glance whether a diocese referred to is ancient, like **Bath-and-Wells,** 'elderly', i.e. Henrician, like Bristol, or modern (post 1836–40) like *Birmingham*, I have set out the names of **Ancient** dioceses (i.e. those existing before 1133) in **bold face**; those of the five permanent Henrician foundations, 1541–1542/5 in roman lower case; those of *modern* foundations or *refoundations* (from 1836 onwards) in *italic* lower case.

THE MAJOR ENGLISH LOCAL RECORD OFFICES

(under counties)

I have been at some pains in trying to indicate the diocesan position of (the greater part of) the parishes in each county during four periods: (*a*) in pre-Reformation times; (*b*) 1541–2 to 1836/40; (*c*) during the nineteenth and early twentieth centuries, and (*d*) at the present day, for even sketchy information on these points has an obvious value to the archivally minded parish historian.

To do this in the limited space available has necessarily involved some rather sweeping generalizations, and the statements made are to be read *exceptis excipiendis*. They are based (*a*) on the *Valor Ecclesiasticus* maps and on Ramsay Muir's map *Ecclesiastical England in the time of Henry VIII*; (*b*) on the convenient summaries given in the various editions of Chamberlayne's *Magnae Britanniae Notitia*; (*c*) on the statements made and maps given in Mr Hill's book, elsewhere referred to, and (*d*) for modern times, on the summary notes given at the head of each diocesan entry in the current *Church of England Yearbook*, and on the map included in the latest *Crockford*. Nevertheless, when any specific parish is concerned, the inquirer will do well to check with his County Archivist whether or not the general statement applies without qualification to his particular instance.

DIOCESES OF ENGLAND
with dates of foundation

An explanation of the different kinds of type used is given at the foot of page 333

Bath-and-Wells (909)
Birmingham (1905)
Blackburn (1927)
Bradford (1920)
Bristol (1542)
Canterbury (?597)
Carlisle (1133)
Chelmsford (1914)
Chester (1541)
Chichester (1075)
Coventry (1918)
Derby (1927)
Durham (990)
Ely (1109)
Exeter (1050)
Gloucester (1541)
Guildford (1927)
Hereford (676)
Leicester (679/1927)
Lichfield (?664)
Lincoln (1072)
Liverpool (1880)

London (601–4)
Manchester (1848)
Monmouth (1921) (Diocese of the Church-in-Wales)
Newcastle (1882)
Norwich (1096)
Oxford (1542)
Peterborough (1541)
Portsmouth (1927)
Ripon (678/1836)
Rochester (604)
St Albans (1877)
St Edmundsbury-and-Ipswich (1914)
Salisbury (1078)
Sheffield (1914)
Southwark (1905)
Southwell (1884)
Truro (1877)
Wakefield (1888)
Winchester (662)
Worcester (680)
York (625)

	To 1541/2 *ecclesiastically, wholly or almost* *wholly in the diocese of*	*1541/2–1836*	*1831/3:* *No. of ancient* *parishes returned* *county +* *major towns*	*1836/40 onwards* *ecclesiastically, wholly or almost* *wholly in the diocese of*	*1968*

BEDFORDSHIRE

Lincoln   **Lincoln**   118 + 5   **Ely**   *St Alba*
 Bedford County Record Office,
 Shire Hall, Bedford
This is recognised as D.R.O. for the archdeaconry of Bedford, mo co-extensive with the county, and in fact it contains on deposit the r 125 parishes in the archdeaconry and county. Diocesan material D.R.O., Hertford.

BERKSHIRE

Salisbury   **Salisbury**   152 + 10   Oxford   Oxfor
 Berkshire Record Office,
 Shire Hall, Reading
This is recognised as D.R.O. for parish records in the archd Berkshire, more or less co-extensive with the county, for archdeacon proper, including wills, etc. Some eighty per cent of the parish regi Reading, the diocesan transcripts are at Salisbury. The Bodleian Oxford, is recognised as D.R.O.

BUCKINGHAMSHIRE

Lincoln   **Lincoln**   206   Oxford   Oxfo
 Buckinghamshire Record
 Office, County Hall,
 Aylesbury
Deposited parish records are normally to be found as above. Th recognised as D.R.O. for the archdeaconry of Buckingham, m co-extensive with the county. Many parish registers are to be f County Museum, Church Street, Aylesbury.

CAMBRIDGESHIRE-and-the-ISLE OF ELY

Ely   **Ely**   152 + 19   **Ely**   **Ely**
Ely   **Ely**   **Ely**   **Ely**
 Cambridgeshire Record Office,
 Shire Hall, Castle Hill, Cambridge.
The two administrative counties were amalgamated in 1965. Th the Isle of Ely, except those in the care of the Clerk of the Peac transferred to Cambridge from County Hall, March.

  This is recognised as D.R.O. for parish records for Cambridges Isle-of-Ely, but the University Library, Cambridge, is D.R.O. and archidiaconal records for the whole of **Ely** diocese.

CHESHIRE

Lichfield   Chester   120 + 10   Chester   Ch
 Cheshire Record Office,
 The Castle, Chester.
This is recognised also as D.R.O. for parochial, archidiaconal archives.

To 1541/2 *ecclesiastically, wholly or almost wholly in the diocese of*	1541/2–1836	1831/3: *No. of ancient parishes returned county +* *major towns*	1836/40 onwards *ecclesiastically, wholly or almost wholly in the diocese of*	1968

ESSEX

London	London	390 + 15	**London** then **Rochester,** then *St Albans*	*Chelmsford*

Essex Record Office,
County Hall, Chelmsford.

The *St Edmundsbury-and-Ipswich* archdeaconry of Ipswich overlaps the county boundary a little, so that a few Essex parishes are in it.

GLOUCESTERSHIRE*

Worcester	Gloucester	319 + 28	Gloucester	Gloucester
Hereford	Bristol		Bristol	Bristol

Gloucestershire Records Office,
Shire Hall, Gloucester.

The Bristol (City) R.O. is recognised also as D.R.O. for those parishes of Bristol diocese which lie within the City of Bristol or the County of GLOU-CESTER, i.e. for ecclesiastical parish records of the three rural deaneries of Bristol archdeaconry which lie in S. Gloucestershire. Similarly, the Gloucester City R.O. (City Libraries, Brunswick Road, Gloucester), is recognised for those parishes of Gloucester diocese which lie within Gloucester City, and is also D.R.O. generally.

HAMPSHIRE†

Winchester	**Winchester**	292 + 15	**Winchester**	**Winchester** *Portsmouth*

Hampshire Record Office,
The Castle, Winchester.‡

HEREFORDSHIRE*

Hereford	Hereford	217 + 6	**Hereford**	**Hereford**

Herefordshire County Record Office,
Shire Hall, Hereford.

Deposited parish registers but not other parish records are normally to be found not as above, but in the recognised D.R.O., at the City Library, Broad Street, Hereford. The diocesan register transcripts are in the Diocesan Registry, Hereford.

---

* GLOUCESTERSHIRE and its neighbouring counties, HEREFORDSHIRE, OXFORD-SHIRE, SHROPSHIRE, WARWICKSHIRE and WORCESTERSHIRE, and Gloucester diocese, with its neighbours **Hereford, Lichfield,** Oxford and **Worcester,** are the best English examples of administrative areas which not only extend—as in it were parochial promontories—beyond their natural boundaries, but also contained or contain 'islands' where jurisdiction, civil and/or ecclesiastical, belongs to a neighbouring county and/or diocese. Some of these anomalies have been 'corrected' in the last century or so, some corrected, then recorrected. When a civil adjustment has been made, this does not necessarily indicate, or even imply, that a corresponding ecclesiastical 'rectification' has been made or ever will be.

† See also note under LONDON, G.L.R.O.

‡ The ISLE OF WIGHT (*Portsmouth* diocese, 1927) has been since 1888 a separate county. It is returned as having its own C.R.O. (at Carisbrooke Castle, Newport, I.o.W.) open two half-days a week, and with an honorary County Archivist. Presumably such I.o.W. parish records as have been deposited must be sought either here or at Winchester.

To 1541/2 *ecclesiastically, wholly or almost wholly in the diocese of*	1541/2–1836	1831/3: *No. of ancient parishes returned county + major towns*	1836/40 onwards 1968 *ecclesiastically, wholly or almost wholly in the diocese of*	

HERTFORDSHIRE

| **London**
and
Lincoln | **London**
and
Lincoln | 127 + 5 | **London**
and **Lincoln**
then
Rochester
then *St Albans* | *St Albans* |

Hertfordshire County Record Office,
County Hall, Hertford.
This is recognised as D.R.O. for the diocese of *St Albans* and for parish records within the county, co-extensive with the modern archdeaconry of St Albans.

COUNTY OF HUNTINGDON-AND-PETERBOROUGH

| **Lincoln**
Lincoln | **Lincoln**
Peterborough | 91 + 2
'c. 24' | **Ely**
Peterborough | **Ely**
Peterborough |

Huntingdonshire County Record Office,
County Buildings, Huntingdon.
The Soke of Peterborough was amalgamated with Huntingdonshire in 1965, but its records in the Northamptonshire County Record Office at Peterborough will continue to be kept there, except the County Council records, which are in the Huntingdonshire C.R.O. (above).

KENT*

| **Canterbury**

Rochester | Canterbury

Rochester | 373 (−9 to
the County
of London
=364) + 27 | **Canterbury**

Rochester | **Canterbury**

Rochester |

Kent Archives Office,
County Hall, Maidstone.
This is the D.R.O. for the whole of the diocese of Rochester, but only for the archdeaconry of Maidstone in the diocese of Canterbury. For parish records in the other (Kentish) archdeaconry, that of Canterbury, the approved repository is the Greater London R.O.

LANCASHIRE

| **York†**
Chester | Chester† | 179 + 32 | Chester,
Carlisle,
then also
Manchester,
Liverpool,
then later still
Bradford,
Blackburn | **Carlisle,**
Manchester,
Liverpool,
Bradford,
Blackburn |

Lancashire Record Office,
Lancaster Road, Preston.
The R.O. is also recognised as D.R.O. for all the Anglican Lancashire dioceses, as also for the R.C. ones.

* See also note under LONDON, G.L.R.O.
† On the archdeaconry of Richmond see note under CUMBERLAND.

| *To 1541/2*   *1541/2–1836* *ecclesiastically, wholly or almost wholly in the diocese of* | *1831/3:* *No. of ancient parishes returned county + major towns* | *1836/40 onwards*   *1968* *ecclesiastically, wholly or almost wholly in the diocese of* |

LEICESTERSHIRE

Lincoln   **Lincoln**   250 + 6   Peterborough   *Leicester*
Leicestershire Record Office,
57, New Walk, Leicester,
is the D.R.O. for parishes within the administrative county. For city parishes
the D.R.O. is
Department of Archives (and City R.O.),
Leicester Museums,
Museum and Art Gallery,
New Walk, Leicester,
which is also the place of deposit for the records of the archdeaconry of
Leicester.

LINCOLNSHIRE*

Lincoln   **Lincoln**   607 + 20   **Lincoln**   **Lincoln**
Lincolnshire Archives Office,
The Castle, Lincoln,
which is also the place of deposit for the diocesan records, and for archidiaconal
records for the archdeaconries of Lincoln and of Stow.

LINCOLNSHIRE: HOLLAND

LINCOLNSHIRE: KESTEVEN

Lincoln   **Lincoln**   **Lincoln**   **Lincoln**
Most county records have been transferred to the (Joint) Archives Office at
Lincoln. A few documents still in regular use for administrative purposes, e.g.
enclosure awards, remain in the care of the Kesteven Clerk of the County
Council, in the County Offices at Sleaford.†

LINCOLNSHIRE: LINDSEY

Lincoln   **Lincoln**   **Lincoln**   **Lincoln**
Most county records have been transferred to the (Joint) Archives Office at
Lincoln. A few documents still in regular use for administrative purposes, e.g.
enclosure awards, remain in the care of the Lindsey Clerk of the County
Council, in the County Offices at Lincoln.

---

* In dealing with LINCOLNSHIRE and the dioceses and counties formerly within the
diocese of **Lincoln** I have had a good deal of help from Mrs J. Varley of the Lincoln A.O.
I hope I have understood correctly the information she has been kind enough to give me. Any
remaining errors in my statements, and any inadequacies in them are to be debited not to her
but to me.

† Small numbers of enclosure records may be consulted at the Lincoln Archives Office if about
a week's notice has been given.

To 1541/2	1541/2–1836	1831/3:	1836/40 onwards	1968
ecclesiastically, wholly or almost wholly in the diocese of		*No. of ancient parishes returned county + major towns*	*ecclesiastically, wholly or almost wholly in the diocese of*	

LONDON (the ancient City area) and GREATER LONDON (the City plus the later L.C.C. and now the Greater London areas)

108 + 1 (City)
+ 9 (Westminster)
+ 52 (County of London— former L.C.C. area),
26 from Middlesex
17 from Surrey
9 from Kent

London	**London**	say 232*	**London**	**London**
			—do— plus parts of **Winchester** then *Southwark Guildford*	—do— plus parts of *Southwark Guildford*
			—do— plus parts of **Rochester** then *Southwark* (on which see † below)	—do— plus parts of *Southwark*

The Corporation of London Records Office, Guildhall, E.C.2, is mainly concerned with the official records of the City and its wards, etc.

The Guildhall Library, Basinghall Street, E.C.2, holds the records of many 'livery' companies, etc. It is one of the D.R.O.s for London, and as such holds deposited the records of many City parishes.

The Westminster Library, Archives Department, Buckingham Palace Road, S.W.1, is recognised as D.R.O. for Westminster parishes only.

There are in the Lambeth Palace Library, S.E.1, some diocesan register transcripts and other diocesan records of parishes in the City of London and in South London, now or formerly among the Archbishop's peculiars.

The Greater London Record Office,† Westminster Bridge, S.E.1, is recognised as D.R.O. for the parishes within the former areas of the counties of LONDON and MIDDLESEX (modern dioceses of *Southwark* and *Guildford*) whose records it has inherited. It holds also the records of the archdeaconry of Surrey in the diocese of Winchester, covering the area of the old county of SURREY and a few parishes in HAMPSHIRE. It is recognised also as D.R.O. for the parish records of that part of the diocese of *Southwark* which lies within the area of the former county of LONDON. It has also some parish records of parishes in S.E. London which were formerly in the county of KENT.

The new county of London was created synthetically only in 1888 from those parts of Middlesex, Surrey and Kent which had been since 1855 within the administrative jurisdiction of the Metropolitan Board of Works. There were major or minor boundary adjustments in 1899, 1903 and 1907. In 1965, following the report of a Commission of 1960, by statute of 1963, the county area was expanded into Greater London, in the process completely absorbing Middlesex (see below), with some further parts of Essex, Hertfordshire, Kent and Surrey (but not, of course, the City of London, though for certain specific purposes the City also now ranks, on occasion, as an Inner London 'borough').

---

* Since Greater London has existed as a local government area only from 1965, it is not of course possible to give figures for 'its' ancient parishes in 1831–3. By courtesy of Miss Darlington, Archivist successively to the L.C.C. and the G.L.C., I give above figures which are fairly comparable with those in the other corresponding entries. I am very particularly indebted to Miss Darlington for her help in revising my draft of what I have tried to make a simplified statement of a very complex situation. If any errors remain in it they are due to my misunderstanding of her statements, and are my responsibility, not hers.

† See also MIDDLESEX, below, also KENT and SURREY.

The 28 (*temp.* L.C.C.) former metropolitan boroughs are generally represented by the present-day 12 Inner London boroughs, and the newly added areas in general constitute the 20 Outer London boroughs. The 32 London boroughs have taken over the surviving records of the civil parishes and/or boroughs of which they are the successors. Usually these are now deposited in the respective borough libraries. Several of these have archivists who look after local collections, deposited records and, in some instances, a selection of the official records.

To 1541/2	*1541/2–1836*	*1831/3:*	*1836/40 onwards*	*1968*
ecclesiastically, wholly or almost wholly in the diocese of		*No. of ancient parishes returned county + major towns*	*ecclesiastically, wholly or almost wholly in the diocese of*	

MIDDLESEX—now in GREATER LONDON

| **London** | **London** | (75 – 26 to County of London = 49) | **London** | **London** |

The Middlesex Section of the Greater London County Record Office, 1 Queen Anne's Gate Buildings, Dartmouth Street, S.W.1, is still physically separated from the Greater London Record Office, a few hundred yards away, but administratively they are closely co-ordinated, and present plans provide for their integration in due course. There was also a local statutory Registry of Deeds which existed 1709–1938. Its contents were apportioned between the former Middlesex C.R.O. and the former L.C.C. C.R.O. Since these are to be amalgamated, the whole contents of the Registry are, or eventually will be, reunited in the Greater London R.O.

The Society of Genealogists, 37 Harrington Gardens, S.W.7, is a private society. It has enormous collections of parish registers for all parts of England in print, TS. and MS. transcript, with much appropriate index material as to registers generally. There is, of course, no general right of public access to these, but the Society on occasion admits non-members to them on payment of a modest daily fee.

MONMOUTHSHIRE

| **Llandaff** | **Llandaff** | 128 | **Llandaff** | *Monmouth* (Diocese of the Church in Wales) |

Monmouthshire County Record Office, County Hall, Newport.

The recognition of the National Library of Wales at Aberystwyth as D.R.O. for all six dioceses of the Province of Wales, means that theoretically many deposited ecclesiastical parish records of Monmouthshire parishes may have to be sought in Cardiganshire, 75 miles or so, even 'as the crow flies', from Newport. In fact, the majority of parish records are still to be found in their parishes, but when ecclesiastical parish records have gone to Aberystwyth civil records have usually been deposited in the appropriate C.R.O.

NORFOLK

| **Norwich** | **Norwich** | 649 + 42 | **Norwich** | **Norwich** |

Norfolk and Norwich Record Office, Central Library, Norwich.

This holds also Norwich diocesan records and those of Norwich and Norfolk archdeaconries, but not deposited parish records.

A few documents still in regular use for administrative purposes, e.g. enclosure awards, remain in the care of the Norfolk Clerk of the County Council, at the County Offices, Thorpe Road, Norwich.

To 1541/2 1541/2–1836	1831/3:	1836/40 onwards 1968
ecclesiastically, wholly or almost wholly in the diocese of	No. of ancient parishes returned county + major towns	ecclesiastically, wholly or almost wholly in the diocese of

NORTHAMPTONSHIRE

Lincoln   Peterborough   'c. 266'   Peterborough   Peterborough
Northamptonshire Record Office,
Delapré Abbey, Northampton.

NORTHUMBERLAND

Durham   **Durham**   91 + 5   **Durham**   *Newcastle*
    '? 109'   then
    Newcastle
Northumberland Record Office,
Melton Park, North Gosforth, Newcastle-upon-Tyne, 3,
which acts also as D.R.O. for parish records in the diocese of *Newcastle*,
virtually co-extensive with the county.

NOTTINGHAMSHIRE

York   **York**   217 + 3   **Lincoln**   *Southwell*
    then
    Southwell
Nottinghamshire County Record Office,
County House,
High Pavement, Nottingham.
This is recognised also as D.R.O. for Southwell diocese, almost co-extensive
with the county. In fact it contains on deposit the records of about half the
parishes in the county—some records from 140 parishes in all. The (archidiaconal) records of the archdeaconry of Nottingham are in the Department
of MSS. in Nottingham University.

OXFORDSHIRE*

Lincoln   **Oxford**   212 + 15   Oxford   Oxford
Oxfordshire County Record Office,
County Hall, New Road, Oxford.
Deposited Oxfordshire parish records are normally to be found in the Bodleian
Library, recognised as D.R.O. for the archdeaconry of Oxford, more or less
co-extensive with the county.

PETERBOROUGH, SOKE of—see under COUNTY OF HUNTINGDON-AND-PETERBOROUGH

RUTLAND

Lincoln   Peterborough   '51'   Peterborough   Peterborough
The (rather scanty) remaining official records of the county are kept at the
County Offices,
Catmose, Oakham,
in the care of the Clerk of the Peace. Concerning such deposited records as
one could fairly expect a larger and wealthier county to provide for also in a
County Record Office, it should be noted that a number of Rutland archive
collections have been deposited in the Leicestershire C.R.O. It would seem
reasonable to address archival and other historical inquiries thither, or to the
Curator of the recently established County Museum, The Castle, Oakham.
Parishes in the county of Rutland are in the archdeaconry of Northampton. It
is understood that a number of Rutland archive collections are in the Northamptonshire C.R.O.

* See note under GLOUCESTERSHIRE.

To *1541/2* ecclesiastically, wholly or almost wholly in the diocese of	*1541/2–1836*	*1831/3:* No. of ancient parishes returned county + major towns	*1836/40 onwards* ecclesiastically, wholly or almost wholly in the diocese of	*1968*

SHROPSHIRE*

Hereford	**Hereford**	225 + 4	**Hereford**	**Hereford**
Lichfield†	**Lichfield**		**Lichfield**	**Lichfield**
also	also		also	also
St Asaph	**St Asaph**		**St Asaph**	**Worcester**
Worcester	**Worcester**		**Worcester**	
	Salop Record Office,			
	Shirehall, Shrewsbury.‡			

SOMERSET

Bath-and-	**Bath-and-**	476 + 10	**Bath-and-**	**Bath-and-**
Wells	**Wells**		**Wells**	**Wells**
	Somerset Record Office,			
	Obridge Road, Taunton,			

which is also D.R.O., and holds all archdeaconry records, and all diocesan records other than the Bishops' Registers. It has deposits of parish records for about one-fifth of the parishes in the county, including parish registers for 33.

STAFFORDSHIRE

Lichfield	**Lichfield**	176 + 7	**Lichfield**	**Lichfield**

The Staffordshire Record Office,
County Buildings, Eastgate Street, Stafford,
which is also D.R.O. for parish records within the archdeaconries of Stafford and Stoke, together more-or-less co-extensive with the county. (It works in association with the William Salt Library, 19, Eastgate, Street, and the Lichfield Joint R.O., Bird Street, Lichfield, which last holds the diocesan? and archidiaconal records, the probate records and the diocesan register transcripts for Staffordshire, Derbyshire and about half of Shropshire and Warwickshire, now transferred from the Diocesan Registry, Lichfield.)

SUFFOLK§

Norwich	**Norwich**	487 + 17§	**Norwich,** **Ely,** ** then *St Edmunds-* *bury-and-* *Ipswich*	*St Edmunds-* *bury-and-* *Ipswich*

EAST SUFFOLK

Norwich	**Norwich**	(327)§	**Norwich**	*St Edmunds-* *bury-and-* *Ipswich***

Ipswich and East Suffolk Record Office,
County Hall, Ipswich.
This is recognised as D.R.O. for Ipswich and Suffolk archdeaconries (i.e. those parishes of the diocese which are in the county). In fact it contains on deposit the records of some parishes in E. Suffolk, and a few from the deanery of Hadleigh in W. Suffolk. A few Suffolk parishes in the deanery of Lothingland are still in **Norwich** diocese, archdeaconry of Norfolk.

* See note under GLOUCESTERSHIRE.
† SALOP W. of the Severn is in **Hereford** diocese; E. of it in **Lichfield**. The diocesan register transcripts are still at Hereford and at Lichfield.
‡ Both the C.R.O. and the Shrewsbury B.L. are recognized as D.R.O.s for the archdeaconry of Salop, diocese of **Lichfield**. Though not recognised as D.R.O. for the archdeaconry of Ludlow (diocese of **Hereford**), the C.R.O. does in fact hold a number of parish deposits for this archdeaconry. The Shrewsbury B.L. holds a few, transferred from Hereford C.L. (formerly recognised as D.R.O. for the whole diocese of **Hereford** but now relinquishing its holdings of parish records).

§ See note * on p. 344.   ** See note † on p. 344.

To *1541/2*	*1541/2–1836*	*1831/3:*	*1836/40 onwards*	*1968*
ecclesiastically, wholly or almost wholly in the diocese of		*No. of ancient parishes returned county + major towns*	*ecclesiastically, wholly or almost wholly in the diocese of*	

WEST SUFFOLK

Norwich	Norwich	(177)*	Ely†	*St Edmunds-bury-and-Ipswich*

Bury St Edmunds and West Suffolk Record Office,
8, Angel Hill, Bury St Edmunds.

This is recognised as D.R.O. for Sudbury archdeaconry (i.e. those parishes of the diocese which are in the county). In fact it contains on deposit the records of some parishes in W. Suffolk.

SURREY

Winchester	Winchester	137 (−17 to the County of London − 120) + 9	Winchester then *Southwark*, *Guildford*	*Southwark*, *Guildford*

Surrey Record Office,
County Hall,
Kingston-on-Thames.

This is recognised as D.R.O. for parishes in Southwark diocese lying outside the former L.C.C. area. See also LONDON. The Museum and Muniment Room, Castle Arch, Guildford, is recognised as D.R.O., and contains on deposit some parish records from parishes in Guildford diocese.

SUSSEX*

Chichester	Chichester	(314)*	Chichester	Chichester
EAST SUSSEX		(148)*		

East Sussex Record Office,
Pelham House, Lewes.

WEST SUSSEX   (166)*
West Sussex Record Office,
County Hall, Chichester,

which holds also the episcopal and archidiaconal records. The three archdeaconries are only approximately co-extensive with the two county divisions. This causes no difficulty, however, for Chichester is the D.R.O. and A.R.O., and all Sussex register transcripts (e.g.) are to be seen there.

WARWICKSHIRE

Worcester	Worcester	199 + 9	Worcester	*Birmingham*,
Lichfield	Lichfield			*Coventry*

Warwickshire County Record Office,
Shire Hall, Warwick,

which is also D.R.O. for *Birmingham* (parish records of parishes outside the city boundary), and *Coventry* dioceses, and in these capacities holds the original registers for the majority of parishes in the county.

There are modern transcripts of many Warwickshire parish registers at Shakespeare's Birthplace Library, Stratford-on-Avon. Birmingham Central Library, Archives Department, is recognised as D.R.O. for those parts of the diocese which are within the city, and in fact it contains some such parish records on deposit. See also note under STAFFORDSHIRE and see note under GLOUCESTERSHIRE.

* On this page, in each of these two divided counties one of the County Archivists, Mr. D. Charman in IPSWICH AND EAST SUFFOLK and Mr. C. G. Holland in EAST SUSSEX has not only allocated the 1831–3 parishes between the two present county areas, but has also corrected and revised them to allow for subsequent boundary changes, etc., so that here the figures are not quite comparable with those given elsewhere—they are in fact considerably more accurate.

† E. SUFFOLK remained in **Norwich** diocese, W. SUFFOLK was in **Ely** 1836–1914.

To *1541/2*	*1541/2–1836*	*1831/3:*	*1836/40 onwards*	*1968*
ecclesiastically, wholly or almost wholly in the diocese of		*No. of ancient parishes returned county + major towns*	*ecclesiastically, wholly or almost wholly in the diocese of*	

WESTMORLAND*

Carlisle,   **Carlisle,**   66 + 2   **Carlisle**   **Carlisle**
York†   Chester
(Archivist-in-Charge),
Westmorland Record Office,
County Hall, Kendal.

WIGHT, ISLE of—see under HAMPSHIRE

WILTSHIRE
Salisbury   **Salisbury**   310 + 8   **Salisbury**   **Salisbury,**
    Bristol   Bristol

    Wiltshire Record Office,
    County Hall, Trowbridge; and
    Wren Hall, 56c, The Close, Salisbury.
(Diocesan Record Office for diocesan, archidiaconal, etc., records relating to Wiltshire, Dorset and Berkshire.)
    Many Wiltshire parish records are deposited at Trowbridge, which is recognised as D.R.O. for Bristol and for Salisbury, except for parishes within the city of Salisbury, some of whose records are at the (City) Council House. The diocesan parish register transcripts are in the D.R.O. at Salisbury.

WORCESTERSHIRE‡
Worcester   **Worcester**   193 + 16   **Worcester**   **Worcester**
Worcestershire Record Office,
Shirehall, Worcester; and
St Helens, Fish Street, Worcester,
this last being recognized as D.R.O. and containing the diocesan and archidiaconal records. The recognition of the whole of the C.R.O. as also D.R.O. means that though all the official county records are preserved at Shirehall, those of the diocese at St Helens, it is possible to follow here the admirable plan of keeping original parish registers in the one building, diocesan transcripts in another, a precautionary measure which it is rarely possible to adopt in other C.R.O.s which have both series of records.

---

    * In effect a branch of the Cumberland, Westmorland and Carlisle Record Office. See note under CUMBERLAND.
    † On the archdeaconry of Richmond see notes under CUMBERLAND and YORKSHIRE.
    ‡ See note under GLOUCESTERSHIRE.

To 1541/2 ecclesiastically, wholly or almost wholly in the diocese of	1541/2–1836	1831/3: No. of ancient parishes returned county + major towns	1836/40 onwards ecclesiastically, wholly or almost wholly in the diocese of	1968
YORKSHIRE		751		
	York City	24		
	and County	15		
	(York Ainsty)			
York*	**York,**		York	York
	Chester*		*Ripon**	*Ripon**
			later also	*Wakefield,*
			Wakefield,	*Sheffield,*
			Sheffield,	*Bradford*
			Bradford	

Archives Department,
York City Library,
Museum Street, York.
The (University of York) Borthwick Institute of Historical Research, St Anthony's Hall, Peaseholme Green, York, has lately collected parish records from various parts of the (present) archdiocese, with one or two borderline cases. It holds also the diocesan parish register transcripts for the present York diocese and other records for the archdiocese ? with some for the province.

YORKSHIRE: EAST RIDING				
York	**York**	189 + 4	**York**	**York**

East Riding County Record Office,
County Hall, Beverley.†

YORKSHIRE: NORTH RIDING				
York	**York**	225 + 2	**York**	**York**
	Chester*			*Ripon,**
				Wakefield,
				Sheffield,
				Bradford

North Riding County Record Office,
County Hall, Northallerton.†

YORKSHIRE: WEST RIDING				
York	**York**	292 + 15	**York**	**York,**
	Chester*		*Ripon*	*Ripon,**
				Wakefield,
				Sheffield,
				Bradford

There is no proper C.R.O. in the County Hall at Wakefield,† though it holds, in the custody of the Clerk of the Peace, the official records of the county.

* The Archdeaconry of Richmond was transferred from York to Chester by Henry VIII. Much of it is co-extensive with the present diocese of *Ripon*.
† Each of the three Ridings has in the county town an ancient statutory Registry of Deeds, these dating from, respectively, 1707, 1734 and 1703. A great many enclosure awards, particularly, were enrolled here, not, as elsewhere, with the Clerk of the Peace for the county.
In these circumstances the City Libraries at Leeds and at Sheffield, each with a qualified archival staff, do a great deal of the work which in a normal country would fall to the C.R.O. They have informally 'partitioned' the Riding between them, so far as concerns the deposit of unofficial records, etc., Sheffield taking the southern half of the area, Leeds the northern half.

Bibliography

I give below notes upon a few of the principal works dealing with the various subjects touched upon. The range of topics covered in the text is so wide that it would be impossible to give a full and detailed bibliography. These are the books that I have found most interesting and most helpful. The editions noted are not necessarily the best. They are those to which I have found it possible to obtain access.

For help in obtaining many of these I am very grateful to the former City Librarians of Stoke-on-Trent and of Leeds.

Preface   Works on Parish Records   *p.* xiv

General Works :

Burn, J.S., *History of Parish Registers in England*, 2nd edn., 1862.
Cox, J.C., *Parish Registers of England*, 1910.
——*Churchwardens' Accounts*, 1913.
Dyer, T.F. Thiselton, *Old English Social Life as told by Parish Registers*, 1898.
Muncey, R.W., *Romance of Parish Registers*, 1933.
Smith, Joshua Toulmin, *The Parish*, 2nd edn., 1857.
Trotter, Eleanor, *Seventeenth Century Life in the Country Parish*, 1919.
Waters, R.E. Chester, *Parish Registers in England*, new edn., 1887.

Barley, M.W., *Parochial Documents of the East Riding*, Yorks. Archaeol. Soc., vol. c, Beverley, 1939.
Buckland, W.E., *Parish Registers and Records in the Diocese of Rochester, Kent Records*, 1912.
Erith, E.J., *Essex Parish Records*, new edn. ed. Emmison, F.G. 1966. Chelmsford.
Fearon, W.A. and Williams, G.F., *Parish Records and Parochial Documents in the Archdeaconry of Winchester*, 1909. Winchester.
Gray, I. and Ralphs, Miss E., *Parish Records of Bristol and Gloucestershire*, 1963.
King, J.E., *Inventory of Parochial Documents in the Diocese of Bath and Wells and County of Somerset*, Taunton, 1938.
Lincoln, Lord Bishop of, Committee on Parochial Records, *Exhibition Catalogue*, Lincoln, 1939.
Peele, E.C. and Clease, R.S., *Shropshire Parish Documents*, Shrewsbury (n.d.).
Powell, D.L., *Guide to Surrey Archives—List of Parish Archives*, Surrey Record Soc., vol. xxvi,* 1928.
Redstone, Miss L. and Steer, F., *Local Records*, 1952.
Woodruff, C.E., *Inventory of Parish Records in the Diocese of Canterbury*, Canterbury, 1922.

* See also note in General Index.

Introduction : Works on the English Parish & Village   *p.* 1

Most of the works given above, especially Toulmin Smith, have some reference to the history of the parish. Many of those noted below *passim* relate to one aspect or another of parochial history. The treatise above all others is :

Webb, S. and B., *The Parish and the County, English Local Government*, 1, 1906.
Bullard, J.V., *The English Parish and Diocese*, 1936, is also very useful for the early history of the parochial organisation.

There must be many hundred books on the English village. The following are specially recommended :

DARTON, F.J.H., *English Fabric* (n.d.).
DITCHFIELD, P.H., *English Villages*, 1901.
GARDINER, C.H., *Your Village and Mine*, 1944.
HARTLEY, D., *Countryman's England*, 1935.
MASSINGHAM, H.J., *The English Countryman*, 1942 (and other books by the same author).
PAKINGTON, H., *English Villages and Hamlets*, 1936.

THE ENGLISH PARISH AND ITS OFFICERS   *p.* 9

Works dealing with all the functionaries named will be found under the appropriate headings below.

THE MINISTER OF THE PARISH   *p.* 12

Various text-books of ecclesiastical law noted below, especially Burn and Lawrence, deal with the legal side of the incumbent's position. The best literary study of the ideal country parson is :

HERBERT, GEORGE, *A Priest to the Temple*, 1652 (available in several modern reprints).
DITCHFIELD, P.H., *The Old-time Parson*, 1908 (gossipy but very valuable).
BARING GOULD, S., *Old Country Life*, 1913 (covering all the rural dignitaries and notabilities from squire to village musician, but dealing especially with the country clergy).

THE VESTRY MEETING   *p.* 13

This is dealt with below, *sub* p. 162.

RATES AND RATING   *p.* 25

CANNAN, G., *History of Local Rates in England*, 1927, will probably supply all the detail the reader needs.

If he wishes to go into the matter of rating in recent years:

PROBYN, J.W., *Local Government and Taxation in the United Kingdom*, 1882.
DAVEY, H., *Law of Rating*, 1924.
DURMSDAY, W.H., *Overseer's Handbook*, 4th edn., 1920.
MACKENZIE, W.W., *Overseer's Handbook*, 9th edn., 1925.

THE CHEST ITSELF   *p.* 35

LEWER, E.W. and WALL, J.C., *Church Chests of Essex*, 1913.
ROE, F., *Ancient Church Chests and Chairs*, 1929.
ROE, F., *Ancient Coffers and Cupboards*, 1902.
HART, C.J., 'Old Chests' (in *Trans. of Birmingham and Midland Institute*), 1894.

Most books on church woodwork etc. have something to say of chests. Good examples are :

CAUTLEY, H.M., *Suffolk Churches and their Treasures*, 1937 (pp. 311–13).
COX, J.C., *English Church Fittings, Furniture, and Accessories*, 1923 (pp. 274–82).
COX, J.C. and HARVEY, A., *English Church Furniture*, 1907 (pp. 291–307).
HOWARD, F.E. and CROSSLEY, F.H., *English Church Woodwork*, 1917 (pp. 346–50).

GROVE, H., *Alienated Tithes in Appropriated and Impropriated Parishes*, 1896.
LIBERATION SOCIETY, *The Case for Disestablishment* (new edn.), 1894.
SELBORNE, ROUNDELL PALMER, EARL OF, *Defence of the Church of England against Disestablishment*, 1886.
   (These last two works should be read together.)
SELDEN, J., *History of Tithes*, edns. from 1618.
P.P. (H.C.), 214 (1887), *Return of all Tithes Commuted and Apportioned . . .* (embodying earlier returns).

CHURCH COURTS, VISITATION RECORDS, FACULTIES AND LICENCES *pp.* 144, 150, 154

The standard history of the Church of England is Stephens, W.R.W. and Hunt, W. (ed.), *History of the English Church*, 9 vols., 1912.

The works of W. Andrews, especially *Church Treasury of History, Custom, and Folklore*, 1898, and *Curious Church Customs*, 1895, are well worth turning up. Legge, H.W., *Hierurgia Anglicana*, 1842, revised edn., ed. Staley, V., 1902–4, is a more academic work. It takes a strongly 'Anglo-Catholic' point of view. Other works dealing with various aspects of the matter are:

AYLIFFE, J., *Parergon Juris Canonici Anglicani*, 1726.
BURN, R., *Ecclesiastical Law*, 1760.
Canons and Constitutions Ecclesiastical, 1604 (and numerous reprints).
CARDWELL, E., *Synodalia 1842, Documentary Annals of the Reformed Church of England*, 1842.
CRIPPS, H.W., *Law Relating to Church and Clergy* (and numerous later edns.; I have used the 7th edn., Lawrence, A.T. and Cripps, Sir Stafford, 1921).
DANSAY, W., *Horae Decanicae Rurales*, 1835.
GASQUET, A., *Parish Life in Mediaeval England*, 1907.
GIBSON, E., *Codex Juris Ecclesiastici Anglicani*, 1761.
JOHNSON, J., *Collection of Ecclesiastical Laws . . . and Canons . . .*, 1720.
LYNDWOOD, W., *Provinciale*, 1433, ed. Bullard, J.V. and Bell, H.C., 1929.
MAITLAND, F.W., *Roman Canon Law in the Church of England*, 1898.
Notes from a Ruri-decanal Register, ed. Fairbank, F.R., *Surrey Archaeological Collections*, vol. XXV, 1912.
OLLARD, S.L. and CROSS, G., *Dictionary of English Church History*, 1912.
'Register of the Archdeacon of Richmond', ed. Hamilton-Thompson, A., *Yorks. Arch. Journ.*, vols. XXX, XXXII, 1931, 1936.

SOCIETIES FOR THE REFORMATION OF MANNERS *p.* 152

WEBB, S. and B., *History of Liquor Licensing in England*, 1903, App., pp. 137–51.
WOODWARD, J., *Account of the Societies for the Reformation of Manners . . .*, 1699.

THE KING'S EVIL *p.* 157

BECKETT, *Free and Impartial Enquiry into the Antiquity and Efficacy of Touching for the King's Evil*, 1722.
BLACKMORE, SIR R., *Treatise on the King's Evil*, 1735.
(Broadside), *The Manner of His Majesties Curing the Disease called the King's Evil* (with an engraving of the ceremony, reprinted in Crawfurd), 1679.
CRAWFURD, R., *The King's Evil*, 1911.
WISEMAN, R., *Treatise of the King's Evill*, 1676, in *Eight Chirurgical Treatises*, 3rd edn., 1691, p. 239, reprinted in Major, R., *Classic Descriptions of Disease*, Springfield, Ill., U.S.A., 1932, pp. 49–52.

The beautifully illustrated detailed inventory: Morgan, F.C., 'Church Chests of Herefordshire', in *Woolhope Field Club Trans.*, 1947, is the best county survey I know of.

PARISH REGISTERS *p.* 43

The principal works on these are noted above, *sub* p. xiv.

On various points mentioned in the text these works:

H.M. Registrar-General, *Story of the General Register Office*, 1937; Public Records Commission, 1912–19, *Report III*, Pt. III, 1919; HILL, G., *English Dioceses*, 1900; Institute of Historical Research, *Bulletin Supplements*, 1–8, 1930–7; and *The Book of Common Prayer* will be found to give a good deal of additional information.

I deliberately repeat here the note on p. 53 that all the references given will be out of date on the completion of Mr. Steel's series (above p. 289, fns. 39/40).

CHURCHWARDENS' ACCOUNTS *p.* 84

Works relating to the churchwardens' duty of presentment will be found below *sub* 'Church Courts', p. 144.

COX, J.C., *Churchwardens' Account*,* 1913 (most valuable).

The lists appended to Cox are superseded by those in Blair, J., *A List of Churchwardens' Accounts* (p.p.), Ann Arbor, Mich., U.S.A., 1939.

PRIDEAUX, H., *Practical Guide to the Duties of Churchwardens*, 16th edn., ed. Mackarness, F.C. 1895.

On Church Ales see Dr Blair's other study: *English Church Ales . . .* (p.p.) Ann Arbor, Mich., U.S.A., 1940.

THE CIVIL DUTIES OF CHURCHWARDENS *p.* 105

The books mentioned above give some information as to the civil functions of churchwardens, interspersed with details of their ecclesiastical duties. Most of their purely poor-law duties are dealt with in the book list given below 'The Poor Law', p. 189. The articles and pamphlets mentioned below give particulars of their statutory functions as to the destruction of vermin.

BRUSHFIELD, T.N., 'The Destruction of vermin in rural parishes', *Report and Transactions of Devonshire Association*, vol. XXIX, p. 291, 1897.
ELLIOTT, J.S., 'Extracts from churchwardens' accounts of Bedfordshire', *Zoologist*, Ser. 4, vol. X, pp. 161 *et seq.*, 253 *et seq.*, 1906.
ELLIOTT, J.S., *Bedfordshire Vermin Payments*, Luton Museum, 1936.
OLDHAM, C., 'Payments for vermin by some Hertfordshire churchwardens', *Trans. East Herts. Nat. Hist. Soc. and Field Club*, vol. XIX, p. 79, 1931.

CHARITY ACCOUNTS, ETC. *p.* 109

GRAY, B.K., *History of English Philanthropy*, 1905.
EDWARDS, H., *Collection of Curious Bequests . . .* 1842.

The reader wishing to investigate the history of local charities should turn up also

Public Record Office, *List of Proceedings of Commissioners of Charitable Uses,** appointed pursuant to the Statutes 39 Eliz. c. 6, and 43 Eliz. c. 4, (1899).
The Charity Commissioners' *Reports*, 32 vols., 1819–40.

    * See my cautionary note above, p. 294, fn. 7.

And the abstracts of these :

The County Reports (one volume per county).
The Analytical Digests (Returns of Charities for Distribution among the Poor, Statistics of Grammar Schools, Schools not Classical, and of Educational Gifts not attached to Endowed Schools), 2 vols., 1832–5.
Final Digest (Digests of the General Charities, and Summaries of the whole of the Charity Property Income), 4 vols., 1842.

Based upon these again are a whole variety of county volumes, e.g.

GRIFFITH, G., *Free Schools and Endowments of Staffordshire*, 1859.
GRIFFITH, G., *Free Schools and Endowments of Worcestershire*, 1852.

with sundry pamphlets and volumes issued in more recent years under the authority of the County Councils, e.g.

KENYON, R.LL. (Chairman of Endowments Committee of Shropshire County Local Education Authority), *Shropshire Charities for Elementary Education*, 1906.

There are also a great many excerpts from these reports in various county directories, from the early nineteenth century issues of White and his rivals to the modern Kelly volumes. The modern, and it seems to me over-publicised, American works on English charities, edited by Professor W. K. Jordan (three major volumes, and several locally-produced county studies) are to be used with some caution. They certainly contain many hundreds of useful (and verifiable) references, not readily accessible elsewhere. It is fair to say that they represent a remarkable achievement for an American scholar, surveying England in the main from Boston, Mass. This is true even if, presumably, Professor Jordan has had the help of numerous American Ph.D. candidates, doing their research years in England (though I do not see that anywhere Professor Jordan acknowledges his obligations to any such).

A great many of Jordan's 'facts' are, however, quite certainly wrong. So I think may well be some of his theories. His work, which finishes c. 1660, is continued by another American, Dr D. Owen, *English Philanthropy, 1600–1960*. Dr Owen is more modest in his aim, and he achieves it. His book gives a most interesting and readable account of the background of English charitable endeavour, and charity law, from the resettlement of English affairs generally in 1660 to the passing of the last great charities act, that of 1960, referred to in some detail on p. 294.

WORKS ON BRIEFS

BEWES, W.A., *Church Briefs or Royal Warrants for Collecti
    Purposes*, 1896.
BRUSHFIELD, T.N., 'Devonshire Briefs', report in *Trans. Dev*
SMITH, J.E., *Bygone Briefs*, 1896.
WALFORD, C., *King's Briefs, their Purposes and History*, rep
    circulation from *Royal Hist. Soc. Trans.*, vol. x, 1882.

TERRIERS

For references to Terriers in the Canons, see the text. detailed references I have come across are in the *Repor* Records Commission of 1912–19:

Terriers in Parish Chests : in general, Rep. II, p. 22; at Abinger,
    p. 86; in Lincolnshire parishes, Rep. III, p. 55.
Terriers among Diocesan Records : in the Peculiars of Cante
    p. 102; at Gloucester, Rep. III, p. 87.
Terriers in Archidiaconal Records : at St Albans, Rep. II, p. 1
    Rep. II, p. 108; at Buckingham, Rep. III, p. 89; at Bed
    p. 89; at Huntingdon (including some Cambridgeshire par
    p. 90.

    * Now transferred with the rest of the archidiaconal records to the dio
record office at Bedford Shire Hall.

Since this book first appeared, several scholars have pub tions of glebe terriers *in extenso* or in abstract. Sometimes interest has been the information which the terriers aff economic history of the church and its clergy. Sometime rather the material available in terriers, but often nowhe the agrarian history of the village communities, a poi Ballard drew attention as long ago as 1908, and Gray in 19 examples of very well-edited series of terriers are to be M. Barratt's Warwickshire volumes, and in various Yor edited by Professor M. Beresford, and appearing in tl *Archaeological Journal*.

THE PARISH CLERK

DITCHFIELD, P.H., *The Parish Clerk*, 1913 (a mine of curious inf
    quaint anecdotes).

Other material on the Parish Clerk will be found in the te ecclesiastical law noted below.

TITHE

There are many scores of books on the history of tithes. All tl histories of agriculture, especially Lord Ernle and Mr Cu below, have much to say about it.

VENN, J.A., *Foundations of Agricultural Economics*, 1923.
DEGGE, SIR S., *The Parson's Counsellor*, edns. from 1676.
FLOYER, G. K., *Studies.*, *Studies in the History of English Church E*
    1917.

Much more important than any of these is Bloch, M., *Les Rois Thaumaturges*, Strasburg (and Oxford), 1924. This contains a mass of material not only about the king's evil, but on other aspects of the priestly nature of the royal office. It was purely from ignorance that I did not cite it in my first edition.

THE VESTRY *p.* 162

Toulmin Smith's *The Parish* and S. and B. Webb's *The Parish and the County* are the main sources on this subject.

A very valuable little work with extensive extracts from the Finchley Vestry Minutes is :

STEPHENS, H.C., *Parochial Self-Government in Rural Districts*, 1893.

Vestry minute books, e.g.

Kettering, Northants, 1797–1853, ed. S.R. Peyton, Northants Record Soc., vol. VI, 1933.
Pittington, Durh. (*Churchwardens' Accounts*, etc.) Surtees Soc., vol. LXXXIV, 1888.
Walthamstow, Essex (1710–94), (*Vestry Minutes* . . . etc.), ed. S.J. Barns, 3 vols., Walthamstow Antiq. Soc., vols. 13 and 14, 16, 1925–7.

PETTY CONSTABLES *p.* 176

All the law books give much detail upon the office of constable. Specially interesting are the accounts in Dalton, M., *The Country Justice*, edns. from 1619, Blackstone, Sir William, *Commentaries* . . ., 1765–9; Hone, N.J., *The Manor and Manorial Records*, 1906 (deals with the function of the constable in the manorial economy).

Other works:

BACON, F., *Office of Constable*, 1618 (*Works*, Spedding's edn. of 1857–9, vol. VII).
LAMBARDE, W., *Eirenarcha*, Bk. I, 1602, etc.
MERITON, G., *Guide for Constables* . . ., 1679.
RITSON, J., *Office of Constable*, 1791.
W—, E—, *Exact Constable*, 1682.
SIMPSON, H.B., 'The Office of Constable', in *Eng. Hist. Rev.*, Oct. 1895, pp. 625–41.

THE POOR LAW *p.* 189

All the standard social and economic histories have much matter on the poor law. The indispensable book is Webb, S. and B., *The Old Poor Law, English Local Government*, VII, *English Poor Law History*, Pt. I.

Lighter works:

GAUNT, W., *English Rural Life in the Eighteenth Century*, 1925.
MARSHALL, D., *English Poor in the Eighteenth Century*, 1926.

AA*

Local studies :

ASHBY, A.W., *A Hundred Years of Poor Law Administrations in a Warwickshire Village*, Oxford, 1912.
CUTLACK, S.A., *Gnosall (Staffs.) Records*, 1678–1837, Staffs. Record Soc. Collections, 1936.
EMMISON, F.G., 'Poor Relief in Two Rural Parishes in Bedfordshire, 1563–98', *Econ. Hist. Rev.*, vol. III, 1931.
——*Relief of the Poor at Eaton Socon, Beds.*, 1706–1834, in Beds. Hist. Record Soc., 8vo. Pubns., 1933.
HAMPSON, E.M., 'Settlement and Removal in Cambridgeshire, 1662–1834', *Camb. Hist. Journ.*, vol. II, pp. 273–7, 1928.
NOLAN, M., *Treatise of the Laws for the Relief and Settlement of the Poor*, 1808.
BURN, R., *History of the Poor Laws*, 1764.
——*Justice of the Peace and Parish Officer*, 1755 (many edns.).

Other works to be consulted :

ASCHROTT, P.F. and PRESTON THOMAS, H., *English Poor Law System*, 1888.
EDEN, SIR F.M., *State of the Poor*, 1797 (a useful condensed reprint, ed. A.G.L. Rogers, appeared in 1928).
LEONARD, E.M., *Early History of English Poor Relief*, 1900.
NICHOLLS, SIR G., *History of English Poor Law*, 1854 (new edn. 1898–9).

Government returns and reports on the poor law. The most generally useful are :

Report from Select Committee on . . . *Overseers' Returns*, 1777, Reprints, Ser. I, vol. IX, p. 297.
Report of Returns made by Overseers of Poor . . ., Reprints, Ser. I, vol. IX, p. 553.
Abstract of Answers and Returns on Maintenance of Poor, S.P. no. 175, 1803–4
Report and Evidence on Operation of Poor Laws, S.P. no. 462, 1817, reprinted, no. 532, 1819.
Report from Lords Committees on Poor Law, S.P. no. 400, 1818.
Report from Select Committee on Relief of Able-bodied Persons, no. 494, 1828.
Report from Lords on Poor Laws, with Index and Appendices, no. 227, 1831.
Report of H.M. Commissioners on Poor Law, no. 44, 1834.

SETTLEMENT *p.* 198

All the old books on the Poor Law have many references to settlement.

BURROWS, Sir G., *Settlement Cases*, 1768.
DAVEY, H., *Poor Law Settlement and Removal*, 3rd edn., 1925.

VAGRANCY *p.* 211

RIBTON-TURNER, C.J., *History of Vagrants and Vagrancy*, 1887.

THE HIGHWAYS *p.* 242

Most of the parish officers' guides given above *sub tit*. Constable have chapters relating to the work of the Waywarden. The Board of Agriculture *General Views* . . . (about a hundred volumes published in the 1790's and 1810's) say a good deal about the parish highways at this time.

WEBB, S. and B., *The Story of the King's Highway*, 1913 (a detailed study).
COSSONS, A., *Turnpike Roads in Nottinghamshire*, 1934.

The legal aspect of highway maintenance :

GLEN, W.C., *Law relating to Highways*, 1897.
PRATT, H.C. and MACKENZIE, W.W., *Law of Highways*, 1923.
SHELFORD, L., ed. SMITH, C.M., *Law of Highways*, 1865.

Index